300 Most Important Tactical Chess Positions

Study five a week to be a better chessplayer

Thomas Engqvist

First published in the United Kingdom in 2020 by
Batsford, an imprint of Pavilion Books Company Limited
43 Great Ormond Street
London
WC1N 3HZ

ISBN: 9781849946124

A CIP catalogue record for this book is available from the
British Library.

26 25 24 23 22 21
10 9 8 7 6 5 4 3 2 1

Reproduction by Rival Colour Ltd, UK
Printed and bound by CPI Books, Chatham, UK

This book can be ordered direct from the publisher at
www.pavilionbooks.com, or try your local bookshop.

Contents

Introduction

The book you are holding in your hand, dear reader, is a follow-up to my previous *300 Most Important Chess Positions – Study five a week to be a better chess player* (Batsford 2018). However, the two books are not dependent on each other since their respective focus is on different territories of chess. The former book dealt with positional methods whereas this one focuses on **tactical ideas**. They can therefore be integrated as part of a training scheme and be studied as a single course. It's a matter of taste in which order you wish to read them or whether you even prefer to work with them concurrently. However, one advantage of starting with the positional methods is that when you move on to the tactics you will come across numerous references to the former book, which you will recognise if you have been ambitious enough to remember the many key concepts given there.

The most important thing is to do the work in a step-by-step fashion. Once you have set off on your path of study you can expect to enrich your chess understanding and acquire more and more tactical and positional weaponry. But, most importantly, you will develop a good habit that will progressively and significantly improve your playing strength over the coming weeks and months. Learning to play good chess is like learning a language or a musical instrument. It does take time to gain a sufficient understanding of the ideas but afterwards you'll never forget them. Indeed, when you have finished reading the books you will have gained sufficient experience to truly understand what to my mind are the most important factors concerning tactical and positional chess.

300 most important chess tactics in the opening, middlegame and endgame was originally an email course which started with the help of my Swedish homepage Schacksnack.se at the beginning of 2019 and lasted for approximately a year. The course was labelled "Less is more – The 300 most important tactical positions" and was primarily aimed at Swedish chess players, since the course was written in the Swedish language. The main idea was to study five tactical positions very carefully every week. All positions have thus been thoroughly explored by the participants as well as myself with the assistance of the latest versions of Komodo, especially Komodo11. There the positions were presented randomly whereas in this book they are thematically arranged in the opening and middlegame section and according to the specific endgame in the endgame section. For example, in pawn endings, stalemates, breakthroughs, passed pawns, pawn races and transitions to queen endings come to the forefront and are therefore the most common tactical ideas to be explored. Both methods, random and structured,

have their own merits. If the positions are solved randomly it's more like a real game situation. However, in the book you will not know the result or the level of difficulty beforehand. The advantage of a thematic order is that you can practice a specific theme. The advantage of a specific endgame is that you can focus on the tactical peculiarities of a particular endgame as well as the peculiarities of the piece which is defining what kind of endgame it is.

I discovered this clever concept of studying a useful but limited number of positions by coincidence as a junior at the end of the 70s when my club SK-33 in the small town of Enköping helped to arrange a couple of meetings with Robert Danielsson. At the time he was a well-known chess specialist in Stockholm, teaching the game to children. Danielsson has written books and study materials for beginners on a high pedagogical level. In Sweden he is most famous for his categorisation of five basic tactical tricks with the help of just one word. The Swedish key word is GABIÖ and it is indeed a clever acronym. Every letter stands for one fundamental and common tactical trick. G stands for Gaffel (Fork), A for Avdragare (Discoverer), B for Bindning (Pin), I for instängning (Trapping) and the last letter Ö means Överlastning (Overloading) If the letters are put in a more convenient order in the English language an equivalant word might be **DPFOT**. It might be a helpful acronym to help remember the five most common tactical tricks in the English language.

During one of our meetings in Stockholm, Danielsson and I agreed to follow a disciplined and structured scheme which meant I had to study five positions from *Pachman's Mittelspielpraxis im Schach* and *Endspielpraxis im Schach* every week. If you work diligently and follow such a schedule ambitiously it will take approximately one year to assimilate the content from all the positions. You will learn all this for a lifetime if you are careful and slowly repeat the positions from time to time, maybe even up to at least 10 times, especially if the position is unfamiliar to you, until you have the specific positions at your fingertips. The main reason to study only a limited number of five positions each week is to restrict your focus to only the most important ones and concentrate solely on them. If you study too many positions, and too quickly, the risk increases that sooner or later you lose discipline and forget what you once tried to learn. The key is to learn slowly but surely and take time to reflect on the positions. If you can discuss these with your friends then so much the better. The best way to learn is actually to teach others, so if you have this opportunity, and it comes natural to you, then you should take advantage of that.

The reason for the limit of 300 tactics in the present book is motivated by the phrase "Less is more". It's according to the principle that the less you know the less you will forget. It will be easier to remember 300 tactical ideas in a systematic manner than 1,000 random ones, since you will have a limited number of tactics on which to concentrate and continually study and revise on a regular basis. Such a learning process will be more effective in the long run and help you to focus on the most important tactical ideas.

It's not enough to learn tactical play in itself. One also needs the mental tools to solve problems effectively. The groundbreaking book *Play like a Grandmaster* by Alexander Kotov impresses upon its readers the need for mastering three abilities to become an exceptionally good player. These abilities are fast and correct **calculation** of variations, a deep **feeling for combinations** and a correct **evaluation** of different kinds of positions. In the present book the focus will be mostly on the second ability, a deep feeling for combinations, since it's an ability which by nature is more tactical. However, to be good at executing and preparing combinations you obviously must be good at calculating complicated variations as well. In a sense tactics is a hybrid of these two abilities and both must be mastered if your aim is to become a really strong tactician at the board.

When a position has been reached where a **combination** is possible then the time has come to execute it. To be able to do this effectively, a great arsenal of tactical and combinational ideas is needed as well as high level calculating ability. When it comes to the definition of a combination it's obviously not enough to quote Alekhine's "The combination is the heart of chess:" It's not consensus in the chess world

that defines what a combination really is. According to the *Sahovski Informator* system in Belgrade, which has produced five editions of the *Encyclopaedia of Chess Middlegames/Combinations* beginning in 1980, a combination is "a forced variation with a **sacrifice** which leads to a positive result" This definition originates from Botvinnik ("The combination is a forced variation with sacrifices") and is the most popular one but it's not entirely correct. I believe that Averbakh, who in his book *Chess Tactics for Advanced Players* stipulates that a combination is a double threat, is on the right track since it also covers the **manoeuvre** as well as the **exchange**.

Consider the following miniature which I won with a tactical trick after an exchange.

Engqvist – Dzevlan
SCT Åland/Åkersberga 1997

1 ♘f3 ♘f6 2 c4 g6 3 b3 ♗g7 4 ♗b2 0–0 5 g3 c5 6 ♗g2 ♘c6 7 0–0 d6 8 e3 ♗f5 9 ♕e2 e5 10 d3 a6 11 ♘c3 ♖b8 12 h3 ♕c8 13 ♔h2 b5 14 ♖ac1 ♖e8 15 ♖fd1 h6 16 ♘d2 ♕d7 17 ♘de4

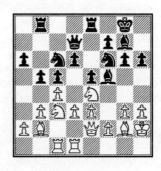

Black to move

17...♗e6??

Correct was 17...♞h7 making the e4-knight as well as the g2-bishop temporarily redundant.

18 ♞xf6+ ♝xf6 19 ♛f3

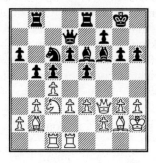

And **Black resigned** due to the double threat on f6 and c6. Dzevlan presumably made the tactical mistake of focusing too much on positional considerations such as controlling the d5-square that he missed a simple fork with the queen only two moves ahead. According to Botvinnik's definition this isn't a combination since before the fork an exchange took place and not a sacrifice. This proves how problematic it is to define a combination, especially if it must contain a sacrifice. Exchanges or manoeuvres can be part of a tactical trick as well, as long as there is a double threat in the position.

So the heart of all tactics is the double threat and as I have already described in *300 Most Important Positions* with regard to Réti's famous pawn ending from 1921, position 158, Averbakh used that famous position containing the immortal manoeuvre ♚g7-f6-e5 to explain that the double threat is the heart of all tactics and combinations.

On e5 the king is threatening to support the c6-pawn with ♚d6 as well as reach the enemy pawn on h4 with ♚f4.

There are a lot of books on the market which teach you how to carry out combinations so the aim of this book is not only to focus on this rather well-covered tactical aspect. More important is the underestimated, almost forgotten topic of how to reach a position where a combination is possible. This is actually the true art of chess and shows the big picture of how to relate to tactics as a whole. If the most important aspect in positional play is how to manoeuvre to achieve your objective, the question with regard to tactical matters is how to direct your play towards achieving your tactical objective.

Some say that tactics is 99 percent of the game and others that this is the case for positional play. The truth of the matter is that tactical and positional play are intertwined. In the above mentioned miniature my opponent made the mistake of focusing too much on the positional side of the game and on this particular occasion was punished for that. I'm sure this has happened to all of us at some time when playing in serious chess competitions. It happened to me in position 298 but I was lucky not to be punished, at least not on this occasion. Or as Euwe expressed it in *Strategy and Tactics in Chess*: "One is constantly faced with two problems: What must I do and how must I do it? In some cases one of these two problems may possibly surpass the other in importance to such an extent that it seems as if we only had one problem to deal with; in reality, however, both problems are always present." This is the key: we must always simultaneously focus on two kinds of chess, tactical and positional. Otherwise, sooner or later, we will give away points to opponents who understand this better than us.

Although the present book will mainly deal with the answer to the second question, "How", rather than "What", the most advanced notion in the tactical field is actually to know **how to reach the position where you can execute a tactical idea.** (Of course this is also valid for prophylactic chess when we try to figure out in advance how our opponent might execute a tactical idea.) Famous in this respect are Rudolf Spielmann's words regarding Alekhine's combinational vision: "I can comprehend Alekhine's combinations well enough, but where he gets his attacking chances from and how he infuses much life into the very opening – that is beyond me. Give me the positions he obtains, and I shall seldom falter. Yes, I continually get drawn games, even out of the King's Gambit".

If you have an advantageous position and you feel that the position is ripe for a hidden combination it's sometimes a matter of "religiously" believing that a combination in this or that position can be found, especially when you are close to giving up the search for an ingenious tactical solution. The main idea, psychologically speaking, is to have a profound belief that it's possible to transform an advantageous position by means of a combination or some other kind of tactical solution to extract a win.

A strong belief, combined with tactical skill, is really what top master chess is all about. "Anyone" can learn and deliver required tactics but most of us, including the great Spielmann, are not able to reach the desired positions. We mustn't forget that Spielmann was a great player in the field of tactics and on top of that wrote the classical *The Art of Sacrifice in Chess*. Included in the present book are therefore tactical positions as well as some initial phases of games designed to cover this highly important but nevertheless less explored topic of how to reach a position where a combination is possible. There isn't a single book dealing with this highly underestimated subject. *How to create combinations* by Vladimir Pafnutieff has an appropriate title but one which is too ambitious since in fact this book only scratches the surface. This and other works mostly deal with different types of combinations, but that is not the most important component. More important is to understand what the pieces can do, the individual peculiarities of the pieces. But, in this respect, also important are the peculiarities when pieces and pawns are working together. In the absence of any book concentrating on the issue of how to reach a position where a combination is possible, you will only be able to find this out by studying famous games by great masters. For example, great attacking and combinative players like Anderssen, Chigorin, Alekhine, Tal, Nezhmetdinov, Kasparov and Shirov come to mind.

After you have gained sufficient expertise in the field of tactical motifs and their calculation, what could be more important than to know the underlying mechanism of how to strive for a combination? On a basic level it's possible to study this important process by looking at miniature games with specific openings, those under 20, 25 or 30 moves depending on your definition of a miniature game. What you learn from miniature games you can use in other positions as well and this includes all phases of the game, since your play can proceed along the same lines using minor operations or manoeuvres with a specific purpose in mind. The advantage of studying important miniature games is that they effectively teach you how to construct opportunities for combinative blows and that is why they are included in the present book. It's not the hidden trap in itself that is important, it's how to create the right conditions to set that trap. This is the heart of Alekhine's successful combinational vision. However, as in the above mentioned game, sometimes it is your opponent who creates the right conditions and then the tactical opportunity is served on a silver platter. We must

always be ready to play normal moves too as these may sometimes be enough to prepare a tactical blow, even against strong opposition. Consider the following miniature:

Engqvist – Wallace
Stockholm International 1997

1 ♘f3 d5 2 g3 c6 3 ♗g2 ♗g4 4 0–0 ♘f6 5 b3 ♘bd7 6. ♗b2 e6 7 d3 ♗c5 8 ♘bd2 0-0 9 e4 ♕e7 10 a3 a5

Here Wallace offered a draw which I declined.

11 h3 ♗h5 12 ♕e1

Black to move

12...♖fe8??

An amazing mistake.

13 e5 Black resigned.

The f6-knight is trapped by the pawn.

This is clearly a case of a loss of concentration by my opponent and perhaps the early proposal of a draw was a telling signal. I declined, but I could never have imagined the psychological impact that it would have. Sometimes a draw offer might indicate that the player isn't feeling motivated enough to play chess on that day and that in itself is a trigger to continue the game, regardless of the colour of the pieces.

Which of the three phases of the game is the most important to study if your main goal is to learn tactics as effectively as possible? Tactical ideas are obviously important in all phases of the game but the middlegame is the most productive one for study, especially if you are interested in more advanced tactics. (Here one can draw a parallel to the Chinese school which believes that the middlegame is the most important phase of the game. This is contrary to the western world which tends to focus more on openings and endings, especially when teaching chess, but as Averbakh has mentioned "the theory of the middlegame lags perceptibly behind the two other phases of the game.") Tactics in the opening mainly relate to straightforward traps, whereas tactics in the endgame focus more or less on passed pawns, breakthroughs or stalemates. In the middlegame, as well as in multi-piece endings, there will be several active pieces involved and this is the main reason tactics may not only be complicated but at worst lead to such insurmountable variations that even highly experienced players have problems successfully dealing with them. Such "impossible" variations are really like climbing up a high ice-clad mountain with a pick until the inevitable fall.

How do we know which are the most important tactical positions to study and learn for a lifetime's use? Of course that's a relative notion depending on your talent for tactics and your previous knowledge and experience. For a novice, a position illustrating the way to win with Greco's bishop sacrifice on h7 followed by a mating attack with knight and queen, is important, but if you are already familiar with the main mechanism you will need to study and comprehend more advanced positions with the same concept. The ability to create complex combinations requires prior mastery of basic positions in order to be able to solve the specific tactics demanded in more difficult positions. Since this book is aimed to a rating category ranging from 1000 to 3000, all levels of player have to be satisfied. This implies that the lower the individual player's level the more basic positions he or she is required to master. On a higher level it means that in a complicated position you must figure out whether Greco's gift is correct or not correct. To find the solution obviously demands a high level of skill in the calculation of variations. The area of calculation will also be touched on since it's an extremely important part of tactics, if not the most important part, especially when dealing with complex positions. The famous concept of **"stepping stones"** developed by the Norwegian grandmaster Jonathan Tisdall in his book *Improve Your Chess Now* will also be explained.

We mustn't forget that many positions will be more difficult to solve if we are not aware of the concept of **motif** and **theme** as developed by Kotov. To find the motif is actually to find an answer to the what-question and is a good example why positional and tactical thinking constantly integrate with each other. Most of the time when analysing combinational possibilities the motif is noticed before the theme but sometimes it's the other way around. When motifs and themes have been established it's easier to find the **candidate moves**. Only after these preliminary stages have been considered can we start the concrete calculation of variations where we try to establish the various stepping stones on which to focus. After the establishment of stepping stones the tree will grow until the final stepping stone results in an evaluation. Only after we have compared the different evaluations from the different trees can we be relatively sure which is the best choice of move.

It is not only knowledge of the most relevant positions that is important but also the solutions, provided they are explained in a pedagogical and easy-to-learn manner, since you need to learn the ideas in the most straightforward manner. After all, you are supposed to learn, understand and remember the tactical ideas for a lifetime and therefore you need to embed the positions into your conscious mind

of chess thinking as early as possible in your chess career. Of course this means that if you have been unable to learn appropriate chess thinking early in your life, it's better to learn the ideas later regardless of your age. To be able to carry out this approach to learning successfully it's vital to **revise the positions** from time to time by looking at them again to see if you remember the tactical idea(s) instantly. If you have forgotten the solution in a particular position you should check it again until the relevant idea is permanently stuck in your mind. For the most part, the reason you forget things is because you didn't understand them properly in the first place. What you understand you will remember more easily, especially if you regularly revise the positions. Don't forget to do this as it's the most important piece of advice I can give regarding the technique of studying these important positions. After all, repetition is the mother of knowledge.

When you have finished reading the book, feel free to contact me at **thomasengqvist@protonmail.com**. I would really appreciate your feedback for possible future editions or workbooks.

Part 1:

150 most important tactical positions in the Opening and the Middlegame

1-27: *Five Basic Tricks:* Fork, Discoverer, Pin, Trapping and Overloading

As mentioned in the Introduction the Swedish chess teacher Robert Danielsson gathered together five tactical tricks in a Swedish compendium for beginners: fork, discoverer, pin, trapping and overloading. These tricks should be mastered on a fundamental level before one undertakes the task of solving different combinations. The reason is that the tricks may be intertwined with each other and sometimes be concealed a couple of moves ahead in the position. We cannot expect the combinations to be served on a silver platter even though that will occasionally be the case.

To find combinations is like mining for gold in Alaska. This is also the reason why even very good players sometimes overlook one of the five basic tricks.

Here follow three positions from top level chess where one highly qualified player missed a **fork** at a certain point. It pays to study positions where a strong player missed a tactical solution.

1

Euwe – Smyslov
World Championship,
The Hague/Moscow 1948
White to move

Here Euwe played 27 ♕e3 which received a question mark from Keres even though White still has a technically winning position. Indeed, Euwe went on to win the game after 42 moves.

There are two tactical solutions which would have won the game much quicker. The most efficient would have been 27 ♕xf7+! ♖xf7

13

28 ♖c8+ ♗d8! (*28...♖f8 29 ♖xf8+* followed by a knight fork (double threat) would have been too easy to find.) 29 ♖xd8+ ♖f8 30 ♘e6 (The point of the bishop move to d8 is that *30 ♖xf8+??* loses to *30...♕xf8*). After the fork Black loses a piece since there is no saving queen check. This was no standard combination since the knight decided the game with a fork without a check and maybe this is why Euwe missed it.

Euwe could also have won with the tactical knight fork 27 ♘e6 fxe6 28 ♕xe6+ ♔g7 (*28...♔h8 29 ♖c8*) 29 ♕e4 ♕xe4 30 ♗xe4 ♗xb2 31 ♖c6 but it would have taken longer compared with the queen sacrifice on f7.

2

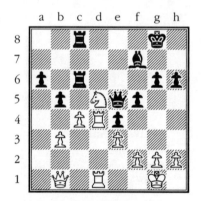

Ding Liren – Giri
Sinquefield Cup, St Louis 2019
White to move

Black had just moved the rook from c7 to c6 instead of to a7 and that gave Ding Liren the opportunity to produce a nice finesse which exploits the forking possibilities hidden in the position.

33 c5!

Giri must have missed this nice move which gives Ding Liren the chance to show what the knight can do if the pawn sacrifice is accepted.

33...a5

33...♖xc5? fails to 34 ♘b6 where the knight not only threatens to win the exchange but also to deliver a knight fork at d7. The idea of the text move is obviously to prevent White from playing b3-b4. The other way of doing this was 33...b4 but then White has good winning chances with the strong knight manoeuvre 34 ♘b6 ♖e8 35 ♘d7.

34 b4 axb4

34...a4 35 ♘c3! is convincing evidence of the knight's versatility in this position.

35 ♕xb4 ♖b8

35...♖xc5? is still met by 36 ♘b6 ♖8c7 37 ♘d7.

36 ♘b6 ♗e6

After 36...♕xc5 37 ♕xc5 ♖xc5 38 ♘d7 Black is forked.

37 ♘d7!

White allows his super knight to be exchanged and in addition sacrifices his c5-pawn to exploit the diagonals and the seventh as well as the eighth rank. A nice transformation of advantages in the spirit of Capablanca and Fischer!

37...♗xd7 38 ♖d5

This intermediate move wasn't necessary. An immediate 38 ♖xd7 was also fine.

38...♕e7 39 ♖xd7 ♕xc5 40 ♕b3+

By exploiting the classical a2-g8 diagonal White forces Black's queen to c4, thereby creating a future invasion square on a7.

40...♕c4 41 ♕b2 ♕c3 42 ♕a2+

A very nice triangulation of the white queen!

42...♖c4

42...♕c4 43 ♕a7 threatening mate on both the seventh and eighth rank.

43 g3

White wants some air for his king so as to enable his d1-rook to become active on d6 with decisive effect. However, even more decisive was to focus on delivering a mate on g7 by means of the continuation 43 ♕a7 ♖f8 44 g3 followed by 45 ♖1d4, cutting off the black queen

from its defence of the g7-square. Then 44...♖a4 loses to 45 ♕b6.

43...♖bc8 44 ♖1d6 ♔f8 45 ♖xg6 b4 46 ♖xh6 f4 47 gxf4 Black resigned.

3

Hermansson – Engqvist
Swedish Championship,
Borlänge 1992
Black to move

I was able to find a most aesthetic move in this game from the Swedish Championship.

20...♘h3!!

I had never seen such an idea before but anyway I realised I had to do something extraordinary in this position. My opponent undoubtedly expected the routine move 20...♘e4? which could have been met by 21 gxf5 (*21 h5? g5*) 21...♗xf5 22 ♘xf5 ♖xf5! with mutual chances.

21 ♖xh3

21 ♗e3 is best answered by the pawn fork 21...f4! 22 h5 (*22 ♖xh3 ♗xg4*) 22...♘g5!! and Black wins since the bishop on e6 is defended.

21...fxg4

A line-opening move to set up a fork with a rook and a pawn is not an everyday occurrence.

22 h5

22...♖xf4!

22...gxh3? leads by force to a position with dynamic equilibrium after 23 ♕xg6+ ♔h8 24 ♗xh6 ♕f6 25 ♗xg7+ ♕xg7 26 ♕xe6 ♕xg3 27 ♕h6+ ♔g8 28 ♘xd5 ♖ae8 29 ♘f6+ ♖xf6 30 ♕xf6.

23 hxg6+

Stronger than 23 ♕xg6+ ♔h8.

23...♔h8

23...♔g8 was also fine. Black won after 24 ♖h5 ♖f3 25 ♕e2 ♕f6 26 ♖e1 ♗g8 27 ♕d2 ♕xg6 28 ♖eh1 ♗h7 29 ♘ge2 ♖af8 30 ♖xd5 ♖f1+ 31 ♖xf1 ♖xf1+ 32 ♘d1 g3 The passed pawns in combination with the bishop pair will decide the game. 33 ♖d8+ ♖f8 34 ♘f4 ♕e4 35 ♖xf8+ ♗xf8 36 ♘c3 ♕h1+ 37 ♕d1 g2 38 ♘ce2 h5 White resigned.

The knight is a tricky piece to handle and normally takes up an outpost in the centre. However, chess is full of exceptions and this position demonstrates that one must also carefully check out decentralising moves, since one of them might turn out to be devastating! Chess would be too easy a game if played by generalisations alone and that is why we must focus on the exceptions. Réti understood this – in contrast to a player like Euwe who was indeed very knowledgeable but not so focused on exceptions.

Here follows six positions where the **discoverer** is the focus. With a discovery three pieces are involved. The first one is sacrificed (or exchanged) and the second one enables a decisive discovery for the third piece.

4

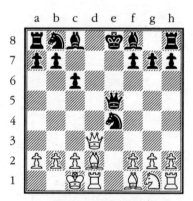

Réti – Tartakower
Vienna 1910
White to move

As a young amateur, Réti managed to beat Tartakower with the most famous discoverer in history.

9 ♕d8+! ♔xd8 10 ♗g5+

Of course the double check 10 ♗a5+?? would be a huge mistake leading nowhere after 10...♔e8 or 10...♔e7.

10...♔c7

10...♔e8 11.♖d8 mate is the so called Opera mate after the Morphy – Duke of Brunswick and Count Isouard game played at a Paris theatre in 1858:

1 e4 e5 2 ♘f3 d6 3 d4 ♗g4 4 dxe5 ♗xf3 5 ♕xf3 dxe5 6. ♗c4 ♘f6 7 ♕b3 ♕e7 8 ♘c3 c6 9 ♗g5 b5 10 ♘xb5 cxb5 11 ♗xb5+ ♘bd7 12. 0–0–0 ♖d8 13 ♖xd7 ♖xd7 14 ♖d1 ♕e6 15 ♗xd7+ ♘xd7

16 ♕b8+! ♘xb8 17. ♖d8 mate.

This game is the most famous of all games and should be learned by heart since it's a very illuminating example of how to play when ahead in development.

11 ♗d8 mate.

Because of this game the beautiful finish is called Réti's mate.

How did the position arise and how could Tartakower fall into this trap?

Well, it arose after **1 e4 c6 2 d4 d5 3 ♘c3 dxe4 4 ♘xe4 ♘f6 5 ♕d3 e5?**

Black makes a mistake which was very common before Morphy entered the arena, i.e. opening up the game when White has more pieces in play. Surprisingly Tartakower commits the same kind of "ancient" error.

6 dxe5 ♕a5+ 7 ♗d2 ♕xe5 8 0–0–0 ♘xe4?? (8...♗e7 was necessary).

One speculation is that Tartakower saw the obvious Opera finale but overlooked the unusual Réti mate.

5

```
   a   b   c   d   e   f   g   h
8      ♜   ♛
7          ♚
6          ♗   ♟       ♜       ♟
5          ♞   ♙       ♙   ♟   ♕
4      ♖           ♟
3  ♟       ♙       ♙       ♖   ♙
2  ♙                           ♙
1                          ♔
```

Mason – Winawer
Vienna 1892
White to move

40 ♖xg5!!

A very strong line-opening move which enables the queen to penetrate to the seventh rank.

40...hxg5

If Black tries to prevent the threatened incursion by 40...♕f8, White wins by controlling the sixth rank instead. After 41 ♖g6 ♖xf5 White can force a winning pawn endgame with 42 ♕xf5! ♕xf5 43 ♖g7+ ♘d7 (*43...♔c8 44 ♖g8+ ♔c7 45 ♖bxb8* and White wins.)

44 ♖xd7+ ♔c8 45 ♖xb8+ ♔xb8 46 ♖b7+ ♔c8 47 ♗d7+ ♕xd7 48 ♖xd7 ♔xd7 49 g4 etc.

41 ♕h7+ ♘d7

41...♔d8 42 ♕h8+ and the rook on f6 falls after 42...♔e7 43 ♕g7+ ♖f7 44 f6+.

42 ♗xd7 ♕g8

42...♕xd7 43 ♖c4+ ♔d8 44 ♕h8+ ♕e8 (*44...♔e7 45.♖xe4+ ♔f7 46.♕h7+*) 45.♕xf6+ and White wins.

43 ♖b7+!! ♔xb7

The rook is overloaded since after 43...♖xb7 44 ♕xg8 the capture of the bishop by 44...♔xd7 is met by 45 ♕g7+

44 ♗c8+!!

The rook check followed by this discovered double check is incredibly beautiful. 44 ♗c6+?? doesn't work since Black has two escape squares on the sixth rank.

44...♔a8 45 ♕xg8

Mason now won easily with queen and bishop against Black's two rooks. Mason has never been known as a famous tactical player which makes this combination even more impressive. Moves 43 and 44 make

this Mason's immortal game and one that is impossible to forget.

6

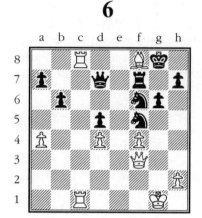

Reshevsky – Fine
New York State Championship
1941
White to move

The best and the most spectacular continuation **48 ♕xd5!!** was unfortunately missed by Reshevsky. This surprising and rare kind of move rests on the notion that sometimes it's better not to exploit a discovered check at once, since now Black will be mated if the queen sacrifice is accepted.

A slower win was by the prosaic 48 ♗h6+ ♘e8 49 ♕xd5 ♘xh6 50 ♕xd7 ♖xd7 51 ♖xe8+ ♔f7 52 ♖ec8 with a technically winning position. In the actual game Reshevsky played the weaker 48 ♗d6+ ♘e8 49 ♗e5 and the game finished in a draw after 61 moves.

48...♘e8

This prolongs his life a little whereas 48...♘xd5 allows mate in three beginning with 49 ♗h6+ and 48...♕xd5 permits mate in four beginning with 49 ♗h6+.

49 ♕xd7 ♖xd7 50 ♖xe8 and White enjoys an extra rook.

7

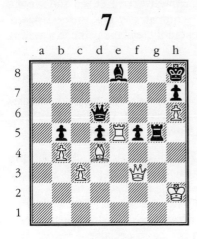

Duras – Spielmann
Pistyan 1912
White to move

45 ♕g3!!

It was not only Marshall who could play beautiful queen moves to g3, as in position 111. Duras knew how to do it as well. His move makes it impossible to parry the threat of ♖xe8+. Note that White cannot release the pin with 45 ♔h1?? since then he would be mated after 45...♕xh6+. However, the tricky text move makes it all possible.

45...♕xh6+ 46 ♕h3 ♕d6

46...♕xh3+ 47 ♔xh3 doesn't help and leads to the loss of a piece.

47 ♔h1

Now this move is fine since the h6-square is protected.

47...♔g8 48 ♖xe8+ ♔f7 49 ♖h8 Black resigned.

8

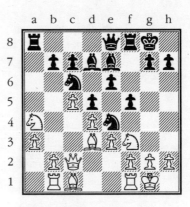

Sjugirov – Dubov
World Rapid Championship 2019
Black to move

16...♖xa4!!

16...♘xd4 is not as strong. After 17 exd4 ♗xa4 the game is equal. If White permits, Black has the possibility of exchanging bishops with 18...♗b5, or else he can advance on the kingside with 18...g5. Dubov played 16...♖f6? 17 ♘c3 ♖h6 and won after imprecise play by White. Black wouldn't have had enough compensation for the pawn after 18 h3!.

17 ♕xa4 ♘xd4 18 ♕d1

The point of the exchange sacrifice is that White cannot play 18 ♕xd4 since the queen would then be trapped in the middle of the board after the forced sequence 18...♗xc5 19 ♕e5 ♗d6 20 ♕d4 c5. It's always beautiful when a queen is caught in the middle of the board, which is not that common even though it does happen from time to time.

18...♘xf3+ 19 ♕xf3 ♘xc5
20 ♗c2 ♘e4

Black has the slightly better game thanks to his stable position in the centre as well as superior harmony of his pieces.

9

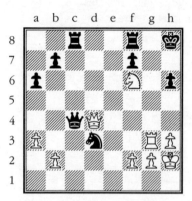

Mittelman – Clausen
Altonaer Schachklub 1929
White to play

White has three pieces in the attack so it's only natural to ask if a mating net can be created? Yes it can!

1 ♖g7!!

An extraordinary move which ignores the fact that the queen is unprotected and at the same time sacrifices the rook. White's main threat is the **Arabian mate** on h7 so Black played...

1...♔xg7

Now if 1...♕xd4 2 ♖h7 mate. To my mind this is the most beautiful example in a practical game of the oldest of all checkmates.

2 ♘e8+

This double check forces the black king to move after which the attacking force of queen and knight, in company with the h3-pawn, inexorably lead the game to a mating finish.

2...♔g6 3 ♕f6+ ♔h5 4 ♘g7 mate.

Note how the tactical themes **discoverer** and **Arabian mate** were intertwined with each other.

The third tactical trick is the **pin** which means that a piece is unable to move due to a bishop, rook or queen pinning the piece. The following five positions illustrate just why a pin can be so decisive.

10

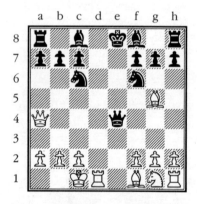

Bronstein – N.N.
Simultaneous display, Sochi 1950
White to move

When pieces are hanging and there are pins involved it might pay handsomely to take a good look around the board. It might just be possible to make a surprise move which exploits the pin(s).

9 ♖d8+!

Exploiting the pin on the c6-knight to set up a pin on the other knight which after **9...♔xd8** will leave the queen undefended after **10 ♕xe4**. So **Black resigned**.

Incidentally, the position arose after 1 e4 e5 2 d4 exd4 3 ♕xd4 ♘c6 4 ♕a4 ♘f6 5 ♘c3 d5 6 ♗g5 dxe4 7 ♘xe4 ♕e7 8 0-0-0 ♕xe4. Bronstein believes that the move which makes the game special, and laid the foundation for a win, was the queen move to a4. It never occurred to Bronstein to go back to d1. What can one learn from this? Normally moving the queen back to its original square should be avoided since that loses time. Instead one should endeavour to annoy the opponent as much as possible with an active queen. This is actually a general advice given by Znosko-Borovsky in *The Middle Game in Chess*. Bronstein even goes so far as to mention the slightly bizarre 4 ♕d2 as a possibility. All this can be read in his classic *200 Open Games*.

11

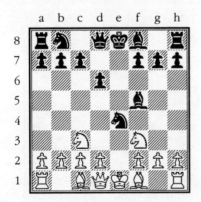

Zapata – Anand
Biel 1988
White to move

The most famous example of a deadly pin in modern top-class chess arose after the following moves: 1 e4 e5 2 ♘f3 ♘f6 3 ♘xe5 d6 4 ♘f3 ♘xe4 5 ♘c3 ♗f5??

6 ♕e2 Black resigned.

If Anand can fall into this trap then anyone can. It's very easy to focus on the e4-square but after 6...♕e7 7 ♘d5 decides.

Anand made the mistake of not taking into account the whole range of movement of the queen's knight, because he was distracted by his primary focus on the e4-square.

I can understand this mistake because it is only natural to focus on the e4-square and the e-file. The knight move to d5 in itself was irrelevant but when the queen arrived on e7 the significance of this move changed to such an extent that it became decisive.

This micro-miniature game actually teaches us how mistakes are born and such knowledge is as vital for the attacking side as well as for the defending side.

What we must do is use this knowledge as a formula of how to win and how to avoid losing in other positions.

An example of how such a formula can be elaborated is the comment to move 16 in position 15, where Keres made a similar tactical mistake as Anand.

These kinds of mistakes will be repeated again and again so do study them!

12

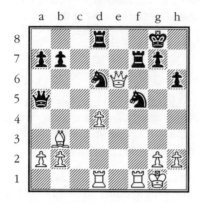

Ståhlberg – Capablanca
Moscow 1935
White to move

The Swedish grandmaster Gideon Ståhlberg played Capablanca four times in serious games and on one occasion he even reached a won position. However, all the games ended in a draw and it can be interesting to learn what mistake Ståhlberg made when he missed the win in their first meeting.

23 g4?

The idea is to win material by 24 ♖xf5 but it seems that Ståhlberg forgot that Black could simply move the king into the corner and neutralise the pressure on the f-file and the classical a2-g8 diagonal.

If Ståhlberg had played 23 ♕e5! he would have achieved maximum pressure on Black's position and most probably would have won the game since Black cannot avoid material loss. 23...♕b6 (*23...♕xe5 24 dxe5 ♔f8 25 ♗xf7*) 24 g4! (*24 ♗xf7+ ♔xf7 25 g4 also wins*) 24...♘h4 25 ♕e7! with threats on f7

and h4. White wins at least the exchange in this variation.

23...♔h8! 24 ♕e5

Now it's too late for this move since the king is no longer on g8. 24 gxf5 ♖xf5 is nothing for White.

24...♕xe5 25 dxe5 ♘e3!

It's because of this tactical move that Black manages to free himself from White's tactical grip.

26 ♗xf7

26 ♖xf7 ♘xf7 27 ♖e1 ♘xe5 28 ♖xe3 ♘xg4 results in a drawish game since Black has active play as well as an extra pawn.

26...♘xd1 27 exd6

27 ♗g6?! ♘e3 28 ♖e1 ♘dc4 29 e6 ♖d1 30 ♖xd1 ♘xd1 31 e7 ♘d6 leads to a position where White is fighting for a draw.

27...♖xd6 Draw.

13

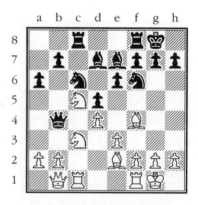

Dus-Chotimirsky – Capablanca
St Petersburg 1913
Black to move

Capablanca was famous for his small but effective combinations and this is one of them.

15...②xd4!

Such a combination can certainly be overlooked since the queen is exploiting the seemingly closed fourth rank.

Capablanca's move actually eliminates the e3-pawn (not the d4-pawn!) which will then leave the bishop on f4 unprotected.

Dus-Chotimirsky probably expected the inferior 15...♗xc5?, which he might have answered with the practically forced continuation 16 a3 ♕a5 17 dxc5 ♕xc5 18 ②e4 ♕b6 19 ②xf6+ gxf6 20 ♗d3.

White has his bishop pair directed at Black's weakened kingside and that in itself should be enough compensation for the sacrificed d4-pawn.

16 exd4

16 ②xd7 ②xe2+ 17 ②xe2 ②xd7 would have been a better defence since White has only lost one pawn compared with two in the game.

16...♗xc5 17 a3

17 dxc5 ♕xf4 loses only one pawn but the price is too high after 18 b4 d4 19 ②d1 e5 since Black has not only taken over the centre but practically the whole board.

17...♕xd4 18 ♗g3 ♗e7

And **Black won** easily with his two extra pawns in the centre.

14

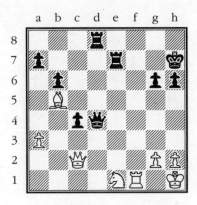

Aronsson – Engqvist
Stockholm 2018
Black to move

Decentralising moves are sometimes harder to find as I experienced in the following position where I didn't find the killer-move...

32...♕a1!

White has no defence since Black's next move will be the devastating 33...♖d1. In the game I played the centralising 32...♕e5? but White parried the double threat easily with 33 ♕b1 and eventually managed to draw.

33 ♕f2 ♖d1 34 ♗e8!!

White's last chance to stir the pot.

34...♕b1!!

This nice queen move keeps up the pressure on e1 as well as defending the critical g6-square. Of course not 34...♖exe1?? 35 ♗xg6+! and Black is mated in three moves. 34...♖dxe1? is also bad and leads to a perpetual check after 35 ♗xg6+! ♔xg6 36 ♕f5+ ♔g7 37 ♕f8+ ♔h7 38 ♕f5+.

15

Kotov – Keres
Candidates tournament,
Budapest 1950
White to move

White has very strong pressure along the b1-h7 diagonal and it's possible to increase this still further with the pretty move **16 ♘f4!!** exploiting the fact that both the g6-knight and the g5-pawn are pinned. Four white pieces are participating in the attack against the king. "A brilliant turn" wrote the fellow-participant Swedish grandmaster Gideon Ståhlberg in the tournament book.

16...gxh4

Keres had forgotten to calculate that 16...♕e8 is met by 17 ♘h5! (Here we have a tactical mistake which echoes the miniature Zapata – Anand, position 11, and where Keres was focused on g6 just like Anand was focused on e4. Keres missed the knight move to h5 and Anand the knight move to d5. The knight move to h5 wasn't dangerous when the bishop was threatened on h4 but when the queen moved to e8 it

became strong.) threatening a deadly royal fork on f6. White is clearly better after 17...♕e7 18 ♗f2 ♗xc4 19 h4 when a fifth piece is introduced into the attack, the h1-rook, but this was still Keres's best option.

17 ♘xg6 ♖e8

18 ♘h8!!

This knight is a true hero since it exploits every opportunity on the board. It not only opens the b1-h7 diagonal but puts pressure on another weak spot – f7. In this original manner the knight maintains its strong attacking position. It's quite something to jump all the way from h3-h8, especially when these manoeuvres are based on tactics, since the knight has been immune from capture on the f4, g6 and h8 squares. What a knight! And that is an understatement...

18...♖e7 19 ♕h7+ ♔f8

White cannot have everything. Now the knight is in the way of the queen so there is no mate on h8. So White needs other pieces to decide the game.

20 f4!

"Kotov plays the whole game in his best style and doesn't give his opponent any breathing space." (Ståhlberg).

20...♘xc4

It's not possible to escape with the king because after 20...♔e8 21 ♘xf7! ♖xf7 22 ♗g6 ♕e7 23 f5 decides. According to the computer the best move is 20...♗xc4 but White is still winning after 21 f5.

21 f5 exf5

Otherwise White plays the f-pawn to f6, which would be a tremendous wedge in Black's position.

22 0–0! ♗c8 23 ♗xf5 ♗xf5 24 ♖xf5 ♔e8 25 ♖xf7

25 ♘xf7 wins too but why allow Black the tricky 25...♔d7? The computer suggests the incredible 25 ♖f6!! when the idea is to be able to play 27 ♕f5+ after 26 ♘xf7 ♔d7. White has now broken through and wins easily.

25...♔d7 26.♕f5+ ♔c6 27.♕f6+ ♔d7 28.e6+ ♔c6

28...♔d6 29 ♖xe7 and now 29...♕xe7 isn't possible because of 30 ♘f7+.

29 ♖xe7 ♕xh8 30 ♖xc7+! ♔b5

Or 30...♔xc7 31 ♕e7+ ♔b8 32 ♖f1.

31 ♕e7 a5 32 ♕d7+ ♔a6 33 ♖b1

It's a forced mate in nine moves. A very beautifully played game by Kotov. What will remain in the memory though is the incredible knight manoeuvre!

Next follow five positions where **trapping** is the theme. All chess

pieces are able to trap an enemy piece so this is a tactical trick to look out for all the time.

16

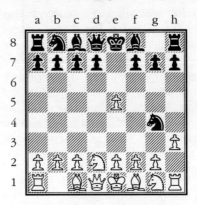

Gibaud – Lazard
Paris 1924
Black to move

This famous and important position arose after the moves 1 d4 ♘f6 2 ♘d2!? e5 3 dxe5 ♘g4 4 h3??. It's probably the most famous micro-miniature ever played. White obviously expected 4...♘xe5 but instead the shocker...

4...♘e3!!

appeared on the board. White had to resign on the spot since his queen is trapped and 5 fxe3 is met by the diagonal mate 5...♕h4+ 6 g3 ♕xg3 mate.

Why can this position be regarded as important, since surely 99.9 percent of relatively experienced chess players would go for 4 ♘gf3? Besides, Breyer's 2 ♘d2!? is pretty unusual too. We can be fairly certain that this game will not be repeated. I checked the latest Mega Database

(2020) which contains more than 8,000,000 million games and only 21 games reached the position after 1 d4 ♘f6 2 ♘d2 e5 3 dxe5 ♘g4. No one played 4 h3 since the game is so universally well-known. So why should we still have to learn this game by heart? We cannot deny the fact that this miniature is aesthetically appealing. After all, the contrast between the two ladies is astonishing, considering that the white queen cannot move at all whereas Black's queen is much more mobile. This fact alone increases the beauty value. However, there are also some lessons to be learned.

First of all it does show the effectiveness of maximal co-operation between an active knight and an active queen. This idea in itself is fundamentally important since it can be used as an overall strategy in other positions as well. There are always two pieces which lay the foundations for making a combination possible: one which is sacrificed and one which decides the game. If a knight and a queen enter the game early it's sometimes possible to use them to exert tactical pressure on the opponent. It's important to be aware of the fact that under ideal circumstances combined play with queen and knight can be decisive, since these two pieces work so well together in view of their different movements which complement each other. A queen and a bishop don't have the same ability to co-operate unless the queen and the bishop are placed on different coloured squares. In the miniature game the black queen operated on the black squares (a potential check to the king on e1) while the black

knight would decide the game on a white square (...♘xd1).

Another interesting lesson from this miniature is that the queen on d8 hasn't moved at all but still plays a key role. Many times it's clever not to move the queen in order to save time for other moves. So it can be rewarding to allow the queen to remain on its original square, as it can swing over to the kingside in one move, in this case to h4 and checkmate the king on e1. It's important to understand that the queen, on its original square, can reach the enemy king in one move regardless of whether it is placed on e1, g1 or c1. To be able to take advantage of the fact that the queens are placed on the same colour as the opposing king is sometimes of crucial importance. An instructive example is the move 16...♕a5! as played in the game Alekhine – Réti, position 20, where 17...♕b6+ was crucial to saving half a point.

17

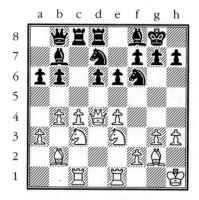

Renman – Kasparov
European Team Championship,
Skara 1980
Black to move

23...♘c5!

A tricky knight move exploiting the centralised position of the white queen. It's pretty well masked since on move 22 Kasparov moved his queen from a8 to b8 while Renman went for waiting moves with his king between h2 and h1 on moves 22 and 23. It seemed that both were just playing waiting moves but Black had a poisoned arrow ready to shoot if the Swedish player continued his wait-and-see game.

24 ♖c2

White must firstly defend against the knight fork on b3 and secondly against ...e6-e5 which wins the e4-pawn. Capturing the knight is taboo because of the queen on b8, After 24 bxc5? dxc5 the escape square e5 is under Black's control.

24...e5 25 ♕d1 ♘cxe4 26 ♘xe4 ♗xe4 27 ♗xe4 ♘xe4 28 ♕f3 ♘f6

Despite the fact that White has good control of the light squares it's not enough compensation for the lost e4-pawn. Kasparov capitalised on his extra pawn and won after 45 moves.

The moral of the story is to play in such a way that subtle traps are laid for the opponent but are masked by apparently just playing a waiting game. Then it's easier to hide real intentions from the opponent just like Kasparov did against Renman. Most of the time great players have more than one idea behind their moves: one which is relatively easy to see and one which demands a higher level of chess culture.

18

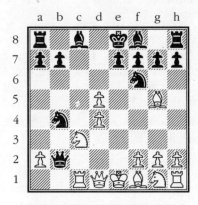

Botvinnik – Spielmann
Moscow 1935
White to move

When Black enters complications such as capturing the "poisoned" b2-pawn, both players must keep control of all variations linked to a possible trapping of the queen. Nevertheless here it seems that Rudolf Spielmann, a high-calibre combinative player, made a mistake in his calculations. This was probably due to the fact that the trap was slightly different and therefore tricky. It's easy to focus on the b5-square (Remember the formula from Zapata – Anand!) but that square isn't the key to trapping the queen in this particular position.

9 ♘a4! ♕xa2

9...♕a3 10 ♖c3 ♕xa2 11 ♗c4 also wins the queen.

10 ♗c4 ♗g4

As we have seen, 10...♕a3 11 ♖c3 wins but obviously not 11 ♖a1?? ♕xa1 12 ♕xa1 ♘c2+ when Black decides with a fork.

11 ♘f3 ♗xf3 12 gxf3 Black resigned.

According to Botvinnik's comments, Spielmann thought for a long time before resigning. He could have continued playing on a piece down by 12...♕a3 13 ♖c3 ♘c2+ but probably he was patently depressed after trying to fool Botvinnik and getting fooled himself.

19

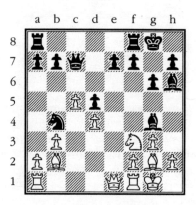

Böök – Sköld
Scandinavian Championship 1956
Black to move

16...♘c2 17 ♕e5

The Finnish player probably thought that this riposte would save him from losing the exchange but Black had seen further...

17...♕d7!

17...♕xe5? 18 ♘xe5 ♗e2 (Of course not *18...♘xa1?? 19 ♘xg4* and two minor pieces are hanging.) 19 ♗xd5 ♘xa1 20 ♖xa1 ♗a6 21 b4 and White has the slightly better game thanks to his strong position in the centre and active pawn majority on the queenside.

18 ♖ad1?

18 h3 ♗xf3 19 ♗xf3 ♘xa1 20 ♖xa1 was a better continuation but Black obviously remains clearly on top with his material advantage after 20...e6.

18...♘e3! White resigned.

It was this diabolical trap that the Swedish player, a very strong tactician, planned with his seventeenth move. If White captures the knight with the pawn then his queen will be trapped in the middle of the board by ...f7-f6. However, Black will play ...f7-f6 regardless of White's next move so White resigned. I have managed to get my queen behind bars myself on the e5-square on two occasions so I know the feeling. It's easy to think that the queen is stronger when centralised but if there are numerous pieces still on the board you must always be mindful of possible finesses which cut off any retreat for the queen.

20

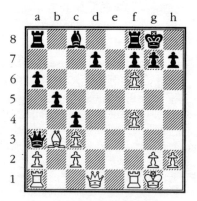

Alekhine – Réti
Vienna 1922
White to move

Here is seems that White's bishop on b3 is doomed but White can miraculously save it by means of tactical resources.

16 ♕d5!

Now it looks like Black is in trouble due to the double threat of 17 ♕g5 and 17 ♕xa8.

16...♕a5! 17 fxg7

White has to change plan since none of his threats work now. After 17 ♕g5? ♕b6+ followed by 18...♕xf6 Black wins since the bishop on b3 is trapped. 17 ♕xa8? is also met by the decisive check 17...♕b6+ followed by 18...♗b7 winning material.

17...♕b6+

This check is crucial to saving half a point. 17...♔xg7? loses after 18 ♕g5+ ♔h8 19 ♕f6+ ♔g8 20 ♖f3 and Black's king will succumb to White's queen and rook. 20...♖e8 (or *20...♖d8 21 ♖g3+ ♔f8 22 ♕d6+ ♔e8 23 ♖e3 mate.*) 21 ♖g3+ ♔f8 22 ♕d6+ ♖e7 23 ♕h6+ ♔e8 24 ♖g8 mate. Note the co-operation between the queen and the rook. The queen operated on the sixth rank and the d6-f8 and h6-f8 diagonals while the rook decided the game by exploiting

the e- and g-files as well as the eighth rank.

18 ♔h1 ♔xg7

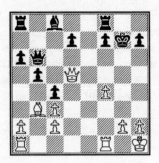

19 ♗xc4!

This is the miracle.

19...♗b7

Not 19...bxc4? 20 ♕xa8 ♗b7 21 ♖ab1! and White wins, for example 21...♕xb1 22 ♕xf8+. Note the importance of the natural move 18 ♔h1 since 18 ♖f2?? would have broken connection with the queen's rook. Incidentally 21 ♖fb1?? is obviously wrong because of 21...♕xb1+ followed by 22...♗xa8.

20 ♕e5+ ♕f6

It's in Black's interest to exchange queens because of his weaker king's position.

21 ♗d3

Now Black should have replied **21...♕xe5!** (Réti played the inaccurate *21...♖fe8?!* which allowed Alekhine to keep queens on the board with *22 ♕h5* thereby maintaining a slight edge. However the game ended in a draw after 61 moves.) **22 fxe5** and continued with **22...♖fc8** when a plausible continuation would have been

23 ♖f4 ♖xc3 24 ♖g4+ ♔h8 25 ♖h4 ♖e8 26 ♖xh7+ 26 ♗xh7?! ♔g7! 26...♔g8 27 ♖h5 ♖c5 and the e5-pawn is lost with an equal game, as 28 ♖e1 is met by 28...d6.

Overloading is the last fundamental tactical trick and it means that one piece is unable to control two vital squares at the same time. We will look at seven positions to illustrate this relatively common tactical idea.

21

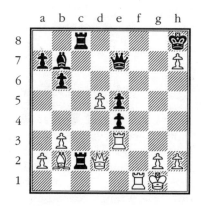

Zukertort – Blackburne
London 1883
White to move

28 ♕b4!! ♖8c5

28...♖e8 loses to the spectacular 29 ♖f8+!! (The computer suggests the simple *29 ♕xe7 ♖xe7 30 ♖h3*) 29...♕xf8 30 ♗xe5+ ♔xh7 31 ♕xe4+ ♔h6 32 ♕h4+ ♔g6 33 ♖g3+.

The queen is immune from capture since after 28...♕xb4 it's game over in seven moves after 29 ♗xe5+ ♔xh7 30 ♖h3+ ♔g6 31 ♖f6+ ♔g5 32 ♖g3+ ♔h5 33 ♖f5+ ♔h6

34 ♗f4+ ♔h7 35 ♖h5 mate.

29 ♖f8+!!

In his annotations Steinitz states that this move, together with the previous one, represents one of the most attractive combinations ever played.

29...♔xh7

29...♕xf8 30 ♗xe5+ ♔xh7 31 ♕xe4+ ♔h6 32 ♕h4+ ♔g6 33 ♕g4+ ♔h7 34 ♖h3+ and mate next move.

30 ♕xe4+ ♔g7 31 ♗xe5+!!

The computer recommends the faster and more spectacular 31 ♖g8+!! which leads to mate in six moves after 31...♔xg8 32 ♕g6+ ♕g7 33 ♕e8+ ♕f8 34 ♖g3+ ♔h7 35 ♕d7+ ♔h8 36 ♗xe5+ etc.

31...♔xf8 32 ♗g7+! ♔g8

32...♕xg7 33 ♕e8 mate.

33 ♕xe7 Black resigned.

22

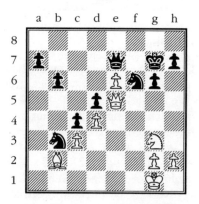

Botvinnik – Capablanca
AVRO tournament, Holland 1938
White to move

30 ♗a3!!

The point of this sacrifice is that the queen will be lured away from e7, thereby weakening the defence of the f6-knight. Later Botvinnik wrote that this famous position was used when he constructed the chess program *Pioneer*. "In my opinion, the process of playing (and probably, of any game) consists in a generalised exchange. A generalised exchange is what we call an exchange where (in a general sense) the changes have both material and positional (invisible) values. The aim of a generalised exchange is a relative gain of these material or positional values. There are and cannot be any other aims. In this position the black queen has the greatest positional value, while for White it's the bishop on b2 that has the least value (of those pieces which a chess master takes into account in his calculations). It should be mentioned that for an exchange of these positional values (in contrast to an exchange of the average material values of the pieces), it is not essential for the pieces to be removed from the board, they only need to leave those squares on which they are placed. Therefore in the variation 30 ♗a3 ♛xa3 the exchange of positional values increases the strength of the position of the white pieces, since the black queen leaves the square e7."

30...♛xa3

Botvinnik gives 30...♛e8 31 ♛c7+ ♔g8 32 ♗e7 ♘g4 33 ♛d7 but it's no improvement on the game continuation.

31 ♘h5+!

31... gxh5

Botvinnik must have calculated 31...♔h6 32 ♘xf6 ♛c1+ 33 ♔f2 ♛d2+ 34 ♔g3 ♛xc3+ 35 ♔h4 ♛xd4+ 36 ♘g4+! since he mentioned it in his comments but above all it was important for him to see the variation was forced before sacrificing the bishop on a3.

32 ♛g5+ ♔f8 33 ♛xf6+ ♔g8 34 e7

This was most probably a stepping stone position (positions 55-56) where Botvinnik calculated the variations, since he had to calculate precisely how his king could eventually escape Black's queen checks.

34...♛c1+ 35 ♔f2 ♛c2+ 36 ♔g3 ♛d3+ 37 ♔h4 ♛e4+ 38 ♔xh5 ♛e2+ 39 ♔h4 ♛e4+ 40 g4 ♛e1+ 41 ♔h5 Black resigned.

An instructive example showing how bad pieces should be sacrificed – in the way that Botvinnik so insightfully expressed it in his annotations to his immortal 30th move.

23

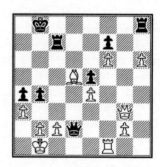

Carlsen – Kotronias
Olympiad, Mallorca 2004
White to move

22 ♘xf6!! ♚xf6 23 ♖xd6+!

This overloading combination is rather unusual since it involves two sacrifices instead of one.

23...♚e7

If 23...♛xd6 then 24 ♛xe3 with a double threat on g5 and a7.

24 ♖xc6 ♛xc6 25 ♛xe3 ♖c7 26 f6+

White is clearly winning with three pawns and a bishop for a rook and moreover Black's king is exposed. However, Carlsen failed to win this position and it can be worthwhile to analyse what happened.

26...♚d8 27 ♛d3+ ♚c8 28 ♗d5 ♛b6 29 ♛g3

It's better to defend the h4-pawn economically with 29 g3 which literally kills off the rook's function on h8.

29...♛d4

29...♛a6 was a better queen move.

30 h5 ♚b8 31 h6?

Here the pawn becomes a weakness and provides a telling example of why one shouldn't break Philidor's famous rule which states that pawns should advance in a phalanx. It would have been better to play pragmatically with 31 ♛f3 followed by g2-g4.

31...a4?

31...♛c5 was better since it's not possible to defend the c3-pawn without losing the h6-pawn.

32 a3

White prevents ...a3 once and for all.

32...♛d2

32...♛c5! was more precise.

33 axb4?

The turning-point in the game for White since Black now grabs a lifeline. Correct was 33.♖c1 with a winning position since Black's king is in a very precarious position.

33...♛xc2+ 34 ♚a1

34 ♚a2! with the idea of meeting 34...a3 with 35 ♖f2 was correct.

34...a3!

Probably Carlsen underestimated the consequences of this move. 35 ♖f2?? obviously doesn't work now since 35...axb2 is check.

35 bxa3

The alternative 35 ♕xe5 axb2+ 36 ♕xb2 ♖a7+ 37 ♗a2 ♕xe4 leads to a position of dynamic equilibrium.

35...♖xh6 36 ♕xe5 ♕d3!

The key move which saves Black half a point and reveals the main idea behind his 34th move. The double threat against f1 and a3 cannot be parried. Carlsen has to be satisfied with a perpetual check.

37 ♕e8+ ♖c8 38 ♕e5+ ♖c7 39 ♕e8+ ♖c8 40 ♕e5+ Draw.

24

Karpov – Taimanov
USSR Team Championship 1977
Black to move

38...♘g3+! White resigned.

The queen is overloaded and if 39 hxg3 then 39...♖a8 followed by 40...♖h8 mate.

Remember this idea because it will return in a more advanced form in the endgame section, position 268.

25

Morphy – Harrwitz
Paris 1858
White to move

Tactical play is often a matter of the principle of the two (tactical) weaknesses. A fundamental example is the following. Morphy played...

30 c5!

A crushing move which attacks the base of Black's pawn centre and exploits the fact that both the d6-pawn and the c7-rook are overloaded. The forced variation 30 ♖xh7+? ♔xh7 31 ♕h5+ ♔g8 32 ♘h6+ (*32 ♔h1!?*) 32...♔g7 33 ♘f5+ leads to a perpetual check.

30...♖xc5

The computer suggests 30...♖d7 as the best defence but after 31 ♘xd6 ♗xd6 32 cxd6 e4 33 ♕e3 ♖dxd6 34 ♕d4+ ♔g8 35 ♖e5, followed by 36 ♕xe4, the situation is hopeless for Black.

31 ♖xh7+ ♔xh7 32 ♕h5+ ♔g8 33 ♘xe7+

This is the reason why the c7-rook was overloaded. White can now profit from the fact that it no longer protects the e7-square and so has left Black's queen overloaded.

33...♔g7 34 ♘f5+ ♔g8 35 ♘xd6 Black resigned.

The rook is pinned and will be lost after the queen moves. A simple example but nevertheless one that is instructive when explaining fundamental tactics and how several tactical ideas such as overloading and the pin interlink. Here this was illustrated by the knight on moves 33 and 35.

26

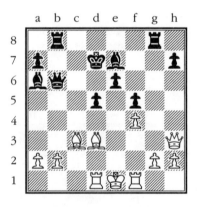

Menchik – Graf
Women's World Championship,
Semmering 1937
White to move

Graf's last move was the fatal 20...♘g4?? to which Menchik responded with the thunderbolt...

21 ♖d7!! Black resigned.

21 ♕xh5? was inferior due to 21...♕xh2+! 22 ♕xh2 ♘xh2, though White is a clear pawn up after 23 ♘xf7 ♔xf7 (*23...♘xf1? loses to 24 ♘h6+ ♔h7 25 ♖d7 ♔xh6 26 ♖xe7.*) 24 ♔xh2.

Menchik's devastating continuation is a good illustration of overloading. The main point is that Black's queen cannot protect the vital d7 and h2 squares at the same time. Graf resigned on the spot since 21...♕xd7 is met by 22 ♕xh5! gxh5 23 ♗h7 mate. Of course it was no longer possible to reply 22...♕xh2+.

27

a b c d e f g h

Reggio – Mieses
Monte Carlo 1903
Black to move

Black's dream is to play the queen to e3 and checkmate on e2. What's amazing is that the dream can be fulfilled by means of two spectacular sacrifices.

22...♖g3!!

The main purpose of this astonishing sacrifice is to force the queen to a fatal square.

23 ♕xg3

After 23 hxg3 ♕e3+ Black's dream comes true.

23...♗h4! White resigned.

A very beautiful finish since it turns out that White must give up the queen to avoid mate. However, White could in fact have continued the game with 24 ♗xa6 (Not *24 ♕xh4 ♕e3+ 25 ♗e2 ♕xe2* mate.) 24...♗xg3+ 25 hxg3 ♕xa6 26 ♖h1 since Black must still prove that he can win the game.

28-45: Mating Combinations

28-39: The magnet sacrifice and back rank mate.

An important area within tactics is an attack on the king. After castling a king is normally thought to be in a safe position because of the three (home) pawns that protect it. One of the most important tactical problems to solve, especially for a player who is fond of storming the castled position, is how to get at a relatively safe king. Generally there are three methods to keep in mind:

1) Try to get some kind of strategic advantage on the same side as the castled king. For example it may be that you have more pieces than your opponent on the same flank where the enemy king is situated.

2) Try to provoke weaknesses in the castled position, for example with the help of sacrifices or favourable piece exchanges and with the aim of penetrating the defensive castle wall. The most common hero in the black defence is the f6-knight which defends h7 but there are other important squares such as h5 and g4 from which White would like to launch an attack with his queen.

3) Learn different mating procedures, i.e. manoeuvring which leads to mate. In the following position White has a clearly winning position and the only question is how to win in the most effective manner.

28

Leiser – Buscaglia
Swiss Championship 1957
White to move

1 ℤc3

The logical move which takes under control an open file with gain of tempo and prepares the following knight sacrifice on e6, the weakest point in Black's position. It was possible to sacrifice at once on e6 and then play the rook to c3 but that would "only" lead to material gain, whereas now it's probable that Black will be mated. A more positional way of playing was by 1 h5, squeezing Black's position. To squeeze is an expression which was popularized in Gelfand's book *Positional Decision Making in Chess*.

1...♛d8 2 ♞xe6!

This is the most logical and elegant continuation. White sacrifices his knight in the heart of Black's position and thereby follows

36

the famous attacking principle developed by Steinitz. According to this principle the player who has a great advantage must attack at once and against the weakest point, otherwise the opponent might improve his position. The tactical idea is to lure the "relatively" safe king out in the open where it will be more insecure.

2...♔xe6

3 ♕xd5+!!

The second sacrifice is no less than a queen sacrifice and this is the climax of the combination because now the black king is in such an exposed position in the centre of the board that it will succumb to mate.

3...♔xd5 4.♖d1+ ♔e4

4...♔e6 allows 5.♗c4 mate and this has been made possible because the most important pawns at e6 and d5 have been eliminated and left the king exposed on the classical a2-g8 diagonal.

5 ♖c4+ ♔f3 6 ♖d3+ ♔g4 7 ♗e2+ ♔xh4 8 ♖cc3

Now it's not possible to prevent 9 ♖h3 so **Black resigned.**

We have just seen an example of a magnet sacrifice, which in this case

worked as a mating operation, i.e. method No.3 mentioned above. We have also illustrated method No.2 since the purpose of the two sacrifices was to weaken the pawn cover in front of Black's king, along the classical a2-g8 diagonal. Black's king hadn't castled but its position could still be regarded as relatively secure due to the black pawn wall h7-g6-f5-e6-d5 which protected it. If we go back to the first diagram we can see that six pieces had the potential to attack Black's king so there was never any doubt that the strategic foundations had already been laid and the position was ripe for a decisive combination. This reasoning indicates that we also have played according to method No.1.

29

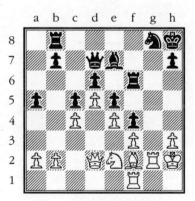

Averbakh – Kotov
Candidates tournament,
Zürich 1953
Black to move

In the tournament book Bronstein writes that the creative element in chess consists of four things: logic, calculation, technique and intuition (imagination). The following move

37

shows when it's important to trust your intuition since it's too complicated to rely on calculation alone.

30...♕xh3+!!

The combinational point is to lure the king to f5 where it will be abandoned by its own pieces while Black attacks with his two rooks and two minor pieces.

31 ♔xh3

After 31 ♔g1 ♖h6 32 ♗e1 ♕h1+ 33 ♔f2, by introducing a third piece in the attack White is massacred by the killer-blow 33...♗h4+.

31...♖h6+ 32 ♔g4 ♘f6+

32...♖f8 also wins but the knight must go to f6 on the next move anyway so it makes sense to play it there immediately.

33 ♔f5

33.♔g5 is met by 33...♖h5 mate.

33...♘d7

Kotov was in time trouble and didn't want to spoil his position before move 40. Nevertheless he made a strong move. The natural 33...♖f8?? would have lost after 34.♔e6 since there is no mate.

In post mortem analysis, Ståhlberg recommended 33...♘g4 which, like the move in the game, wins. The purpose is to prevent White from placing his rook on g5. The knight is immune from capture because of mate by the enemy rooks. The only way to avoid mate is by 34 ♘xf4 but then Black wins after 34...♖g8! (*34...♖f8+? looks like it's winning but White is all right after the incredible continuation 35 ♔xg4 ♖g8+ 36 ♘g6+ ♖gxg6+ 37 ♔f5 ♖h5+ 38 ♖g5 ♗xg5 39 ♔g4!! ♗xd2+ 40 ♔xh5 and an equal endgame has arisen out of nowhere.*) 35.♘h5 ♖hg6! 36.♕g5! ♗xg5! (*36...♖xg5+?? loses to 37 ♔e6*) 37 ♔xg4 ♗f4+ 38 ♔h3 ♖xg2 etc. Bronstein writes that since Kotov didn't play this variation the sacrifice on h3 isn't based on calculation but on intuition. Of course it's not easy to see this continuation if one is not of the same calibre as a computer.

34 ♖g5!

The best way to avoid the mate in three by ...♖f8+, ...♖g8+ and ...♖f6.

34...♖f8+ 35 ♔g4 ♘f6+ 36 ♔f5 ♘g8+ 37 ♔g4 ♘f6+ 38 ♔f5 ♘xd5+

Kotov eliminates any risk of a draw by repetition as move 40 draws closer and closer.

39 ♔g4 ♘f6+ 40 ♔f5 ♘g8+ 41 ♔g4 ♘f6+ 42 ♔f5 ♘g8+ 43 ♔g4 ♗xg5 44 ♔xg5 ♖f7!

Black is threatening mate in two moves with the rooks and White must give back his material advantage to defend against this.

45 ♗h4

This is relatively best – to control f6.

45...♖g6+ 46 ♔h5 ♖fg7 47 ♗g5

White must prevent the mate on h6.

47...♖xg5+ 48 ♔h4 ♘f6

Black is threatening mate on h5 and so White must continue sacrificing.

49 ♘g3 ♖xg3 50 ♕xd6 ♖3g6 51 ♕b8+

White has been checked thirteen times and one can understand his desire to give one last spite check to Black's king!

51...♖g8 White resigned.

This game won first prize for the most beautiful game in the tournament. This queen sacrifice on

h3 will always be regarded as Kotov's immortal combination and never forgotten.

30

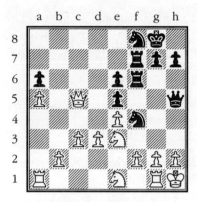

Hermann – Hussong
Frankfurt 1930
Black to move

When analysing the position the first thing to check is whether the magnet combination **23...♕xh2+** works. 23...♖h6?? is too slow. After 24 ♘f1 White wins thanks to his material advantage. The other candidate move to look at is 23...♘e2? followed by 24...♕xh2+ and 25...♖h6 mate. But White calmly replies 24 ♘f3 with a slight advantage so this move can be excluded from any further analysis.

24 ♔xh2 ♖h6+ 25 ♔g3 ♘e2+ 26 ♔g4 ♖f4+ 27 ♔g5

Now, as White has entered the fifth rank with his king, Black should be able to mate with so many pieces at his disposal. In fact he can decide the game in several ways and there are even two different paths to checkmate in four moves.

27...♜h2

Quicker was 27...♜fh4! 28 ♛xf8+ ♚xf8 29 g4 ♞xg1 followed by 30...♞h3 mate. The alternatives 29...♜h3 or 29...♜h2 are also good enough since 30...♜g6 mate cannot be prevented. Another quick finish would be 27...♜ff6! 28 ♛xf8+ ♚xf8 29 ♚g4 ♜fg6+ 30 ♚f3 ♞xg1 mate.

28 ♛xf8+ ♚xf8 29 ♞f3

White's position is totally lost but after this move Black has a forced mate in four.

29...h6+ 30 ♚g6 ♚g8! 31 ♞xh2

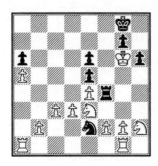

31...♜f5!!

Black is threatening mate on both g5 and f4.

32 exf5

32 g3 ♜g5 mate.

32...♞f4 mate.

So the active knight on f4 was the man of the match, except in the variation where 27...♜fh4 was played because the knight wasn't needed as Black also had the option of playing 29...♜h3 or 29...♜h2 followed by 30...♜g6 mate.

But, on the other hand, it would have been impossible to drive the king to g4 if it weren't for the knight check on e2 which by the way also freed the f4-square for Black's most passive rook. Apart from the knight's movements it's fascinating to see the capabilities of the rooks which weaved a mating net vertically as well as horizontally. Finally, one might think that the h7-pawn was necessary for the grand finale but this wasn't the case as the knight on f8 could have also mated the king on g5 by exploiting the vacant h7 square.

31

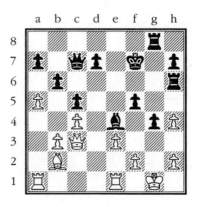

Svidler – Andreikin
World Rapidplay Championship,
St Petersburg 2018
Black to move

Here Black has four pieces aiming at White's kingside as well as two aggressively placed pawns. We can also see that White's king is poorly defended. It's logical to look for a breakthrough, indeed there are several options for this but which one is the most appropriate?

25...♛xh2+!!

Obviously 25...♜xh4?? fails to 26 ♛f6+ and the rook falls. 25...g3 is possible, although it complicates the win after 26 hxg3 ♖xg3+ 27 ♔f1.

26 ♔xh2 ♖xh4+ 27 ♔g3

27.♔g1 ♖h1 mate.

27...♖h3+ 28 ♔f4 ♖f3+

It's important to play the moves in the right order because if first 28...♖g6? White has the saving move 29 ♕g7+! with an equal game.

29 ♔e5 ♖g6!

It's not possible to prevent 30...♖e6 mate so **White resigned**. Such a combination is not that hard to find if you are familiar with mating operations from similar positions. It was most difficult to discover the quiet 29th move which reminds us of 8 ♖cc3 from Leiser – Buscaglia, position 28.

32

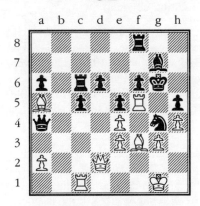

Matlakov – Kokarev
Russia 2019
White to move

30 ♖xh5!

The prelude to a nice combination in which the black king is drawn

into the white position like a magnet.

30...♔xh5 31 ♗xg4+ ♔h6

31...♔xg4? falls into a mate in four: 32 ♕e2+ ♔h3 33 ♕f1+ ♔g4 34 ♕f5+ ♔xg3 35 ♗e1 mate. White's combination becomes more stylish due to the fact that it's easy to forget that the bishop on a5, placed on the queenside, is an attacking piece. Karpov had a clever metaphor stating that a bishop manoeuvre where the edges of the chessboard are utilised is like playing billiards. Such a metaphor is obviously good to be aware of since it will be easier to discover bishop moves along the edges (from a5 to e1) when you compare them with the movement of a billiard ball.

32 ♗f5

Black is lost since all his pieces are misplaced and unable to resist the attack on the white squares.

32...♖cc8 33 ♖f1 ♖b8 34 g4 ♗h8 35 g5+ ♔g7 36 ♗c7 ♕c6 37 gxf6+

Even stronger is 37 ♗xb8 ♖xb8 38 ♕d1.

37...♔f7 38 ♗xb8 ♖xb8 39 ♕g2 ♗xf6

41

If 39...罝g8 then 40 奧e6+.

40 豐g6+ 當e7 41 豐xf6+ Black resigned.

It was also possible to win with the evolutionary (rather than revolutionary) 41 奧e6! 罝f8 42 奧d5 followed by 43 罝xf6.

33

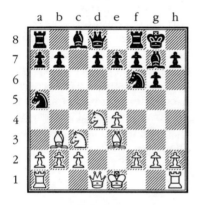

a b c d e f g h

Fischer – Reshevsky
USA Championship,
New York 1958
White to play

9 e5 ❺e8

Relatively best was 9...❺xb3 10 exf6 ❺xa1 11 fxg7 當xg7 12 0–0 d5 13 豐d2 and White is clearly better due to his advantage in development and strongly centralised position. 9...❺h5 would lose a piece after 10 g4.

10 奧xf7+!! 當xf7

If 10...罝xf7 then 11 ❺e6 and the queen is trapped, since the d7-pawn is pinned by the white queen.

11 ❺e6!

It's pretty amazing that this magnet combination – which lures the king into the open by threatening to capture the queen with the knight on e6 – works despite the fact that the f7- and e6-squares are overprotected.

11...dxe6

And White won easily after 42 moves. A comfortable victory for Fischer who used Russian analysis he had studied in a Russian magazine. Such a combination is easy to overlook if you are not familiar with it, but then when you see it you don't forget it since it makes such a strong impression with the double piece sacrifices. In this particular case it teaches us that Steinitz's theories about weak points sometimes don't help us. Fischer actually attacked two strong points by exploiting the dynamic activity of his pieces and the tactical co-ordination between them.

Comparison can be made with the forerunner Tarrasch – von Holzhausen, Paris 1924, which went 1 e4 e5 2 ❺f3 ❺c6 3 奧c4 奧e7 4 d4 exd4 5 ❺xd4 ❺f6 6 ❺c3 d6 7 0–0 0–0 8 罝e1 罝e8 9 b3 ❺d7?

10 奧xf7+! 當xf7 11 ❺e6! and Black resigned because of his

trapped queen, since he would be subjected to a forced mate after 11...♗xe6 12 ♕d5+ ♔f6 13 ♕f5.

Here it wasn't difficult to see that f7 and e6 were weak points – in comparison with Fischer – Reshevsky where these squares were overprotected. So in the first case Steinitz's method didn't help you but it certainly did in the second scenario as f7 and e6 really were weak points. One should strike where the opponent is weakest yet sometimes it pays to hit the strongest points! An interesting paradox, or exception to the classical rule, because most of the time Steinitz was right.

34

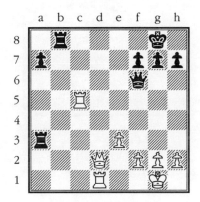

Guldin – Bagdatiev
USSR 1963
White to move

One of the most important mating combinations on which to concentrate and know deep down to its roots is that which involves the exploitation of the back rank. This is because it's a very common combinational theme: after all, most of us have succumbed to a back rank

mate just as we have won by placing a rook on the eighth rank and announcing checkmate. As beginners, we learn to make a pawn move in our castled position so as to give the king an escape square and not get mated should an enemy rook happen to land on our first rank. However, as we progress we learn that seemingly innocent flank pawn moves like h2-h3 can be weakening and a loss of time. This is the reason that even advanced players can fall into this trap.

The most famous example of this is the exhibition game Capablanca – Bernstein, Moscow 1914. However here we have a back rank combination between two lesser known players. A well-trained combination solver will find White's first move pretty easily but it's the elegant defensive moves which are the most interesting since White has a weak back rank as well. In this position it's obvious that the back rank is the main motif as well as the loose rook on a3.

White played **1 ♕b4!**

This "Zukertort move" isn't the only one which is winning. Less spectacular is the "Rubinstein move" 1 ♕c1 with a double threat on c8 and a3. If Black defends with 1...♕a6 then 2 ♖c6 ♕b7 3 ♖cd6!! is decisive because the double threat on the back rank and the loose rook on a3 remains. In many ways the quiet manoeuvring moves ♕d2-c1 and ♖c5-c6-d6 are more beautiful than the explosive continuation in the game.

1...♖d8

The only way to avoid an immediate loss but now the next problem arises. How should White react to the threat on his back rank?

2 ⌶cd5!

Now we can see that Black has an obvious problem with his back rank. It's not possible to capture the rook due to the queen check on b8.

However Black can try the imaginative **2...⌶d3!** which is the culmination of the position since both players' back ranks are exposed.

White must reply **3 ⌶5xd3** as 3 ⌶1xd3?? fails to 3...♕a1+ 4 ⌶d1 ♕xd1+ 5 ⌶xd1 ⌶xd1+ and mate next move. A very nice x-ray attack by Black.

3...⌶xd3

Now it's White who decides with an x-ray attack.

4 ♕b8+ ♕d8 5 ♕xd8+ ⌶xd8 6 ⌶xd8 mate.

I believe this position is very powerful in both the pedagogical as well as the aesthetic sense. The reasons are as follows:

(1) both players' back ranks are weak

(2) all major pieces are on the board, and

(3) the play revolves around x-ray attacks which the human brain has problems handling because of their illusory effect. When we analyse the movements of the pieces in our head whilst contending with an x-ray, they penetrate or jump like knights. So we must learn that major pieces as well as bishops can "jump" when opportunities for an x-ray present themselves.

35

Adams – Torre
New Orleans 1920
White to move

Are there any combinational motifs here? Yes, the last rank looks rather vulnerable due to White's strong pressure on the e-file.

17 ♗xf6! ♗xf6

17...gxf6 was necessary which goes to prove that in a bad position only bad moves are available. After the disruption of the kingside pawn structure, White can simply play 18 g3 followed by 19 ♘h4 when he will soon have an "eternal knight" on f5.

18 ♕g4!

Placing the queen en prise works since a capture on e2 means nothing as the e1-rook is defended.

18...♕b5

The only move which protects the rook on e8.

19 ♕c4!!

Note that 19 a4?? fails to 19...♕xe2 20 ♖xe2 ♖c1+ and it's White who will fall into a back rank mate!

19...♕d7

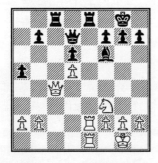

20 ♕c7!!

Such beautiful queen moves one after another.

20...♕b5

20...♕a4 21 b3 ♕b5 22 a4 leads to the same thing.

21 a4!

Care must be taken as if 21.♕xb7?? then 21...♕xe2 and Black wins.

21...♕xa4

21...♕xe2 22 ♖xe2 is ineffective

since the queen blocks the path of a decisive check on c1.

22 ♖e4! ♕b5 23 ♕xb7! Black resigned.

This should be the most beautiful back rank combination of all time. But do let me know if you find one that is more beautiful than this! Not only are the amazing queen moves fascinating but also the fact that there was only one way to win. If White made one slip he would be mated himself on the back rank!

If this can be regarded as the most beautiful back rank combination ever, then the most famous is undoubtedly that seen in the game Bernstein – Capablanca, Moscow 1914, which does not appear here due our limited number of 300 positions. However it might be published in a later workbook containing additional tactical positions to those presented here.

36

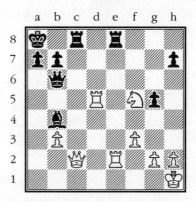

Teschner – Portisch
Monaco 1969
Black to move

As mentioned in position 1, if we want to fine-tune our own tactical ability to greater heights it will pay to look at specific positions where a strong player has missed a tactical solution. In this position Lajos Portisch, "the Hungarian Botvinnik", missed...

29...♕f2!

Chess players who are familiar with the back rank and pinning motif will surely find this winning move without any particular effort. But here one must also see the x-ray idea which can be rather illusory unless you look at the whole board from a to h. The game actually continued 29...♕a6? and the players agreed to a draw.

30 ♘g3

30 ♖xf2 is met by 30...♖e1+.

30...♕e1+!

Sometimes x-ray moves like this are overlooked since it can be somewhat difficult to see the connection between the rook on e8 and the e1-square. After all, the white rook on e2 seems to break the connection but this is not the case. What is required is the ability to see through the pieces, the e8-rook penetrating the e2-rook to the e1-square, which is why it's called an x-ray. By the way, it's not the first time a player of Portisch's calibre misses what is really a rather simple combination. This only points to the fact that he probably hasn't solved enough tactical exercises, especially with specific themes. Even though the main theme here involves a back rank mate, which even beginners know well, the whole combination

also embraces other themes such as pin and x-ray.

37

Durovic – Engqvist
Titograd 1991
Black to move

22...♘c5!

It's always a pleasure to decide the game with the queen's knight, especially when it seems to come out of nowhere. Comparison can be made with Capablanca's ingenious 14 ♘c4!! (position 72). Things move very fast when knights start to jump around even though they might be coming from the lower regions of their half of the board. But in this case all White's tactical weaknesses like f2 and e1 become exposed as well as his pieces, except the knight on d1. Note that it's because the d1-knight stands in the way of the c1-rook that there is a strong motif for a back rank mate.

23 ♖xc5

23 ♖xd4 ♘xb3 leads to a decisive knight fork after which Black wins a whole rook. 23 ♕c3 is met by

23...♕xd3! and the c5-knight is immune from capture due to the back rank mate.

23...♕xc5 24 ♘c3

If 24 ♘xc5 then 24...♖e1 mate.

24...♕xf2+! Black resigned.

Sometimes a knight is not a king's best friend just like here when it is in fact no better than a pawn because of the inevitable back rank mate on e1 after 25.♘xf2 ♖e1. Note that all this has been made possible by the strong placement of the rook on e2, which forces White to recapture on f2 with the knight. This is the finest combination I have ever had featuring the back rank motif and I'm particularly proud of my 24th move since it also helped me to gain my first IM-norm. A pleasant memory that I now want to share with you all!

38

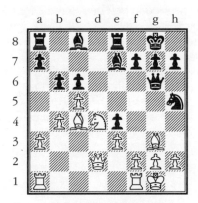

a b c d e f g h

Engqvist – Bronstein
Gausdal 1990
White to move

Here I played 22 ♘xc6! ♕xc6 23 ♗d5 and after 23...♕d7 I was

forced to make the decision where to place my queen to get out of the pin on the d-file.

24 ♕a2??

Unfortunately I missed the best move 24 ♕d1!! with a double threat on a8 and h5 which forces Black to continue 24...♘xg3 25 fxg3 ♗f6 but then after 26 ♖xf6 gxf6 27 ♗xa8 White has good winning chances thanks to his passed c-pawn.

24...♘xg3?

In our calculations we both missed the fact that Black could play 24...♕f5! which offers winning chances since 25 ♗xa8 is met by 25...♗e6 with a double threat on a2 and a8. This would have given Black two minor pieces for rook and pawn.

25 fxg3

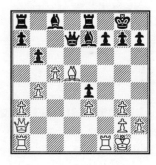

25...♖b8?

25...♗b7 was forced. Then after 26 ♗xf7+ ♔h8 27. ♖ad1 ♕a4 28 ♗xe8 ♕xe8 29 ♖f7 White has a slight advantage because of the superior activity of his pieces. Black must defend against the further incursion 30 ♕e6.

26 c6

White's c-pawn serves as bait to lure the queen from its defence of the king's rook.

26...♛d6 27 c7

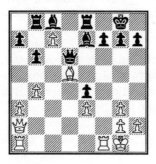

27...♖a8!?

This beautiful move came as a shock to me during the game and I was reminded of Bronstein's genial creativity and originality. I have only experienced a similar rook move on one other occasion and that was in Gausdal 1995 against Nick de Firmian who also placed his rook on a square where I could capture it in a similar fashion.

28 ♗xf7+

28 ♗xa8 is obviously met by 28...♗e6.

28...♔h8 29 ♖ad1 ♛e5 30 ♗xe8 ♗e6

31 ♖d8!

An amusing back rank finesse which exploits the outpost on d8. White's queen is hanging on a2 but after this move other pieces are hanging too! It's always a pleasure to find moves which increase the tension even further.

31...♗xa2 32 ♖xa8 ♛xc7 33 ♗f7+ ♗d8 34 ♖d1 g6 35 ♖axd8+ Black resigned.

I think the play from the first diagram was very instructive in

respect of the theme "loose pieces". It's also very unusual that the a8-square attracted so much attention. That's usually only the case when the king has castled queenside.

39

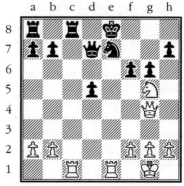

Steinitz – von Bardeleben
Hastings 1895
White to move

22 ♖xe7+!

The second best option is 22 ♘xh7 ♖xc1 23 ♘xf6+ ♔f7 24 ♖xc1 ♛e6 and now the elegant...

25 ♘d7!! practically forces the exchange of queens in spectacular fashion to reach a clearly advantageous rook and knight ending.

22...♔f8!

Black attempts a clever boomerang combination by exploiting White's back rank weakness while all his pieces are hanging. 22...♗xe7 loses to 23 ♕b4+! ♔e8 (*23...♕d6 24 ♕xb7+ ♕d7 25 ♖e1+ ♔d6 26 ♘e4+!* and the queen is lost.) 24 ♖e1+ ♔d8 25 ♘e6+; and 22...♕xe7 fails to 23 ♖xc8+.

23 ♖f7+!

Inferior is 23 ♘xh7+ ♔xe7 24 ♖e1+ ♔d8 25 ♕b4 ♖c6 26 ♕f8+ ♔c7 27 ♕xa8 ♕xh7 although White still has good winning chances after 28.♕e8!.

23...♔g8 24 ♖g7+!

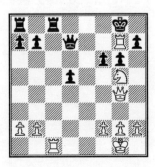

Black resigned.

Black threw in the towel after realising that 24...♔h8 (*24...♔f8 25 ♘xh7+*) can be met by 25 ♖xh7+! ♔g8 26 ♖g7+ ♔h8 27 ♕h4+ ♔xg7 28 ♕h7+ ♔f8 29 ♕h8+ ♔e7 30 ♕g7+ ♔e8 31 ♕g8+ ♔e7 32 ♕f7+ ♔d8 33 ♕f8+ ♕e8 34 ♘f7+ ♔d7 35 ♕d6 mate.

40-45: *Other mating combinations*

40

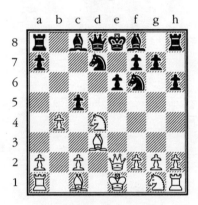

Gershon – Finkel
Ubeda Open 1997
White to move

This position arises in the Caro-Kann after **1 e4 c6 2 d4 d5 3 ♘d2 dxe4 4 ♘xe4 ♘d7 5 ♗c4 ♘gf6 6 ♘g5 e6 7 ♕e2 ♘b6 8 ♗d3 h6 9 ♘5f3 c5 10 dxc5 ♘bd7 11 b4 b6 12 ♘d4 bxc5??**. White now wins the queen or mates after **13 ♘c6 ♕c7 14 ♕xe6+!! fxe6 15 ♗g6 mate**.

The beautiful mate with bishop and knight can easily be overlooked if you are not familiar with it. As a matter of fact, according to the databases, this opening trap has been sprung three times and on one occasion even a 2500-player fell into it, while the two other players had 2200+ Elo ratings. It is certainly one of the most dangerous traps in the Caro-Kann because of its concealed nature and also because the normal looking but suicidal 12...bxc5?? seems such a logical move.

to know, since most of the time the hostile king castles kingside. It's part of every serious attacking or defensive player's make-up to have such mates at their fingertips. If not it would be difficult to see the beautiful rook and queen sacrifice which results in a neatly economical mate.

41

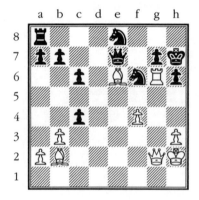

Bauer – Hellner
1956
White to move

1 ♖xh6+! gxh6

1...♔xh6 2 ♕g5+ ♔h7 3 ♕h4+ ♔g6 4 f5 mate.

2 ♕g8+! ♘xg8 3 ♗f5 mate.

If you are familiar with this mating pattern where the bishop-pair alone mates the king you shouldn't have any difficulties in solving the combination. But if you didn't know this mating pattern beforehand you will know it now.

Mates on the long diagonal as well as the b1-h7 diagonal are important

42

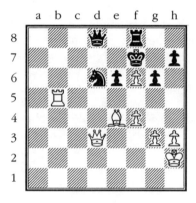

David – Katapodis
Anagia 2019
White to move

47 ♖d5! exd5 48 ♕xd5+ ♔xf6

48...♔e8 49 ♕e6+.

49 ♕e5+! ♔f7 50 ♗d5 mate.

If you haven't seen this mating pattern before it's not certain that you would find the combination. Note how the three pieces co-operate with each other to create this beautiful and economical mate. Without the pawn on f4 this mate could never have been delivered.

43

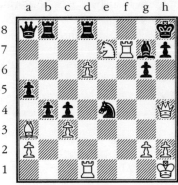

Carlsen – Karjakin
Game 4, rapid playoff,
World Championship 2016
White to move

50 ♕h6+!!

A very beautiful finish which might have been difficult to detect early in the calculation because there wasn't a pawn on h6. In this position Carlsen's move was the only way to avoid a loss so it must have been considered several moves beforehand. After the brilliant queen sacrifice, no matter how Black recaptures he will be mated by one of White's rooks. 50...♔xh6 is answered by 51 ♖h8 mating on the h-file while 50...gxh6 is met by 51 ♖xf7 with mate on the seventh

rank. The two rooks co-operate perfectly to achieve these different kinds of mates.

44

D. Cramling – Engqvist
SCT Taby 2009
White to move

In time pressure my opponent missed a forced mate. I didn't notice it either until after the game. Cramling could have won with the neat **36 ♘xg6+**.

In the game 36 ♗c1?! was played and I managed to draw after 44 moves.

36...♔g8 37 ♕e7 ♗xc3 38 ♖g7+!! ♗xg7 39 ♕e6 mate.

This kind of mate with bishop and knight is more unusual but it's important to remember it even when a queen is involved! The knight is a tricky piece, both for the attacker and defender, therefore it's important to keep such patterns in your head so you can see them instantly, like a bolt from the blue, when the situation arises.

45

Varavin – Zavarnicin
USSR 1991
White to move

**1 ♕xf7+!! ♚xf7 2 ♗e6+ ♚f6
3 e5+!**

3 f4?, with the idea of 4 e5+ followed by 5 ♘e4 mate, is met by 3...♘e5! and instead of mate White can only give a perpetual check by 4 ♗g5+ ♚g7 5 ♗h6+ etc.

3...♚xe5

Of course there is a knight mate on e4 if Black captures with a pawn or a piece.

4 ♖d1!!

This is the key move which makes the combination work and it really

impressed me the first time I analysed the position. It's important to control d4 because if the king manages to escape via that square then the white pieces will find it hard to attack it if it then has access to squares on the queenside such as c4, b4 and a5.

4...♚f6

4...g5 is answered by 5 ♗xg5 followed by 6 f4 mate.

5 ♘e4+

The quiet move 5 f4?? doesn't work on account of 5...g5! and Black's king takes refuge on g6.

5...♚e5 6 ♗f4+ ♚xe4 7 f3 mate.

As we have mentioned before, the difficulty in this kind of combination is to find the fourth move since it's a quiet move with deadly threats.

46-47: Stalemate

46

Kasparov – McDonald
Simul, England 1986
Black to move

Here Black managed to draw by a very beautiful and economical stalemate.

54...♖xg3+!! 55 ♔xg3

55 ♔h4 ♖g4+!! 56 ♔xg4 ♕d7+!! leads to stalemate as well but it's not as beautiful as the main variation since there are three pieces involved and two of them control the h7-square. Compare this with the main variation where each white piece controls a black escape square on its own.

55...♕e5+!!

Note that the other checks only help the king to escape.

56 ♕xe5 Draw.

An extremely beautiful stalemate – which you will never forget once you have seen it. In fact it might come in handy when you least expect it!

47

Fehling – Rutschi
Biel 1983
Black to move

It might be hard to imagine that there is a forced stalemate in this position, since there are so many mobile pieces including the king.

1...♔h6!!

The key move which indeed leads to a stalemate by force if White plays for a win.

2 ♕d3 d1♕!! 3 ♕xd1

3 ♕xg3 ♕xg1+ 4 ♔xg1 ♖xg2+ doesn't change the situation.

3...♕xh3+! 4 gxh3 ♖h2+ 5 ♔xh2 Draw.

If you can see the slightest motif to play for a stalemate it's important to check if it is possible to put the idea into practice. Here it was certainly to the black player's advantage.

48-49: Composing and Solving Problems

48

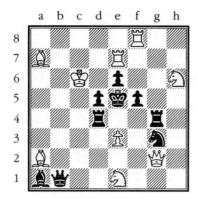

Engqvist
Expressen 1978
White to move

A good training method to develop an awareness of tactical ideas is to compose your own problems or studies. This problem I composed when I was 14 years old and it was published on my 15th birthday in 1978. I'm still proud of it. It was actually my father who persuaded me to send it to the Swedish evening paper *Expressen* and Kristian Sköld, who conducted the chess column, was very happy to publish it.

1 ♕e4+!!

Even though Black can capture the queen with seven pieces, it will be mate in two moves.

1 ♗xd4+ ♖xd4 shows why it's important to have a black rook on g4 in the problem, otherwise it would be mate with the queen on d5.

1...♕xe4

1...♖gxe4 2 ♘f3 mate.

1...♖dxe4 2 ♘f3 mate.

1...♔xe4 2 ♖xe6 mate.

1...♘xe4 2 ♘f3 mate. (2 ♖xf5 mate.)

1...fxe4 2 ♘xg4 mate.

1...dxe4 2 ♖xe6 mate.

2 ♗b8 mate.

Before the problem was published Sköld asked me in a polite letter why the bishop on a1 was necessary. I replied that otherwise White could win with 2 ♘xg4+ fxg4 3 ♗xd4 mate.

49

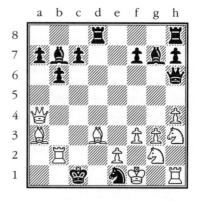

Loyd
New York Sunday Herald 1889
White to move

How do you go about finding the solution to this two-mover by the legendary Sam Loyd (1841–1911)? It's natural and easy to stare blindly at prosaic solutions where the h1-rook delivers the mate but the trick is to find the key-diagonal and the key-file.

By playing **1 ♗f8!!** White threatens 2 ♕a1 mate, which can only be prevented in two ways, either by 1...♗xb2 which allows 2 ♗xh6 mate or by 1...♔xb2 permitting 2 ♕a3 mate.

The key-diagonal was h6-c1 and the key-file the open a-line leading to the back rank, where mate is delivered by the queen, not the rook. The rook on h1 was superfluous and had no other function than to make the problem more difficult. Solving problems by Loyd is strongly recommended since it will help to develop your imagination and teach you how to find key weaknesses. In this case the diagonal and the file were the keys to the solution.

Apart from solving two-movers a very effective way of improving your ability to see everything within the range of three moves is to solve three-movers. The American grandmaster Samuel Reshevsky is said to have seen everything within the range of three moves and if you manage to do that your chess skill will be on a very high level indeed. It's not so easy as Reshevsky proved himself in position number 6. Try to solve the following three-move-problem by Wormald which I found in Wilhelm Steinitz's The Chess Columns of *The Field* Edited by Wilhelm Steinitz Volume 1: 1873-1876:

It's pretty obvious that White needs to improve the position of his rook to be able to mate in three moves because 1 ♗d2 fails to 1...c1♕+. The first instinct tells you that the rook should manoeuvre in such a way that it will be possible to mate with the bishop on f4. However Black's knight on a1 will destroy this plan after for example 1 ♖b6 ♘xb3 and White doesn't have time to manoeuvre to f6 due to the threat on c1. If this plan doesn't work we have to look at something completely different. How about trying to exploit the third rank with 1 ♖a5!! ♘xb3 (1...cxb3 2 ♖a3!! leads to a zugzwang as well) 2 ♖a3!!. Black is under the compulsion to move and mate cannot be avoided on the next move. An extraordinary beautiful problem which not only improves your calculating ability but also the ability to play with the rook. In this problem the third rank is the key rank and the main tactical idea is the zugzwang. The value of solving three-movers on a consistent basis cannot be underestimated. In the book *The Art of Planning in Chess – Move by Move –* by Neil McDonald the following can be read: "In fact, if you are serious about improving your play, you should train yourself every day by solving puzzles of 'mate in three moves' variety." So, don't forget the three-movers!

50-59: Calculation of Variations

Before starting the actual calculation of variations Kotov recommends that you begin by figuring out reasonable candidate moves. Here follows a couple of positions where it's necessary to work in that order, otherwise mistakes might occur. In positions 50 and 51 this method is correct, however in position 52 it's not.

To learn the art of calculating variations one should strive to master the handling of **candidate moves**, 50-52, **motif** and **theme**, 53-54, **stepping stones**, 55-56, **evaluations**, 57-58, **pragmatism** See also the later position 65 where calculation relates to material.

50-52: Candidate moves

50

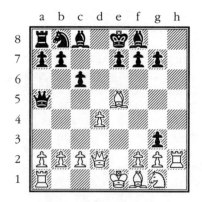

Schuster – Carls (Analysis)
Bremen 1912
Black to move

This is a typical position where all candidate moves have to be checked before calculating any variations.

10...gxf2+

This simple move was found by two railwaymen. One week before, a Soviet chess magazine had analysed the far inferior 10...♕xe5+?? 11 dxe5 gxh2 12 0–0–0 ♗d7 13 ♘h3 h1♕ 14 e6! fxe6 15 ♗d3 ♕h2 16 ♗g6+ ♔d8 17 ♘f4 ♕h6 18 ♘xe6+ ♔c8 19 ♕xh6 gxh6 20 ♘xf8 and wins.

This example exemplifies well Lasker's famous words that when you have found a good move you should try to find an even better one. This is also true of candidate moves. It's easy to get stuck in a standard way of thinking but each position is unique. In the actual game 10 c3 was played when 10...♕xe5+! was the winning move. Some readers of the Soviet chess magazine wanted to improve with 10 ♕d2 but the editorial team missed the simple refutation 10...gxf2+ whereas the less dramatic 10...♕xd2+? 11 ♔xd2 gxh2 12 ♗xh2 ♗f5 leads only to an equal game.

Also Eero Böök missed this simple move in the Finnish chess column "SJ:s personalblad". It was Böök who got the letter from the two railwaymen and then related the anecdote in his entertaining book *Odödliga partier* (Immortal games).

51

Dvoretsky – Schüssler
Tbilisi 1980
White to move

16 ♕g3

At first Dvoretsky planned the tempting bishop sacrifice 16 ♗xh7+ ♚xh7 17 ♖h5+ ♚g8 18 ♕h3, forcing Schüssler to consider whether to advance the f-pawn one or two squares. But later Dvoretsky realised that the bishop sacrifice wasn't as convincing as it first seemed. After 18...f6 Dvoretsky planned 19 ♖e1 ♘f7 20 ♕f5 but overlooked the strong defensive move 20...♖e8 giving the black king an escape square to f8. Similarly 18...f5 19 ♖h8+ ♚f7 20 ♕h5+ ♚e6 or 18...f5 19 ♖e1 ♘e4 20 ♖h8+ ♚f7 21 ♕xf5+ ♗f6 or 21...♘f6 leave Black okay in all variations.

When he understood that the variations after the bishop sacrifice didn't work he looked at natural continuations, such as 16 ♖ae1, but failed to find anything convincing and returned to the bishop sacrifice. He thereby made a cardinal mistake in calculating variations. He broke

Kotov's famous principle which stipulates that one should always calculate variations to the end, one by one, as he should have done after the bishop sacrifice and not jumped between different candidate moves, After having hopped around he finally decided to play the text move which threatens to capture on e7.

Another candidate move, not mentioned by Dvoretsky, was 16 ♕h3 g6 17 ♕h6 threatening 18 ♖h5. However Black has 17...f5! threatening the fork 18...♘f7. Then if 18 ♖e6 Black has 18...♖f6!.

16...♗h4?

Dvoretsky writes that after the best continuation 16...♘e8! perhaps he wouldn't have had enough energy left to see the favourable variation 17 ♖ae1 ♗f6 18 ♖h5 g6 19 ♕h3! ♗xd4 20 ♖xh7.

17 ♗xh7+

Now the bishop sacrifice certainly works

17...♚xh7 18 ♖h5+ ♚g8 19 ♕h3!

Of course not 19 ♖xh4? ♘f5.

19...g5 20 g3

Stronger was 20 ♗e5!.

20...♕c8 21 ♕xc8 ♘xc8 22 ♗d2 ♘e7 23 gxh4 gxh4 24 ♚h1! Black resigned.

Dvoretsky teaches us that he should have decided on the candidate moves much earlier, before he started to analyse the complicated variations after the bishop sacrifice. Only if a forced win can be seen should one focus on the bishop sacrifice, but since this wasn't the case it would have been better to analyse the other candidate moves thoroughly. This way of thinking would have given Dvoretsky the opportunity to play 16 ♕g3 much quicker. In the event it took too long and a lot of energy was wasted on less important analysis, leading in the worst case scenario to exhaustion.

According to Yusupov it's extremely important to make clear to yourself which candidate moves you should focus on before embarking on a calculation of variations. Calculation of variations is essentially a matter of getting an overview of the different candidate moves, because then it will be easier to use your time wisely and understand the position in broader terms and not limit yourself to analysing one branch of a variation tree in depth.

52

a b c d e f g h

Ernst – Hellers
Stockholm TV tournament 1994
White to move

51 ♖d1!

In the Swedish tournament book *Snilledrag i Schack* (Ingenious moves in chess) this move is called a surprising sneaker. Such an insidious move can only be discovered as a possible candidate move after the more direct and concrete variations have been thoroughly and correctly analysed.

The rook move is indeed logical since it has no function at all on the closed e-file, but now the decisive threat 52 ♕d6+ becomes a reality. Black has no defence. In the game, the inferior 51 ♕h7+? was played. After 51...♔d8 Black threatens the decisive rook move to h8 so White's next move is forced. 52 ♕xb7 ♖h8 53 ♕a8+ (*53 ♕d5+?! ♕xd5 54 ♗xd5 ♘f3 55 ♖e2 ♔c7 leads to a position which is easier to play for Black due to his more active pieces.*) 53...♔e7 54 ♕b7+ ♔d8 55 ♕a8+ and the players agreed to a draw.

51...e3

This is regarded as the best reply according to the tournament book but then White has the possibility of winning the knight on d4 in a more efficient way due to the fact that the fourth rank has been opened for White's queen. 51...♖d8 leads to mate in five after 52 ♕h7+ ♔f6 53 ♕h4+ ♔g7 54 ♖g1+ etc. and 51...♔d8 52 ♕e3 loses the knight instantly.

52 ♕h4+!

Weaker is 52 ♕d6+ ♕xd6 53 cxd6+ ♔d7 54 ♖xd4 e2 55 ♗xe2 ♖xe2 56 h4 f4 57 ♖xf4 ♔xd6 58 h5 ♖e6 59 ♖h4 even though White has a won rook ending. But why complicate when it's not necessary?

This position provides good proof that sometimes it's not possible to know all the candidate moves beforehand. Only after having analysed the necessary variations to their end do we know if we need to find and analyse a better candidate move.

The key to understanding how to deal with the question of candidate moves is to know when the method is applicable and when it is not. This is something Kotov didn't deal with in his books and so we must elaborate on it ourselves. I do believe, though, it's important to think in this manner because it saves time and disciplines one's thinking.

53-54: Motif and Theme

An important method of dealing with combinations, the most important element in tactics, is to adopt Kotov's method and use motif and theme. What motif or motifs are there for a combination in the following position?

53

Maslov – Babahanov
USSR 1970
White to move

We can see that it's possible to fork on e4 if the f6-knight is eliminated. Besides that we note that White has a lead in development which needs to be exploited quickly before Black catches up.

1 ♖xf6!

1 ♖ae1 improves the position and is the second-best option if White doesn't manage to calculate the variations associated with the text move. This preparatory move obviously makes the ♖xf6 idea even stronger. However you need to calculate the following variations before playing it: 1...♘h5 (*1...♘d7 2 ♘e4*) 2 ♕f3! with a clear advantage. Note that the routine reply 2 ♘e4?? runs into 2...♖xe5 3 ♘xc5 ♖xe2 4 ♖xe2 ♘g3+ so don't forget the opponent's forks!

1...♗xf6

The tricky move 1...♕e7, exploiting the pin on the e-file, needs to be analysed as well. It is best answered by 2 ♖e6! ♗xe6 3 ♗xg7 ♔xg7 4 dxe6 ♕xe6 when the computer's choice is 5 ♕xe6 (It's logical to keep queens on the board with 5 *♕f3!?* since White has two minor pieces and good chances of attacking Black's king.) 5...♖xe6 6 ♗xb7 ♖b8 7 ♗d5 followed by ♗b3 with a winning position. After 7...♖e3 White can play 8 ♖g1 threatening a fork on f5. If you have looked at 1...♗xh3 2 ♗xh3 ♗xf6 (*2...♕xd5+ 3 ♗g2 ♕xe5 4 ♕xe5 ♖xe5 5 ♖d6* wins a knight for a pawn.) 3 ♘e4 ♕xd5 4 ♕f3!! ♕xe5 5 ♘xf6+ followed by 6 ♘xe8 you are certainly very good at calculating variations.

2 ♘e4 ♕f8 3 ♗xf6 ♗f5!

Black has dangerous counter threats which White must analyse in advance. Everything works for White despite the fact that Black has an annoying pin on the e-file. The reason for this is the super bishop on f6. Such a bishop is worth more than a rook or a knight as Bronstein once put it. 3...♖xe4 4 ♕xe4 ♕xf6 is answered by the pawn sacrifice 5 d6!! which releases all the energy inherent in White's position. White wins after 5...♕xd6 6 ♕e8+ ♕f8 7 ♕e5 h6 8 ♖e1.

4 ♖f1!

A clever move which defends the bishop with the help of an x-ray. Beware of the trap 4 ♗c3? ♖xe4! 5 ♗xe4 ♖e8 and Black is back in the game.

4...♖xe4 5 ♗xe4 ♖e8

5...♕xf6 6 ♗xf5 gxf5 7 c4 is a technical win for White.

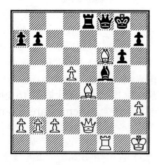

6 ♖xf5!! gxf5 7.♕h5!

This silent move is the hardest to see but 7 ♕g2+ ♔f7 8 ♕g5! fxe4 (*8...♖xe4 9.♕xf5*) 9 ♗c3 is also convincing. The queen and bishop battery plus the d5-pawn is far stronger than Black's army so

Bronstein was certainly right with regard to the strength of the bishop.

7...fxe4

After 7...♖xe4 8 ♕g5+ ♔f7 9 ♕xf5 Black is forced to play 9...♖e1+. Then 10 ♔g2!. White must be aggressive and go nearer the enemy rook. 10...♕g8+ (*10...♔g8 11 ♕g4+ ♔f7 12 ♗c3! or 10...♔e8 11 ♔f2!*) 11 ♗g5+ ♔e8 12 ♔f2! The key to winning is to exploit the king as an active force. Black can no longer control the e-file and White wins due to the decisive checks on c8 and e6. Such beautiful play with the king is important to remember and fortunately hard to forget.

8 ♕g5+ ♔f7 9 ♗c3

White is threatening a decisive check on f6, followed by further checks on h8 and h7. In this variation we clearly see the importance of the d5-pawn controlling e6.

9...♖d8 10 ♕h5+! ♔g8

10...♔e7 is met by 11 ♗b4+.

11 ♕g4+

It's mate next move.

Note the importance of the d-pawn in this last variation as well. The position is graphic proof that three pieces (four pieces if we include the king!) most of the time are enough to mate but we mustn't forget the pawn which in this case counts as a piece! The overall theme of the whole combination was to mate with queen, bishop and pawn against king, queen and rook. Learning how to win with different dynamic forces is crucial, but as a general rule rook(s) are poor defenders against active knight(s) and/or bishop(s), especially when co-operating with a queen in an organised attack.

54

Cserna – Smyslov
Copenhagen 1986
White to move

Positions that are rewarding to work on systematically are those where the attacking side has missed a tactical and more efficient solution. One secret among others is to use Kotov's famous and ingenious vocabulary and try to find the theme of the position. For most players it's pretty obvious that here it's a strong back rank motif but if you don't think about the theme(s) at all the risk increases dramatically that you will not find the move. However, as Kotov mentions in his eminent book *Play like a Grandmaster*, you might miss it anyway as Cserna did. It's all about the need to have a finely tuned feel for combinations. The right move is **21 ♕d6!.**

In fact the positional move 21 ♗b5 was played and White went on to win a fine game. Nevertheless he could have saved himself a lot of effort if he had seen that there was an immediately decisive tactical solution.

Note that another candidate move is 21 ♗g6? but the problem is that Black has the defensive move 21...♘d7. It doesn't help to sacrifice with 22 ♗xf7+ because after 22...♔xf7 23 ♕d6 e5 24 ♕xd5+ ♔g6 Black controls the position. Note that 24...♕e6?! is worse due to 25 ♖xd7+! ♖xd7 26 ♕xa8.

21...♘a6

21...♖xd6? 22 ♖c8+ Many chess players would probably calculate this far but now comes the beautiful...

22 ♖xa7!

And White wins by continuously elaborating on the back rank theme. If one fails to see the tactical motif in the position, then 22 ♖d7 is a good move which indeed leads to a clear advantage for White, but maybe not to a win in a practical game. The main variation goes 22...♖xd7 23 ♕xd7 ♘b4 24 ♗b1 ♕g4 25 a3 ♕xd4 26 axb4 ♕xb4 27 ♕b7 ♖f8 28 ♕xa7 ♕xb2 and the position is not easy to win.

When you are not sure which move to play, the trick is to check which theme or themes are the most relevant. This obviously assumes that you have a fundamental knowledge of combinations. Many players can surely see the first move in the combination but to see the second move you must have acquired the habit of solving back rank combinations (positions 34-39). There are many pitfalls when analysing moves, motifs and themes and the white player, who surely must have felt inspired when playing a great player like Smyslov, couldn't find the best solution to win the game more quickly and beautifully.

55-56: Stepping stones

55

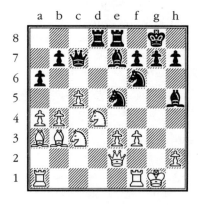

Riazantsev – Rublevsky
European Championship,
Warsaw 2005
White to move

19...♗xc5!

The move order 19...♖xd4! 20 exd4 ♗xc5 also works, since it's bad to play 21 dxc5? after which Black continues the same way as in the game by 21...♘xf3+ 22 ♕xf3 ♗xf3 23 ♖xf3 ♘g4 24 ♗xf7+ ♔h8 25 ♗xe8 ♕xh2+ 26 ♔f1 ♕h1+ 27 ♔e2 ♕g2+ 28 ♔d3 but now exploits the fact that the d4-pawn is on c5 by 28...♘e5+! 29 ♔d4 ♘xf3+ 30 ♔d5 ♕c2 and the ♘c3 cannot be defended without losing material.

20 bxc5 ♖xd4! 21 exd4 ♘xf3+ 22 ♕xf3 ♗xf3 23 ♖xf3

White has a rook and two bishops, which normally are worth more than

a queen and a pawn, but here Black has the opportunity to attack the enemy king with two pieces, since White's forces on the queenside are rather too distant to help the defence.

23...♘g4! 24 ♗xf7+ ♔h8

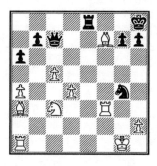

Presumably many can visualise the variation up to here but will still be unsure of the correct evaluation. Without this attacking move it would not be stimulating to dig deeper into the variations. You have to continue the calculation and use this position as a "stepping stone", to use the words of Jonathan Tisdall, focus on it mentally and try to make at least an intuitive evaluation. Strong players might even continue the calculation since the variation is pretty much forced.

25 ♗xe8 ♕xh2+ 26 ♔f1 ♕h1+ 27 ♔e2 ♕g2+ 28 ♔d3 ♕xf3+

This position can be regarded as stepping stone No. 2.

29 ♔c4

29 ♔c2 ♕f5+! 30 ♔b2 (*30 ♔b3* is prohibited because of the reply *30...♕e6+*) 30...♘e3 31 ♖c1 ♘c4+ 32 ♔a2 (*32 ♔b3 ♘d2+ 33 ♔b2 ♕e6 34 ♔c2 ♘f3* and White's bishop is trapped on e8 since *35 ♗h5* is met by *35...♕f5+*) 32...♕d3! 33 ♔b3 ♘xa3 34 ♔xa3 ♕e3 and White has no defence against the double threat on c1 and e8. If you have seen this far you really are a calculating machine!

29...♘e3+ 30 ♔b3 ♕f5!

Stepping stone No.3. If you had visualised this position already at move 19 you might have made the evaluation that Black has good winning chances. This isn't surprising because White's king and bishop on e8 are placed on sensitive squares. The rest of White's army is passive compared to Black's queen and knight which are very active.

White now lost quickly after **31 ♖a2?** However, he had defensive resources to save the game. After the forced variation 31 ♖c1 ♕e6+ 32 d5 ♘xd5 (Note that *32...♕xe8??* loses to the decisive pin *33 ♖e1* and

Black has no defence to *34 ♗c1*.) 33 ♘xd5 ♕xd5+ 34 ♖c4 ♕e6 Black's e8-bishop is trapped. White's best shot is 35 ♗b5!! (*35 ♗h5? ♕h3+*) 35...axb5 36 axb5 and his counterplay with c5-c6 should secure half a point.

31...♕e6+ 32 d5 ♘xd5

If 32...♕xe8?? then 33 ♖e2 followed by 34 ♗c1.

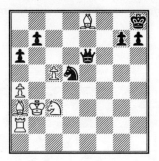

33 ♖e2

An incredible variation is 33 ♗d7 ♕f7! (*33...♕xd7? 34 ♖d2*) 34 ♗e8 ♕g8!! and Black wins.

33...♘e3+ 34 ♔b2 ♕xe8 35 c6 ♕xc6

The point of this example was to show in what type of a position a queen can be stronger than a rook and two minor pieces. It's all about activity and the possibility of playing on weaknesses. In this position it was the bishop on e8 which was the problem, combined with White's passive pieces and king on the run.

If your intuition is well developed you could make the evaluation that Black has the attack after the first stepping stone (24...♔h8) as well as after the second stepping stone (28...♕xf3+). Pragmatically speaking it's not necessary to calculate until the third stepping stone (30...♕f5!) since so-called quiet moves are often difficult and time-consuming to find. A high level calculator might find it since matters are pretty forced. However, this position is rather very much about making correct evaluations. Sometimes it's easier to calculate moves than to evaluate unbalanced positions as we saw in this example.

56

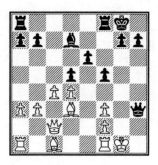

Van Hoorde – Fichtl
Gijon 1954
Black to move

If you think along the lines of Kotov's terminology, candidate moves, motifs, and themes, there is still no guarantee that you will find the best move or continuation in the position, even if you know the motif. Here it's very clear that a combination is in the air due to the tactical weaknesses on h2 and d2. How can White exploit this in the best way?

1...♕h6!

In the game the tempting 1...♗xh2+? 2 ♔xh2 ♕h6+ 3 ♔g1 ♘xd2 4 ♗c1 ♘f3+! 5 gxf3 ♕h3!

…with the deadly threat ...♖f6-g6 was played but White could have saved himself with 6 ♗g5!. In the game White played the losing move 6 ♗f4? and after 6...♖f6 (threatening 7...♖g6+ 8 ♗g3 ♖h6 followed by 9...♕h1 mate) 7 ♗g5 ♖g6 8 f4 h6 had to resign. However after 6 ♗g5! ♖f6 7 f4 (7 ♗xf6? gxf6 wins for Black due to the open g-file. For example 8 f4 ♔f7 9 f3 ♖g8+ 10 ♔f2 ♖g2+ wins the white queen.) 7...♖g6 8 f3 h6 9 ♔f2 and Black has to react against 10 ♖h1 winning the queen. The only continuation is 9...♕h2+ 10 ♔e3 ♕xc2 11 ♗xc2 hxg5 but White has good drawing chances after 12 ♖g1 despite the pawn deficit.

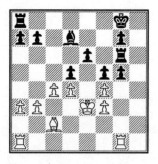

If White had responded correctly Black would probably not have won the game. Black had to calculate correctly and see the quiet move 5...♕h3 (the first stepping stone) as well as the only defensive continuation starting with 6 ♗g5 and ending with 12 ♖g1, which is the second stepping stone, since an evaluation is necessary to decide whether or not the variation should be played.

2 ♘f3

Worse is 2 f4? ♗xf4.

2...♘d2!

A nice little knight move that wins material by force since 3 ♕xd2? obviously loses to 3...♗xh2+ 4 ♔h1 ♗f4+.

3 ♘e5 ♗xe5 4 dxe5 dxc4 5 ♗xc4

After 5 bxc4 Black can play the intermediate move 5...♗c6! before capturing the exchange, since 6 ♗c1?? is met by 6...♘f3+! 7 gxf3 ♕g6+. It is important to be aware of such moves as 5...♗c6 since they utilise the power of the knight placed on d2. Remember how long a time Alekhine's rook was placed on e3 in his game against Réti (position 103) and how he exploited its power along the third rank. Here the knight exploits the possibility of checking on f3 with deadly effect before cashing in on the exchange. It's better to checkmate the opponent than to be satisfied with an extra exchange.

5...♘xf1

Black has won the exchange. He could have played the intermediate move 5...♗c6 here, threatening a deadly check on f3, and after 6 f3 (6 ♗xe6+? ♔h8) take the exchange with 6...♘xf1.

57-58: Evaluations

57

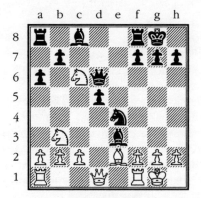

Reshevsky – Euwe
World Championship,
The Hague/Moscow 1948
White to move

When practicing tactical ideas it's an excellent idea to analyse positions where pieces are hanging because then it's mandatory to calculate variations and be tactically alert. In this position it's important to hold your tongue regarding candidate moves, calculation of variations and evaluations of critical positions. Reshevsky played **14 fxe3**.

The question is what would have happened after 14 ♕xd5. At first sight it looks like White wins a pawn if Black captures the queen or the knight. However, Black has a boomerang combination with 14...♘xf2! which forces 15 ♕xd6

65

♘e4+ 16 ♔h1 ♘xd6 17 ♘e7+ ♔h8 with equal play. White has the possibility of eliminating the black bishop-pair but Reshevsky most probably thought the game would be too simplified after all the exchanges and therefore chose the text move. Maybe he shouldn't have done that because he lost the game after 72 moves.

14...bxc6

The position is equal. The conclusion one can draw is that it's a matter of taste whether one chooses the tactical variation 14 ♕xd5 or the calmer 14 fxe3. This example is distinguished by the fact that there are not so many variations to calculate and that it's more a matter of making correct evaluations after the tactical skirmishes.

58

Capablanca – Villegas
Buenos Aires 1914
White to move

This position is excellent for practicing the calculation of variations. If you are endeavouring to play at the same level as the young Capablanca, it will be necessary for you to calculate eight moves ahead and then evaluate the position correctly. This is not so difficult for an experienced player since the variation is forced.

18 ♘xd7!!

As we have mentioned in position 13, Capablanca was a master of so called small combinations. Here he exploits the latent energy inherent in White's four active pieces. The prosaic 18 ♗xd4 leads to a game with only major pieces on the board after 18...♘xe5 19 ♗xe5 ♗xe5 20 ♖xe5 but after 20...♖fd8 White's pawn majority is neutralised due to Black's control of the only open file.

18...♕xd7

Necessary, since 18...dxe3? is met by 19 ♘xf6+ ♔h8 (*19...gxf6 20 ♖g4+ ♔h8 21 ♗xf6* is a well-known checkmate pattern.) 20 ♖h4 h6

21 ♖xh6+! This move leads to a deadly discoverer and is the heart of the combination because of the special circumstance that the queen is placed on c7. 21...gxh6 22 ♘d5+ (The other discoverer *22 ♘e8+* works too since c7 is the target.) 22...♔h7 23 ♘xc7 e2 24 ♖e1 ♖ad8

25 f3 (*25 ♗c3* with the idea *25...♖d3 26 ♗b4* is also clearly advantageous for White.) 25...♖d2 26 ♗c3 with excellent winning chances for White.

If you had calculated this far, or at least eight moves ahead and made a correct evaluation you are good at calculating forced variations as well as evaluating positions. If you didn't manage it this time you can try to calculate the main variation in your head and focus on the position at the end of it. Next time you repeat this position you will have greater chances of managing the task of calculation.

19 ♗xd4 ♗xd4 20 ♖xd4 ♕c7 21 ♖fd1

In comparison with the position after the 18th move if White had captured on d4 instead of d7, here it is White who is in charge of the only open file and in combination with the pawn majority he has two small advantages to work on, which forces Black to be careful in his defensive play.

21...♖ad8

Here Capablanca didn't play the strongest continuation which was to put more pressure on the d-file by tripling up his major pieces with the

queen or quietly playing the g-pawn to g3 to avoid back rank mates in the future. If you gain an understanding of this position from beginning to end you will have practiced the three most important things in chess:

1) calculation of variations

2) feeling for combinations

3) evaluations.

59: *Pragmatism or deep analysis?*

A fundamental question to answer when we are conducting a game of chess is whether we should be pragmatic or aim for perfection. The shorter time control, the more pragmatic must be our thinking and playing. But if we ignore the question of time it's really a matter of understanding what kind of position merits deep thought and which not. Here is one example which allows us to discuss this interesting topic.

59

Ivanchuk – Romanishin
USSR 1988
White to move

1 ♕g4!!

When analysing this position it's logical first to analyse the forced variation 1 ♗xe4? ♖xc1 2 ♕xc1 ♕xd4 3 ♗xh7+ only to realise that it's nothing special for White after 3...♔f8! 4 ♖xe8+ ♔xe8 with equal play, since 5 ♕c8+ ♔e7 6 ♕xa6 ♕xb4 7 ♗d3 ♕e1+ 8 ♗f1 b4 leads to an ongoing equal game. But why play this variation when we also run the risk from the sixth move of getting the bishop shut in with ...g7-g6?

We need to find a better continuation and if we look hard enough and take our time we can see that the text move creates a double threat and needs to be analysed thoroughly to determine whether or not it leads to advantageous variations. It's obviously natural and normal to look at the given forced variation first and only abandon it if one sees that it doesn't lead to anything desirable.

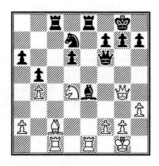

1...♗xc2

(1) 1...♕xd4 2 ♕xd7 leads to tactical pressure on e4, both rooks and, in the long run, also the back rank. In fact Black has no defence as shown by the following variations:

(a) 2...♖f8 3 ♖cd1 ♗c6 4 ♕xc8! ♕xd1 5 ♕xf8+ wins a rook.

(b) 2...♖ed8 3 ♗xe4! and White wins due to Black's weak back rank.

(c) After 2...g6 White must be careful not to play 3 ♗xe4? (Correct is *3 ♖cd1* or *3 ♗b3* with a win.) since Black has the boomerang combination 3...♕xe4!!

(d) 2...♖cd8 is met by 3 ♖xe4! ♕xe4 4 ♕xd8! and White is a piece up.

(2) 1...♕g6 is answered by 2 ♖xe4 ♕xe4 (*2...♖xe4 3 ♕xd7* and White wins a piece.) 3 ♗xe4 ♖xc1+ 4 ♔h2 ♘f6 5 ♕g5! The queen's long arm decides. 5...♖xe4 6 ♕xc1 and the d4-knight is immune from capture due to the back rank mate.

(3) 1...h5 2 ♕xd7 ♖ed8 3 ♕a7! and White keeps the extra piece. Black can try 3...♗xc2 4 ♘xc2 (4 ♖xc2? ♖a8 5 ♕b6 ♖db8 and the d4-knight will hang when the queen moves.) 4...♕b2 but 5 ♕e7! ♖f8 6 ♕e2 followed by ♕d1 decides. A very beautiful defensive queen manoeuvre to release the pressure on the c-file!

(4) 1...d5!? is the trickiest move Black can try, since it contains some traps.

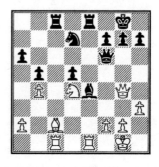

Now 2 ♕xd7? is a draw by repetition after 2...♖cd8 3 ♕a7 ♖a8 4 ♕d7 ♖ad8 (*4...♕xd4??* fails to *5 ♖xe4! ♖xe4 6 ♗xe4* and a back rank mate is in the air. However correct is 2 ♗xe4! ♖xc1 (*2...dxe4 3 ♖xc8 ♖xc8 4 ♕xd7 ♖d8 5 ♖xe4! ♖xd7 6 ♖e8* mate.) 3 ♖xc1

(a) If 3...♘e5 then 4 ♕c8!! wins but not 4 ♖c8? because of the boomerang combination 4...♕xf2+!! 5 ♔xf2 ♘xg4+ 6 hxg4 ♖xc8 7 ♗xd5 ♖d8 8 ♘c6! leaving White with only a small advantage.

(b) 3...♕h6 doesn't help either after 4 ♖c7 ♘f6 (*4...♖xe4 5 ♖xd7!* or *4...♘e5 5 ♖c8!*) 5 ♖c8! dxe4 (*5...♕d2 6 ♖xe8+ ♘xe8 7 ♗f3*) 6 ♘f5 ♕g6 7 ♘e7+.

2 ♕xd7

White must be careful! After 2 ♖xe8+? ♖xe8 3 ♕xd7 ♖f8! 4 ♘xc2 ♕b2 Black wins back the piece since the rook cannot be defended. This was the trap Black was hoping for but at the same time it's illogical to exchange on e8 before capturing on d7.

2...♖ed8 3 ♖xc2! ♖xd7 4 ♖xc8+ ♖d8 5 ♖e8+

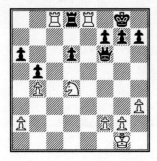

A nice x-ray attack which leads to mate next move. A lot of calculation was necessary to avoid mistakes in the variations of the tree that arose after the text move 1 ♕g4. However, Black made it pretty easy for his opponent since he declined to play the tricky move 1...d5!?. From a pragmatic point of view White could have played 1 ♕g4 without any deeper analysis, since it was obvious that White was never at risk of getting the worse position. When we calculate variations we must always strike a balance between pragmatic chess and deeply accurate analysis. By playing the text move relatively quickly, after ensuring that it cannot be worse than 1 ♗xe4?, we could put more pressure on Black who would have to take more options into account.

60-74: Knight Manoeuvres and Knight Sacrifices

60

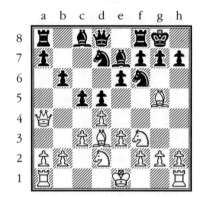

Bellon – Engqvist
Team Championship,
Stockholm 2014
White to move

The position arose after 1 d4 ♘f6
2 ♘f3 e6 3 ♗g5 c5 4 e3 d5 5 c3
♘bd7 6 ♘bd2 ♗e7 7 ♗d3 b6 8 ♕a4
0-0.

9 ♘e5

White adopts the soundest plan in
chess history. As stated by Emanuel
Lasker in his *Manual of Chess*,
this idea was first played by
De la Bourdonnais in his mammoth
match against McDonnell, London
1834.

9 ♕c6 ♖b8 10 ♗f4 doesn't
achieve anything after 10...♗b7 or
even the interesting 10...♖b7!?

9...♕c7

9...♗b7 was playable but not
9...♘xe5?? 10.dxe5 ♘d7 because of
the venomous trap…

11 ♕h4! with a decisive double
threat on h7 and e7. Particularly
when suffering from fatigue, even
experienced players can miss long
queen moves along the fourth rank –
so keep this tactical idea in mind
when both defending and attacking.

10 f4

White now has a Pillsbury setup
where, in return for conceding the
e4-square, White has established a
strong knight on e5, which can form
the basis for a future kingside attack.

What can be more venomous than
to play in accordance with a
positional plan which at the same
time contains a sneaky trap? The
only drawback with the white setup
is that the queen is actually worse
placed on a4 then on d1, since it will
lose two tempi if it returns to d1 en
route to the kingside.

61

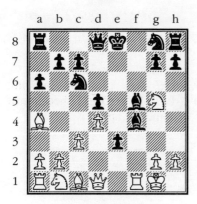

Sköld – Keres
Stockholm 1960
White to move

12 ♘h3!!

According to the Alekhine/Fischer-rule which was dealt with in *300 Most Important Chess Positions*, positions 76 and 77, knights should go forward, but obviously there are exceptions to this rule. It can sometimes be harder to see backward moves/manoeuvres in positions of a highly tactical nature. The natural continuation 12 ♖xf4 ♕xg5 13.♗xe3 ♕g6 is not as strong as what was played in the game.

12...♗xh3

Keres pondered more than 50 minutes on his response.

13 ♕h5+ g6 14 ♕xh3 e2 15 ♕e6+?

Best was first 15.♗xc6+! bxc6 16 ♕e6+ ♕e7 17 ♕xc6+ ♔f7 18 ♖xf4+ ♔g7 19 ♗d2 e1♕+ 20 ♗xe1 ♕xe1+ 21 ♖f1 ♕e3+ 22 ♔h1 ♖f8 23 ♕xc7+ ♔h6 24 ♘a3

and White wins.

15...♕e7 16 ♗xc6+ ♔d8! 17 ♕xd5+ ♗d6 18 ♖e1 bxc6 19 ♕g5

If 19 ♕xc6 ♗xh2+ then 20 ♔h1 (not *20 ♔xh2?? ♕h4+* and White is mated in three moves by Black's second queen!) 20...♖b8 21 ♕d5+ ♔c8 22 ♗g5 ♕d6 23 ♕e4 and White is clearly better.

19...♘f6 20 ♘a3?

20 c4 followed by ♘c3 was the strongest continuation, securing control of the centre.

20...♖b8 21.♗f4

21...♖xb2??

Black has no time for such adventures. White gains extra tempi for a decisive attack. After 21...♗xf4 22 ♕xf4 ♘d5 White must consider whether or not to defend the b2-pawn. According to the computer the position is completely equal (0.00).

22 ♘c4 ♗xf4 23 ♕xf4 ♖c2 24 ♘e5

The knight is really quick to jump into Black's position!

24...♕e6

Not 24...♖xc3? 25 ♕d2.

25 ♕f3 ♖f8

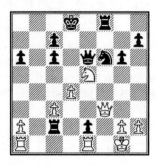

26 ♖ab1?

Immediately winning was 26 ♕d3! with a double threat on c2 and a6 while exploiting the finesse 26...♖xa2 27.d5!

26...♔e7?

26...♕f5! was the only chance to stay in the game.

27 c4?

27 ♖xe2 ♖xe2 28 ♕xe2 was the simplest way to win as Black is left with a vulnerable king and weak pawns.

27...♕f5?

27...c5 should have been played.

28 ♕a3+ ♔e6

If 28...♔e8 then 29 ♖b8+.

29 ♕xf8

And White won after **29...♕f4 30 ♕c8+ ♔d6 31 c5+ ♔d5 32 ♕d8+ ♔e4 33 ♘f3 ♘d5 34 ♕e8+ ♔d3 35 ♖b3+ ♘c3 36 ♕xc6 ♖xa2 37 ♕e6 ♖c2 38 ♕xa6+ ♔e4 39 ♕e6+ ♔d3 40 ♔f2 g5 41 ♖xe2 g4 42 ♕a6 mate.**

62

Poitoranov – Stein
USSR 1955
Black to move

This is a position where we are in the middle of an exchange of blows. The question is whether Black should capture on g7, d2 or g3?

17...♘xd2!

Stein's move is stronger than 17...♔xg7?! which would give Black only a small advantage in view of his fine outpost on c5 and passed a-pawn.

17...♘xg3 is also inferior to the move played, although Black remains slightly better after 18 ♗xf8 ♘xf1 19 ♗xe7 ♗f5 20 e4 ♕xe7 21 ♖xf1 ♗d7.

18 ♗xf8 ♘xf1 19 ♗xe7 ♗f5 20 e4 ♕xe7 21 exf5 ♘e3!

21...♘xh2 or 21...♘xg3 were also possible but Stein's move is more beautiful since it secures permanent control of the e5-square with the prospect of a positional win.

22 fxe3 ♕xe3+ 23.♔h1 ♘c5

Black's knight is superior to the white bishop and his distant passed pawn combined with dark-square control will decide the game.

24 ♕b2?

24 ♗f1 was tougher but White would still be doomed in the long run.

24...♘d3 25 ♕a2 ♘c1! White resigned.

A very nice miniature game by Stein. The recipe was to play as actively as possible with his knights. Incidentally, this is how the game began:

1 d4 ♘f6 2 ♘f3 g6 3 g3 ♗g7 4 ♗g2 0–0 5 0–0 d6 6 c4 ♘c6

Black's knights are perfectly placed and control all the four squares in the centre of the board.

7 d5 ♘a5 8 ♘fd2 c5 9 a3 b6 10 b4 ♘b7

It's hard to think that this knight will decide the game!

11 ♗b2 ♗d7 12 ♕c2 axb4 13 axb4 a5

Black secures the c5-square for his knight.

14 bxa5 bxa5 15 ♘c3 ♕c7 16 ♘ce4 ♘xe4 17 ♗xg7 thereby reaching the starting point for our calculations.

A very instructive game which should be learned by heart, paying close attention to Stein's play with the knights. The king's knight was sacrificed to pave the way for the queen's knight to decide the game. Other great players showing great dexterity in handling the knight pair have been Chigorin, Pillsbury and Anand. As a matter of a fact the knight duo has always been underestimated throughout chess history, in strong contrast to the many who promote 'the advantage of the two bishops'. Of course, you may be able to benefit from such a biased perspective if you keep hold of your knights and become particularly adept at handling them!

63

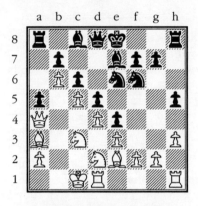

Reshevsky – Keres
World Championship,
The Hague/Moscow 1948
White to move

Here we have a position where one of the players has a big lead in development but still has to find a way to open up the position. There are two options: to sacrifice on e4 or break with f2-f3. Reshevsky made the correct choice.

16 ♘dxe4!

It's quite easy to understand that it's the d2-knight rather than the c3-knight which should be sacrificed on e4. The c3-knight is more actively placed and is needed for the pawn push d4-d5 which will also open the d-file for the d1-rook. The positional method 16 f3 doesn't open up the position as much after 16...exf3 17 ♘xf3 h4 and in addition weakens the g3-square which Black can exploit by ...♘h5.

16...♘xe4

Worse is 16...dxe4 17.d5 and White has a dream position with pressure on the d-file and the a4-e8 diagonal.

17 ♘xe4 h4

Keres didn't accept the piece sacrifice and preferred to play on a pawn down rather than choose the continuation 17...dxe4 18 d5 ♗xc5 19 dxc6! ♗xa3+ 20 ♔c2 (*20 ♕xa3? ♕xb6*) 20...♕xb6 (*20...♗d6 21 ♖xd6!*) 21 cxb7+ ♔e7 22 ♕xa3+ and White wins. An illuminating example how a locked centre can become dynamic. Amazingly Black managed to win the game after 63 moves despite the fact that Reshevsky won the strongest pawn on the board for free.

64

Nezhmetdinov – Kamyshov
Russian Federation Championship,
Yaroslav 1951
White to move

A typical tactical idea to keep in mind when Black has a doubled f-pawn on the kingside is to sacrifice a knight on f7 or e6. Note that a sacrifice on e6 leads to the same damaged pawn structure as a sacrifice on f7 if Black accepts the sacrifice, which is generally forced. The motif of such a sacrifice is to exploit weaknesses on the h5-e8 and a2-g8 diagonals as well as the central files.

Of course this sacrifice can also be made with the f6-pawn on g7. Black can even have the h7-pawn on h6 or g6. These kingside pawn structures are very common and it's important to master the tactical ideas associated with them.

Here the strong tactician Nezhmetdinov played the tempting **17 ♘xf7**. However the best continuation was 17 cxd5! fxe5 18 dxe6 which would have destroyed Black's position even more than Nezhmetdinov's knight sacrifice. All diagonals and files are opened and it will be easier for White to get his pieces out. In addition White wins a couple of pawns. The main variation goes 18...fxe6 (After *18...♗e7 19 ♕d7+ ♔f8 20 ♕xb7 ♕d8 21 ♕f3* and Black cannot do anything against White's domination of major pieces and strong pawn on e6.) 19 ♕h5+ ♔e7 20 ♖xe5. Now White has all his pieces in play an can try to exploit a number of weaknesses such as the e6- and b7-pawn, while Black has problems creating harmony in his position.

17...♔xf7 18 ♕h5+ ♔e7 19 cxd5 e5 20 f4 ♕xd5?

It was not necessary to help White open a second central file. A better defence was 20...♖d8 and then try to escape with the king to the queenside.

21 fxe5

21 ♖ad1 ♕c5+ 22 ♔h1 also improves White's attack.

21...f5 22 e6 ♔f6 23 h4!

It's interesting that White never seems to play the queen's rook to d1. It really shows how strong White's position is if that rook isn't needed. Now it's the h-pawn which is used to prepare a mate on g5 or f7.

23...♗c5+ 24 ♔h1 ♕xe6

There is no defence. To play the computer move 24...♕xg2+ would be degrading for a human.

25 ♕h6+ Black resigned.

In position 65 another way is presented, relating to material (pieces or pawns?), which might be an alternative to the Kotov/Tisdall method (positions 50-59), especially when you are attacking the enemy king.

65

Kasparov – Nikolic
Olympiad, Manila 1992
White to move

Capablanca and Kasparov liked to have a knight on f5 when attacking because it is easy to get at the king from that square.

17 ♘xg7!

It's interesting to compare this knight sacrifice on g7 with Tal – Vasjukov, position 141. The computer prefers the preliminary move 17 ♘g5!, for example 17...♘e5 18 ♘xg7 ♔xg7 19 ♕f5 with at least as great attacking prospects as in the game.

17...♔xg7 18 ♕f5 ♘f8

On Chessbase, Chandler states that this is the most logical way to parry the threat of 19 ♖xd7 – but it's not the best. 18...♖ad8! develops Black's last piece but if White finds 19 ♕g5+ ♔h8 20 g4! Black is nevertheless in a difficult situation. On the other hand 18...♔f8 19 ♘g5! makes White's task far more straightforward.

19 h4

It would be easier to attack with pieces rather than pawns and play 19 ♘e5 followed by ♖df1 and ♘g4 with enormous pressure on f6.

19...h6?

Better defences were 19...♕b6 or 19...♖ad8.

20 g4

Again it would be simpler to play just with the pieces as shown by the forced variation 20 ♕g4+ ♔h7 21 ♘g5+ ♔g8 22 ♗xf6.

20...♕c8! 21 ♕xc8 ♖axc8 22 g5 ♘8h7 23 e4

23 gxf6+ ♗xf6 24 ♘d4 was more precise.

23...♖cd8 24 ♖df1 ♔f8 25 gxf6 ♗xf6 26 e5 ♗g7 27 ♖hg1 c5 28 ♔c2!?

White stops the possibility of ...♖d3 once and for all and steps off of the h6-c1 diagonal. The variation 28 ♖g4 h5 29 ♖f4? ♗h6 shows why it's not advisable to have the king on c1.

28...♖e6 29 ♖g4 ♗h8 30 b4 b6 31 bxc5 bxc5 32 ♖b1 ♖a6 33 ♖b2

Decisive was 33 ♖b7 ♖xa2+ 34 ♗b2!.

33...♗g7?

If 33...♖b6 then 34 ♖b5! ♖xb5 35 cxb5.

34 ♖b7 ♖xa2+ 35 ♔b3 ♖a6 36 e6! ♖xe6

36...♗xc3 37 e7+ ♔e8 38 ♖g8+ ♘f8 39 exf8♖ mate.

37 ♖xg7 Black resigned.

What's interesting about Kasparov's play is that he missed more precise variations which only involved piece-play. Comparison can be made with the game Tal – Vasjukov, position 141, where Tal also attacked purely with pieces.

What we can learn from this example is that it might pay to check variations involving only pieces first and if you are not satisfied with the variations you can include pawns as well. This is a another kind of technique we can develop to help us calculate variations in a more structured way in addition to the well-known process developed by Kotov/Tisdall, seen in positions 50-59.

66

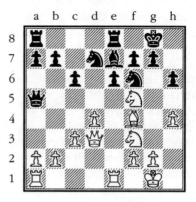

Tal – Keres
USSR Team Championship 1959
White to move

The question here is what White should do with his knight on f5.

15 ♘xg7?

(2) Correct was the positional continuation 15 ♘xe7+ ♖xe7 16 ♘e5 with mutual chances.

(2) 15 ♘d6 ♘d5 16.♗h2 ♗xd6 17.♗xd6 was also playable.

(3) Tal most probably analysed 15 ♖xe6 fxe6 16 ♘xh6+ gxh6 (*16...♔f8? 17 ♕g6 ♕h5* gives White the opportunity to show off with the decisive...

18 ♘g5!! since *18...♕xg6* is answered by *19.♘xe6* mate.) 17 ♕g6+ ♔h8 but White cannot get anything more than a draw after 18 ♕xh6+ (*18 ♘e5 ♘xe5 19 ♗xe5 ♖ec8 20 ♗xf6+ ♗xf6 21 ♕xf6+* and the queen gives a perpetual check horizontally or vertically, depending on Black's reply.) 18...♘h7 19 ♘e5 ♘df8 20 ♕h5 (*20 ♘g4 ♘d7 21 ♘e5 ♘df8* leads to a draw by repetition.) and White has enough compensation for the sacrificed material.

15...♔xg7 16 ♘e5

Tal plans the clever 16 ♗xh6+ ♔xh6 17 ♘xf7+ ♔g7 18 ♖e5!! but Black has a strong defensive move.

16...♖h8! 17 ♕h3

Tal now focuses on the fragile pawns on f6 and e6 but even here Black has a strong defensive move.

17...♖h7!

Incredible play with the king's rook! Such unusual moves can easily be missed by the attacker. White is lost since White has committed suicide by sacrificing too much material.

18 c4

18 ♘xf7 ♔xf7 19 ♕xe6+ ♔f8

20 ♗xh6+ ♖xh6 21 ♕xe7+ ♔g8 leads nowhere for White. The game concluded:

18...♘f8 19 ♖ad1 ♖d8 20 ♗d2 ♕b6 21 ♗c3 ♔g8! 22 ♖e3 ♘e8 23 ♖g3+ ♘g7 24 ♖dd3 f6 25 ♘g6 ♘xg6 26 ♖xg6 ♔f7 27 h5 ♕a6! 28 b3 ♕xa2 29 d5 cxd5 30 cxd5 ♖xd5 31 ♖xd5 exd5 32 ♕d3 ♕a6 33 ♕xd5+ ♕e6 34 ♕f3 ♖h8 35 ♗d2 ♖d8 36 ♗xh6 ♕e1+ 37 ♔h2 ♕e5+ 38 ♔g1 ♘f5 39 ♗f4 ♕e1+ 40 ♔h2 ♖d1 41 ♔h3 ♖d4 42 ♖g4 ♕d1 43 h6 ♖d3 44 h7

44 ♗e3 ♕h1 mate.

44...♖xf3+ 45 gxf3 ♕xf3+ 46 ♗g3 ♘xg3 White resigned.

67

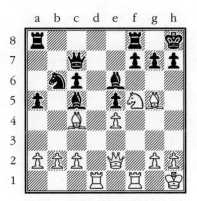

Stein – Portisch
Interzonal tournament,
Stockholm 1962
White to move

19 ♘xg7!!

One of the most beautiful knight sacrifices on g7. This must have come as a shock to Portisch who probably expected the positional continuation 19 ♗xe6 fxe6 20 ♘h4 with a clear advantage to White due to his more favourable pawn structure.

19...♗xc4

If 19...♔xg7 20 ♗f6+ ♔g8 21 ♕d2 (*21 ♖d3 allows mate in six moves*) 21...♖fb8 22 ♕h6 ♗f8 23 ♕g5+ ♗g7 24 ♕xg7 mate.

20 ♗f6!

The point of the sacrifice was to set up a well-known mating pattern.

20...♗e7

If 20...♗xe2 then 21 ♘f5+ ♔g8 22 ♘h6 mate, which is an important mating pattern to keep in mind when attacking with knight and bishop.

21 ♕f3 Black resigned.

This game was rewarded with the first beauty prize and then published all over the world.

Normally three pieces are enough to deliver mate but here White has four! Smirin played the beautiful and absolutely decisive move...

26 ♘g6+!! hxg6 27 ♕xg6

After this quiet move White has three pieces in the attack and is threatening 28 ♗e5+. Black has only one decent move.

27...♘c6

But now comes the Alekhine-move, seen in positions 103-104.

28 ♖e6!

This decides like a knife in the heart. The minor pieces have prepared the way for the major pieces so now Black's best option is to sacrifice her royal highness for the king's rook. But instead **Black** politely **resigned**.

68

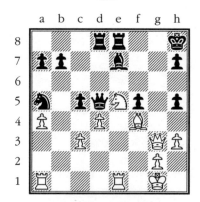

Smirin – Volokitin
Fügen 2006
White to move

69

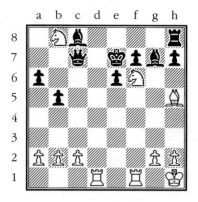

Pedersen – Gallmeyer
Denmark 1971
White to move

21 ♘c6+!

After this, the strongest move in the position, White can announce mate in five. 21 ♘g8+ ♔e8 22 ♘c6 also wins but it's not as forcing as the move played by Pedersen and leads only to a material advantage rather than mate.

21...♕xc6

21...♔f8 22 ♘d7+ ♗xd7 23 ♖xf7+ and mate next move.

22 ♘g8+!

What knights!

22...♔e8

If Black accepts the second knight sacrifice he will be mated after 22...♖xg8 23 ♖xf7+ ♔e8 24 ♖c7+ ♔f8 25 ♖d8+.

23 ♗xf7+ ♔f8 24 ♖d8+ Black resigned.

It's mate next move. The combination was perhaps not difficult to solve if you are familiar with the fundamental tactical tricks.

What's more interesting is how such a hair-raising position could arise. This was another example how to play maximally with knights, just like the miniature game Poitoranov – Stein.

The diagram position arose after:

1 e4 c5 2 ♘f3 d6 3 d4 cxd4 4 ♘xd4

The king's knight is already placed in a centralised and flexible position.

4...♘f6 3 5 ♘c3 a6 6 ♗g5 e6

Black has for the moment neutralised both White's knights

with the pawn on e6, which controls d5 and f5, and a6 which controls b5.

7 f4 b5

The sharp Polugaevsky variation demands a lot of preparation by both players.

8 e5 dxe5 9 fxe5 ♕c7 10 exf6 ♕e5+ 11 ♗e2 ♕xg5 12 0–0 ♕e5 13 ♗f3 ♖a7 14 ♘c6 ♕c5+?!

It was better to exchange White's active knight for Black's passive one. Black's decision proves to be fatal.

15 ♔h1 ♖d7

A typical rook manoeuvre in this variation, but here it ignores the dangerous c6-knight.

16 ♘xb8! ♖xd1 17 ♖axd1 gxf6 18 ♘e4

Now even the queen's knight will take an active part in the attack.

18...♕c7?

18...♕f5! was the best defence.

19 ♘xf6+ ♔e7 20 ♗h5!

The last minor piece – Bobby Fischer's favourite – reinforces White's attack.

20...♗g7

And we have reached the diagram position.

This miniature not only demonstrates a successful attack against an uncastled king, but more importantly helps us to understand how to play with the king's knight, which in this game showed it was clearly stronger than the queen's knight, since it paved the way for the other pieces to enter the fray. This kind of model game may help you to develop a close relationship with your king's knight and win in the same manner. Remember position 16 where the king's knight decided the game after only four moves, due to its perfect co-ordination with the black queen. It is most important to understand the great potential of such a knight. It was a giant on d4 and performed like a real hero in the game. In fact most games have one outstanding piece whose mission is to pave the way for the rest of the army.

70

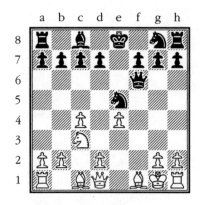

Novotny – Kalendovsky
Brno 1973
Black to move

The position arose after **1 c4 e5 2 ♘c3 ♘c6 3 ♘f3 ♗c5 4 ♘xe5?! ♗xf2+! 5 ♔xf2 ♘xe5 6 e4 ♕f6+ 7 ♔g1?** whereupon Black exploited the overloaded queen on d1.

7...♘g4!

Black wants to mate on either f2 or d4 so White is forced to sacrifice the queen to avoid mate.

7...♕b6+?? would have been a huge mistake because of 8.c5! ♕xc5+ 9.d4 ♕d6 10.♗f4 and White wins.

8 ♕xg4

The only way to avoid mate was by 8 ♕f3 ♕d4+ 9 ♕e3 ♘xe3 10 dxe3 but then White would only have one dark-squared bishop for the queen.

8...♕d4 mate.

All White's moves look pretty natural which is why even skilled players can fall into such a venomous opening trap. White could have improved with 4 e3, while 7 ♔e1 was forced.

I checked Mega Database (2020) and didn't find a single game with 6...♕f6+!. It's actually the best move in the position and sets the trap. One 2295-player continued 6...d6 instead and missed the chance to win with this trap. Instead Black lost after 27 moves against an unrated player.

It's possible to win miniature games by mobilising your queen and knight rapidly which may enable you to exert immediate tactical pressure on your opponent. This is an important concept to bear in mind, since it's possible to create chaos in the enemy position by fast mobilisation of these particular pieces.

71

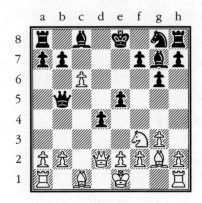

Sörensen – Kistrup
Uppsala 2018
White to move

In this position, one of my students, the talented Hampus Sörensen, played the amazing move…

11 ♘xd4!!

Opening the long light-squared diagonal.

11...exd4

And the silent sneaker…

12 ♕d3!!

Now it is striking that wherever Black moves the exchange of queens is unavoidable.

12...♕xd3

(1) 12...♕a4 is answered by 13 ♕b3!.

(2) 12...♕b6 by 13 ♕b3!.

(3) 12...♕b4+ by 13 ♗d2 since 13...♕xb2? is met by 14 ♖b1 and White breaks through on the queenside. The best continuation was…

(4) 12...♕c5! 13 ♕a3! (Note that *13 cxb7? ♗xb7 14 ♗xb7 fails to*

14...♕b4+) 13...♕xa3 14 bxa3 ♗h3!! 15 ♗xh3 bxc6 and White must be satisfied with only a slight advantage because of his doubled pawn on the a-file.

13 exd3

Despite the fact that Black is a piece up there is no way to retain it in this particular case.

13...♘e7

Black's best move 13...♗h3!! reminiscent of Shirov's immortal and unforgettable bishop move to h3 in his ending versus Topalov (position 195). Then 14 ♗xh3 bxc6 leads to a positional advantage for White although that was still the best defence for Black.

14 cxb7 ♖b8 15 bxc8♕+ ♖xc8 16 ♔d1

White has exploited his extra pawn and won after 48 moves. Such imagination says something about this young man's bright future!

72

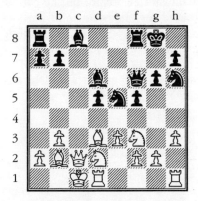

Capablanca – Baca Arus
Havana (Blindfold) 1912
White to play

In this position Black has weakened both the long and classical diagonals and Capablanca exploited these weaknesses beautifully with the amazing and unforgettable move…

14 ♘c4!!

Such energetic moves are evidence that the knight is the soul of chess.

14...dxc4

Objectively 14...♘hf7 is better but it doesn't save the game after 15 ♘fxe5 ♘xe5 16 f4. For example 16...♘xd3+ 17 ♖xd3 (*17 ♕xd3? dxc4 18 ♕xc4+ ♗e6*) 17...dxc4 18 ♗xf6 cxd3 19 ♕c4+ ♖f7 20 ♗b2 and White wins.

15 ♗xc4+ ♘hf7 16 ♖xd6 ♕xd6 17 ♘xe5 ♗e6 18 ♖d1 ♕e7 19 ♖d7!!

The most beautiful move in the whole combinational sequence. White sacrifices both rooks for the purpose of exploiting the diagonals of the bishops all the way down to the vital squares in the king's castled position.

19...♗xd7 20 ♘xd7

Surprisingly Capablanca missed the elegant 20 ♘xg6! but he can be excused for this because of the fact that he was playing blindfold. White then wins by setting up a deadly battery along the a1-h8 diagonal so that after 20...hxg6 21 ♕c3 Black is unable to stop the mate on g7.

20...♖fc8

If 20...♕xd7 then 21 ♕c3.

21 ♕c3 ♖xc4 22 bxc4 ♘d6

22...♘e5 was a better defence but it would not hold if White plays 23 ♘xe5 ♕f6 24 c5 threatening a check on b3 or c4.

23 ♕h8+ ♔f7 24 ♘e5+ ♔e6 25 ♕xa8 Black resigned.

73

Engqvist – Ängskog
Team Championship,
Stockholm 2003
White to move

After **26 ♕xa4??** I thought I was winning but I had overlooked a devilish move.

With hindsight it would have been correct to capture the stronger knight on d3. After 26 ♕xd3 ♕xa5 the pin looks pretty annoying but there is no tactical way for White to profit from this. 27.♖a3 is answered by 27...♘b2! and 27 ♕c2 by 27...♕c3!. Black handles the pin gallantly with tactical retorts which exploit White's unprotected pieces.

26...♗g5!!

This shock move came as a bolt from the blue and is very instructive since it shows how a smothered mate can arise when one least expects it! At least I didn't on this particular occasion.

27 ♗b6

27 ♗xg5 ♕a7+ 28 ♔h1 ♘f2+ 29 ♔g1 ♘h3+ 30 ♔h1 ♕g1+!

31 ♖xg1 ♘f2 mate is the famous smothered mate discovered already in the 17th century by the Italian genius Gioachino Greco (1600-1634). It's one the most beautiful combinations resulting from a perfect co-ordination between a queen and knight.

27...♗xd2 and Black won.

This game taught me that it's not enough to have a thorough knowledge of tactical motifs. One must also have a good feel for when and how combinative positions can arise. I could have given some thought to the weakened move f2-f3 and the fact that Black had a super knight on d3 which could co-operate with the queen on the g1-a7 diagonal, particularly if the e3-bishop disappeared from that vital diagonal. From a psychological perspective, it's also true that the combination is somewhat easier to discover for an attacker than a defender.

74

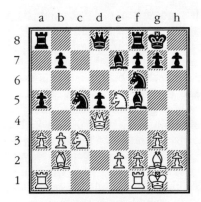

Benkö – Horowitz
USA Championship,
New York 1968
White to move

14 ♘xd5!

The logical move which keeps the initiative but necessitates a temporary exchange sacrifice. The variations are not particularly complicated to calculate since there is a natural flow to the moves. The passive 14.♕d1?! is met simplest by 14...♕b6 since 15 ♘xd5 ♘xd5 16 ♗xd5 ♖ad8 leads to a position where Black's more active pieces compensate for the minus pawn.

14...♘xb3 15 ♕f4 ♘xd5?

Black should have ignored the exchange and played 15...♗e6 16 ♘xe7+ ♕xe7 when after 17 ♖ab1 White retains a slight advantage due to his strong bishop-pair in an open position, as well as other active pieces on good squares.

16 ♕xf5 ♘xa1 17 ♘xf7!

This is the tactical finesse White had to see before sacrificing the exchange.

17...♕c8

A better defence was offered by 17...♖xf7 18 ♗xd5 ♗f6 even though Black is a pawn down and has no counterplay after 19 ♗xa1.

18 ♘h6+! ♔h8

If 18...gxh6 then 19 ♗xd5+ and the game is decided on the classical and long dark-squared diagonal.

19 ♕xd5 ♘c2

Black invites White to deliver the famous smothered mate. 19...♕e8 is obviously torture after 20 ♗xa1.

20 ♕g8+! Black resigned.

20...♖xg8 allows 21 ♘f7 mate.

75-96: Bishop Manoeuvres and Bishop Sacrifices

75

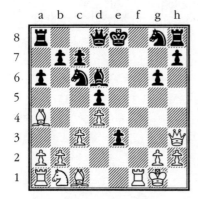

Sköld – Haave
Radio game 1949
White to play

15 ♗d1!!

Such a rare bishop retreat can be difficult to see in a tactical position where there are several possible continuations. It looks strange to release the pin on the knight but the idea is to prevent Black from moving the queen to d7 followed by castling queenside. It's a very beautiful manoeuvre since you don't expect it and it's a prophylactic move as well as an attacking one. Backward thinking is sometimes important when we manoeuvre our pieces to the best squares. We must exploit the whole board or think like Karpov that we are playing billiards with the bishop.

The continuations 15 ♗xe3 ♕d7 or 15 ♕xe3+ ♕e7 are fully playable

but increase Black's defensive possibilities. Sköld's move is the best while at the same time being the most aesthetic.

15...♕d7?

Black is undeniably in a tough spot but why give White such a dream move for free? A better option was 15...♘ge7 16 ♗xe3 (or *16 ♗g4 e2*) 16...♖f8 releasing the pressure on the f-file and preparing 17...h5. Play might continue 17 ♖xf8+ ♔xf8 18 ♗g4 h5 19 ♗e6 ♔g7 20 ♘d2 and White is positionally winning thanks to his more active pieces. These can easily manoeuvre and improve their positions move by move, using the weak e6 and g5 squares as pivots to quote a famous term by Nimzowitsch.

16 ♗g4 ♕e7 17 ♗xe3 h5 18 ♗c8!

It's not often one sees a bishop manoeuvre from f1–b5–a4–d1–g4–c8 in the opening phase of a game so there is no doubt which piece is the hero here. The bishop is like a razor blade in Black's position. 18 ♗e6! was also good and one can imagine that Sköld had a good think whether the bishop should go for the pawn on d5 or the exchange. I think players who don't care how they win would play the latter while more artistic players would prefer the former.

18...♖xc8

What else? White was actually threatening to move his other bishop to g5, because if Black captures it then it's mate on d7. This is one of the points of drawing the bishop to c8 instead of e6 which a computer would have done. Fortunately a human is more aesthetically inclined and can play more artistically than a computer.

19 ♕xc8+ ♘d8 20 ♕h3

Here we leave the game which Sköld went on to win after 49 moves.

76

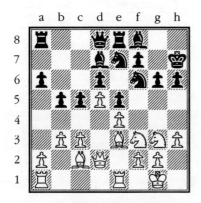

Tal – Ghitescu
Miscolc 1963
White to move

With the help of a piece sacrifice it's possible to blow up a blocked centre and thereby create one that is mobile. Here Tal played **19 ♗xc5!?** which isn't a move a computer would suggest because it thinks it's better to keep the position blocked and so would choose a move such as 19 ♘h2, with the idea of f2-f4, or play on the queenside with 19 b4. Tal, who was a highly-acclaimed magician, most probably had

psychological/pragmatic reasons for his choice. One mustn't forget Lasker's words that chess is a struggle between humans. Sometimes it's better to play an objectively inferior move if it means that the opponent will have more problems to solve as well as feel more uncomfortable. If that adds up to a significant psychological advantage, then half the battle is already won.

19...dxc5 20 ♘xe5 ♘c8

The natural and most probably the best move was 20...♔g8, although White has enough compensation in the form of his strong and mobile centre after the consolidating 21 ♖ad1.

21 f4

Tal probably analysed 21 ♘xf7 ♕e7 22 ♘g5+ hxg5 which destroys Black's pawn structure. After 23 e5...

Black has the super move 23...♘d6!!. How often does a player fork himself? This is a really clever move because the e5-pawn cannot attend two weddings at the same time and must make a choice which knight to capture. (The more human but still fully playable continuation

23...♘xd5 24.♕xd5 ♘b6 would have left chances for both sides.) 24 ♕xg5 ♕f7 25 exf6 ♗h6 26 ♕h4 ♖xe1+ 27 ♖xe1 ♗e8 and White has full compensation for the pawn but no more than that.

21...♕e7 22 c4! ♗g7

An important alternative was 22...♘d6.

23 ♘f3 bxc4

Tal had calculated 23...♘h5 24 ♘xh5 ♗xa1 25 e5! with a winning attack. Inferior is 25 ♖xa1 gxh5 26 e5+ ♚g8 27 ♕d3 f5 as Tal mentions, for example 28 e6 ♘d6 29 exd7 ♕xd7 30 ♘e5 and White's has rather the better game.

Now the seemingly natural…

24 bxc4?

…was played but it's actually a mistake. Tal avoided 24 e5 ♘xd5 25 ♕xd5 ♘b6 mainly on general grounds but White is winning after 26 ♕e4 with the idea f4-f5.

24...♘d6

With the double threat of capturing on c4 or e4.

25 e5

25 ♗d3? fails due to the discoverer…

25...♘fxe4! 26 ♗xe4 ♗xa1 and White's rook on e1 is overloaded. White has to play the discoverer 27 ♗xg6+ fxg6 28 ♖xe7+ ♖xe7 and accept a slightly worse position.

25...♘xc4 26 ♕c3 ♗b5

26...♘b6 was an important alternative in order to put pressure on White's centre.

27 ♖ad1 ♖ad8 28 d6

White expands in the centre and wins back the piece.

28...♘xd6 29 exd6 ♕b7

29...♕f8 is met by 30 ♕xc5.

30 ♘e5 ♘d7?

30...♘d5 31 ♕f3 ♖xd6 was necessary to keep the position alive. The text move loses and is the turning point in the game.

31 ♘h5! ♗h8 32 ♕g3

White's threats against g6 and f7 can in principle only be eliminated by an exchange on e5 after which the pawns will be connected again.

32...♘xe5

If 32...♘f8 then 33 a4.

33 fxe5 ♕d7 34 ♘f4! ♗xe5 35 ♗xg6+ ♚h8

Or 35...fxg6 36 ♕xg6+ ♚h8 37 ♖xe5 ♖xe5 38 ♕f6+.

36 ♗xf7 ♗d4+

Otherwise 36...♕xf7 37 ♘g6+ or 36...♗xf4 37 ♖xe8+ ♖xe8 38 ♕xf4.

37 ♖xd4 ♖xe1+ 38 ♕xe1 ♕xf7

After 38...cxd4 follows 39 ♕e5+ ♚h7 40 ♕e4+ ♚h8 41 ♕g6 ♕xd6 42 ♘e6 and Black cannot avert mate in three moves.

39 ♕e5+ ♕g7 40 ♕xc5 ♗c6 41 ♖d2 Black resigned.

77

Tal – Polugayevsky
USSR Championship, Tbilisi 1959
White to move

White must declare his intentions with regard to his minor pieces on the c-file. So how best to proceed from here?

14 ♘xa4

This seems to be the best solution, however an interesting alternative was the more complicated 14 ♘f5!? which leads to incredibly complicated variations after 14...♕xc4 (More logical than *14...exf5 15 exf5* which opens further white files and diagonals and in addition liquidates the most important defensive e6-pawn.) 15 ♘xg7+ ♔f8 16 ♘xa4 ♗xa4 17 ♗h6.

14...♗xa4

14...b5? is answered by 15 ♗d5! exd5 16 exd5 bxa4 17 ♗xf6 gxf6 18 ♕h6 and White is threatening a massacre of the black position with a capture on f6 or e7. 14...♕xc4? is obviously met by the fork 15 ♘b6.

15 ♗xe6!

A typical sacrifice in the Sicilian where the idea normally is that White gains three pawns for a piece as well as the f5-square for a knight. Here the position is more complicated since White doesn't get three pawns for the piece due to the tactical pawn-weakness on c2.

15...fxe6 16 ♘xe6

White has placed his knight in the heart of Black's position. Such a knight Koblencs (Tal's coach) called a Trojan horse. The knight on e6, just like a bishop, prevents Black from castling in either direction, but the drawback, compared to a bishop, is that it is easier to attack a knight with a bishop, queen or a king. After all, a king cannot be placed on f7 with a bishop on e6. Armed with this information, it's now vital to bring up reinforcements and strike while the iron is hot.

16...♕xc2

17 ♕d4

Tal obviously visualised this stepping stone position while calculating the sacrifice on e6. Here it's easy to understand that Black ought to play...

17...♔f7

...but how does White proceed from here? When focusing on the second stepping stone you need to check if Morphy's principles are valid since White is ahead in development as Black's rooks are undeveloped and he has decentralised pieces on a4 and a2. According to Morphy's principles you have to open the central lines if ahead in development so the logical continuation to analyse is...

18 ♖c1 ♕a2 19 e5

The most principled move but according to the computer 19 ♘xg7 ♔xg7 20 e5 dxe5 21 ♖xe5 is more precise and gives White a slight advantage.

19...dxe5

The forced variation 19...♕xe6 20 exf6 ♗xf6 21 ♗xf6 ♕xf6 22 ♕d5+ ♔f8 23 ♕xb7 ♖e8 24 ♕xa6 must also be examined together with an evaluation that White has more than enough compensation for the piece since Black's rook on h8 has problems and the d6-pawn is weak. White's two passed pawns are more than enough compensation for the bishop.

20 ♕xe5

Here we have stepping stone No.3. We can make the evaluation that White's more active pieces and extra pawn should be enough compensation for the sacrificed light-squared bishop. However, one should see the forced variation...

20...♕xf2+

20...♕d5! 21 ♗xf6 ♕xe5 22 ♗xe5 ♔xe6 23 ♗xg7+ ♔d7 24 ♗xh8 ♖xh8 leads to dynamic equilibrium and was Black's strongest continuation.

21 ♔xf2 ♘g4+ 22 ♔g1 ♘xe5

23 ♖xe5

Now the evaluation can be made that White has a slight advantage due to his more active pieces. Koblencs was of the opinion that Tal must have seen this position (stepping stone No.4) already when he sacrificed the bishop on e6. That is ten moves ahead but by focusing on the stepping stones at move 17, 20 and 23 it's not impossible. You can travel far just by good calculation technique coupled with sound chess principles learned from great players from the past. The game continued...

23...♗xg5 24 ♘xg5+ ♔g6 25 ♘e6 ♖he8 26 ♖e3 ♖ac8 27 ♖f1!

White needs to keep both rooks to have any chance of successfully attacking Black's king.

27...♗b5 28 ♖g3+ ♔h6 29 ♘xg7! ♖f8

29...♗xf1 30 ♘xe8 ♖xe8 31 ♔xf1 leads to a technically winning rook ending.

30 ♖e1 ♖f6 31 h3

White has to give the king a flight-square and be able to activate the e1-rook.

31...♖c2??

The bishop no longer has any function on b5 so the appropriate move was 31...♗d7.

32 ♖e4 ♖c4 33 ♖e5 ♖c1+ 34 ♔h2 Black resigned.

There is also a psychological aspect which is important when sacrificing a piece for a pawn as Tal did with 15 ♗xe6!. Tal/Koblencs mention in their annotations to the game: "Of course, you need courage, self-confidence and optimism to play chess like this!"

78

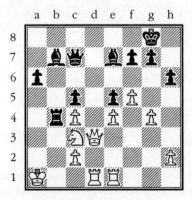

Karachurin – Bennedik
Correspondence 2004
Black to move

34...♗d5!!

One of the most extraordinary sacrifices ever played and it wins on the spot! Black's threat is 35...♗xc4 and whichever piece captures on d5 leads to clear defeat for White.

35 cxd5

The best defence because if a piece lands on d5 White loses material or is quickly mated.

(1) 35 ♘xd5?? ♕a5+ and mate next move.

(2) 35 ♕xd5? ♕a5+ 36 ♘a2 ♖a4 37 ♔b1 ♖xa2 and Black is threatening mate in two, first on a1 and then on a3 so White has to protect the a3-square. 38 ♕d3 ♖a3 and Black wins the queen since it cannot move from the third rank while avoiding mate.

(3) 35.exd5? e4 opens up the long dark-squared diagonal with decisive effect. Then 36 ♕g3 would be met by 36...♗d6 followed by ...♗e5 leading to a deadly pin, since mate soon follows.

35...c4 36 d6

After 36 ♕e2 ♕a5+ 37 ♘a2 Black has the decisive wedge-move 37...c3 cutting White's position in two since there is no communication on the second rank. White has no effective antidote to either 38...♖a4 or 38...♕a3 39 ♖b1 ♖a4.

36...♕a5+ 37 ♘a2 cxd3 38 dxe7 ♖b8 39 ♖b1 ♖e8 40 cxd3 ♖xe7

Now it's only a matter of technique.

41 ♖b8+ ♔h7 42 ♖c1 ♖c7 43 ♔b1 ♖xc1+ 44 ♘xc1 ♕d2 45 ♖b2 ♕d1 46 ♖a2 ♕g1 47 ♖xa6 ♕xh2 White resigned.

79

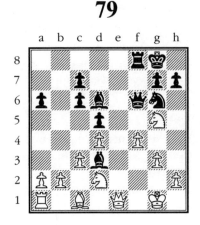

Euwe – Keres
World Championship,
The Hague/Moscow1948
Black to move

Black has a big advantage in development and according to Morphy's principles one should endeavour to open up the game to profit from having more active pieces than the opponent. Black certainly has more pieces on the kingside and it's tempting and logical to check if a sacrifice on f4 works. Here two different pieces can be sacrificed but how do we know which one to choose? Of course calculation of the necessary variations is needed but as a general rule it's probably better to have a knight on f4 rather than a bishop. Both Capablanca and Kasparov liked very much to have a knight on f5 and this kind of reasoning is also valid with a knight on f4, when a king on g1 is an excellent target due to possible checks on e2 or h3. A sacrifice on g2 might be possible as well. Keres played the strongest move...

19...♗xf4!

19...♘xf4? 20 gxf4 ♗xf4 (*20...♕xf4?? 21 ♕e6+ ♔h8 22 ♘df3* and White forces an exchange of queens and wins with his extra piece.) 21 ♕e6+ ♕xe6 22 ♘xe6 ♗e3+ 23 ♔g2! ♖f2+ 24 ♔g3 ♖f6 and Black has enough compensation for the piece but no more than that. Because of this variation it's understandable that Black needs to control the e6-square and not allow an exchange of queens. The advantage of having a knight on f4 instead of a bishop is that the key square e6 is defended.

20 gxf4?

A tougher defence was 20 ♘h3 even though Black has excellent winning chances after 20...♗d6 in view of his far more active pieces.

20 ♕e6+? loses more quickly than the text move, i.e. 20...♕xe6 21 ♘xe6 ♗e3+ 22 ♔h1 ♖f1+! and now White cannot play 23 ♘xf1 because of 23...♗e4 mate, so the knight on d2 is lost after a further rook check on f2.

20...♘xf4 21 ♘df3

Keres gives 21 ♘gf3 ♕g6+, 21 ♕h4 ♘e2+ followed by ...♗e4, and 21 h4 h6 with the correct evaluation that Black wins in all variations.

21...♘e2+ 22 ♔g2 h6

Black wins back the piece with an ongoing attack.

23 ♕d2 ♕f5 24 ♕e3 hxg5 25 ♗d2 ♗e4 White resigned.

This position is a classical example of how to break up White's pawn cover which in this case reminds us of the Leningrad variation with reversed colours.

80

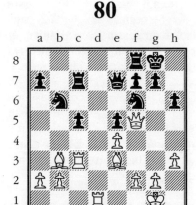

Bykhovsky – Oltean
Berlin 1990
White to move

White has five active pieces and four of them can quickly manoeuvre to the kingside so what are the moves to be played?

24 ♗xh6! gxh6

The intermediate move 24...c4 is relatively best but who wants to play on a pawn down without any chances of counterplay? White has several winning continuations: 25 ♕g5 ♘e8 26 ♗c2, 25 ♗g5 or 25 ♖g3 followed by 26 ♗c2 win too. But not 25 ♗c2?? gxh6 and White cannot organise any attack.

25 ♖d6!!

This is the key move for the initial sacrifice to work. If you saw this move you have good combinational vision because of the pin along the sixth rank.

25...♘bd7

25...♕xd6 26 ♕g6+ ♔h8 27 ♕xh6+ shows the point of the beautiful 25th move. The king's

knight is pinned but is forced to go to h7 to avoid mate on g3 with the c3-rook.

25 g6+ ♔h8 27 ♕xh6+ ♘h7 28 ♖g3 Black resigned.

Black loses after 28...f5 (or *28...♖g8 29 ♖xg8+ ♔xg8 30 ♖g6+ ♔h8 31 ♕g7 mate.*) 29 ♖e6 ♕f7 30 ♖eg6! (*30 ♖e8? c4*) 30...c4 31 ♖g7 etc.

81

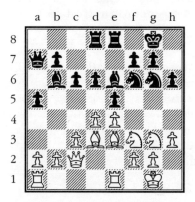

Anand – Ding Liren
Altibox Norway Chess,
Armageddon 2019
White to move

18 ♕d2

With two knights on the kingside it's logical to play for a sacrifice on h6.

18...d5

This is also logical since flank attacks are often effectively met by a counter blow in the centre as Steinitz advocated. 18...♔h7 was a more careful option but obviously it's not to everybody's taste to stand in the firing line of the bishop on d3. This is relevant because although the e4-pawn cannot move, the d3-h7 diagonal may be opened if Black plays for a break in the centre with ...d6-d5.

19 ♗xh6! dxe4

Liquidation of the centre by 19...exd4 20 cxd4 ♗xd4 and after 21 ♗g5 continuing 21...dxe4 22 ♘xe4 ♗d5 23 ♘xf6+ gxf6 24 ♘xd4 ♕xd4 leads to a tangible advantage to White because of his bishop pair, better king's position and superior pawn structure.

20 ♘xe4 ♘xe4 21 ♖xe4

Anand goes all in for this Armageddon game and even manoeuvres his king's rook to Black's kingside. However, better was 21 ♗xe4! exd4 22 cxd4 ♗xd4 23 ♗g5 and White has the advantage.

21...♗d5 22 ♖g4?!

22 ♗g5 ♗xe4 23 ♗xe4 ♖d6 24 ♗xg6 ♖xg6 25 dxe5 was correct with a slight advantage.

22...e4 23 ♘h4 exd3 24 ♘f5??

24 ♘xg6 would have led to a forced draw after 24...fxg6 25 ♖xg6 ♖d7 26 ♗xg7! ♖xg7 27 ♖xg7+ ♔xg7 28 ♕g5+ ♔f8 29 ♕h6+ ♔e7 30 ♖e1+ ♔d7 31 ♕h7+ ♔d8 32 ♕h4+ and Black cannot escape the perpetual check without losing the rook and the game.

24...♗e6??

To a certain extent, one can understand why Ding Liren missed the winning continuation 24...♖e2

25 ♕xd3 ♕a6 26 ♕g3 gxh6 27 ♖xg6+ fxg6 28 ♕xg6+ ♔f8 when Black's king survives despite the lack of pawn cover and two aggressively placed white pieces.

25 ♗xg7 ♗xf5 26 ♕h6 ♖e6

(1) 26...♗xg4 27 ♗f6 and Black is mated on g7 next move.

(2) 26...f6 27 ♖xg6 ♔f7 28 ♖xf6+ ♔e7 29 ♖xf5 and White wins.

27 ♗h8! Black resigned.

The queen's bishop was really the hero in this game. However, what is strange is that the hero survived. Mate will follow on g7.

82

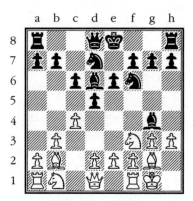

Cekro – Khenkin
Brussels 1998
Black to play

We have mostly seen attacks with queen and knight(s) since they are easier to generate at the beginning of the game, so here is an example of an attack with queen and bishops. White has played the seemingly innocent 8 h3 but Black can exploit it by a tactical sequence.

8...♗xf3 9 ♗xf3 dxc4 10 bxc4?!

It was better to continue his development with 10 ♘a3! and exploit the lost time when Black captured the c4-pawn.

10...♗xg3!

This trap can be easy to fall into in view of all the "natural" moves that preceded it. It's important to understand that the black queen is pretty active on its original square as we have already mentioned in the comments to position 16.

11 fxg3

11 ♗xf6? ♕xf6 and the a1-rook is under attack.

11...♕b6+ 12 ♖f2 ♕xb2 White resigned.

83

Hamppe – Meitner
Vienna 1872
Black to move

After the initial moves 1 e4 e5 2 ♘c3 ♗c5 3 ♘a4 Black played the strongest and most principled continuation **3...♗xf2+!** since it works tactically. Otherwise the quiet 3...♗e7 has to be played.

4 ♔xf2 ♕h4+ 5 ♔e3 ♕f4+ 6 ♔d3 d5!

The best move which opens the centre as well as a venue for the bishop. 6...f5? is met by 7 c4!! ♕xe4+ 8 ♔c3 and it's not easy for Black to develop an attack.

7 ♔c3!

The variation 7 ♘c3? dxe4+ 8 ♘xe4 ♗f5 9 ♕f3 ♗xe4+ 10 ♕xe4 ♕xf1+ shows why it's important to play 6...d5!.

7...♕xe4?

So far both players had played the best moves after the bishop sacrifice but here Black makes a mistake. Correct was 7...d4+ 8 ♔b3 ♕f6! and White has no counterplay in the centre. According to the computer Black stands slightly better.

8 ♔b3?

White misses the opportunity to gain influence in the centre with 8 d4! and thereby also obtain a clear advantage.

8...♘a6?

And Black again misses the chance to play 8...d4!.

9 a3

9 d4! is correct.

9...♕xa4+?

A surprising queen sacrifice which however is incorrect. But pragmatically speaking it might be the best choice compared with the computer suggestion 9...d4.

10 ♔xa4 ♘c5+

Here White played the natural but fatal **11 ♔b4?**

The paradoxical **11 ♔b5!**, entering the fifth rank, actually leads to a forced win and is a refutation of the queen sacrifice. The position after move 10 shows the value of calculating variations correctly and not only to think in general terms that the king would be safer on the fourth rank. Chess is not that simple as everything depends on the concrete circumstances. 11...♘e7! (The best move which was originally found by Johannes Schmedes. Worse is *11...a5* due to *12 b4!* according to Josef Ettner.) 12 c4 d4 13 ♔xc5 a5 14 ♕a4+ ♔d8

15 ♕xa5!! An incredible defensive move which is the only way to secure an advantage for White. After 15...♖xa5+ 16 ♔b4 ♘c6+ 17 ♔b3 White has a dark-squared bishop for a pawn and with a safe king's position also a technical win.

11...a5+ 12 ♔xc5

The alternative was 12 ♔c3 d4+ 13 ♔c4 b6 14 ♕f3 (Vukovic's suggestion 14 ♔d5?? loses to 14...f6 followed by 15...♘e7+ and 16...♗e6 mate/16...♗a6 mate. 15.♔c6 allows mate in three after 15...♔d8!) 14...♗e6+

(1) 15 ♔b5 ♗d7+ 16 ♕c6 (*16 ♔c4 c6*) 16...♗xc6+ 17 ♔xc6 ♘e7+ 18 ♔xc7 (18 ♔b5 c6+ 19 ♔xb6 (*19 ♔c4 allows 19...♘f5 followed by 20...♘d6 mate.*) 19...♘a4+ 20 ♔c7 (*20 ♔b7 ♔d7*) 20...♖d8 21 ♔b7 ♔d7 and Black mates in two moves.) 18...0–0 19 ♔d6 ♖fd8+ 20 ♔xe5 ♖d5+ 21 ♔f4 ♖f5+ 22 ♔g4 ♖xf1 and White wins.

(2) 15 ♕d5 ♗xd5+! (Better than Heidenfeld's *15...♘e7 16 ♕xe6 fxe6 17 ♘f3 ♘c6 18 a4* securing the king's advanced position on c4, or *16...♘xe6* since after *17 ♔b3* followed by *18 ♔a2* White's king is safe.) 16 ♔xd5 f6 and by defending the centre pawn Black plans a cheeky mate with 17...♘e7+ 18 ♔c4 ♘f5 followed by 19...♘d6+ 20 ♔d5 ♔d7 and 21...c6. The computer combats this by 17 ♔c4 ♘h6 18 c3 ♘f7 19 cxd4 ♘d6+ (*19...exd4!?*) 20 ♔c3 ♘ce4+ 21 ♔c2 ♘f2 with equal play.

12...♘e7

Black plans 13...b6+ 14 ♔b5 ♗d7 mate. White has only one defence.

13 ♗b5+ ♔d8

14 ♗c6!!

White's defensive arsenal is imaginative as well as enormous!

14...b6+ 15 ♔b5 ♘xc6

Black continues to threaten mate, now by 16...♘d4+ and 17...♗d7. White has to capture the knight and in this way approach Black's hostile pieces.

16 ♔xc6 ♗b7+ 17 ♔b5

17 ♔xb7? ♔d7 18 ♕g4+ ♔d6 and Black mates with ...♖hb8. White can only offer a spite check with the queen on an optional square.

17...♗a6+ 18 ♔c6

If 18 ♔a4? Then 18....♗c4 followed by 19...b5 mate.

18...♗b7+ Draw.

This game is called "The Immortal Draw" and just like "The Immortal Game" between Anderssen – Kieseritzky, London 1841, there are several mistakes but nevertheless it is a game that will remain in your memory for ever.

84

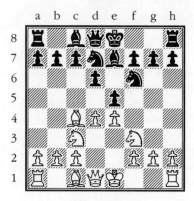

Zelic – Muse
Split 2002
White to move

This position arises in the Philidor Defence and is important to know for e4-players. The position usually arises with the following move order: 1 e4 d6 2 d4 ♘f6 3 ♘c3 e5 4 ♘f3 ♘bd7 5 ♗c4 ♗e7 and here it looks tempting to play **6 ♗xf7+?** which actually is a mistake. This has been known since the game Rabinovich – Ilyin-Genevsky, USSR 1922. Correct is 6 0–0 and now the bishop sacrifice on f7 really is a deadly threat since the g2-pawn is defended.

If 6.dxe5 dxe5 is included then 7 ♗xf7+ ♔xf7 8 ♘g5+ becomes sounder. For example:

(1) Pachman – Guimard, Interzonal, Göteborg 1955, continued 8...♔g8 9 ♘e6 ♕e8 10 ♘xc7 ♕g6 11 ♘xa8 ♕xg2 12 ♖f1 ♘c5 13 ♕e2 ♗h3 14 ♗e3 ♕xf1+ 15 ♕xf1 ♗xf1 16 ♔xf1 ♔f7 and now 17 ♘c7 was simpler to secure equal play. The game actually continued 17 ♗xc5?! ♗xc5 18 ♘c7

95

♖c8 19 ♘7d5 ♗d4 and ended in a draw after 61 moves.

(2) 8...♔g6! looks daring but works when the centre is stabilised. 9 f4 exf4 10 ♘e6 ♕g8 11 ♘d5! (Keres analysed *11 ♘xc7* but missed the strong reply *11...♘e5!*. The idea is that *12 ♘xa8?* is answered by *12...♗g4 13 ♕d4 ♘c6 14 ♕a4 ♗b4! 15 0–0 ♕c4* threatening the decisive *16...♗c5+*. Then after *16 ♗xf4 ♖xa8* Black's position is to be preferred thanks to his strong activity.) 11...♗d6 12 ♘exc7 ♗xc7 13 ♘e7+ ♔f7 14 ♘xg8 ♖xg8 and Black is slightly on top with three minor pieces for the queen.

6...♔xf7 7 ♘g5+ ♔g8!

7...♔g6? would make the piece sacrifice playable because of the king's jeopardised position. 8 f4! (*8 ♘e6? ♕g8!*) 8...exf4 9 h4 leads to a strong attack for White. Black first has to defend against 10 h5+! ♔xg5 11 ♗xf4+! ♔xf4 12 0–0+ ♔g5 13 ♖f5+ ♔h4 14 ♕f3 (a quiet move) followed by 15 ♕h3 mate. So 9...♘h5 is the only move but after the forced sequence 10.♘e6 ♕g8 11 ♕g4+ ♔f7 12 ♕xh5+ g6 (*12...♔xe6? 13 ♕f5 mate.*) 13 ♘g5+ ♔g7 14 ♕e2 White has a clear advantage.

8 ♘e6 ♕e8 9 ♘xc7 ♕g6 10 ♘xa8

10 0–0, as in Mirkovic – Sutorikhin, Kecskemet 1996, is perhaps worth a try because Black's play is too easy now.

10...♕xg2 11 ♖f1 exd4 12 ♕xd4

In the stem-game Rabinovich – Ilyin-Genevsky, USSR 1922, 12 ♕e2?? was played. The game continued 12...dxc3 13.♕c4+ d5 14.♕xc8+ ♔f7 with a winning attack for Black.

12...♘e5 13 f3 ♘h5

Black is clearly better. If you play this variation with the black pieces remember to place your king on g8 when there is tension in the centre and on g6 when the situation in the centre is stabilised.

85

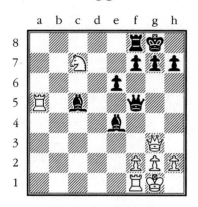

Vallejo Pons – Kasparov
Linares 2005
Black to move

27...♗xf2+!

Black exploits the fact the a5-rook is unprotected.

28 ♕xf2 ♕xa5 29 ♘xe6

And White exploits the fact that the f7-pawn is pinned because of the mate on f8. Has Black been fooled?

29...♗xg2!! White resigned.

No, Black has a beautiful boomerang combination which forces White to resign on the spot.

30 ♔xg2 is met by 30...♕d5+ and 30 ♕xg2 with 30...♕b6+ winning the knight on e6 in both variations while securing two extra pawns (and a far better king's position).

It's important to be aware of the opponent's combinational possibilities so you don't get hit by a boomerang. Such tactics are especially common when several pieces are hanging. In such situations one must always be more careful in the calculation of variations in order to avoid tactical mistakes.

86

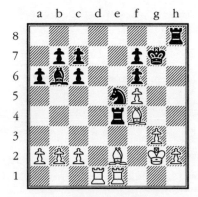

Kasparov – Short
Game 17, World Championship,
London 1993
Black to move

Here Short played the beautiful **24...♗f2!!** which wins a pawn by force. Short commented on the move in this way: "This is my thunderbolt. Kasparov had clearly overlooked it. I was delighted with this move. Later I heard that the Kasparov's Gambit computer which they are using in the press room saw this "cheapo" in a matter of seconds,

even though the man after whom it is named missed it completely."

Yes, it's psychologically more difficult to see sacrifices on empty squares, especially when on the defending side. If Kasparov can miss it anyone can, including Short.

25 ♔xf2 ♖xh2+ 26.♔f1 ♖exe2!

This is the main point of the combination. Combinations which exploit both of the last ranks, from Black's point of view, can easily be missed since there are several steps in such combinations.

27 ♖xe2 ♖h1+ 28 ♔f2 ♖xd1

Short: "I have a won a pawn but unfortunately I have no serious winning chances."

29 b3

29 ♗xe5? fxe5 30 ♖xe5 ♖a1! 31 ♖a5 ♖b1 32 b3 ♖b2 leads to practical winning chances for Black in the rook ending.

29...♖d7 30 ♖d2

30 ♗xe5 fxe5 31 ♖xe5 ♔f6 leads to a win of a pawn.

30...♖xd2+ 31 ♗xd2 c5 32 ♔e3 c6

Kasparov: "My position was so good that I could blunder away a full pawn and still be in no serious danger of losing. This says something about the nature of the position."

33 ♔e4 c4 34 b4 b5 35 ♗f4 ♘d7 36 ♔d4 ♔f8 37 ♗c7 ♔e7 38 g4 ♔f8 39 ♗d6+ ♔g7 40 ♗c7 ♔f8 41 a3 Draw.

87

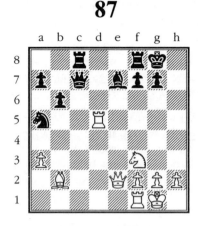

Kasparov – Portisch
Niksic 1983
White to move

Kasparov had already made a sacrifice of his light-squared bishop on h7 on move 19 and now the natural question is whether White can play a classical double bishop sacrifice. In the game, Kasparov did indeed play the spectacular **21 ♗xg7!?** but for him this has to be regarded as a positional exchange rather than a sacrifice. After all, the g7-pawn is the most important pawn in Black's pawn cover and it might very well be worth a minor piece. However the problem is that the move may still not be the most accurate.

21 ♘d2!, with the idea of playing 22.♕g4, could very well be stronger. White has attacking possibilities along the g- and h-files. Besides, the idea of a bishop sacrifice on g7 still remains an option.

21...♔xg7 22 ♘e5 ♖fd8

Black creates an escape square on f8 for the king behind the f7-pawn.

23 ♕g4+ ♔f8 24 ♕f5!

Portisch had only reckoned on 24 ♘d7+ ♖xd7 25 ♖xd7 ♕c4 but then Black is fine. The knight is stronger than the exchange as Kasparov demonstrates with his latest move.

24...f6

24...♗d6 is answered by the strong 25 ♕f6!. White threatens to exploit the potential of the knight as can be seen in the variation 26 ♘g6+ ♔e8 27 ♖e1 ♔d7 28 ♘e5+ ♔e8 29 ♘c4+. This is how the grindstone should be drawn. The knight plays the main part. 25...♗xe5 26 ♖xe5 and Black must sacrifice his queen to avoid mate.

25 ♘d7+ ♖xd7 26 ♖xd7 ♕c5?!

More persistent was 26...♕e5 but White has a strong attack nevertheless after 27 ♕h3.

27 ♕h7! ♖c7 28 ♕h8+!

Now the manoeuvring move 28 ♖d3 would win if it weren't for Portisch's clever trap...

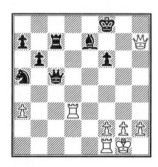

28...♕xf2+!! 29 ♔xf2 ♗c5+ 30 ♔g3 ♖xh7 31 ♖xf6+ ♔e7 and it is White who must fight for the draw.

28...♔f7 29 ♖d3 ♘c4 30 ♖fd1 ♘e5?

A slip which shortens the game but it would have been impossible to defend successfully in the long run anyway.

31 ♕h7+ ♔e6 32 ♕g8+ ♔f5

If 32...♘f7 then 33 ♖e1+.

33 g4+ ♔f4

Or 33...♘xg4 34 ♖f3+.

34 ♖d4+ ♔f3 35 ♕b3+ Black resigned.

88

Caruana – Kasparov
Fischer Random Championship,
Saint Louis 2019
Black to move

Kasparov played the seemingly strong **34...♗xb2??**

34...♖e3! would have maintained his winning position but also rook moves to f3 or d2 were good enough. After 34...♖d2 Black wins with his material advantage after 35 ♖c2 ♖d1+ 36 ♖c1 ♖xc1+ 37 ♔xc1 ♗xb2+.

35 ♖c5 ♕b4 36 ♖xa5+ ♔b6 37.♖a4!!

Kasparov had missed the ingenious rook manoeuvre c5-a5-a4 and he had to resign after **37...♕b3 38.♕xb2 Black resigned.**

A rook move like that to a4 can easily be missed in the calculation of variations. The rooks are normally poor defenders but here we saw an example where the rooks proved to be effective in defence.

89

Colle – O'Hanlon
Nice 1930
White to move

The number one question is obviously "Does the Greek gift, the bishop sacrifice on h7, work in this position?" Superficially it looks like the answer is "No" since White doesn't have a pawn on e5, which would prevent the main defensive move ...♘f6. Black has also already played the useful rook move to e8, thereby securing Black's king a flight-square on f8. In the game Colle did indeed play...

12 ♗xh7+!?

It's understandable that the attacking player Colle couldn't resist offering the Greek gift, especially when it secures at least a draw, which is pretty common if the combination doesn't lead to a win. The solid alternative 12 ♕xd4 might have ensured White a small advantage, thanks to his superior development and more active pieces, but was probably not to Colle's taste.

12...♔xh7 13 ♘g5+ ♔g6?

Necessary was 13...♔g8 14 ♕h5 ♕f6! and White has no win. The critical position arises after 15 ♕h7+ ♔f8 16 ♘e4 ♕e5 17 f4 (*17 cxd4 ♕xh2+ 18 ♔xh2 ♗xh2+ 19 ♔xh2* leads to a balanced position where Black has the better pawn position due to his fewer pawn islands.) 17...♕d5 18 c4 ♕c6 and here both 19 f5 and 19 ♕h8+ ♔e7 20 ♕xg7 are interesting variations to explore.

Of course it's impossible in practical play to go beyond these variations and so over-the-board most players would probably make the evaluation that the arising positions are very complicated. Everything depends on the playing style and how much risk one is willing to take, whether to sacrifice on h7 or not. According to Tal's rule you should sacrifice if you have invested a lot of time on your calculations, since you will then have a better understanding of the different variations than your opponent. Sometimes it's difficult to find the right moves, so the position is certainly complicated for both players.

14 h4!

The standard move 14 ♕g4 doesn't work here due to 14...♘f6 or 14...f5. White doesn't have the standard retreat to g3. Possibly Colle's opponent missed or underestimated the move played in the game.

14...♖h8?!

A standard defensive move in this combination to stop the h-pawn advancing to h5 but now White wins much more quickly. 14...f5 was probably a better practical chance although White wins after 15 h5+ ♔f6 16 ♕xd4+ ♗e5 17 ♕h4!.

15 ♖xe6+! ♘f6

If 15...fxe6 then 16 ♕d3+ ♔f6 17 ♕f3+ wins.

16 h5+ ♔h6

Or 16...♖xh5 17 ♕d3+ ♔h6 18 ♕h7 mate.

17 ♖xd6 ♕a5 18 ♘xf7+ ♔h7 19 ♘g5+ ♔g8 20 ♕b3+ Black resigned.

This is one of many examples where analysis of the Greek gift becomes very complicated and the objective is primarily to ascertain whether the sacrifice is correct or not. If you are interested in studying the Greek gift in depth I can recommend Jon Edwards's *Sacking the Citadel* which is the only book analysing this sacrifice in all its aspects.

90

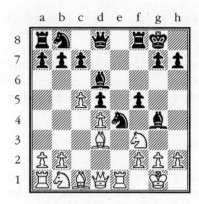

Garcia Gutierrez – Renteria
Barranquilia 2000
Black to move

Here, obviously the question is whether or not Black should sacrifice on h2. Black has three active minor pieces and a queen, not to forget a rook which can easily reinforce the attack, so it is most logical first to analyse if the piece sacrifice on h2 works. In the game followed...

10...♗xh2+!?

10...♗e7 was probably a tad sharper than the text move.

11 ♔xh2 ♘xf2 12 ♕e2 ♘xd3??

Necessary was 12...♘e4 and Black has enough compensation for the piece sacrifice. Black has two pawns for the sacrificed bishop and a very strong knight on e4. The most important kingside pawn is the one on g2 since it provides protection along the g-file, but the elimination of the f2- and h2-pawns means that the g3-square is permanently weak.

13 ♗g5!

It's easy to miss such intermediate moves during an exchanging sequence.

13...♕d7

Not 13...♕xg5? 14 ♕e6+ or 13...♗xf3? 14 ♕e6+.

14 ♕xd3

White is winning. In this position Black has no knight on e4 and that radically changes the evaluation compared with 12...♘e4.

91

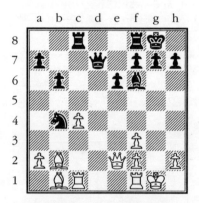

Aagaard – Barkhagen
Swedish Team Championship 2004
White to move

18 ♗xh7+?!

18 ♕e4? is even worse since Black in "Andersson-fashion" continues 18...♖fd8!. The check on h7 is completely harmless and only helps Black's king to go to e7 where it is relatively safe. A plausible continuation is 19 ♕xh7+ ♔f8 20 ♗xf6 gxf6 21 ♗g6 ♕e8! and Black can play for a win after 22 ♖fe1 ♖c5 with a clear advantage.

But not 22...fxg6?? 23 ♕h8+ ♔e7 24 ♕g7+ ♔d6 (*24...♕f7?? 25 ♖xe6+ ♔xe6 26 ♖e1+ wins.*) 25 ♕xa7 and White has enough compensation due to Black's exposed king..

Best was 18 ♗xf6 gxf6 followed by 19 ♕e3 or 19 ♔h1 and White has enough compensation for the pawn.

18...♔xh7 19 ♕e4+ ♔g8 20 ♗xf6 ♕d3!

The logical continuation is to minimise White's attacking prospects on the kingside by an exchange of queens. 20...gxf6 leads to a draw by perpetual check after 21 ♕g4+ ♔h8 22 ♔h1 ♕d3 23 ♕h4+ ♕h7 24 ♕xf6+ ♕g7 25 ♕h4+ ♕h7 26 ♕f6+.

Komodo suggests the interesting 20...e5!? as a more tactical way of preventing the decisive 21 ♕g4 g6 22 ♕h4 which was on White's agenda.

21 ♔h1

21 ♕g4 is answered by 21...♕g6 22 ♕xg6 fxg6 and if now 23 ♗e7 Black has the counter threat 23...♘d3.

(1) Tactical skirmishes like 24 ♖c3? is answered by 24...♖xf3 25 ♖d1 ♘xf2! and

(2) 24 ♖cd1? ♖xf3 25 ♔g2 ♖f7 or 25...♘e5 26 ♗d6 ♖f5 are both in Black's favour.

(3) Best is 24 ♗xf8 ♘xc1 25 ♖xc1 ♔xf8 when Black plays for two results in the rook ending due to his superior pawn structure.

21...♕xe4 22 fxe4

22...♘d3!

It's fascinating that the knight, which was placed so far away from the kingside, can now help the defence at just the right moment.

22...gxf6?? 23 ♖g1+ ♔h7 24 ♖c3 leads to mate and 22...♘xa2? is answered by 23 ♖cd1! followed by 24 ♖g1 and it's clear that the knight cannot help the defence so far away. But not 23 ♖g1? which leads to a draw in a well-known manner after 23...♘xc1 24 ♖xg7+ ♔h8 25 ♖xf7+! ♔g8 26 ♖g7+ ♔h8 27 ♖f7+!.

23 ♖c3 ♘f4

More precise is to play according to Andersson's formula and evacuate the f8-square for the king with 23...♖fe8!.

24 ♗g5 ♘g6

The play is approximately equal but due to the fact that the promising Swedish IM played such beautiful knight manoeuvres we cannot leave the game at this stage! Play continued...

25 ♖fc1 ♖c6 26 a4?

Correct was immediate activity byh 26 c5 b5 27 ♖b1 a6 28 a4! with ongoing equal play.

26...♖fc8 27 c5?

Necessary was 27 ♗e3, preparing either 28 c5 or 28 a5 depending on Black's reply.

27...bxc5 28 ♗e3 c4 29 a5

Or 29 ♗xa7 ♖a8 30 ♗e3 ♖xa4.

29...a6 30 ♖b1 ♘e5 31 ♖b7 ♘d3 32 f3?

32 ♖b6 or 32 ♔g2 were better tries. It's all about activity, especially in the defence.

32...♘c5! 33 ♖b4

The forced continuation 33 ♗xc5 ♖xc5 34 ♖b4 ♖xa5 35 ♖bxc4 ♖xc4 36 ♖xc4 ♖a2 shows why 32 f3? was a mistake. White has no drawing chances whatsoever with the king confined to the back rank.

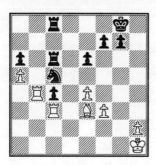

33...♘b3

Note the nice knight manoeuvre from d3-c5-b3 utilising both outposts provided by the c4-pawn.

34 ♗b6

It was better to sacrifice the a5-pawn and go for improved piece placement, especially with regard to the king, but also the pawns on h2,

f3 and e4 are more important than the a5-pawn and should be activated.

34...e5!

Excellent technique! Black creates further outposts for his knight.

35 ♔g2 ♘d4

This knight is certainly taboo!

36 ♔f2 ♘b5

Here we see a fourth outpost being used by Black to administer the advance of the c-pawn.

37 ♖c2 c3 38 ♔e3 ♖d6 39 ♔e2 ♘a3 40 ♖a2

40 ♖c1 ♖d2+

40...c2 41 ♗e3

41...♘b1!! White resigned.

It's not common that a knight utilises so many outposts as it did in this game and with such effect! The main purpose was to promote the advance of the passed pawn while after Black's final move White cannot avoid loss of material. Note what a hero the knight proved to be in this game. It was placed on b4 when we started to look at the game and look where it is now and above all what a journey it has made! It actually manoeuvred via d3-f4-g6-

e5-d3-c5-b3-d4-b5-a3-b1! Such a performance shows how super a knight can be when the circumstances are right. To conduct a knight like this is a dream we all have and for Barkhagen it has already come true and with it a well deserved win.

92

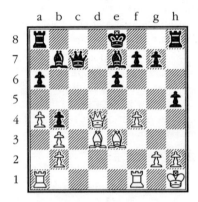

Ulybin – P. Cramling
Rilton Cup, Stockholm 2004/5
Black to move

19...♖d8!?

Despite the apparent vulnerability of the h5-pawn, 19...0–0 was a good way to defend the g7-pawn The move played in the game is cleverer since it involves an unusual trap.

20 ♕xg7?

Black falls into Cramling's original trap. 20 ♕c4 was better but Black is slightly better of after 20...♕xc4 21 ♗xc4 h4 22 ♔g1 ♖h5.

20...♗f6!! 21 ♕xf6 ♖g8

This is the point with the sneaky double sacrifice. Black has a double attack on g2 and d3. Black now won quickly.

22 ♖g1

22 ♖fc1 ♗xg2+ 23 ♔g1 ♕b7! and the game will soon be over.

22...♖xd3 23 ♗f2 ♖d2 24 ♕h4 ♗d5 25 ♗g3 ♕b7 26 h3

26 ♕h3 is met by 26...h4! when the white queen is overloaded.

26...♗xg2+ 27 ♔h2 ♗f1+ White resigned.

Interestingly this wasn't the first time Cramling had the opportunity to play the combination. 15 years before the present game she had the chance to carry out the same combination in a different position against Joel Benjamin. She missed the stunning idea but won the game nevertheless. However, she never forgot the unusual tactical idea and eventually this paid off in her game against Ulybin. This concept is especially important to keep in mind since even experienced grandmasters can miss Cramling's ingenious bishop sacrifice.

93

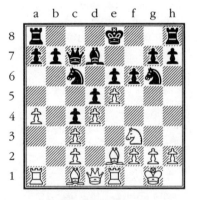

Fischer – Larsen
Candidates match, Denver 1971
White to move

13 ♗a3!

A modern example showing the effectiveness of the Morphy-diagonal when Black hasn't had time to castle kingside.

13...fxe5

Otherwise White plants his bishop on d6 but the text move has the drawback of giving White the d4-square. 13...0–0–0 14 ♗d6 ♕a5 15 ♕d2 followed by 16 ♖eb1 would have also led to a difficult position for Black.

14 dxe5 ♘cxe5 15 ♘xe5 ♘xe5 16 ♕d4! ♘g6 17 ♗h5!

Stronger than 17 ♕xg7 0–0–0 18 ♕d4 ♔b8.

17...♔f7?

17...0–0–0! would have offered better chances of a successful defence since 18 ♕xa7 forces the exchange of queens after 18...b6 19 ♕a8+ ♕b8 20 ♕xb8+ ♔xb8.

18 f4 ♖he8 19 f5!

According to Morphy's fundamental principles one ought to open up the game when ahead in development or in possession of more active pieces.

19...exf5 20 ♕xd5+ ♔f6

The alternatives were:

(1) 20...♗e6 21 ♖xe6 ♖xe6 22 ♕xf5+ ♖f6 23 ♕d5+ ♖e6 24 ♖f1+.

(2) 20...♖e6 21 ♕xf5+ ♖f6 22 ♕d5+ ♗e6 23 ♖xe6 ♖xe6 24 ♖f1+.

21 ♗f3?

Surprisingly, Fischer missed a win by 21 ♗d6 ♕d8 22 ♗f3 and gives Black the chance to centralise the knight.

21...♘e5!

Fischer managed to win the game all the same since Larsen failed to follow up his strong move in the best way.

An instructive example which shows how Morphy's principles can be adopted against the French defence. As long as there are possibilities of opening up the game and profiting from having more pieces in play it doesn't matter if the game is semi-open or even blocked. Remember Tal's 19 ♗xc5!? against Ghitescu, position 76.

94

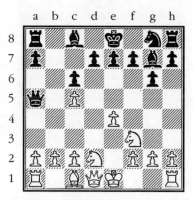

Anand – Carlsen
Sinquefield Cup, St Louis 2019
Black to move

Carlsen correctly played 7...♕xc5.

Also playable was 7...♘f6 8 0–0 ♕xc5. The tempting 7...♗a6 prevents White from castling kingside and looks like the logical move in the spirit of Morphy, but here it would have been answered by the hard-to-find move 8 ♖b1!! ♕xc5 9 c4 followed by b4 with comfortable play for White. Or 8...♕xa2 9 b4 planning the rook manoeuvre ♖b3-a3 trapping the queen; then if 9...♗c4 (*9...♕e6? 10 ♘g5*) 10 e5 followed by ♗b2 with the slightly better game.

8 0–0 d6 9 ♖e1 f6 10 a3 ♘h6 11 b4 ♕h5 12 c4 0–0 13 ♕a4 ♗d7 14 ♘f1

White stands slightly better thanks to his space advantage.

95

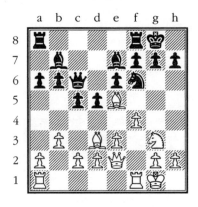

Lasker – Bauer
Amsterdam 1889
White to move

White has more pieces in the attack than Black and if we count the pieces that can be easily deployed in an attack against h7 or g7 there are four in total. If we also count the rook on f1 as a potential attacking force White has in fact five. Black's defence hangs primarily on the f6-knight which is protected by the e7-bishop so White's next move is easy to find.

14 ♘h5

It's a fairly common concept to exchange the queen's knight for the opponent's king's knight so as to weaken the opponent's kingside, although in this particular case White has undertaken a four-move manoeuvre (b1-c3-e2-g3-h5) with his queen's knight to create favourable tension between the rival knights.

14...♘xh5?

It was necessary to evacuate the f8-square for the king to give it more air and just abandon the h7-pawn in the process. A plausible variation is 14...♖fc8 15 ♘xf6+ ♗xf6 16 ♗xh7+ ♔f8!. White is obviously clearly better but in a practical game there are some counter-chances on the semi-open files on the kingside as well as on the long light-squared diagonal. The king will be pretty safe on e7. By the way, king safety is one of Ulf Andersson's specialities and in Sweden I have been taught that this clever evacuation idea was typical of him when he was one of the strongest defensive players in the world, especially in the 80s and 90s. A nice variation for White after 16...♔xh7? is 17 ♕h5+ (A serious mistake would be 17 ♗xf6?? gxf6 18 ♕h5+ ♔g7! followed by ...♔f8-e7.) 17...♔g8 18 ♗xf6 gxf6 19 ♕h6! preventing Black's king from escaping to e7 and with 20 ♖f3 to follow.

15 ♗xh7+!

This is how the grindstone should be employed! If instead 15 ♕xh5? f5! and Black is absolutely fine with no weaknesses on the kingside.

15...♗xh7 16 ♕xh5+ ♔g8

17 ♗xg7!

This position is actually the prototype for the double bishop sacrifice.

17...♔xg7

Black has to accept the second sacrifice as well, since 17...f6 allows mate in eight moves beginning with 18 ♖f3 ♕e8 19 ♕h8+ ♔f7 20 ♕h7. Here Black must prevent mate on the next move by evacuating the e8-square for the king, for example 20...♕b8 21 ♕h5+ ♔g8 22 ♖g3 etc.

17...f5 also leads to mate in eight moves if 18 ♗e5! is played. After 18...♖f6 19 ♖f3 ♔f8 20 ♖g3 it's mate in five. Note that 18 ♖f3 ♔xg7 19 ♖g3+ ♗g5! 20 ♖xg5+ ♔f6 unnecessarily prolongs the game, although White still wins after 21 ♕h4 ♔f7 22 ♕h7+ ♔e8 23 ♖g7 ♖b8 24 ♖c7 ♕d6 25 ♖xb7 with his two extra pawns and safer kingside.

18 ♕g4+

It's important to force the king to the edge of the board as soon as possible. If 18 ♖f3? Black has good winning chances by 18...♖h8 19 ♖g3+ ♗g5!. This bishop is certainly a mighty good defender as

we have seen a couple of times! Apart from the knight on f6 it's very common that a dark-squared bishop on e7 is the most important defender when Black has castled kingside. Here we see how Black makes use of it to create space for the black king after 20 ♕xg5+ ♔f8 or 20 ♖xg5+ ♔f6.

18...♔h7 19 ♖f3 e5

The only move to prevent mate.

20 ♖h3+ ♕h6

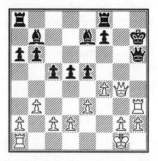

21 ♖xh6+

In a good position there are often several ways to win, as also is the case here. An additional possibility is 21 ♕f5+ ♔g7 22 ♖xh6 ♔xh6 23 ♖f1 but the pragmatic, most instructive and cleanest continuation is the one adopted by Lasker.

21...♔xh6 22 ♕d7

And Lasker won with his material advantage. The position is fundamental to understanding and controlling more complicated cases of the double bishop sacrifice, as well as other sacrifices associated with pawns on h7 and g7. For example Steinitz – Lasker, discussed in the next position. There were five main reasons the double bishop sacrifice worked here:

107

(1) One rook was immediately available,

(2) The hostile troops couldn't help the defence,

(3) The king couldn't escape via the f-file (the Andersson plan)

(4) It wasn't possible to ignore the second sacrifice without serious consequences,

(5) White had a material advantage at the end of the combination. Other famous double bishop sacrifices in history are Nimzowitsch – Tarrasch, Saint Petersburg 1914 and Alekhine – Drewitt, Portsmouth 1923. Do take a look at them if you have access to the games.

96

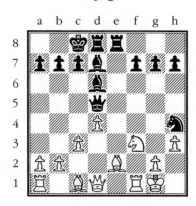

Steinitz – Lasker
London 1899
Black to move

After you have familiarised yourself with the classical game Lasker – Bauer it will be useful to look at another Lasker game where two pieces are sacrificed for the h- and g-pawns. This time it's a knight and a bishop which pave the way for

the other pieces.

15...♘xg2!

In the prototype game Lasker – Bauer it was the h-pawn which was captured first, here it's the g-pawn and that changes the circumstances slightly.

16 ♔xg2

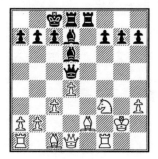

16...♗xh3+

John Nunn has mentioned in his book about Lasker (*John Nunn's Chess Course*) that 16...♖e6! is more precise. This move is also logical considering that the g-pawn is better to protect the king than the h-pawn so Black doesn't necessarily need to sacrifice the bishop for the h-pawn, at least not immediately. A plausible continuation is 17 ♗d3 ♖f6! 18 ♗d2 ♗xh3+! 19 ♔xh3 ♕e6+ 20 ♔g2 ♕g4+ 21 ♔f2 and now the quiet move 21...♖e8! which cuts off the king on the e-file. One can understand that Lasker sacrificed on h3 since he most probably had his own game against Bauer in mind. Besides, the continuation 17...♖f6 was not easy to find, since it's a quiet move. On top of that Black had to play an additional quiet move 21...♖e8 in this variation so we can understand that it wasn't easy to find this continuation. Such tactics are often harder to detect and analyse compared with forced and more explosive moves.

17 ♔f2

White cannot accept the other sacrifice with 17 ♔xh3 due to 17...♕f5+ 18 ♔g2 ♕g4+ 19 ♔h1 ♕h3+ 20 ♔g1 ♕g3+ 21 ♔h1 ♖e4 22 ♗g5 ♖g4 etc.

17...f6!

A nice quiet move which prepares the push of the g-pawn. The king is stripped off all of his protecting pawns and has no defence against Black's pawn roller on the kingside.

18 ♖g1?!

It was better to play the relatively forced variation 18 ♖h1 ♕f5 19 ♗d3 ♗g3+! 20 ♔g1 ♕g4 21 ♖xh3 ♗d6+! 22 ♔f2 ♕xh3 23 ♕g1 g5 24 ♕g2 ♕e6 25 ♗d2 ♔b8 although ultimately White has nothing against Black's play on the kingside.

18...g5 19 ♗xg5?!

It might be mentally satisfying to make a move which eliminates Black's strong pawns but it hardly improves White's position. Black won easily after:

19...fxg5 20 ♖xg5 ♕e6 21 ♕d3 ♗f4 22 ♖h1 ♗xg5 23 ♘xg5 ♕f6+ 24 ♗f3 ♗f5 25 ♘xh7 ♕g6 26 ♕b5 c6 27 ♕a5 ♖e7 28 ♖h5 ♗g4 29 ♖g5 ♕c2+ 30 ♔g3 ♗xf3 White resigned.

97-99: Exchange Sacrifices

The question whether positional exchange sacrifices should be counted as tactical or positional is tricky. It's a tactical move since a sacrifice is made but also positional since the reward is long-term. It's rather a matter of correct evaluation than precise calculation. The exchange sacrifice is clearly a case where the positional and the tactical are intertwined. Petrosian, a well-known specialist in the exchange sacrifice, was of the opinion that this kind of sacrifice was an exchange rather than a sacrifice. This reminds us of Kasparov who gladly "exchanged" a bishop for the g-pawn in front of the enemy king. Such personal opinions show very clearly the relative notion of the material relationship between the pieces. True genius is actually to be on another planet or in another dimension and have an individual scale of correct values in various positions. Eventually it's really about forgetting the numerical evaluations and rather embracing movement, activity and energy in a long-term perspective. It's like being a fish in water in a world which is infinite.

In the next position Petrosian sacrificed a rook for bishop. The main idea is to eliminate the key defender of the black squares in White's camp. It's a struggle for squares of a certain colour rather than material, which gives the exchange sacrifice a positional dimension. This kind of move shows

that tactics and positional play are different sides of the same coin. Ulf Andersson, also a famous exchange sacrifice specialist, has made many similar sacrifices. He's sacrificed a rook for a bishop on e3 even against such giants as Karpov and Kasparov and been successful. As long as the white rooks don't get serious play along the open files there are good chances for success with such an exchange sacrifice.

97

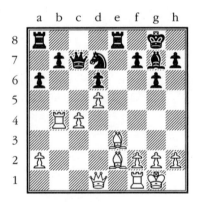

Polugaevsky – Petrosian
USSR Championship 1983
Black to move

19...♖xe3! 20 fxe3 ♞c5

Here the knight ensures that any of White's major pieces on the b-file will be virtually useless. It's the same situation when a white rook on the b-file bites on a b6-pawn defended by an a7-pawn. It bites on granite and has a decreased value on that specific file.

110

21 ♕c2 ♖e8 22 ♖f3 ♗h6 23 ♕c3 ♕e7 24 ♖b6??

Under psychological pressure, Polugaevsky tries to prove that the rook has some value on the b-file after all by occupying the weak b6-square but on this particular occasion the knight controls this square too, albeit indirectly. 24.g3 followed by ♔g2 should have been played but obviously Black has more than enough compensation since it's impossible for White to create any activity.

24...♘a4 White resigned.

Slightly unexpectedly the c5-knight was the piece to decide the game but it's not the first time we have witnessed such an effective queenside knight as we have seen another in the hands of Stein, position 62.

98

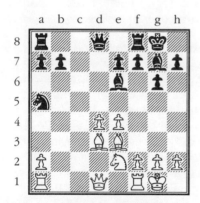

Sokolsky – Tolush
Omsk 1944
White to move

This is an instructive position where an exchange sacrifice is made to gain control of a diagonal.

13 d5

Some believe that Bronstein introduced the exchange sacrifice in the Grünfeld Defence but it was actually Sokolsky in this very game. It's a clever way to avoid the complications after 13.♖c1 ♗xa2 which arose in Ghitescu – Korchnoi, Zagreb 1970.

13...♗xa1

It's mandatory to accept the exchange sacrifice, otherwise White would have a very comfortable position after 14 ♖c1 together with a superior central concentration of pawns and pieces.

14 ♕xa1 f6

Black exploits the fact that the d5-pawn is momentarily pinned.

15 ♗h6 ♖e8?

It was better to give back the exchange with 15...♗f7 16 ♗xf8 ♔xf8 when White is only a little better due to his centralised position. The move in the game is too passive.

16 ♘f4 ♗d7

Black keeps the exchange but the price is too high. 16...♗f7 allows 17 ♗b5 as in Enevoldsen – Flores Alvarez, Olympiad, Dubrovnik 1950.

17 e5

White has a very strong attack in the centre as well as on the kingside. You only have to count how many pieces are concentrated on Black's kingside, so it's only a matter of time before his position collapses.

17...e6 18 dxe6 ♗xe6 19 ♗b5 ♗d7?

A better defence in a hopeless position was 19...♕c7 although after 20 ♗xe8 ♖xe8 21 ♘xe6 ♖xe6

22 exf6 the position of the king is too weak for any realistic chances of survival in the long run.

20 exf6 ♔f7

Black probably overlooked 20...♗xb5 21 f7+ ♔xf7 22 ♕g7 mate.

21 ♗xd7 ♕xd7 22 ♘h3

A nice backward move.

22...♔e6

Black is desperate to commit suicide. The normal continuation 22...♔g8 23 ♘g5 ♖f8 24 ♖d1 ♕f5 25 ♗xf8 ♖xf8 (*25...♕xg5 26 f7+ ♔xf8 27 ♖d7!* followed by mate on h8.) 26 f7+ ♖xf7 27 ♘xf7 ♔xf7 28 ♕h8 would have prolonged the suffering.

23 f7 Black resigned.

The long dark-squared diagonal became the key factor after Black was forced to accept the exchange sacrifice.

99

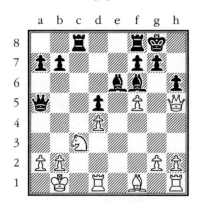

Pillsbury – Lasker
St Petersburg 1895/96
Black to move

17...♖xc3

The simple 17...♗d7! 18 ♕f3 ♗c6, followed by ...b5-b4, was actually more dangerous for White.

18 fxe6

18 bxc3? ♖c8 19 fxe6 ♕xc3 20 exf7+ ♔f8 21 ♕e2 ♗xd4 and Black wins.

18...♖a3!! 19 exf7+?

Once you have seen this incredible rook manoeuvre from c3 to a3 it will be hard to forget. However, it's important to remember the tactical idea which is founded on the fact that the middle pawn in the king's castle wall is eliminated. When the b2-pawn disappears the b-file is weakened as well as the long dark-squared diagonal.

Here we can learn from Kasparov that Black is actually exchanging his rook for White's most important pawn cover.

Black has three pieces left to deliver checkmate or win by material superiority or at least have more than enough compensation after the correct 19 bxa3 ♕b6+ 20 ♗b5! (*20 ♔a1? ♗xd4+ 21 ♖xd4 ♕xd4+ 22 ♔b1 fxe6 wins.*) This clever intermediate move pulls the queen off the dark squares, especially d4, and after 20...♕xb5+ 21 ♔a1 fxe6 22 ♕h3 ♕e2 23 ♕c3 (*23 ♔b1 ♖c8*) 23...♕xg2 and Black has the slightly better of it because of his more comfortable position.

19...♖xf7 20 bxa3 ♕b6+ 21 ♗b5 ♕xb5+ 22 ♔a1

22...♖c7?

This is a mistake due to time pressure. The time control was at move 30. White gets the opportunity to use the h1-rook in the defence. Compare 22...♕c4!. It's important that Black exerts pressure on White's position before he has time to bring over his kingside rook to help in the defence. 23 ♕g4 ♖e7! Black is now threatening both ...♖e4 and ...♖e2 and White has no effective defence, since the h1-rook is too far away.

23 ♖d2!

White defends the second rank while at the same time giving the h1-rook a chance to help with the defence.

23...♖c4 24 ♖hd1?

Too passive, correct was 24.♖e1 with mutual chances. White is threatening 25 ♕e8+.

24...♖c3?

24...♕c6! 25 ♔b1 ♗g5 26 ♖e1 ♔h7 and Black wins back the exchange with a clear advantage thanks to the better position of his king and superior pawn structure.

25 ♕f5 ♕c4 26 ♔b2?

26 ♔b1 would have led to a clearly advantageous position for White.

26...♖xa3! 27 ♕e6+

It's too late for 27 ♔b1 because of 27...♗xd4!.

27...♔h7

27...♔h8! wins at once.

28 ♔xa3

28 ♕f5+ ♔g8! 29 ♕e6+ ♔h8! 30 ♕e8+ ♔h7 31 ♔b1 ♗xd4! and Black wins. Or 31 ♔xa3 ♕c3+ 32 ♔a4 a6! and the innocent a-pawn decides the game, e.g. 33 ♖b1 ♕xd2 and Black wins.

28...♕c3+ 29 ♔a4 b5+ 30 ♔xb5 ♕c4+ White resigned.

Because if 31 ♔a5 then 31...♗d8+ and mates next move. Whether Lasker would have captured with the bishop or the pawn is open to debate.

Despite a few bad moves in a complicated positions, what makes this game so extraordinary is that Black repeats the incredible rook manoeuvre from c3 to a3. What a feat for the rooks! Lasker was really a great master of playing with rooks along the rank as he demonstrated so many times, for example against Marshall and Tarrasch. But here he trod even deeper into enemy territory.

100-109: Rook Manoeuvres and Rook Sacrifices

100

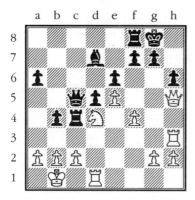

Kuzmin – Kondevsky
Krasnodar 1970
White to move

21 ♖dd3!!

After this particularly strong move **Black** thought for 90 minutes without finding any effective defence and **lost on time**. White's idea is to play 22 ♖g3 with the threat of 23 ♖xg7+ ♔xg7 24 ♕xh6+ ♔g8 when it's mate in four different ways! According to the computer the best defence is to sacrifice the queen on d4 but obviously no normal human would want to lose in this torturous way. Note that the white queen controls the d1-square so White can ignore any back rank issues if the rook captures on d4. This is another example showing how three pieces closing in on an enemy king can deliver a mate. The first piece is sacrificed and the other two work together to mate.

101

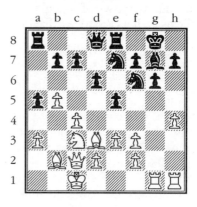

Krasenkow – Kholmov
Voskresensk 1992
White to move

In this position it's more difficult for Black to open the position in front of White's king. However for White it's quite easy.

15 h5!

Note that the h1-rook hasn't yet moved but is now activated by the h-pawn. A peculiarity of the corner rook is that it can be placed on its original square for so long and still exercise decisive power, especially when it controls the whole file down to h8.

15...♘xh5

Black cannot prevent the kingside opening up but at least he will force White to sacrifice. Krasenkow writes in his book *Learn from Michal Krasenkow* that 15...c6 gives

White the possibility of continuing his attack with 16 f4 followed by 17 f5 and that 16...exf4 17 exf4 doesn't change anything.

16 ♖xh5!

A logical sacrifice of the exchange with the purpose of opening the g-file as well as the b1-h7 diagonal.

16...gxh5 17 ♗xh7+ ♔f8

After 17...♔h8 18 ♖h1 ♗f6 19 ♖xh5 ♔g7 20 f4 White launches a decisive attack.

18 f4!

The next step is to open the long dark-squared diagonal for the b2-bishop.

18...♕d7

18...exf4? 19 ♘e4 leads to an immediate collapse on the long diagonal.

19 ♘e4

The queen's knight manoeuvres to the kingside, via the centre, while opening the diagonal for the dark-squared bishop. White now has several decisive ideas, such as an exchange sacrifice on g7, an exchange on e5 followed by f4, and

a queen manoeuvre to d1. Black is defenceless.

19...♕e6

The alternatives were:

(1) 19...♘g6 20 ♘g5!.

(2) 19...h4 20 ♕d1! ♕e6 21 ♘g5 ♕xc4+ 22 ♗c2 threatening 23 ♘h7+ or 23 ♕h5.

(3) 19...♖ad8 20 ♕d1! ♕h3 21 ♘g5 ♕h4 22 ♗e4 ♔g8 23 ♕f1 and White's queen is in danger.

20 ♘g5 ♕h6 21 ♗e4

This move introduces new tactical opportunities such as ♘h7+ or ♗xb7.

21...♖eb8 22 ♗d5!?

"A good deal" according to Krasenkow, since the e7-knight is an important defensive piece. 22 ♘h7+ was also strong as can be seen after 22...♔e8 23 fxe5 ♗xe5 (23...dxe5 24 f4) 24 f4.

22...♘xd5 23 cxd5

White is threatening to penetrate with his queen to f5.

23...♖e8

(1) 23...♗f6 24 ♘h7+ ♔e8 25 ♕f5 is absolutely decisive.

(2) 23...♔e8 is met by 24 ♘xf7! ♔xf7 25 fxe5 ♗xe5 26 ♗xe5 dxe5 27 ♕f5+ ♔e7 28 ♕xe5+ ♔f7 29 ♖g5!.

24 fxe5 dxe5 25 ♕f5 ♗f6

25...♖e7 26 ♗xe5! ♗xe5 27 ♘h7+ and White wins the queen or mates.

26 ♘h7+ ♔e7 27 a4!

The Morphy-diagonal a3-f8 can be useful when the king is placed on e7.

27...♖ad8

27...♖ed8 is answered by the beautiful...

28 ♖g8!! (28 ♗a3+ ♖d6 29 b6 also wins but Krasenkow's variation is more aesthetic.) 28...♖xg8 29 ♗a3+ ♔d8 30 ♘xf6 and Black will soon be mated.

28 ♗xe5 Black resigned.

28 ♗a3+ ♖d6 29 b6 would have been more beautiful and more convincing according to Krasenkow.

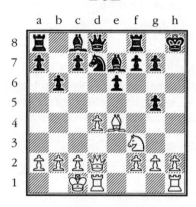

102

Judit Polgar – Berkes
Budapest 2003
White to move

14 g4!!

If White should be able to open the h-file then the g-pawn must first be blocked.

An immediate 14 ♗xa8?? is met by 14...g4 and Black has good winning chances. The knight cannot move because of ...♗g5 pinning and winning the queen.

14 h4?? is obviously met by 14...g4.

14...♖b8 15.h4 g6

15...gxh4? is met by 16 g5 and Black must prepare himself for different attacking moves such as 17 ♕f4, 17 ♖xh4+ or 17 ♘xh4.

16 hxg5+ ♔g7 17 ♕f4

Despite the fact that Black has an extra piece there is nothing he can do against White's onslaught. This is a good example of piece majority since White has more pieces in the relevant sector, the kingside, than

Black has to defend himself on that side of the board.

17...♗b7

17...♖h8, to prevent the deadly rook check on h7, doesn't help after 18 ♖xh8 ♕xh8 19 ♘e5! ♕f8 (*19...♘xe5 20 ♕xe5+ ♔g8 21 ♕xc7 ♗xg5+ 22 ♔b1 [22 f4? ♕h2! 23 ♖f1 ♗a6 24 ♕xb8+ ♔g7] and Black can only save his rook by 22...♗f4 23 ♕xf4 e5 but with two extra pawns White has an easy win.*) 20 ♖h1 ♔g8 21 ♘xf7! ♕xf7 22 ♖h8+ ♔g7 3 ♖h7+.

17...♗d6 prevents the rook check on h7 but the knight manoeuvre to e5 is decisive after the continuation 18.♘e5 ♗e7 (*18...♗xe5 19 dxe5 ♖h8 20 ♖h6!*) 19 ♘xf7!.

18 ♖h7+!!

This combination even works when the f7-pawn is defended!

18...♔xh7 19 ♕h2+ ♔g8 20 ♖h1 ♗xg5+ 21 ♘xg5 ♕xg5+ 22 f4 ♕xf4+

Black cannot defend both h7 and h8 and desperately sacrifices his queen.

23 ♕xf4 ♗xe4 24 ♕xe4 Black resigned.

103

Réti – Alekhine
Baden-Baden 1925
Black to move

Alekhine's tactical play from the diagram includes one of his most famous combinations.

26...♖e3!!

To quote Alekhine, this is a "spectacular move" which penetrates deep into the heart of White's position. White is weak on e3 and g3 and must parry the acute threat on g3.

27 ♘f3?

(1) Correct was 27 ♗f3. Alekhine had planned 27...♗xf3 28 exf3 cxb5 29 ♘xb5 ♕a5! 30 ♖xd5 ♖e1+ 31 ♖xe1 ♕xe1+ 32 ♔g2 ♖a1?? (*32...♘xd5 33 ♕xd5 ♖a1 leads to perpetual check after 34 ♕d8+ ♔h7 35 ♕h4+ and is the correct continuation.*) but it loses after 33 ♖d8+ ♔h7 34 ♕h4+ ♔g6 35 f4! since White can escape from the mating threat and keep his extra piece.

(2) 27 ♖d3 is met by 27...♖xe2!.

(3) 27 ♗g2? is refuted by 27...♖xg3! since 28 fxg3 fails to 28...♘e3 and White is defenceless against the threats on g3 and c4.

(4) Alekhine also analyses 27 ♔h2 which he had planned to answer with the logical but over-optimistic 27...♖aa3? (Better was *27...♖ae8* to keep the balance in the position. If White then plays *28 fxe3?!* Black's threat after *28...♘xe3* is not only to catch the queen but also to play the super move ...*♗c8!!* which evacuates the g4-square for the f6-knight.) with a strong attack on g3, but the simple 28 ♘d3! cuts the communication between Black's two rooks. Alekhine seems to have missed this possibility since he doesn't mention it in his annotations.

(5) It's obviously impossible to capture the rook since after 27 fxe3? ♕xg3+ 28 ♗g2 ♘xe3 the mate on g2 cannot be parried.

27...cxb5 28 ♕xb5 ♘c3

Note that the rook on e3 is the key to Black's strengthening of the attack. This piece is controlling the third rank and exploits it maximally. Just like Marshall exploited the rook on h3 with the wonderful move 23...♕g3!!, position 111.

29 ♕xb7

It doesn't help to defend the e2-pawn with 29 ♕c4 due to 29...♖a4 and White loses material.

29...♕xb7 30 ♘xb7 ♘xe2+ 31 ♔h2

After 31 ♔f1 Alekhine gives the forced winning line 31...♘xg3+ 32 fxg3 ♗xf3 33 ♗xf3 ♖xf3+ 34 ♔g2 ♖aa3 35 ♖d8+ ♔h7 36 ♖h1+ ♔g6 37 ♖h3 ♖fb3!.

31...♘e4!

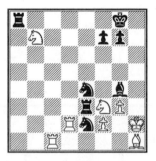

It's fascinating how long the rook can remain on e3 without the f2-pawn even touching it! The f2-pawn is only breathing on this brave piece.

32 ♖c4!

Réti finds the best defensive move.

32...♘xf2

The e3-rook has at last been stabilised.

33 ♗g2 ♗e6!

Black evacuates g4 with gain of tempo.

34 ♖cc2 ♘g4+ 35 ♔h3 ♘e5+ 36 ♔h2 ♖xf3! 37 ♖xe2 ♘g4+

38 ♔h3 ♘e3+ 39 ♔h2 ♘xc2 40 ♗xf3 ♘d4 and **White resigned** because of the inevitable scenario 41 ♖f2 ♘xf3+ 42 ♖xf3 ♗d5 and Black wins a piece.

The important idea to remember is that the main tactical goal is to penetrate into the heart of the opponent's position and by placing "a Trojan horse" there to prepare the way for a decisive attack for the rest of the army. Remember Tal – Polugaevsky, position 77, which employed the same idea as well, albeit with a knight.

104

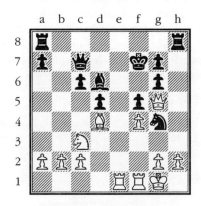

Alekhine – Rosanoff
Moscow, 1907
White to move

Here is a simpler example with the same idea as in the game against Réti.

23 ♖e6!!

White penetrates the heart of the enemy position.

23...♔xe6?

23...♖h6! was the best defence but after 24 ♖fe1 one must see the extraordinary continuation 24...♖b8! 25 h3 ♖b4! 26 hxg4 ♖xd4 which leads to a forced draw after either 27 gxf5 (or *27 ♖f6+ gxf6 28 ♕xh6 ♖xf4 29 ♕h7+ ♔f8 30 ♕h8+ ♔f7 31 ♕h7+* and White draws by perpetual. Quite amazing variations!) 27...♖xf4 28 fxg6+ ♔g8 29 ♕xf4 ♗c5+ 30 ♕e3 ♗xe3+ 31 ♖1xe3 ♕h2+ 32 ♔f2 ♕f4+ 33 ♖f3 ♕d4+ 34 ♔e2 ♕c4+ 35 ♔d2 ♕d4+ and Black draws by perpetual.

Inferior continuations are:

(1) 24...♗xf4? 25 ♖e7+ ♔g8 26 ♖xc7 ♗xg5 27 ♖xg7+ ♔f8 28 ♖b7! ♔g8 29 h3 ♗f6 30 ♗xf6 ♘xf6 31 ♖e6 and White wins at least a pawn while maintaining his two active rooks versus Black's disorganised rooks.

(2) 24...♘xh2 25 ♖f6+! gxf6 26 ♕xh6 and White wins. Obviously not 26 ♕xf6+?? ♔g8,

24 ♕xg6+ ♔d7 25 ♕xf5+ ♔d8 26 ♕xg4

White has the slightly better prospects and went on to win after 42 moves after too passive play from the opponent.

26...♗f8 27 ♖e1 ♕d7 28 ♕g5+ ♔c7 29 ♖e3 ♔b7 30 ♘a4 ♖e8 31 ♖b3+ ♔a8 32 ♕g3 ♖h6 33 ♕d3 ♖he6 34 ♗e5 c5 35 ♖b5 ♖c8 36 c4 a6 37 ♘b6+ ♖xb6 38 ♖xb6 ♔a7 39 ♕g6 ♕a4 40 ♖b3! ♕c6 41 ♕f7+ ♔a8 42 cxd5 Black resigned.

105

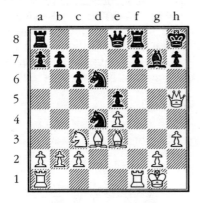

Fischer – Benkö
USA Championship,
New York 1963/64
White to move

18 ♗xd4!

A surprising exchange but the idea is to be able to mobilise the e4-pawn and open up the d3-h7 diagonal for the bishop.

18...exd4 19 ♖f6!!

An incredibly beautiful move. Fischer writes in *My 60 Memorable Games* that Benkö expected 19.e5 f5!. The rook move to f6 has some similarities with Pillsbury – Lasker, St Petersburg 1896, position 99, where Lasker played the famous move 17...♖xc3 and then continued 18...♖a3!! with the same rook, despite the fact that White had a pawn on b2. Another example is Marshall – Rubinstein, Lodz 1908, position 106, where Rubinstein played 37...♖xf3. Decisive rook sacrifices on the squares f6, c6, c3 or f3, leading to mate, are not that common. What makes Fischer's move so appealing is that the rook is played to an empty square. This was actually one of Fischer's specialities, to exploit empty squares. Comparison can be made with Lasker's move which captures a knight on c3 and Rubinstein's which captured a pawn on f3. However, Lasker's rook move to a3 was to an empty square. By associating with famous examples it's easier to memorise such rook moves and perhaps have the pleasure of playing one yourself when something similar turns up in your own games.

19...♔g8

19...dxc3 20 e5 or 19...♗xf6 20 e5 both lead to a forced mate in three moves.

20 e5 h6

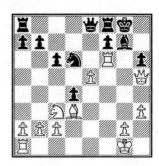

21 ♘e2! Black resigned.

This is Fischer's exclamation mark but Komodo11 actually

considers 21 ♘d1 to be the most precise move. According to Fischer Black was hoping for an ending after 21 ♖xd6 ♕xe5!. The ending is certainly winning after 22 ♕xe5 ♗xe5 23 ♘e4 ♗xd6 24 ♘xd6 but obviously Fischer preferred to win as quickly as possible to save energy for the other games in the Championship. Note that following in the footsteps of Pillsbury – Lasker with 21 ♖xh6 could be met by 21...f5. Benkö resigned after the 21st move since there is no defence to ♖xd6. The knight on d6 cannot move because then the white queen goes to f5 and the rook cannot be captured because of ♕xh6. By the way, it was this Championship Fischer won with 11 points of 11. He was certainly in a great shape then!

106

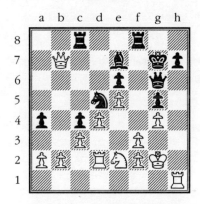

Marshall – Rubinstein
Lodz 1908
Black to move

37...♖xf3

This move has for a long time been regarded as one of Rubinstein's immortal combinations but Marshall

didn't defend in the best way. Simpler was to put pressure on the f-file with 37...♕f7 when White has no good way to defend the f3-pawn. 38.♘g1 (*38 ♖h3 h5!*) is met by 38...a3 when White's position collapses.

38 ♕xc8?

The rook sacrifice should have been accepted. After 38 ♔xf3 ♖f8+ 39 ♔g2 (*39 ♔g3? ♕e4 40 ♖f1 ♖f3+ 41 ♔h2 ♕xg4 42 ♘g3 ♔f7* followed by ...*♘f4* leads to a win.) 39...♕e4+ 40 ♔g1 ♕b1+ 41 ♔g2 ♖xf2+ 42 ♔xf2 ♕xh1 Black has only a slight advantage which indicates that Rubinstein's 37th move wasn't the best.

38...♕e4 39 ♔g1 ♘e3!

Black exploits this knight's mobility now that White's queen is no longer exerting pressure on the black bishop.

40 ♘g3

White defends against the threat of 40...♖g3+ followed by 41...♕g2 mate.

40...♖xg3+ 41 fxg3 ♕b1+ 42 ♔f2

42 ♔h2 leads to mate in all variations after 42...♘xg4+ 43 ♔g2 (*43 ♔h3 ♕xh1+ 44 ♔xg4 h5 mate.*) 43...♕e4+ 44 ♔f1 (*44 ♔g1 ♕e1+ 45 ♔g2 ♕xd2+ 46 ♔h3 ♘e3*) 44...♕xh1+ 45 ♔e2 ♕g2+ 46 ♔e1 ♕g1+ 47 ♔e2 ♕f2+ 48 ♔d1 ♕f1+ 49 ♔c2 ♘e3 mate.

42...♘xg4+ 43 ♔e2 ♕e4+ White resigned.

Marshall gave up because Black has a forced mate in six moves.

107

Naiditsch – Gustafsson
European Championship,
Dresden 2007
Black to move

23...♖e2!

The main idea is to cut off the queen so that after 23...♕h3 there is no longer the defence 24 ♕f1.

24 ♖xe2 ♕h3 25 ♘e3

White cleverly uses the defensive potential of the e2-rook but Black also has a clever move.

25...♖f4!! White resigned.

A very beautiful rook sacrifice which forces White's immediate resignation since there is no defence against the decisive 26...♖h4!!. A nice swing to the most vital sector on the kingside, and what rooks! Note that the swing from f4 to h4 is essentially the same kind of manoeuvre as c3 to a3 in Pillsbury-Lasker but here Black is exploiting White's fourth and not third rank.

White was hoping for 25...♘xe3? 26 fxe3 and the mate on g2 is now covered by the rook. 25...♖f6?

26 ♕e4! ♘xe3 27 fxe3 would also have led to a position where White is in no danger.

108

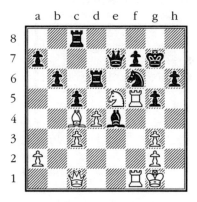

Kapetanovic – Kurcubic
Yugoslavia 1991
White to move

1 ♖xg5+!

White plays with the rook as if it is a knight only going forward into battle. The retreat 1 ♖5f2? would be a mistake because of 1...b5!.

1...hxg5 2 ♕xg5+ ♗g6

After 2...♔f8 3 ♗xf7 ♕xf7 4 ♘xf7 ♔xf7 the strongest move is 5 ♕e5! ♖e6 6 ♖xf6+ ♖xf6 7 ♕xe4 with excellent winning chances. However Kapetanovic had planned 5 g4!? which wins after 5...cxd4 (If *5...♖e6 6 d5!* and White wins material after *6...♖d6 7 ♕e5* with a double threat against d6 and e4.) 6 ♕f4 ♖e6 7 g5 dxc3 8 gxf6.

3 ♘xf7!

White is threatening mate starting with a queen check on h6 followed by mate in the corner. The natural

3 ♗xf7? doesn't work on account of 3...♘d5! and Black is fine. Incidentally, according to *Chess Informant* 3...♘g8?? wins for Black, however, the annotator missed the following mating combination:

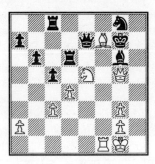

4 ♗xg6! ♕xg5 5 ♖f7+ and mate next move on h7.

3...♕xf7?

A better defence was offered by 3...♘g8 4 ♕xe7 ♘xe7 5 ♘xd6 ♖c6 6 dxc5 ♖xc5 7 ♖f4 and the game still isn't decided because of White's pawn islands.

4 ♗xf7 ♔xf7 5. g4! ♖f8?

5...cxd4 6 cxd4 ♗d3 was correct. Now Black's position goes downhill.

6 ♕h6!

Black cannot avoid further material loss.

6...♗d3 7 ♖f2 cxd4 8 cxd4 ♔e7 9 ♕e3+ ♗e4 10 g5 ♖e6 11 gxf6+ ♖fxf6 12 ♕g5! ♔f7 13 d5 ♖d6 14 ♕e5 ♖xf2 15 ♕xd6

15 ♔xf2 is met by 15...♖f6+.

15...♖xg2+ 16 ♔f1 ♖g6 17 ♕d7+ ♔f8 18 d6 ♗g2+ 19 ♔f2 ♗h3 20 ♕xh3 ♖xd6 21 ♕a3 ♔e7 22 ♕xa7+ ♔e6 23 ♕b7! Black resigned.

109

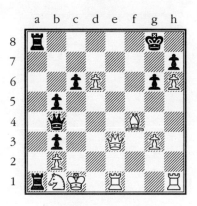

Vester – Krejcik
Vienna 1937
Black to move

1...♖xb1+! 2 ♔xb1 ♖a1+!

Both of Black's rook sacrifices have the purpose of luring the white king to the a-file so that Black's queen can gain a tempo by a check on the a-file.

3 ♔xa1 ♕a4+ 4 ♔b1 ♕a2+ 5 ♔c1 ♕a1+ 6 ♔d2 ♕xb2+ 7 ♔d3

If 7 ♔d1 then 7...♕c2 mate. Note the importance of the b3-pawn which provided the queen with two nice outposts on a2 and c2.

7...♕c2+

Observe how for every check Black utilises the power inherent in the pawns on b3, b5, c6 and g6!

8 ♔d4 ♕c4+ 9 ♔e5 ♕d5+ 10 ♔f6 ♕f7+

10...♕f5+?? 11 ♔e7 leads nowhere.

11 ♔e5

11 ♔g5 ♕f5+ 12 ♔h4 ♕h5 mate.

123

11...♛f5+ 12 ♚d4

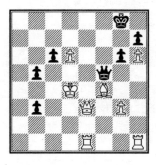

12...c5+!

The tempting 12...♛d5+?? loses after 13 ♚c3 ♛c4+ 14 ♚b2 (14 *♚d2?? ♛c2* mate.) 14...♛c2+ 15 ♚a3 ♛a2+ 16 ♚b4 ♛a4+ 17 ♚c5 ♛c4+ (*17...♛a7+ 18 ♚xc6*) 18 ♚b6.

It's not enough to control the light-coloured squares, at least one dark square must be under Black's control to secure a mate.

13 ♚c3 ♛c2 mate.

A very aesthetically pleasing position where all the pawns, except the one on h7, were necessary to create a mating net.

The moral of the story is that one must always look closely how the pawns are configured before embarking on a kingside attack, since their location is often crucial for an effective attack. Even "insignificant pawns" might turn out to be a decisive factor in a successful mating attack.

110-113: Queen Manoeuvres and Sacrifices

110

Spassky – Bronstein
Candidates tournament,
Amsterdam 1956
Black to move

This well-known position arises in the Saemisch variation of the King's Indian Defence after the moves 1 d4 ♘f6 2 c4 g6 3 ♘c3 ♗g7 4 e4 d6 5 f3 e5 6 d5 ♘h5 7 ♗e3 ♘a6 8 ♕d2 ♕h4+ 9 g3.

9...♘xg3!

Stronger than 9...♕e7 10 ♗g2 with comfortable play for White.

10 ♕f2

Not 10 ♗f2? ♘xf1.

10...♘xf1!

After 10...♘b4 11 ♕xg3 ♕xg3+ 12 hxg3 ♘c2+ 13 ♔f2 ♘xa1 14 ♗d3 the knight on a1 has trouble getting out of the corner, while White has an easy game compared to that after Bronstein's spectacular sacrifice.

11 ♕xh4 ♘xe3

This is the point of the queen sacrifice, since the triple threats against g2, c2 and c4 secure enough material for the queen.

12 ♔f2 ♘xc4

The bishop pair and two pawns may not seem to be enough compensation but in this position this material relationship works since Black has no target(s) against which the white queen can take aim.

13 b3 ♘b6

More active was 13...♘a3! with the idea of ...b7-b5.

14 ♘ge2 f5 15 ♖hg1 0–0 16 ♔g2 ♗d7 17 a4 ♗f6 18 ♕g3 ♘b4 19 a5 ♘c8 20 exf5 ♗xf5 21 ♖a4 ♘d3 22 ♖c4 ♘c5?

Correct was 22...♗d8 with dynamic equilibrium.

23 ♘e4

Spassky went on to exploit his advantage and won after 48 moves. Dynamic long-term sacrifices of this type are the most difficult to conduct since they demand that one is highly skilled at making correct evaulations.

111

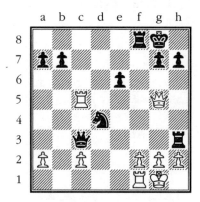

Lewitski – Marshall
Breslau 1912
Black to move

Marshall said about the following sacrifice: "The most elegant move I have ever played!" and it's impossible not to agree.

23...♛g3!! White resigned.

This move reminds us of a surfboard riding the wave along the third rank, from c3 to g3, while delivering a serious threat on h2.

White resigned on the spot since any capture of the queen has a devastating effect due to a decisive knight check on e2.

The defence 24 ♕e5 fails to 24...♘e2+ (or *24...♘f3+*) 25 ♔h1 (*25 ♕xe2 ♕xh2* mate.) 25...♖xh2 mate.

A quiet combinational move like this, where the queen is sacrificed for several pieces without giving check or capturing any piece, is

difficult to foresee. However, once you have seen it, you will find it easier to apply it in your own practice – if you are lucky enough to have the opportunity!

Note that the aesthetic effect becomes greater with the rook already placed on h3 (Compare Lasker's rook on a3 in his game against Pillsbury!) and it's actually the placement of this rook which laid the foundation for Marshall's immortal queen move. It represents perfect co-ordination between all of Black's four pieces.

Incidentally, Alekhine played a similar queen sacrifice on g6 in a blindfold simultaneous game against Supico in Lisbon 1941. This miniature went:

1 e4 e5 2 d4 exd4 3 c3 dxc3 4 ♘xc3 ♗b4 5 ♗c4 ♕e7 6 ♘e2 ♘f6 7 0-0 0-0 8 ♗g5 ♕e5? 9 ♗xf6 ♕xf6 10 ♘d5 ♕d6 11 e5 ♕c5 12 ♖c1 ♕a5? 13 a3 ♗xa3 14 bxa3 c6 15 ♘e7+ ♔h8 16 ♕d6 ♕d8 17 ♘d4 b6 18 ♖c3 c5 19 ♘df5 ♗a6

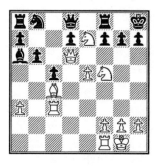

20 ♕g6!! And Black resigned since it's mate in three moves after 20...fxg6 (*20...♖g8 21 ♕xh7+!*) 21 ♘xg6+ hxg6 22 ♖h3+ etc.

126

112

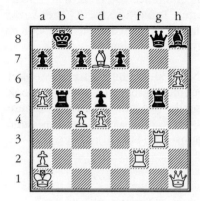

Varavin – Golicyn
USSR 1990
White to move

White wins by the spectacular
1 ♕xd5!! ♕xd5.

1...♖bxd5 is met by 2 ♖b2+ ♖b5
(*2...♔a8 3 ♗c6 mate.*) 3 ♖xb5+
♖xb5 4 ♖xg8+ and 1...♗xd4+ by
2 ♕xd4 ♖xg3 3 cxb5.

2 ♖f8+ ♔b7 3 ♗c8+ ♔a8!

A strong defensive move that can
easily be missed and which is the
main reason I wanted to show this
position, because it's this move in
combination with the initial queen
sacrifice which impressed me when I
saw this position the first time. Now
White wins after…

**4 ♗e6+! ♔b7 5 ♗xd5+ ♖bxd5
6 ♖b3+!**

A strong intermediate check that
decides the game.

6...♔a6 7 cxd5 ♗xd4+ 8 ♔b1
♖h5 9 ♖f4! ♗f6 10 ♖c4 ♖xh6
11 ♖c6+ ♔xa5 12 ♖xc7 a6 13 ♖c5+
♔a4 14 ♖c6 ♖h1+ 15 ♔c2 ♖h2+

16 ♔d3 ♖xa2 17 ♖bb6 a5 18 ♖c4+
♔a3 19 ♖b5 a4 20 ♖bb4 **Black
resigned.**

113

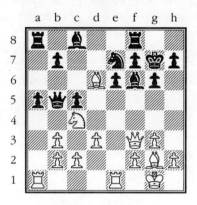

Petrosian – Pachman
Bled 1961
White to move

Petrosian played **18 ♖e4?** which is
a winning move but he criticizes
himself that he didn't think for a
longer time.

As a matter of fact Petrosian
missed the spectacular combination
18 ♕xf6+!! ♔xf6 19 ♗e5+ ♔g5
20 ♗g7!!. Petrosian overlooked this
beautiful 20th move which leads to a
forced mate in seven moves. The
fantasy variation goes like this:
20...♕c6 21 ♘e5! ♕xg2+ 22 ♔xg2
♘d5 23 h4+ ♔h5 24 g4+ ♔xh4
25 ♖h1+ ♔g5 26 ♔g3 f6 27 ♘f3
mate.

**18...♖d8 19 ♕xf6+! ♔xf6 20 ♗e5+
♔g5**

Or 20...♔f5 21 ♖f4+ ♔g5 22 ♗f6+
♔h6 23 ♖h4 mate.

21 ♗g7! Black resigned.

127

White makes a quiet move (no check) and such a move is sometimes difficult to find when calculating a combination many moves ahead. The nice bishop move controls both of the retreat squares, f6 and h6, and makes it easier to deliver a checkmate with the relevant pieces on the kingside: the rook, the pawns and the light-squared bishop. In the final position, the toughest defence according to the computer is 21...♖xd3 22 cxd3 ♘f5 23 h4+ ♘xh4 24 gxh4 and Black will be mated on h5 or f5 with White's g2-bishop.

Note that 21 ♖h4 was less effective due to 21...h5 when it will take ten moves to checkmate against the best defence. The initial move is obviously 22 ♗g7!.

114-116: King Manoeuvres

114

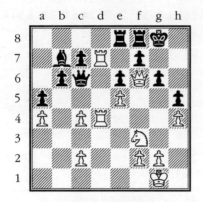

Short – Timman
Tilburg 1991
White to move

31 ♔h2!!

White has the ambitious plan to manoeuvre his king to h6 via h2-g3-f4-g5. It's not often one sees the king take such an active part in a kingside attack, but here it works since Black's pieces are powerless to do anything against it.

31...♖c8

In the actual game Timman plays two waiting moves but if he had chosen 31...♗c8 at once then White would have decided the game by a blitz attack with queen, rook and knight starting with 32 ♘g5!!

Then:

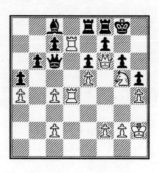

(1) 32...♕xd7 33 ♖xd7 ♗xd7 34.g4! hxg4 35 h5 gxh5 36 ♕h6 or 34...♗xa4 35 gxh5 gxh5 36 ♘e4! ♔h7 37 ♕g5 f6 38 ♘xf6+ ♖xf6 39 exf6 and White wins.

(2) 32...♗xd7 33 ♖f4! White hits at the weakest point, the f7-pawn. 33...♕c5 34 ♘xf7 ♖xf7 (34...♔h7 35 ♕g5) 35 ♕xf7+ ♔h8 36 ♕xg6 ♕xe5 37 g3 ♕g7 38 ♕xh5+ ♕h7 39 ♕xh7+ ♔xh7 40 ♖f7+ and White wins the rook ending.

32 ♔g3 ♖ce8 33 ♔f4 ♗c8 34 ♔g5
Black resigned.

This is the most famous example of a kingside attack with the participation of a king and must be regarded as the key position to know with this rare but effective attacking plan. So don't forget to use your king – but make sure your opponent can't attack it!

115

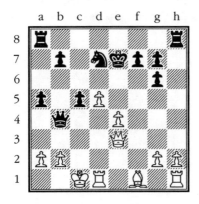

Nyback – Giri
Wijk aan Zee 2010
Black to move

Here White is threatening to expand in the centre with e4-e5, but Black has an original way to stop White's central pawn-push.

21...♔d6!!

It's not very common to centralise the king with all the major pieces still on the board. However here it works thanks to Black's firm control of the dark squares. The knight is certainly the king's best friend, since it can effectively parry any threat along the h2-b8 diagonal with ...♘e5.

22 a3 ♕a4 23 ♖d3?!

Presumably White wants to provoke Black into playing ...♘e5xd3 because that would give White attacking chances, but Giri obviously doesn't want to oblige.

White has only one break to play for in this position and that is h4-h5. Therefore correct was 23 h4! or developing the bishop with 23 ♗e2!.

23...b5 24 ♖c3 ♖hc8 25 ♗e2 ♘e5 26'♔d2?

White's king was safer on the queenside and there is certainly no time to carry out artificial castling to the other flank.

26...b4 27 ♖c2 bxa3 28 bxa3 ♖ab8

Black has already opened up the queenside and is ready to penetrate along the file. A strong continuation would be 28...♕d4+! 29 ♕xd4 cxd4 with a positional endgame win. Black's next move would be ...f7-f5.

29 ♖hc1 c4 30 ♖c3 ♖b2+ 31 ♖1c2?

31 ♔e1was more logical.

31...♕b5 32 ♖xb2 ♕xb2+ 33 ♖c2 ♕b1 34 ♕c3? ♖c5 35 g3 f5

The decisive break.

36 ♖b2 ♕xe4 37 ♔c1 ♘d3+ White resigned.

116

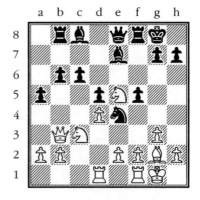

Hjelm – Engqvist
Swedish Team Championship,
Stockholm 2011
Black to move

14 ♘xc6!?

Oops! As a matter of a fact I overlooked this surprising move in my calculations. I thought I had played relatively decent moves up to now so it would be very surprising if a combination suddenly turned up. However, as we have seen in earlier examples, one must always be alert when two knights (as well as the queen) are out on green pastures.

A more positional continuation was 14 ♘xe4 fxe4 15 f3 with the slightly better game for White. Note that 15 ♗xe4? is wrong due to 15...a4 16 ♗xd5+ cxd5 17 ♕xd5+ ♔h8 and Black's light-squared bishop will be very dangerous.

14...♕xc6 15 ♘xd5 ♔f7!!

It's the second time in my life I have had the chance to play a super move with the king to f7. The first was in the Winawer Counter Gambit after the moves 1 d4 d5 2 c4 c6 3 ♘c3 e5 4 cxd5 cxd5 5 ♘f3 e4 6 ♘e5 f6 7 ♕a4+ ♘d7 8 ♘g4

8...♔f7!!.

Anyway, back to the main position. It's not very often you can allow discoveries to the right and the

left but here it works because of the position's inherent soundness – or was I just lucky?

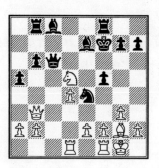

16 f3

The discoveries lead to nothing tangible for White:

(1) 16 ♘c3+ ♕e6 17 d5 ♕d6!

(2) 16 ♘b4+ ♕e6 17 d5 ♕d6 18 ♘c6 ♖b7

(3) 16 ♘xe7+ ♔xe7

(4) 16 ♘f4+ ♔e8

(5) The best continuation was probably 16 ♗xe4 fxe4 17 f3 e3 18 ♘xe7+ ♔xe7 19 ♕xe3+ ♕e6 with chances for both sides.

16...♘f6 17 ♘b4+??

Correct was 17 ♘xe7+ ♔xe7 18 e4 with some compensation for the sacrificed piece.

17...♕e6 18 d5 ♗c5+ 19 ♔h1 ♕e3 20 ♘d3 ♗d6

And having a dark-squared bishop for just two passive pawns makes the win for Black only a matter of time.

117-139: Pawn Play

117-128: The unexpected Pawn Break

117

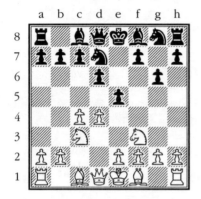

Hodgson (Analysis)
Secrets of Spectacular Chess 1995
White to move

Sometimes it's possible to play creatively very early in the game, as in the following position where the English grandmaster Julian Hodgson suggested...

5 c5!!

An incredibly creative move which I think most players wouldn't find, unless they possess exceptional creativity which was what Hodgson was famous for. I played him in Gausdal 1990 and was very impressed by his creative abilities after he had crushed me in 22 moves. In a grandmaster game there followed...

5...♘gf6

(1) 5...♗g7 6 cxd6 cxd6 7 e4 leads to some problems with the weak d6-pawn and this is the main idea of the early pawn break. 5...dxc5? 6 dxe5 ♗g7 7 ♗g5 is clearly favourable for White since 7...♘e7? cannot be played because of 8 ♘d5 and White wins.

(2) 5...exd4 6 ♕xd4 leaves White ahead in development.

6 cxd6 ♗xd6 7 e4

White should be a little better because of the positional weaknesses on the dark squares on the kingside, according to GM Jonathan Levitt in his *Secrets of Spectacular Chess*. However, the question is whether 7 g3 isn't better? It has the point of maintaining the e4 square for knight manoeuvres after the normal moves 7...0–0 8 ♗g2 ♖e8 9 0–0 c6 10 ♗g5, as well as keeping the h1-a8 diagonal open for the bishop.

118

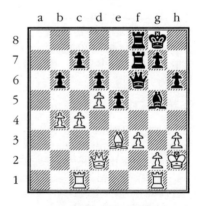

Schlechter – Pillsbury
Germany 1900
Black to move

In this position it can be hard to decide which move to play. Pillsbury chose what is probably the best from the pragmatic point of view.

33...e4!?

An interesting alternative was the simplifying 33...♕f4+ 34 ♗xf4 ♗xf4+ 35 ♕xf4 ♖xf4 followed by ...♖a8. After the game continuation a double rook ending also arises and bearing this in mind Pillsbury's choice feels right.

34 fxe4

More precise was 34 ♗xg5! hxg5 35 ♖ce1! exf3 36 gxf3 ♕xf3 37 ♖xg5 with equal play. This variation can be difficult for a human to find since it requires some precise moves. Besides, the h3-pawn is a worse protector of a king than its counterpart on g7, although in this position the g5-rook has no problems defending the king. It is for this reason that Pillsbury's move really was the best pragmatically.

34...♕e5+ 35 ♔h1 ♖f2!

This finesse, exploiting the fact that the e3-bishop is pinned by the g5-bishop, is an important point. Black gains a tempo to break through to White's second rank.

36 ♕c3 ♕xc3

36...♗xe3 37 ♕xe3 ♖8f4 leads to simplification after 38 c5 ♕xe4 39 ♕xe4 ♖xe4 40 cxb6 cxb6 41 ♖c6 ♖xb4 42 ♖xd6 ♖d2 43 ♖e1 ♖bb2 44 ♖g6 ♔h7 45 ♖ee6 with good drawing chances for White.

37 ♖xc3 ♗xe3 38 ♖xe3 ♖c2 39 e5?!

More precise was 39 c5 bxc5 40 bxc5 ♖xc5 since, compared to the game continuation, White has only two pawn islands instead of three. This makes his position easier to defend in practice.

39...dxe5 40 ♖xe5 ♖xc4

Pillsbury managed to win the double rook ending after 56 moves because Schlechter played some imprecise moves. What we can learn from Pillsbury's play is the way he placed his opponent under maximum pressure by forcing him to calculate complicated variations and play as uncomfortable positions as possible. By comparison, if Pillsbury had chosen the computer's suggestion 33...♕f4+ then Schlechter most probably would have secured the draw without any problems.

119

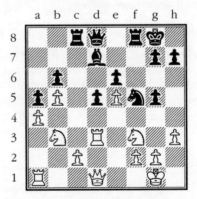

Anand – Mamedyarov
Tata Steel, Holland 2019
White to move

Mamedyarov had just played the incorrect 19...b6? instead of 19...♕c7 which would have prevented Anand's beautiful reply on the c-file.

20 c4!!

A surprising pawn thrust like this can easily be missed. Apart from exerting pressure on the d-file it also opens the classical a2-g8 diagonal.

20...♖xc4

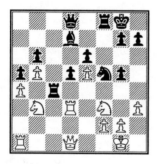

21 ♖xd5

This is the main point. Black cannot recapture due to the double threat against g8 and c4.

21...♖f7

Black finds the best defensive move but in the long run he cannot withstand the pressure on the d-file. The acceptance of the rook sacrifice by 21...exd5? 22 ♕xd5+ ♔h8 23 ♕xc4 is obviously winning for White who is a dangerous passed pawn up.

22 ♖d3 g4 23 ♘fd2 ♖b4 24 hxg4 ♘e7 25 ♘f3 ♘d5 26 ♘bd4 ♖f4 27 ♘c2 ♖be4 28 ♖xd5 exd5 29 ♕xd5+ Black resigned.

Since 30 ♖d1 will follow.

So always look out for combinations which exploit an exposed king on g8. This is

especially common when an f7-pawn has advanced or been captured.

120

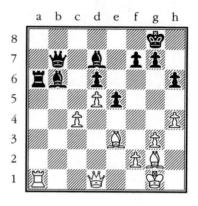

Carlsen – Grischuk
Stavanger 2015
White to move

26 c5!!

A nice tactical/positional pawn sacrifice by which White liberates his bishop on g2 and also creates a dangerous passed pawn on the sixth rank.

26...♗xc5

26...dxc5 27 d6 ♖xa1 (27...♕a7 28 ♖xa6 ♕xa6 29 ♕d5) 28 ♕xa1 ♕a7 29 ♕b2!!. A nice prophylactic move. It's more important to prevent Black playing 29...c4 than to take the pawn on e5. Indeed after 29 ♕xe5 c4 Black has enough counterplay to provide him with an equal game. 29...f6 30 ♕b3+ ♔f8 31 ♗e4 and White's clearly better placed pieces ensure him the better game despite his pawn deficit.

27 ♗xc5 dxc5 28 d6 ♕b6

28...♖xa1 29 ♕xa1 e4 30 ♕e5 and White wins back one of the pawns.

29 ℤxa6 ℤxa6

30 ♗d5!

30 ♕d5? would have been a mistake because after 30...♕a1+ 31 ♔h2 ♕d4 Black has control of all the pawns in the central zone. The text move is a beautiful centralisation, since f7 is a weak point in Black's position. The pawns on e5 and c5 are tactical weaknesses as well and White has good chances of winning back one of the pawns while retaining the initiative.

30...♕c8?!

Stronger is 30...♕b6 to prevent White from setting up a battery along the classical diagonal.

31 ♕b3 ♗e8 32 ♕c3

White will now win back either the e- or the c-pawn.

32...c4?!

32...♕f5 was a better try although White would stand slightly better after 33 ♕xc5 g5 34 hxg5 hxg5 35 ♗g2 but not 35 ♗c6? ♕c8.

33 ♗xc4 ♗d7 34 ♕b3 ♕e8?!

Economical defence with 34...♗e8 was preferable.

35 ♕f3 ♔f8

36 h5?

More precise was to follow Nimzowitsch's famous principle, as elaborated in *My System*, and impede Black's pawn majority with 36 ♗d5. Thereafter White can gradually strengthen his position on the kingside.

36...♔g8?

Black could have equalised with 36...e4. After 37 ♕a3 Black has the possibility of the positional pawn sacrifice 37...e3! 38 ♕xe3 (*38 fxe3 ♕e5* provides Black with enough compensation for the pawn.) 38...♕xe3 39 fxe3 ♗g4 and the bishop ending is a draw.

37 ♕e4 ♗c6 38 ♗d5 ♗d7 39 ♔g2 ♔h8 40 f4!? exf4??

Black either misses a tactical finesse or makes a fatal misjudgement of the arising endgame. He could have kept his position together by continuing 40...f6 41 fxe5 fxe5 42 g4 ♕c8 43 ♔g3 ♕c5 44 ♕f3 ♔h7!.

41 ♕xe8+ ♗xe8 42 ♗xf7! ♗c6+ 43 ♔f2 fxg3+ 44 ♔xg3 ♗d7 45 ♗g6 Black resigned.

Black is powerless against the forthcoming king manoeuvre to c7 followed by a decisive bishop manoeuvre to c8.

121

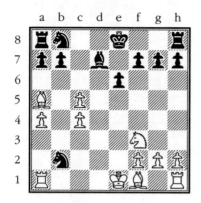

Marshall – Lasker
Paris 1900
White to move

15 c6!!

A strong pawn sacrifice which creates chaos in Black's position. Compare with the two variations where Black has no problems whatsoever:

15 ♗c3 ♘xa4 16 ♗xg7 ♖g8 17 ♗d4 ♘a6 and the c5-pawn falls.

15 ♘e5 ♘c6 and Black has no problems.

One can sense that Lasker has calculated everything precisely but has forgotten Marshall's ingenious pawn move.

15...♗xc6

15...♘xc6?? 16 ♗c3 and it's not possible to capture the pawn on a4 since the other knight is blocking the bishop on d7.

16 ♘e5

16 ♘d4 with the threat 17 ♖a2 is an alternative. After 16...♗e4 with the idea to manoeuvre the b2-knight to d3 White can play 17 ♘b5 with a certain initiative.

16...♗e4?

16...♘d7 shows the drawback of Marshall's move since the e5-knight must explain itself. 17 ♘xc6 bxc6 18 ♗c3 ♖b8 19 ♗xg7 (Teichmann gives *19 ♖a2 ♘xc4! 20 ♗xc4 ♖b1+*) 19...♖g8 20 ♗d4 leads to mutual chances and was the move Marshall intended to play.

17 ♗c3?

Marshall overlooks an instant win with 17 ♖a2 f6 18 f3 ♗f5 19 g4 fxe5 20 gxf5.

17...f6 18 f3 ♗c2?

18...♗f5 19 ♗xb2 fxe5 20 ♗xe5 ♔f7 with a slight advantage to White was to be preferred. Now White is winning instead.

19 ♔d2 ♘xa4 20 ♔xc2 ♘xc3 21 ♘d3 ♘d5 22 cxd5 exd5 23 ♘c5

Here White's position is too active and Black's three pawns are not enough material for the bishop. Lasker eventually had to resign after 58 moves.

122

a b c d e f g h

(board diagram)

Podgaets – Novak
Bratislava 1967
White to move

According to Steinitz's classical principles one should attack where the opponent is weakest but there are exceptions to the rule as this instructive position shows.

22 d5!!

Black has overprotected the d5-square so it is paradoxical that the attack should be aimed at Black's strong-point but the reason is it will create temporary chaos due to the fact that the black pieces will step in each others' way.

(1) 22 ♘xf6+? ♕xf6 23 ♕xh7+ ♔f8 leads nowhere, since the d-pawn is in Black's hands and his pieces are centralised.

(2) 22 ♗xg6? fxg6 23 ♘xf6+ ♕xf6 24 ♕xh7+ ♔f8 isn't correct because the black bishop controls the important f3-square. It's necessary to analyse this variation since a slight nuance in the position might mean that the combination is playable in another position.

(3) 22 ♕g5? ♘d5 23 ♘h6+ (*23 ♕h6 f5*) 23...♔g7 24.♘f5+ (*24 ♘xf7? ♕xf7 25 ♕h6+ ♔g8 26 ♗xg6 ♕g7! 27 ♗xh7+ ♔f7 28 ♕h5+ ♔e7 and Black wins.*) 24...exf5 25 ♕h6+ ♔f6 26 ♕h4+ ♔g7 27 ♕xh7+ ♔f6 28 ♕h4+ leads only to a perpetual check.

22...♗xd5

(1) 22...♖xd5 leaves the c8-rook undefended and this can be exploited by 23 ♗xg6! fxg6 24 ♘xf6+ ♕xf6 25 ♕xh7+ ♔f8 26 ♕h8+ ♕xh8 27 ♖xh8+.

(2) 22...exd5 23 ♕g5 (*23 ♗xg6 fxg6 24 ♘xf6+ ♕xf6 25 ♕xh7+ ♔f8 26 ♖f3 also wins since the d5-pawn stands in the way of the c6-bishop.*) 23...♖d6 There is no other defence due to the fact that Black cannot move the knight to d5. 24 ♖f3 ♔g7 25 ♕h6+ ♔g8 26 ♘xf6+ ♖xf6 27 ♖h3 and White wins.

(3) 22...♗e8 23 ♗xg6! fxg6 24 ♘xf6+ ♕xf6 25 ♕xh7+ ♔f8 26 dxe6! (More precise than *26 ♖f3*) 26...♕xe6 27 ♕h6+ ♔f7 28 ♖f3+ ♔e7 29 ♖e3.

23 ♕g5 Black resigned.

Since it's not possible to move the knight to d5. If 23...♔g7 the black king will be overloaded after 24 ♘xf6 ♕xf6 25 ♖xh7+.

123

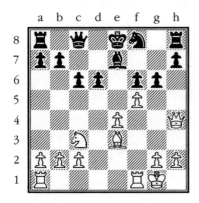

Schlechter – Blackburne
London 1899
White to move

17 e5!

A typical tactical central breakthrough to release the e4-square for the queen's knight. The most famous example of this idea is the game between Lasker and Capablanca played in Saint Petersburg 1914 which Lasker won with the exchange variation of the Ruy Lopez. You should check it out if you have access to the game.

17...fxe5?

Hoffer gives the slightly more resistant alternative 17...dxe5 18 ♘e4 gxf5 19 ♘xf6+ ♔f7 20 ♕h5+ and White wins. After 20...♔xf6 (Worse is *20...♘g6? 21 ♖xf5 ♗xf6 22 ♖af1 ♕d8 23 ♗g5* with a clear win.) the forced variation 21 ♕g5+ ♔f7 22 ♖xf5+ ♔e8 23 ♖xe5 ♕d7 24 ♕h5+ ♘g6 5 ♗c5 ♔d8 26 ♖d1 ♘xe5 27 ♗xe7+ ♔c8 28 ♖xd7 ♘xd7 29 ♕a5 decides.

18 f6 ♗d8

Black has now reached a so called Steinitz-position where all the pieces are placed on the back rank!

19 ♘e4 ♔d7

19...♕e6 20 ♕h6 hardly helps since White breaks through via g7 next move and decides the game.

20 ♖ad1 d5 21 c4 ♗b6

21...d4 is obviously met by 22 ♗xd4 exd4 23 ♖xd4+ since the best defence leads to a forced finish after 23...♔c7 24 ♕g3+ ♔b6 25 c5+ ♔a6 26 ♖a4+ ♗a5 27 ♖xa5+ ♔xa5 28 ♕a3+ ♔b5 29 ♘d6 mate.

22 ♗xb6 axb6 23 cxd5 c5

The reason Black continues the game is because Blackburne, just like Bogoljubow, was an optimist at the chessboard. Optimism is undoubtedly to be preferred rather than pessimism but the drawback comes when the optimist has to handle an inferior position.

24 ♕h6 ♔c7 25 d6+ ♔b8 26 d7 ♘xd7 27 ♕g7 ♖d8 28 ♕e7 ♔a7 29 ♖f3 Black resigned.

124

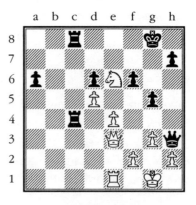

Duda – Xiong
FIDE World Cup 2019
White to move

Black has weakened his kingside with 34...g5 and the question is whether White can exploit it and, if so, then how.

35 e5!!

35 ♕a7 leads to nothing after 35...♕h6 since it's not possible to generate any more energy in White's position.

35...dxe5

35...fxe5? is met by the forcing 36 ♕xg5+ ♔f7 37 ♕g7+ ♔e8 38 ♕f8+ ♔d7 39 ♕f7 mate.

36 ♕a7 ♕h6 37 d6!

The strength of the passed pawn is the reason why the pawn break to e5 was so strong.

37...♖c1

If 37...g4 then 38 d7 wins material.

38 ♖xc1 ♖xc1+ 39 ♔g2 g4

Black's attack looks dangerous but White wins with an "only move".

40 h4!

A typical defensive idea with the h-pawn which is worth remembering.

40...gxh3+

Tarrasch used to call such a pawn an intruder but in reality it shields

the white king since the h-file is now closed.

41 ♔h2 ♕g6 42 ♕a8+!

Also this move is the only way to win. White has to take the control of the long diagonal.

After 42 d7?? ♖h1+ 43 ♔xh1 ♕e4+ White is mated in two moves.

42...♔f7 43 d7

And **Black resigned** because of the threat of mate on e8. White had to calculate exactly eight moves ahead and two of these moves where "only moves" which had to be played to avert the loss of the game.

125

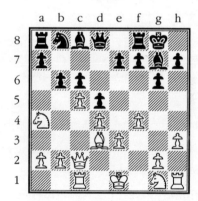

Wang Yue – Carlsen
Nanjing 2009
Black to move

13...e5!!

More effective than the preparatory 13...f6 which can be answered by 14 h4! e5 15 h5 when Black is practically forced to lock the situation in the centre by 15...e4 in order to release the pressure against g6. This is not something Black really wants to do since he has the bishop pair.

14 dxe5

Worse is 14 fxe5 which weakens the h6-c1 diagonal and can be exploited by 14...♗h6! when White has no comfortable way of defending the e3-pawn, since Black has the break ...f7-f6 next move.

14...f6 15 exf6 ♕xf6 16 ♘f3 ♕e7 17.♔f2

It's safer to defend the pawn with 17 ♕e2 to keep options open for castling kingside. Now the king is placed on the same file as the enemy rook, which is unpleasant as well as lacking in harmony. 17...♖e8 would force the king to f2 but then the king's rook is misplaced since Black, in the spirit of Morphy's style of play, prefers to have the queen's rook there.

17...b5 18 ♘c3 ♘a6

18...♕xc5 is inferior since it slows down his development.

19 ♕d2?

Better is 19 a3 ♘xc5 20 ♘e2 ♘xd3+ 21 ♕xd3.

19...♘xc5 20 ♗b1 ♔h8 21 b4 ♘b7 22 ♘e2 ♘d6 23 ♘ed4 ♘c4 24 ♕d3 ♗d7 25 h4 ♖ae8 26 ♖ce1 ♕xb4 27 h5 ♘d6 28 hxg6 ♘e4+ 29 ♔g1 h6

Black has a slight advantage. The game ended in a draw after 58 moves.

126

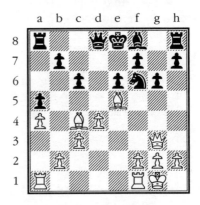

Carlsen – Utegaliyev
World Rapid Championship 2019
White to move

In clearly favourable positions it's sometimes easy to miss strong tactical turns, since relatively simple pragmatic moves progressively increase the advantage. This is probably the reason why the world champion missed the decisive tactical break in this rapid game.

18 d5!!

Carlsen played 18 f4 and eventually won the game but if Black had replied 18...♗e7! White would only have had the slightly better prospects.

18...♗g7

The relatively best but Black is clearly lost after…

19 dxe6 0–0 20 exf7+ etc.

Note that capturing the d5-pawn is taboo since 18...exd5 is met by 19 ♖fe1 or Morphy's favourite setup 19 ♖ae1. Black is unable to escape material losses since his king cannot run away from the e-file with 19...♔d7 due to 20 ♕h3+.

Then again, 18...cxd5 19 &b5+ &e7 loses after the beautiful break...

20 c4!! Pawns are certainly the soul of chess even if in this case they are mainly cannon fodder for opening files and diagonals. White's main threat is the long queen move to a3. For example, 20...♘e4 21 ♕a3+ ♘d6 22 &xh8 and White wins with an ongoing attack.

Of course the pragmatic move is 20 &c7 winning the queen, since 20...♕c8 fails to 21 ♕d6 mate.

127

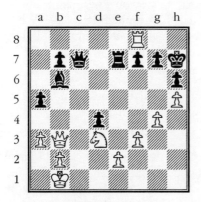

Petrosian – Peters
Lone Pine 1976
White to move

Petrosian has outplayed his opponent whose position is in ruins. Now it is a matter of deciding the game for which often concrete and tactical means are necessary. The key to winning the position lies in the pawn-push g4-g5, either immediately or after preparation. Petrosian chose the latter. The very best move is an immediate...

48 g5!!

...which takes advantage of the fact that Black has weakened his kingside with ...h7-h6. The threat is plain and simple: to advance another square with the g-pawn since the classical diagonal would then be opened and a mate would suddenly become possible on g8.

Playing 48 ♕d5 at once has the drawback of only threatening a queen check on f5, thereby comparing unfavourably with the text move which threatens mate in two moves. 48...g6 (After *48...♕d7 49 ♘f4 ♕xd5 50 ♘xd5 d3 51. exd3 ♖e1+ 52 ♔a2 &d4 53 ♖xf7* White wins but it would take longer and be less dramatic.) 49 hxg6+ ♔xg6 50 g5! This is the key move if White succeeds in breaking up the king's position. 50...♔g7 51 ♖a8 ♖e6 (*51...h5 avoids the opening of lines but loses quickly after 52 ♕f5 ♕d6 53 ♘f4*) 52 gxh6+ ♖xh6 53 f4 and White is winning thanks to his active pieces and Black's weak king's position.

Petrosian, who was known to play in slow motion, to use Botvinnik's words, instead came up with another winning plan. 48 f4 &c5? (*48...g6 was better but Black would still not be able to save the game after 49 g5!*) 49 ♕d5 ♖e5 50 ♖xf7 and Black resigned.

48...hxg5 49 ♕d5

The point of the pawn sacrifice is that when Black plays 48...hxg5 the pawn itself becomes a tactical weakness on g5. This is a very important tactical idea to keep in mind since it's applicable in many other positions. The fact that a pawn sacrifice can saddle the opponent with weaknesses is very significant. White's plan is twofold, either to check with his queen on f5 or capture on g5 with the queen and follow with the decisive break h5-h6. What White wants to do next is to force the g7-pawn to move so that the f6-square becomes weak and White's queen will then be able to exploit it.

49...♕d7

If Black plays 49...g6 to take advantage of the fact that the queen cannot occupy the f6-square at once, then White wins with 50 hxg6+ ♔g7

51 ♕xg5!! ♔xf8 (or *51...fxg6 52 ♕f6+ ♔h6 53 ♕h4+ ♔g7 54 ♕h8 mate.*) 52 g7+ ♔g8 53 ♕h6! How a queen and a pawn on the seventh rank can co-operate under ideal conditions is a good tactical idea to remember.

50 ♕xg5 ♕e6

If 50...♖xe2 then 51 h6 f6 52 hxg7 ♕xg7 53 ♕h5+ and White wins the queen.

51 ♘f4 ♕f6

52 ♘g6!!

It's incredibly aesthetic that the "frog" jumps from d3 to f4 to g6 and decides the game, exploiting the fact that the f7-pawn is pinned by the f8-rook. An instructive example showing that a knight, placed on the third rank, can attack the king pretty quickly. There is no defence to the mate on h8 other than by giving up too much material.

128

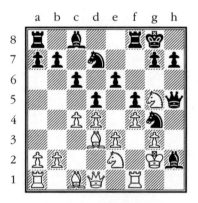

Glucksberg – Najdorf
Warsaw 1930
Black to move

This position arose after the following moves: 1 d4 f5 2 c4 ♘f6 3 ♘c3 e6 4 ♘f3 d5 5 e3 c6 6 ♗d3 ♗d6 7 0–0 0–0 8 ♘e2 ♘bd7 9 ♘g5 ♗xh2+ 10 ♔h1 ♘g4 11 f4 ♕e8 12 g3 ♕h5 13 ♔g2.

13...♗g1!! 14 ♘xg1

White must accept the sacrifice, otherwise White will lose the e3-pawn or be mated in two moves.

14...♕h2+ 15 ♔f3

Najdorf writes: "My calculations had gone this far. When attacking, the material deficit does not matter, the important thing is the position of the king, which here is exposed. I had learned that in such cases one must open up the position, and without hesitation I played…"

15...e5!!

A very beautiful move taking control of the e5-square by one of Black's knights. Note that Black is threatening 16...e4+ followed by 17...♘de5+!!. Another important tactical idea to know.

On the other hand 15...♕h1+? 16 ♔e2 ♕g2+ 17 ♔e1 would only help White's king to find a safe haven.

16 dxe5 ♘dxe5+

It doesn't matter which knight recaptures on e5 but on principle it's better to begin with the one that is most passively placed.

17 fxe5 ♘xe5+ 18 ♔f4 ♘g6+ 19 ♔f3

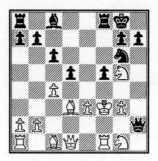

19...f4!!

Another beautiful, seemingly impossible pawn break which threatens mate with the knight on e5. In view of all its beautiful moves, it's easy to understand why the game was baptized "The Polish Immortal" by Tartakower. Later this was changed to "The Najdorf Immortal".

20 exf4 ♗g4+!

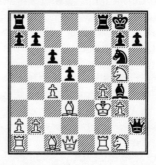

The king will be lured to the fourth rank where it will be caught in a mating net.

21 ♔xg4

143

White can prolong the game by 21 ♔e3 ♗xd1 22 ♖xd1 but Black will clear the kingside of all its pawns and pieces whilst pursuing an ongoing attack by 22...♕xg3+ 23 ♘1f3 ♕xf4+ 24 ♔f2 ♕h2+ 25 ♔e3 ♖ae8+ 26 ♔d4 ♕f2+ 27 ♔c3 ♖xf3 28 ♘xf3 ♕xf3. The queen surely makes a good impression of a vacuum cleaner! No other piece can perform this role as well as the strongest piece on the board.

21...♘e5+! 22 fxe5 h5 mate.

If Black didn't have the h-pawn the combination wouldn't work at all which just goes to shows how important a humble foot soldier can be for the effective conclusion of an attack. Remember the previous example, position 127, where a rook pawn also played a vital role in the overall construction of the mating net. Now we know what rook pawns are really worth and the glory they are waiting for in every game – and our mission is must be to fulfil their secret dreams! How many players realise that it is the rook pawns that are also the soul of chess?

Najdorf said later: "In the Najdorf Immortal I saw fourteen moves ahead, but sometimes these immortals are much simpler than positional games, even though the latter do not earn such fame."

129-132: The unexpected pawn push

129

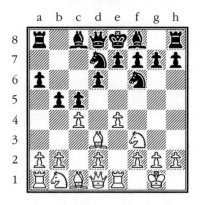

Carlsen – Topalov
Sinquefield Cup 2015
Black to move

This position arose after the moves 1 e4 c5 2 ♘f3 d6 3 ♗b5+ ♘d7 4 0–0 ♘f6 5 ♖e1 a6 6 ♗d3 b5 7 c4. Here Topalov played the ultra-aggressive **7...g5!?** which is actually a very strong move quite in the spirit of his style. Black tries to exploit the fact that White cannot open the centre by taking the initiative himself on the kingside. This very instructive example demonstrates the principal difference between strategy and tactics. It comes in the same category as model examples such as Dubois – Steinitz, London 1862 and Aronian – Kramnik, Candidates, Berlin 2018 (positions 138–139 in *300 Most Important Chess Positions*).

Indeed comparison can be drawn between Topalov's pawn sacrifice 7...g5!? and the above mentioned games where ...g7-g5 was prepared either by ...h7-h6 (Dubois – Steinitz) or ...♖g8 (Aronian – Kramnik). Incidentally, Nakamura preferred the quieter 7...♘e5 in a rapid game against Carlsen at Zürich 2014.

8 ♘xg5

Otherwise Black plays the pawn to g4. Note that it's impossible to open up the position in the centre due to the x-ray attack from Black's queen, aiming at the unprotected bishop on d3. After 8 e5?! dxe5 9 ♘xe5?? (*9 ♘xg5 ♖g8 10 ♘e4 is better and maintains equal chances.*) 9...♘xe5 10 ♖xe5 ♕xd3 is decisive for Black.

8...♘e5

Stronger than 8...♖g8?! 9 ♘f3 which takes back control of the e5-square.

9 ♗e2 bxc4 10 ♘a3?!

Stronger was 10 ♘c3 ♖g8 11 d4 cxd3 12 ♗xd3 ♘xd3 13 ♕xd3 with a slight advantage thanks to White's advantage in development.

10...♖g8 11 ♘xc4?!

11 d4 cxd3 12 ♗xd3 was correct

with mutual chances – but Carlsen has other ideas.

11...♘xc4

11...♖xg5? 12 d4 ♘xc4 13 ♗xg5 leads to a clear advantage to White.

12 d4 ♘b6 13 ♗h5?

Correct was 13 dxc5 dxc5 14 ♕xd8+ ♔xd8 15 ♘xf7+ ♔e8 16 ♘g5 e5 but White doesn't have full compensation for the piece sacrifice.

13...♘xh5 14 ♕xh5 ♖g7?!

More active was 14...♖g6! with a clear advantage, although Topalov still retained a slight edge which he converted to a win after 40 moves.

130

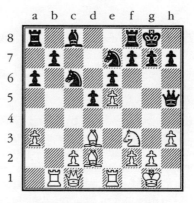

Kudinovsky – Kuprikov
Russia 1991
White to move

1 g4!!

It takes a while for the computer to come up with this super move. It needs to think 27 half moves ahead before it has calculated deep enough to offer it as the best continuation.

1 ♔h2 is too slow. Black equalises after 1...f6 which creates escape squares for the queen along the h5-e8 diagonal.

1...♕xh3 2 ♘h2

By defending the g4-pawn in this way White is threatening to win Black's queen after the sequence 3 ♗f1 ♕h4 4 ♗g5 so Black's next move is easy to understand.

2...h6

(1) The idea of exchanging knights on f3 by playing 2...♘d4 can be forestalled by 3 ♖e3! ♕h4 4 ♖g3 and White is threatening 5 ♗g5 as well as 5 c3 followed by 6 ♘f3.

(2) 2...f6 can be met by 3 ♖e3 ♕h4 4 ♖g3. This beautiful rook manoeuvre behind the g4-pawn should be remembered since it generates different ideas how to trap Black's queen. For example one idea is to play 5 ♔g2 followed by 6 ♖h3 or 5 ♗f1 followed by 6 ♖h3.

3 ♗f4!!

This move is certainly worth two exclamation marks!

3...♘f5?

The best defence was 3...h5. Presumably White would have continued 4 ♖e3 ♕h4 5 ♖g3 hxg4 6 ♖xg4 ♕h5 7 ♖g5 ♕h8 8 ♕d1 g6

9 ♘g4 with a clearly winning position.

4 gxf5 exf5 5 ♖e3 ♕h4 6 ♖g3 ♖e8 7 ♘f3 ♕h5 8 ♗xh6 g6 9 ♗f4 ♘d8 10 ♘d4 ♘e6 11 ♘xe6 ♗xe6 12 ♔g2 Black resigned.

131

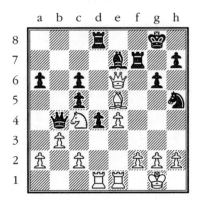

Capablanca – Marshall
New York 1909
White to move

Typical of Capablanca's style was that he regarded the initiative as more important than material. A good example is the following position where he played...

23 g4!

The pawn advance to g4 was one of Capablanca's favourite moves and sometimes he even played it when it wasn't really the best choice, although always made with the intention of taking the initiative. Here, however, g2-g4 is indeed the best.

A more materially inclined player would probably have played 23 ♕xc6 and there is nothing wrong with holding on to the two extra pawns, although it does lose some initiative. What's interesting here is that Capablanca didn't in fact play that way which reveals one of the keys to his way of thinking about the problems in the position. In Capablanca's mind the initiative comes ahead of material.

Note that 23 &c7 followed by ♘e5, winning the exchange, doesn't work here due to the intermediate move 23...♘g7 and White's pieces lose their harmony. Capablanca didn't like that. Harmony, as well as initiative, was more important than winning material. In this sense Capablanca wasn't a materialist even though his playing style could be regarded as materialistic, according to the theory of accumulation,

23...&h4

Black's available knight moves have no future since 23...♘g7 is met by 24 &xg7 &xg7 25 ♘e5 and the rook on f7 cannot move due to the fact that it must defend the bishop.

23...♘f6 is answered most simply by 24 &c7 followed by ♘e5 winning the exchange. Note how strong the knight was on c4 in both these variations since it can jump to e5 and create chaos in Black's disorganised position.

24 gxh5

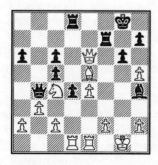

24...&xf2+

24...♛c3 first can be answered by 25 hxg6 (The careful and pragmatic player would choose *25 &g3*) 25...&xf2+ 26 &f1 The king move looks dangerous but Black has no harmful checks because of the strong queen on e6. 26...hxg6 27 ♛xg6+ &f8 28 ♛h6+

Then:

(1) 28...&e7 29 &d6+ ♖xd6 (*29...&d7 30 ♘b6+ &e8 31 ♛e6+ ♖e7 32 ♛g8 mate.*) 30 ♛xd6+ &e8 31 ♛e6+ &f8 32 ♘e5.

(2) 28...&e8 29 ♛e6+ &f8 30 &d6+ ♖xd6 31 ♘xd6 ♛f3 32 ♖e2!.

25 &h1 ♛c3

25...&xe1 is completely hopeless, e.g. 26 hxg6 hxg6 27 ♛xg6+ &f8 28 ♘d6 ♖f1+ 29 &g2 ♖f2+ 30 &g1 and it's a forced mate in 14 moves.

26 ♖e3!

Marshall's mating threat on f3 is parried by a crushing and spectacular move which Capablanca might have already had in mind when he moved his pawn to g4. Capablanca was very skilful at calculating variations so it's most probable that he saw everything in advance.

26...♕xc2

If 26...♗xe3 then 27 hxg6 hxg6 28 ♕xg6+ ♔f8 29 ♘d6 ♖dd7 30 ♘xf7 and it's mate in eight moves.

27 ♖ed3!

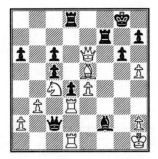

White's rook, which was originally placed on e1, is a real hero in the defence. First it parries the mate threat on f3, then it defends the rook on d1 with a gradual lateral manoeuvre. Capablanca always handled the rooks superbly in every phase of the game.

27...♕e2

If 27...gxh5 then 28 ♖g1+! ♗xg1 29 ♖g3+ ♔f8 30 ♗g7+! ♔g8 (*30...♖xg7 is met by 31 ♖f3+ another lateral rook move.*) 31 ♗h6+ ♔h8 32 ♕e5+.

28 ♘d6 ♖xd6 29 ♗xd6 ♗e1 30 ♕e8+ ♔g7 31 h6+ Black resigned.

Starting from a fine position, Capablanca has steadily increased his initiative and eventually developed an overwhelming attack, while simultaneously defending against Black's threats. Finally, seeing that White defends against the mate on f1 after capturing the rook on f7, Marshall resigned.

132

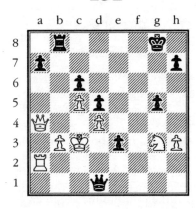

Spraggett – Kindermann
Lugano 1988
Black to move

46...a5!

In the *Informant* Kindermann and Botsaris attach two exclamation marks to this strong move and it's certainly more appealing then the computer's suggestion since it introduces the rook pawn into the attack. Black is threatening the decisive ...♖b4 so White's next move is forced.

Komodo11 suggests with "brute force" (15 moves ahead) the continuation 46...♕e1+ 47 ♔b2! as White needs the escape square on a3. (Not *47 ♔d3 ♖b4 48 ♕a3 ♕d1+* and the d4-pawn is lost with devastating effect. Nor *47 ♔c2 ♕xg3 48 ♕xc6 ♕f2+* leading to a forced mate in seven moves.) 47...e2! (*47...♕xg3 48 ♕xc6 ♕f2+ 49 ♔a3*) 48 ♘xe2 ♕xe2+ 49 ♔a3 ♕e1 Preventing White from taking the pawn on c6 because of the decisive queen check on b4. 50 ♖g2 ♕a1+ 51 ♖a2 ♕c3 and Black wins since there is no defence to the rook manoeuvre 52...♖b5 followed by 53...♖a5.

47 ♘e2 ♖b4 48 ♕a3

48 ♕xa5 ♖xb3 mate.

48...♕e1+ 49 ♔d3 a4!

The point is to weaken the c4-square.

50 bxa4

50 ♖b2 ♖xb3+ 51 ♖xb3 ♕d2 mate. Note that Black has two pawns which help to produce the beautiful mate.

50...♕b1+ 51 ♔xe3

It's no longer possible to play 51 ♔c3 because of 51...♖c4 mate.

51...♖b3+ 52 ♔f2 ♕f5+ 53 ♔e1

53 ♔g1 ♕d3! and Black's queen is trapped. Incidentally, 53...♕xh3 also wins after 54 ♕c1 ♕g4+ 55 ♔f1 ♕f5+ 56 ♔g2 ♕e4+ 57 ♔h2 ♕h4+ 58 ♔g2 ♖h3. Note how Black's major pieces can avoid the e2-knight and thereby render it completely helpless in the defence. When Andersson defeated Karpov in Milano 1975 White had a similar setup of pieces but Black also had a white-squared bishop!

53...♕xh3

White's queen is trapped.

54 ♕b2

54 ♕c1 is met by 54...♖b1!.

54...♖xb2 55 ♖xb2 ♕a3 56 ♖b7 ♕xa4

Black's two passed pawns will decide the game and so White could obviously have resigned here.

Spraggett seems to belong to the category of optimistic players!

57 ♖e7 ♕b4+ 58 ♔f2 ♕d2 59 ♖e6 ♔f7 60 ♖h6 ♕c2 61 ♖xc6 g4 62 ♖c7+ ♔f6 63 ♖c6+ ♔g5 64 ♖c7 g3+ 65 ♔e1 ♕b1+ 66 ♔d2 ♕a2+ 67 ♔d1 ♕a4+ 68 ♔c1 ♕a5 69 ♖e7 ♔f6 White resigned.

133-138: The passed pawn

133

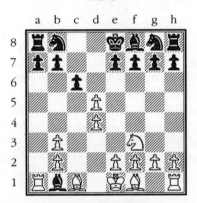

Schlechter – Perlis
Carlsbad 1911
White to move

The initial moves were 1 d4 d5 2 ♘f3 ♗f5 3 c4 c6 4 ♕b3 ♕b6 5 cxd5 and White has won a pawn since 5...♕xb3 6 axb3 ♗xb1 (*6...cxd5 loses a pawn due to 7 ♘c3 with the double threat of 8 ♘xd5 and ♘b5*) is met by...

7 dxc6!

7.♖xb1 cxd5 is nothing special since White's bishop pair is balanced by Black's inferior pawn structure.

7...♘xc6

Black cannot keep the extra piece by playing 7...♗e4? due to the amazing 8 ♖xa7!! ♖xa7 9 c7 and the pawn promotes either on c8 or b8. In the heat of battle it can be easy to forget the significance of the semi-open a-file and the fact that on the seventh rank the pawn cannot be stopped from queening. If the rook hadn't moved from a8 Black could just move his knight. The golden rule is always to look extra carefully when a pawn is only two moves from promotion!

8 ♖xb1

White has an extra pawn, but what a pawn it is on d4 – the strongest on the board. Schlechter obviously didn't have any problems winning this position. We will in fact be returning to the rook ending which occurred later in the game. It is certainly worth memorising this opening trap.

134

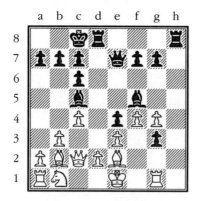

Larsen – Spassky
USSR vs. Rest of the World,
Belgrade 1970
Black to move

14...♖h1!

A really strong move which would have been even stronger with the inclusion of the preliminary 14...♗xe3!! 15 dxe3. Then after 15...♖h1!! 16 ♖xh1 g2 the point is that the white king is now stuck on e1, since it cannot cross the d-file. Perhaps this is just pedantry since Black wins quite easily anyway.

15 ♖xh1 g2 16 ♖f1

Spassky gives the spectacular variation 16 ♖g1 ♕h4+ 17 ♔d1 ♕h1 18 ♕c3 ♕xg1+ 19 ♔c2 ♕f2 20 gxf5 ♕xe2 21 ♘a3 ♕d3+ (*21...♗b4* was simpler but Spassky's line is undeniably more beautiful.) 22 ♕xd3 exd3+ 23 ♔c3 ♗xe3! 24 dxe3 d2 25 ♖d1 ♖h8.

16...♕h4+ 17 ♔d1 gxf1♕+ White resigned.

There is no question which piece was the hero, since the h-pawn managed to promote on the remote square f1 and with such incredible speed. Isn't this what is called a home run in American football? Here the hero will be sacrificed, as (almost) all heroes, since mate follows shortly after 18 ♗xf1 ♗xg4+ etc. and therefore Larsen immediately resigned.

So Spassky defeated Larsen, one of the best players in the world during this period, in only 17 moves and it's natural to ask how it happened and above all how the h-file was opened. Here are the initial moves of the game:

1 b3 e5 2 ♗b2 ♘c6 3 c4 ♘f6 4 ♘f3 e4 5 ♘d4 ♗c5 6 ♘xc6 dxc6

150

7 e3 ♗f5 8 ♕c2 ♕e7 9 ♗e2 0-0-0
10 f4 ♘g4 11 g3 h5!

This move is the prelude to an amazing sequel.

12 h3 h4!

The h-pawn rushes forward.

13 hxg4 hxg3

Suddenly the h-file is opened and the h-pawn is on g3, only two moves from promotion.

14 ♖g1

And we have reached the diagram position.

Many chess players would undoubtedly find the beautiful rook move but the trick is how to obtain the position. The game shows that if the centre isn't opened it's just as effective to open up the position on a flank, especially the side of the board where the enemy king is located, and in that way exploit a lead in development. So, to repeat, when ahead in development the trick is to open up the game where the opponent's king is situated – but the difference here, in contrast to Morphy's games, is that Spassky did this on the flank.

135

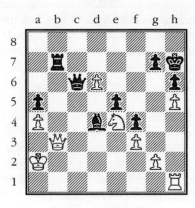

Alterman – Legky
USSR 1989
White to move

This position looks completely lost for White but if one looks more closely it's actually White who is winning. Alterman played the clever move…

1 ♖c1! ♕xc1

(1) 1...♖xb3 2 ♖xc6 ♖b2+ 3 ♔a3 leads to a win since the d-pawn in combination with the knight overpowers Black's position.

(2) 1...♕d7 2 ♘f6+! gxf6 3 ♕xb7 ♕xb7 4 ♖c7+ wins.

2 ♘f6+!

The point of White's last move.

2...gxf6

2...♔h8 is met by 3.♕g8 mate.

3 ♕xb7+

The pawn on h5 helps White to force a decisive exchange of queens on c7. Without the pawn on h5, an important detail in the position, the combination would not have worked. This brings us to something that can be stressed again and again: a really good player knows how to use the rook-pawn, both for tactical (Larsen – Spassky) and positional objectives.

3...♔g8 4 ♕b8+ ♔f7 5 ♕c7+

An instructive example showing how dangerous a knight placed on the fourth rank in the centre can be. Petrosian had already showed this in the fifth game of his world title match against Botvinnik in 1963, but that was from a positional point of view. What we saw here was how a knight placed on e4 can also be a basis for tactical operations. Also remember how in position 127 Petrosian was able to utilise his knight on d3 for tactical operations.

136

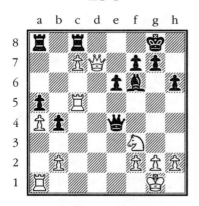

Ståhlberg – Euwe
Olympiad, Stockholm 1937
White to move

27 ♖e1

It's logical to start the analysis with the forced variation 27 ♖xa5 ♗xb2 28 ♖e1 ♕b7 29 ♖xa8 ♕xa8

30 ♖d1 which looks like a win because of the threat 31 ♕xc8+ followed by 32 ♖d8+. But what about the clever defensive move 30...♔h7! (The natural resource *30...♗f6?* loses on the spot due to *31 ♘e5!*) evacuating the back rank. After the further 31 ♕xf7 ♗f6 32 ♕xe6 ♖xc7 the position looks pretty drawish.

27...♕b7 28 ♘d2!

Black must now be prepared for three different knight moves depending on Black's reply.

Ståhlberg played the inferior 28 ♘e5? ♗xe5 29 ♖exe5 ♖a7 and lost the game even though he had a forced draw by 30 ♖xe6! fxe6 31 ♕d8+ ♔h7 32 ♕d3+ as Black cannot escape perpetual checks.

28...♗xb2

(1) If 28...♖a7 then 29 ♖ec1 ♗xb2 30 ♖1c4 and White is threatening not only the winning 31 ♘e4 but also 31 ♖b5 followed by 32 ♕xc8+ and 33 ♖b8.

(2) 28...♕a7 is answered by 29 ♘b3 threatening the a5-pawn as well as the decisive rook manoeuvre ♖c1-c4.

29 ♘c4

After White's knight manoeuvre to c4 Black's position quickly falls apart.

The key to the win was the activation of the passive knight (hampered by the bishop on f6) so it could strike Black's positional weaknesses on d6 and a5. When in possession of such a super pawn on c7 the game plays itself, but there are many pitfalls even for very strong players. We can learn so much from other players' mistakes and it's strange that there is no book focusing on this one important aspect. Where strong players go wrong, all players go wrong which means that we should learn not only from our own mistakes but especially from the mistakes of others. This is the reason we must take all the great players' mistakes on board as well and not just their winning ideas.

137

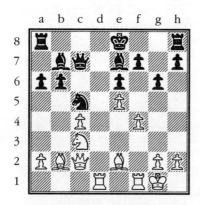

Petrosian – Pfeiffer
Olympiad, Leipzig 1960
White to move

18 ♘d5!

Most probably Philidor would have liked this knight sacrifice since it shifts the emphasis on to the pawns and their lust to expand.

18...exd5

A better practical chance was to activate the queen before capturing on d5. A plausible variation is 18...♕c6 19 ♗f3! (*19 f5!?*) 19...exd5

20 cxd5 ♕a4 21 ♕c3 ♕a5 22 ♕xa5 (*22 ♕c1!?*) 22...bxa5 23 d6 (*23 ♗a3!?* or *23 g3!?* were decent alternatives to avoid the forthcoming endgame) 23...♗xf3 24 ♖xf3 ♗d8 25 e6 ♖g8 26 d7+ ♔e7 27 ♗a3 ♗b6 28 ♖c3 fxe6 29 ♗xc5+ ♗xc5+ 30 ♖xc5 and Black has good drawing chances in the double rook ending. However there were several possibilities for White to avoid this ending at moves 19, 22 and 23 so the variation is far from forced.

19 cxd5

This position is instructive in the sense that here it's easy to see that two well defended pawns on the fifth rank can be valued higher than a minor piece. The same applies for two pawns on the sixth in relation to a rook (D.Cramling – Blomqvist, position 290). Here the pawns are threatening to expand with d5-d6 and e5-e6. Obviously the monster bishop on b2 helps when Black has weakened himself with ...g7-g6.

19...♕c8

It would not have helped to give back the piece with 19...0–0 20 d6 ♕c6 21 ♗f3 ♕d7 22 dxe7 ♕xe7 since White would then have a crushing position after 23 f5.

20 e6

Other strong continuations were 20 d6 ♕f5 21 ♕c3 or 20 f5.

20...0–0 21 ♕c3 f6 22 d6 ♘a4 23 ♕xc8 ♖fxc8 24 ♗a1

The exchange of queens has not helped Black's defence. The pawns will just head for the seventh and eighth ranks.

24...♖c2

24...♗f8 25 ♗xf6 ♘c3 26 ♗xc3 ♖xc3 27 e7 also wins.

25 dxe7 ♖xe2 26 ♖d8+ ♔g7 27 ♖c1! ♖xe6

27...♖xg2+ 28 ♔f1

28 ♖c7 ♔h6 29 ♗xf6 ♗e4 30 ♗g5+ Black resigned.

He did not want to wait for the mate after 30...♔h5 31 e8♕ ♖xe8 32 h3!.

138

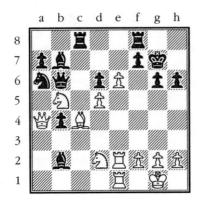

Yedidia – D. Gurevich
USA 1983
White to move

This position made a strong impression on me. It's taken from *Informant 35* which I read a long time ago, since I belonged to the "children of Informator" generation, It's a tactically rich position where only one set of minor pieces has been exchanged. Immediately noticeable is the fact that the e6-pawn is a veritable powerhouse. In the game **1 e7!** was played. White's super pawn actually splits Black's

position into two, since any communication between his pieces on the seventh rank is made impossible.

White could also play 1 ♘e4! at once since 1...♖xc4 is met by 2 ♘exd6 and "everything" hangs. The main variation is 2...♘c5 3 ♘xc4 ♘xa4 4 ♘xb6 axb6 5 e7 ♗xd5 6 ♘c7!. There is no hurry to capture the rook on f8. More decisive (and cleverer) is to endeavour to get a rook to d8 and thereby exploit both outposts on the eighth rank, d8 as well as f8.

Then:

(1) 6...♗c6

is met by 7 ♖e6!!. The threat is not only to capture the bishop but more deadly, as mentioned before, is the rook manoeuvre to d8, in this case via d6. 7...fxe6? reveals another advantage of maintaining the tension of the energy in the e7-pawn, since it now can explode on f8 like an atomic bomb after 8 ♘xe6+. All these tactical variations work thanks to the inherent energy in the e7-pawn, i.e. its lust to expand to f8 or e8 and also its capacity to provide an outpost on d8 for a rook. The pawn really is the soul of chess, as Philidor so insightfully expressed it, but here we are only referring to one pawn, a true hero.

(2) 6...♗c4 is countered by 7 ♖d1!! followed by ♖d8 winning. What's interesting, with all the above mentioned variations, is that White fully utilised the energy in the e7-pawn, since it not only threatened the rook on f8 or to promote on e8, but it also provided an outpost for a rook on d8. The pawn's lust to expand means to all the squares e8, f8 and d8. The rook manoeuvre e6-d6-d8 was made possible because of the e7-pawn's control of f8 and d8. When playing tactical positions where pieces are hanging one must always look further to see if there is any clever intermediate move which makes maximum use of any tactical opportunities. The most common mistake in such positions is to focus solely on forced variations and exchanges of blows. In a practical game it's most common to miss those moves which are not part of any forced variation or exchange. The fundamental method of calculating variations is to look at forced variations first – and it's important to be aware of any illusions in this habit of thinking. It's important not to forget Lasker's insightful words that there might be a better move when you have finished your calculation. An instructive example is Ernst – Hellers, position 52.

1...♖fe8 2 ♘e4!!

Here we see a further example where knights are releasing their energy over the entire board. According to the principle adopted by Alekhine and Fischer, presented in positions 66-67 of *300 Most Important Chess Positions*, one should play with knights in such a manner so as to avoid backward moves. Here it's astonishing that Yedidia sacrifices the pawn like cannon fodder, since this was something ill-advised according to Philidor. Yedidia's thinking might have been that it's not the pawn which is the soul of chess, since in this case it's not part of any chain, but rather it's the knight which is the soul of the game. That a knight is regarded as the soul of the game in highly tactical positions might certainly be true, thereby contrasting with Philidor's principle which is most suited to closed or locked positions, especially when pawn chains are on the agenda.

2...♗e5

2...♖xe7 is met by 3 ♘bxd6 with a double threat on c8 and b7.

3 ♘bxd6!

This is the point. White exploits another weakness, namely the long dark a1-h8 diagonal.

3...♗xd6 4 ♕a1+

Now the queen releases its energy to the maximum.

4...♗e5

Black has to communicate with his queen on the sixth rank.

5 ♕xe5+ f6 6 ♕d6!

The idea is simply to exchange queens and then transfer the knight to d6. White could also have moved the queen to f4 or g3. In the game, the inferior 6 ♘xf6? was played. After 6...♕xf6 7 ♕xf6+ ♔xf6 8 ♖e6+ ♔f7 9 d6 ♘b8 play continued with the suicidal 10 ♖6e3+?? ♖xc4 and White resigned.

In fact the last chance to win the game would have been 10 ♗b5 ♗d5 11 d7 ♗xe6 12 dxe8♕+ ♖xe8 13 ♗xe8+ ♔xe7 14 ♗xg6.

What a pity that White lost such a fine position with a strongly supported dream pawn on e7 as well as two dancing knights.

6...♖xc4

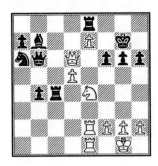

7 ♘xf6!!

The culmination of the tactical operation which exploits the fact that Black has partly lost communication with the sixth rank. 7 ♕xb6 axb6 8 ♘d6 also wins but the text move is undoubtedly more principled as well as more beautiful.

7...♖cc8 8 ♘xe8+ ♖xe8 9 ♕d7 ♘c7 10 d6

Both knights, the heroes in this particular game, were sacrificed, but perhaps White can honour them by promoting to two new knights! Life must go on...

139: Dynamic play with pawns

139

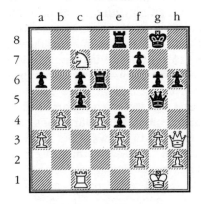

Marshall – Alekhine
New York 1924
Black to move

Alekhine was a master of dynamic tactical pawn play. Here is one example:

25...cxd4!!

In the tournament book Alekhine analyses the inferior 25...♖e7 26 ♕c8+ (*If 26 ♖xc5 ♕f6 27 ♕c8+ ♔g7 28 ♘e8+ ♖xe8 29 ♕xe8 ♕f3 30 ♖c1 ♖f6 31 ♖f1 White is a pawn up but his rook is passive. This may not have been to Alekhine's liking.*) 26...♔g7 27 bxc5 ♖f6 28 ♖b1

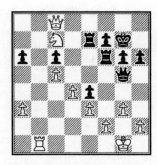

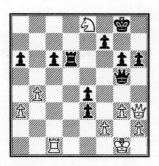

...but here he missed the spectacular 28...♖xf2!! (instead of the weaker *28...♕f5*)

(1) The most entertaining variation after 29 ♔xf2 ♕h5 is 30 ♔e1 ♕f3 31 ♖b3 ♕h1+ 32 ♔d2 ♕xh2+ 33 ♔c1 ♕g1+ 34 ♔b2 ♕f2+ 35 ♔c3 ♕xe3+ 36 ♔c4 ♕c1+ 37 ♔b4 (*37 ♖c3??* even loses after *37...♕f1+ 38 ♔b3 ♖xc7! 39 ♕xc7 ♕b1+ 40 ♔c4 ♕b5* mate. What a queen!) 37...♕d2+ 38 ♔a4 ♕xd4+ 39 ♖b4 ♕d1+ 40 ♔a5 ♕d3! and it's actually White who must fight for the draw.

(2) 29 ♖b8 ♔f6 30 ♕h8+ ♔f5 31 ♕c8+ ♔f6 32 ♘e8+ ♖xe8 33 ♕xe8 ♖e2 34 ♕h8+ ♔f5 35 ♕e5+ ♔g4 36 ♕xe4+ ♔h5 and the position is completely equal. It's quite incredible what variations lay hidden in chess and even a genius like Alekhine couldn't find them. Chess is indeed inexhaustible!

26 ♘xe8 dxe3!

(1) Alekhine gives the funny variation 26...♖d8 27 ♕g4 ♕e7 28 ♕xe4 and White wins, but...

(2) 26...♖e6 27 ♖c5 ♕e7 28 ♕xh6 ♕xe8 29 exd4 e3 30 fxe3 ♖xe3 31 ♖e5 ♖xe5 32 dxe5 ♕xe5 33 ♕c1 leaves equal play.

27 ♘xd6

Alekhine mentions that Marshall could lay a trap by 27 f4 exf3 28 ♘xd6 f2+ (The trap is that *28...e2??* loses to *29 ♕c8+ ♔h7 30 ♕h8+! ♔xh8 31 ♘xf7+* This tactical idea reminds us of Petrosian who played it twice, namely a queen sacrifice on h8 followed by a decisive knight fork on f7. Look at position 300) 29 ♔f1 (Actually the only move as *29 ♔h1??* loses to *29...♕d5+ 30 ♕g2 e2*. Philidor would be happy with a pair of pawns like this, which has at least the same value as a full queen.) 29...e2+! 30 ♔xf2 ♕xc1 31 ♔xe2 ♕b2+ 32 ♔e3 ♕c1+ 33 ♔e4 ♕c2+ 34 ♔d4 ♕f2+ and White cannot escape the perpetual checks without giving up the knight. Alekhine writes that this variation was the hardest to find at move 21!! This says something about Alekhine's calculating abilities. At the same time it's incredible that the variations work so well but that's because White's queen is cut off from the main scene of action and cannot assist the defence. In addition the knight on d6 is undefended, which brings to mind a clever acronym from the English grandmaster and prolific chess writer John Nunn – LPOD which means "Loose Pieces Drop Off"!

27...exf2+ 28 ♔xf2 ♕d2+ 29 ♔g1 ♕e3+!

A nice intermezzo which secures the draw. Not 29...♕xc1+? 30 ♕f1 ♕e3+ 31 ♕f2 ♕b3 32 ♕d4 when White should win.

30 ♔g2! ♕f3+ Draw.

Interestingly it was the b6-pawn which advanced via c5-d4-e3 to f2. This certainly proves Alekhine's ability to play dynamically with his pawns. In his famous game against Bogoljubow at Hastings 1922, where he also had the black pieces, he played incredibly well with the pawns. It was like he was playing checkers instead of chess because his pawns were moving diagonally and criss-crossing the board. His pawn play was truly magical and this aspect of Alekhine's game is worthy of deep study yet, strangely, no one has ever really focused on it. We can still learn so much from the old grandmasters.

140-150: Attacking the King

140: Attacking the king with pawns

140

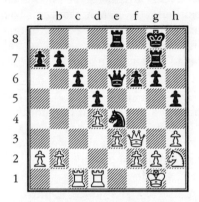

Bobotsov – Petrosian
Olympiad, Lugano 1968
Black to move

From the first world title match game he lost to Botvinnik in 1963, Petrosian learned that it's possible to carry out a pawn storm even if you have castled on the same side as the opponent. Here, White's queen, knight and h3-pawn are the motifs for Black to open lines on the kingside. The knight on e4 (remember the concept by Labourdonnais/Pillsbury, position 60.) ensures that it is indeed possible to attack thanks to having firm control of the centre. Steinitz stipulated that one must unconditionally go for an attack when having the advantage and Black's rook on g7 indicates that he

has more pieces for the attack than White has in the defence. So Petrosian played...

33...g5! 34 ♕xh5

White is forced to accept the gift since it's mandatory to stop the pawn-push to g4.

34...f5

Nothing will stop Black from breaking through on the kingside with ...g5-g4.

35.♖e1?!

A better defence was 35 ♕f3! g4 36 ♕f4 gxh3 37 g3 even though Petrosian might have played his patented exchange sacrifice 37...♖g4! and switched to autopilot!

35...g4

Now White's queen is cut off.

36 hxg4 fxg4 37 f3?

Unnecessarily opening more lines against his own king. White should have strengthened his weakest point on f2 by playing 37 ♖c2.

37...gxf3 38 ♘xf3

If 38 ♕xf3 ♖f8 39 ♕e2 then 39...♖f5! and Black wins since it's not possible to oppose the rooks on the f-file due to the knight fork on g3. Black then plans ...♕h6 followed by ...♖h5.

38...♖h7!

White's queen is caught like a fish in a net and can only flounder for a couple of moves.

39 ♕e5 ♕c8 40 ♕f4 ♖f8 41 ♕e5 ♖f5 White resigned.

Petrosian finishes the game with a beautiful catch of the queen in the middle of the board.

141-143: Attacking the king with pieces

141

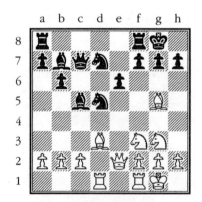

Tal – Vasyukov
USSR Championship 1964
White to move

Tal and Alekhine adopted different methods of attack. While Alekhine often used diversionary tactics on the queenside to achieve something on the other flank, that is playing over the whole board, Tal, on the other hand, was known for "launching" which is an expression from Canadian hockey. Indeed, one can well imagine the puck gliding on the ice towards the goal (the king's position!) to create chances. The piece which acts like a puck in this position is the knight on g3 so Tal played the launching move…

15 ♘h5!

Here the knight is like a sword pointing at the g7- and f6-points. 15 c4 ♘5f6 16 ♘e4 ♘xe4 17 ♗xe4 ♗xe4 18 ♕xe4 would have led to a more simplified game.

15...♔h8!

A useful move since it prevents White from capturing the h7-pawn with check, and prepares a rook move to g8 if the g-file is opened. An illustrative variation showing the strength of controlling the f6-square is the following: 15...♖ae8 16 c4 ♘5f6? 17 ♗xf6! ♘xf6 (*if 17...gxf6?* then *18 ♕d2* and Black cannot prevent the white queen from invading on h6. Here we can clearly see how the puck and the player (the queen) work together in harmony.)

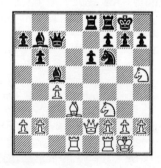

18 ♘g5! White plays another puck to the critical zone and with decisive effect, since the best continuation 18...h6 19 ♘xf6+ gxf6 concedes material after 20 ♘h7.

16 ♗e4 f6 17 ♗h4 ♗d6 18 c4 ♗a6

19 ♘xg7!

This kind of sacrifice is what Kasparov calls an exchange rather than a sacrifice because the knight on g3 and the pawn on g7 are at least of equal value in this specific position. Kasparov carried out a similar exchange against Portisch in Niksic 1983 when he captured on g7 with a bishop. See position 87.

19...♔xg7 20 ♘d4 ♘c5 21 ♕g4+ ♔h8 22 ♘xe6 ♘xe6 23 ♕xe6 ♖ae8 24 ♕xd5 ♗xh2+ 25 ♔h1 ♕f4 26 ♕h5! ♕xe4 27 ♖fe1 ♕g6

In this position Tal lost his advantage by exchanging queens on g6. He could have won immediately by...

28 ♗xf6+!

But Tal still managed to win the game in 58 moves.

142

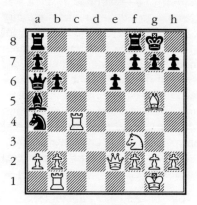

Alekhine – Sterk
Budapest 1921
White to move

As mentioned above, Alekhine often adopted queenside play to achieve something on the kingside, thereby playing over the whole board. This contrasts with Tal who concentrated his pieces on the kingside and prepared launching moves followed by sacrifices.

23 ♗f6!!

White takes control of the long dark diagonal by tactical means, This is more subtle than to play in the style of Zukertort and fianchetto the bishop on b2 early in the game, since Black can then adapt immediately. Alekhine's play is perfectly covert and only now is he revealing his real intention – which is to attack the king on the g7-square. Alekhine writes in *My Best Games of Chess 1908–1937* that the "chief point in these attacks (In the present game as well as Alekhine – Bogoljubow, Triberg 1921, Alekhine – Rubinstein, Carlsbad 1923 and

161

Alekhine – Selesnieff, Pistyan 1922) lies in the fact that none of them was prepared in its immediate vicinity of its objective. On the contrary, all the preliminary manoeuvres which tended to divert the adverse pieces from the defence of their king took place in the centre or on the opposite wing. Furthermore, it is interesting that the deciding move, a real hammer-blow, is played by a bishop and always involves sacrificial variations."

Note that 23 b4?? fails to 23...♘c3 exploiting the pinned c4-rook.

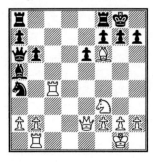

23...♖fc8!

The only move according to Alekhine. Black must defend against the Morphy style 24 ♖g4 ♕xe2 25 ♖xg7+ ♔h8 26 ♖g6 mate. Kotov gives the following variations:

(1) 23...gxf6 24 ♖g4+ and Black's queen is lost.

(2) 23...h5 24 ♖g4 ♕xe2 25 ♖xg7+ ♔h8 26 ♘g5 It's impossible to prevent mate.

(3) 23...h6 gives the black king an escape-square on h7 but after 24 ♘e5 there are too many threats, chiefly 25 ♕g4.

24 ♕e5!

This nice centralisation of the queen, threatening 25 ♕g5, was of course foreseen by Alekhine.

24...♖c5

Alekhine gives the following insufficient variations:

(1) 24...♕xc4 25 ♕g5 ♔f8 26 ♕xg7+ ♔e8 27 ♕g8+ ♔d7 28 ♘e5+ ♔c7 29 ♕xf7+.

(2) 24...♖xc4 25 ♕g5 ♖g4 26 ♕xg4 g6 27 ♕xa4.

(3) 24...gxf6 25 ♖g4+.

25 ♕g3

Nicer than the pragmatic continuation 25 ♖xc5 ♕d3 (25...gxf6 26 ♕g3+) 26 ♖cc1 gxf6 27 ♕xf6.

25...g6 26 ♖xa4 ♕d3 27 ♖f1 ♕f5 28 ♕f4 ♕c2 29 ♕h6 Black resigned.

Interestingly the hero, the bishop on f6, has survived the battle and helps to deliver the mate. But how did Alekhine achieve his objective of luring Black's pieces to the queenside? Let's see the game from the beginning: **1 d4 d5 2 ♘f3 ♘f6 3 c4 e6 4 ♘c3 ♘bd7 5 e3 ♗d6 6 ♘b5 ♗e7 7 ♕c2 c6 8 ♘c3 0–0 9 ♗d3 dxc4 10 ♗xc4 e5 11 dxe5 ♗xe5 12 0–0 b6 13 e4 ♗b7 14 ♗g5 ♕c8 15 ♕e2 ♗b4 16 ♗d3.**

Kotov, who has written a biography of Alekhine, writes that this move is in accordance with the principle of launching a sudden attack since it already prepares to deliver the main blow on the kingside.

16...♗xc3 17 ♖fc1 ♘xe4 18 ♗xe4

♗xe4 19 ♕xe4 ♘c5 20 ♕e2 ♗a5 21 ♖ab1 ♕a6 22 ♖c4 ♘a4 thereby reaching the diagram position.

Don't forget to study the three other games mentioned by Alekhine to gain a deeper understanding of his attacking methods.

143

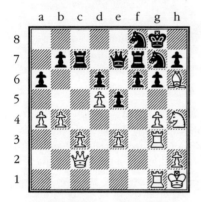

Eliskases – Gruenfeld
Mährisch-Ostrau 1933
White to move

27 ♘f5!

The first time I became acquainted with this typical sacrifice in Benoni structures was when I studied the fascinating book *Pawn Power in Chess* by Hans Kmoch. Unfortunately his original but witty terminology didn't get the recognition it deserved as time went by. He called this knight thrust "The Benoni Jump". It's a typical tactical twist when major pieces are doubled (or sometimes tripled) on the g-file. Maybe the most famous example is when Fischer played this move against the young Ulf Andersson in a newspaper sponsored exhibition

game during the Olympiad at Siegen 1970. Fischer played the knight to f5 after 22 moves and Andersson's position collapsed. In this position the Benoni Jump is decisive as well.

27...gxf5

Practically forced otherwise Black loses the exchange.

28 gxf5 ♕e8 29 ♕g2

It's interesting that the computer prefers the cooler 29 c4 followed by c5. The possibility of playing the queen to g2 doesn't disappear so it's not wrong to improve the position on the queenside even if a human probably wouldn't do that. The move played is the most principled way to profit from the queue on the g-file. After all, it's the breakthrough on the g-file which is the main point of the Benoni Jump.

29...♕d7 30 ♖xg7+ ♖xg7 31 ♗xg7 ♕xg7 32 ♕c2 ♘g6 33 fxg6 h6

Black has played all the best defensive moves but these do not help since White's position is too strong. The newly born pawn on g6 is obviously an unpleasant intruder thrust deep into Black's territory.

34 ♕f5

A very beautiful and decisive queen centralisation which makes good use of the earlier knight jump to f5, since it made that a critical key square.

34...♕f8 35 c4

The pawn avalanche is set in motion according to the principle of the two weaknesses.

35...♔g7

35...♖xc4? 36 ♕e6+ ♔g7 37 ♕d7+ ♔g8 38 ♕h7 mate instructively shows the value of the g6-pawn which has created outposts on f7 and h7, the most intimate part of Black's position.

36 ♖c1!

White needs to provoke another weakness since it's not possible to break through on the kingside.

36...b6 37 e4 ♕e7 38 ♕f2 ♖b7 39 h4

29... a5

Suicidal would be 39...♔xg6? 40 ♖g1+ ♔f7 41 ♕f5 and Black is mated by force in a dozen moves. Or else 40...♔h7 41 ♕f5+ ♔h8 42 ♕c8+ ♔h7 43 ♕g8 mate. Note the beautiful queen manoeuvre via the light f5-c8-g8 squares. It's the knight sacrifice on f5 which has laid the foundations for these rewards.

40 h5 axb4 41 ♖b1 b3 42 ♖xb3

White can now focus on weaknesses on both sides of the board, with the ultimate aim of carrying out a breakthrough on either the queenside or the kingside.

42...♕d7

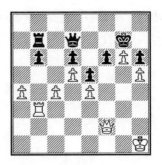

43 ♕f5!

The introduction to a very beautiful queen manoeuvre which leads to a winning rook endgame.

43...♕e7

43...♕xf5 44 exf5 also leads to a winning rook endgame, since a4-a5 cannot be prevented with any other move than 44...♖a7 but then 45 ♖xb6 ♖xa4 46 ♖xd6 ♖xc4 47 ♖d7+ ♔f8 48 ♖f7+ decides.

44 ♕e6! ♕c7 45 ♕f7+!

Again, thanks to the Benoni Jump, White gains maximum profit by exploiting the outposts on f5, e6 and f7!

45...♕xf7 46 gxf7 ♖a7

If 46...♔xf7 then 47 a5.

47 ♖xb6 ♖xa4 48 ♖xd6 ♖xc4 49 ♖xf6! ♔f8 50 d6 ♖xe4 51 d7 ♖d4 52 ♖xh6 ♔xf7 53 ♖h8! Black resigned.

Because after 53...♖xd7 54 ♖h7+ ♔e6 55 ♖xd7 ♔xd7 56 h6 Black's king is outside the square. A beautiful game, not only because of the Benoni Jump but also because of the manoeuvres with the queen, rook and pawns, while the king just remained on h1 and watched everything with the greatest delight.

144: Prophylaxis against an attack on the king with pieces.

144

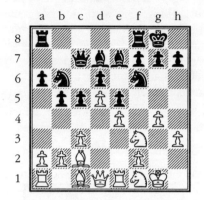

Kasparov – Petrosian
Banja Luka 1979
Black to move

15...h5!

A strong prophylactic move which prevents White playing according to the standard plan ♘g3-f5 as we saw in the last example.

16 gxh5

It's hard to find a better alternative since 16 ♘3h2?! is met by 16...hxg4 17 hxg4 ♘h7 securing the g5-square for Black. If White continues 18 ♘g3 Black can neutralise the g3-knight with 18...g6. Nor is 16 g5?! a good option because of 16...♘h7 17 h4 g6 followed by the break ...f7-f6 which will make White's king's position weaker than Black's.

16...♗xh3

An interesting tactical idea is 16...g6!? but White can easily

disarm it by 17 h6! (*17 hxg6 fxg6* would give Black sufficient compensation for the pawn which ultimately will manifest itself either on the f-file after ...♘h5 or the h-file after ...♔g7.) 17...♗xh3 18 ♘1h2 followed by ♔h1 and ♖g1 with play on the kingside to counterbalance Black's chances on the queen's flank.

17 ♘3h2

17...♗xf1!?

Most players would probably keep the bishop on h3 but Petrosian was fond of such unconventional exchanges with a stronger bishop in order to reduce the potential of White's piece majority on the kingside.

18 ♘xf1 ♕d7 19 ♘g3 ♕h3 20 ♕f3

20 ♘f5?? loses after 20...♘g4 21 ♘xe7+ ♔h7 22 ♗e3 ♘c4 and White has nothing better than to sacrifice his queen for the g4-knight. What knights!

20...g6 21 ♗d1 ♖fe8 22 ♕g2 ♕xg2 23 ♔xg2 and the players agreed a **draw**.

145-146: Attack on the king with major pieces

145

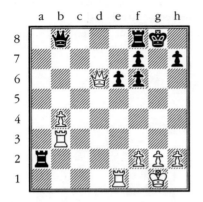

P. Cramling – Kosteniuk
Women's Grand Prix,
Monaco 2019
White to move

Very often tactical solutions are associated with a different move order than the one you first expect. An instructive example is how Pia Cramling missed a win against Alexandra Kosteniuk.

30 ♕d4!

In the game followed 30 ♖g3+? ♚h8 31 ♕d4 ♕d8 32 ♕g4 (After *32 ♕h4 ♖g8 33 ♖h3 ♖g7* Black is safe.) 32...♖g8 33 ♖d1 ♕b8 and White didn't achieve anything special. In fact the game ended in a draw after 34 ♕h4 ♕e5 35 ♖xg8+ ♚xg8 36 h3 h5 37 ♕c4 ♖b2 38 g3 ♕f5 39 ♕d4 ♕e5 40 ♚g2 ♚g7 41 ♖d2 ♖b1 42 ♕xe5 fxe5 43 ♖e2 ♚f6.

30...♕d8 31 ♕h4!

Now it's clear why it's so important to move the queen before the b3-rook since White has the additional possibility of moving the rook to h3 with decisive effect. Black has no defence against 32 ♖g3+ ♚h8 33 ♖h3 or the quiet, but killing, 32 ♕h6. In the game Black was helped by the important inclusion of ...♚h8 and ...♖g8 which wouldn't have been possible if White had made the moves in the correct order.

146

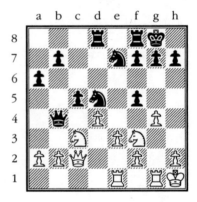

Janowski – Bernstein
Saint Petersburg 1914
Black to move

White has played according to Morphy's plan, which is constructed on the idea of playing the king's rook to g1 (after a preliminary ♚h1) followed by the pawn-push to g4. This was one reason Morphy preferred to place his rooks on f1 and e1. How can Black counter White's intent to open a front against Black's king?

18...cxd4!

(1) After 18...fxg4?! the semi-open g-file is not particularly dangerous but why help the king's rook gain influence on the fourth rank and in the centre? Never help your opponent unnecessarily! A plausible variation is 19 ♖xg4 cxd4 20 ♖eg1 ♘f6! 21 ♖xd4 and White is slightly more active but Black's pawn structure is preferable. But not 21 ♖xg7+? ♔h8 and White has problems meeting the double threat against c3 and ...♘g6 trapping the g7-rook. 21 ♖f4 is answered by 21...♕c5! with a slight advantage to Black.

(2) 18...f4? is a strategic mistake since White can play the pawn to e4 at the right moment. After 19 a3 ♕a5 20 ♘xd5 ♘xd5 21 e4 White's position is slightly preferable.

19 ♘xd4 f4!

After this move the Morphy plan falls flat since the g-file will never be opened. White is now saddled with weaknesses and Bernstein is ready to exploit them with fine technique.

20 ♘f5

Janowski plays the most aggressive move and tries to make as much use of the g4-pawn as he can.

20...fxe3

The correct move order was 20...♘xf5! 21 gxf5 fxe3.

21 fxe3

White should have played 21 ♘xe3!.

21...♘xf5 22 gxf5 ♘xc3 23 bxc3 ♕c4

Tarrasch writes in the tournament book: "White's position now has several weak points and his king is worryingly exposed. One can add that with only major pieces on the board the safety of the king is the most vital factor."

24 e4 ♖d3 25 e5 ♕c6+ 26 ♔g2?!

Better drawing chances were to be found in the double rook ending arising after 26 ♕g2 ♖xc3 27 ♕xc6 ♖xc6.

26...♖fd8 27 ♕f2

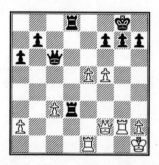

27...♖d2?!

Bernstein missed the decisive 27...♖d1!. When playing with three major pieces one must keep in mind all the relevant files, ranks and diagonals. By playing the front rook to White's first rank Black plans to follow up with the rear rook by 28...♖8d2. Note that Black uses both rooks on the d-file to exercise maximum pressure along the first and second ranks while the queen exerts pressure on the long light-squared diagonal. It's the d8-rook which will deliver the death blow.

Now:

(1) 28.♔g1 ♕xc3 29 ♖f1 ♕a1! and White is defenceless against the threat of 30...♖xf1+ 31 ♕xf1 ♖d1.

(2) 28 ♖eg1 is met by 28...♖xg1+ 29 ♕xg1 (*29 ♔xg1 ♖d1+*) 29...♕f3 and White cannot parry 30...♖d1.

28 ♕g3 ♖xg2 29 ♕xg2 ♕xc3 with a winning position for Black. Bernstein duly forced White's resignation after 39 moves.

147-149: Attack and defence when diagonals are involved

147

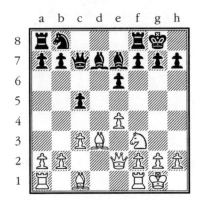

Radjabov – Vachier-Lagrave
World Cup, Khanty-Mansiysk
2019
White to move

This position arose after 1 ♘f3 ♘f6 2 c4 c5 3 ♘c3 d5 4 cxd5 ♘xd5 5 e3 ♘xc3 6 dxc3 ♕c7 7 e4 e6. Here Radjubov played the strong novelty 8 ♗d3!. White has a simple attacking plan in mind. The game continued with the natural moves 8...♗e7 9 ♕e2 ♗d7 10 0–0!. Here I think Vachier-Lagrave was fooled because he would most probably not have considered castling

kingside if White still had the option of playing h2-h4. After 10...0–0, which is probably a mistake, White commenced a strong attack with the indicated but nevertheless strong move...

11 e5!

White plans a battery along the b1-h7 diagonal, with the queen in front on e4, so as to force a weakness in Black's castled position. Therefore Black's next move is practically forced.

11...♗c6

White has four pieces to throw into the attack against Black's king so White's next move suggests itself.

12 ♘g5

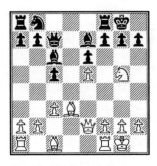

12...h6

12...g6 would have been answered by the knight sacrifice 13 ♘xh7!. Then:

(1) 13...♔xh7? loses to 14 ♕h5+ ♔g8 15 ♗xg6!. The other piece sacrifice prepares the way for White's two remaining attacking pieces to weave a mating net. 15...fxg6 16 ♕xg6+ ♔h8 17 ♕h5+! ♔g8 18 ♗h6! and White wins. An important tactical idea to keep in mind. Note how well the queen

co-operates with the dark-squared bishop.

(2) 13...c4! 14 ♗xg6! fxg6 15 ♘xf8 ♗xf8 16 ♕g4! ♕f7 17 ♕xc4 leaves White with a rook and three pawns for a bishop and knight and therefore the far easier position to play.

13 ♗h7+ ♔h8 14 ♗c2

14 ♗b1!? was probably more precise since White's queen can make use of the c2-square on the next move.

14...c4

Black prevents White's queen from setting up a battery on d3.

15 ♖e1 ♕d8 16 ♘h3 ♕d5 17 ♘f4 ♕c5 18 ♗b1! ♗g5

19 ♘xe6

White plays this logical move but in fact the sacrifice is not the strongest way to continue. White must not forget Black's threat and play 19 ♕c2 g6 20 ♘xe6?? fxe6 21 ♕xg6 ♕xf2+ 22 ♔h1 since then Black can mate in three different ways.

The best continuation, 19 b4! cxb3 (if *19...♕e7* then *20 ♕xc4*) 20 ♕d3 (*20 axb3? ♕xc3*) 20...g6 21 axb3,

would have given Black greater difficulties since White now plays over the whole board, using the Alekhine technique discussed previously. Black must be careful on the kingside but also on the queenside because of moves such as ♗a3 or b2-b4. This is in accordance with the principle of the two weaknesses since Black isn't only weak on the kingside, for example on g6 and e6, but also the queen is exposed on c5 as well as the bishop on c6 after a pawn rush like b4-b5. Stockfish's main variation, eleven moves deep, goes like this: 21...♘d7 22.b4 (Komodo's *22 ♕g3* with the idea of h2-h4 might very well be the strongest.) 22...♕e7 23 b5 ♘c5 24 ♕e2 ♗d7 25 h4 ♗xf4 (*25...♗xh4 26 ♗xg6*) 26 ♗xf4 ♕xh4 27 ♗e3 ♘a4 28 c4 ♘c3 29 ♕d3 ♘xb1 30 ♕xd7 ♘c3 31 ♕xb7 ♕xc4 32 ♗xh6 ♘xb5 33 ♗xf8 and White is winning.

19...fxe6 20 ♗xg5 ♕d5 21 ♕g4 ♘d7

Black had the opportunity to exchange queens by 21...♕xg2+ 22 ♕xg2 ♗xg2 but it would have left Black in a difficult situation after 23 ♔xg2 hxg5 24 ♗g6.

22 ♗e4 ♘xe5 23 ♕h5 ♕b5

The exchange of queens would have led to a catastrophe after the forced sequence 23...♘f3+ 24 ♗xf3 ♕xg5 25 ♕xg5 hxg5 26 ♗xc6 bxc6 27 ♖xe6 when not only is Black a pawn down, he must also play on with five pawn islands versus White's two.

24 ♗xh6 ♗xe4 25 ♗f4+ ♔g8 26 ♕xe5 ♗d5

The best practical chance was to exchange queens at this moment, since 26...♕xe5 27 ♗xe5 would have led to an ending with bishops of opposite colours. White is surely winning but must display good technique and avoid the exchange of all rooks. Black's g-pawn is perfect in Black's defence because it makes it more difficult for White to create a passed pawn. With queens still on the board White's attack will be much more dangerous, since White has effectively an extra piece on the dark squares.

27 ♖e2 ♖f5 28 ♕e3 ♕e8 29 f3

A nice move which eliminates Black's possibilities of attacking White's g2-pawn along the long light-squared diagonal.

29...♕g6 30 h4

White thereby secures an outpost for his bishop on g5.

30...♖af8 31 ♗g5 a6

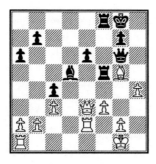

32 ♖d1

Interestingly it took White 32 moves to develop his queen's rook but here it is clear it will do a good job on the g4-square. Note how from now on White manoeuvres all his pieces towards Black's weak pawn on g7.

32...♕e8 33 ♖d4 ♕c6 34 ♖g4 ♔h7 35 ♗f4

The bishop manoeuvres to e5 where it acts in harmony with White's queenside rook.

35...♖8f7 36 ♗e5 ♕b5 37 ♕f2

The queen manoeuvres to g3.

37...♕d7 38 ♕g3 ♖h5 39 ♗d4 ♕c7 40 ♗e5 ♖hf5 41 ♖g5

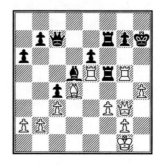

White now has all his pieces on dark squares, which is typical when playing with bishops of opposite colours. Black can do nothing against White's massage of the dark squares nor can he exploit his opponent's light squares, since White has no weaknesses in his position. The pawn on f3 literally kills the bishop as well as the two rooks on the f-file, since it's impossible to sacrifice on f3.

41...♔g8 42 h5

The pawn is on its way to h6 to decide the game, once and for all.

42...♖xg5 43 ♕xg5 ♕e7

An exchange of queens is Black's ultimate dream but it's too late.

44 ♕g4 ♖f5

A blunder but White was threatening ♖g5 followed by h5-h6 against which Black had no effective defence.

45 ♕xf5 Black resigned.

148

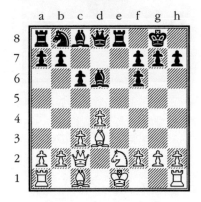

Paehtz – Grandelius
Gibraltar 2018
Black to move

This highly interesting position arises after 1 e4 c6 2 d4 d5 3 ♘d2 dxe4 4 ♘xe4 ♘f6 5 ♘xf6+ exf6 6 c3 ♗d6 7 ♗d3 0–0 8 ♕c2 ♖e8+ 9 ♘e2.

9...h5!?

It may seem strange that Black advances the h-pawn two squares but it's actually been the most popular move since 2017. The customary moves before were 9...g6, 9...h6 and Konstantinopolsky's 9...♔h8!?. Compared to 9...h5 all these moves are more passive. The idea of Konstantinopolsky's clever move is to play according to Steinitz's principles and defend economically by manoeuvring the knight to f8, while at the same time avoiding any pawn weaknesses on the kingside. The other two moves have the obvious drawback that it will be far easier for White to open lines on the kingside after queenside castling. After 9...g6 White can go for h4-h5 while after 9...h6 the pawn break g4-g5 is the dream move.

A relatively recent book by Ivan Sokolov, *Chess Middlegame Strategies – Opening Meets Middlegame*, surprisingly doesn't even mention 9...h5 or 9...♔h8 despite the fact that the book was released during 2018. But then again, maybe it's not so surprising because first of all these moves have not been sanctioned by players from older generations and, secondly, Sokolov only goes back to Wijk aan Zee 1991 when he happened to see 5...exf6 played in a game between Khalifman and Seirawan.

I have always believed in Black's fifth move ever since I was a junior in the 80s and in those days 5...gxf6 was more popular. However, when Viktor Korchnoi played it in the 20th game of his world title match against Karpov in 1978 this was an additional source of inspiration. Korchnoi was ahead of his time and understood that it was possible to play aggressively with 5...exf6 by using the extra pawn available on the kingside. Whether it's the f6-pawn, g7-pawn or the h7-pawn is not important, it's rather the flexibility and dynamic energy inherent in these pawns. Korchnoi advanced all the pawns (except the one on f7) and the f6-pawn landed on f4, the g7-pawn on g3 and the h7-pawn on h4, thereby creating a nice upside-down pyramid.

10 ♗e3

White plans queenside castling but the drawback is that the bishop can easily be attacked by the knight in the future. 10.0-0 has been played in several high level games but then Black just continues with the advance of the h-pawn. After 10...h4 Black prevents White from placing a knight on g3 while White must consider whether or not to stop ...h4-h3. Such annoying little problems for White show why this variation has practical value, since he must take his time and decide how to react against the saucy h-pawn.

10...♘d7 11 ♘g3 ♘b6

11...h4?! is met by 12 ♘f5.

12.0–0–0

12 ♘xh5?! would give Black the slightly better game after 12...♘d5.

12...h4 13 ♘e4 ♘d5 14 ♖de1 ♘f4 15 ♗xf4 ♗xf4+ 16 ♔b1 f5 17 ♘c5 b6

Black can be happy with his choice of opening since he has secured the bishop pair. The position is roughly equal but in fact the very promising Swedish grandmaster went on to win after 47 moves.

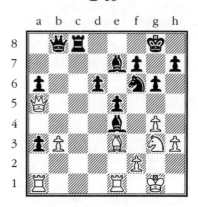

Carlsen – Ding Liren
Game 2, Blitz Final,
Sinquefield Cup 2019
Black to move

32 g5

A less risky alternative was to eliminate Black's most dangerous bishop. 32 ♘xe4 ♘xe4 33 ♕xa3 would have led to a position with mutual chances.

32...♗a8! 33 ♕xa6??

White wants to prevent Black from doubling up the queen with the bishop on the h1-a8 diagonal. Correct was to accept the piece sacrifice and after 33 gxf6 ♕b7 34 ♔f1 ♕g2+ 35 ♔e2 ♕f3+...

(1) Not 36 ♔d2?? ♗d8 which forces White's queen to give up the d5-square with decisive effect, for example 37 ♕xa3 ♕d5+ 38 ♔e2 ♖c2+ mating in two moves.

(2) But 36 ♔f1 ♕g2+ and Black only has a draw by a perpetual check.

33...♘d5 34 ♗a7

If White tries to exchange queens Black can neatly avoid it by using the fourth rank as a springboard to the kingside: 34 ♕a7 ♕b4!? 35 ♕xa3 (*35 ♕a4 ♕b7!*) 35...♕h4!.

34...♕c7 35 ♖ec1

Carlsen wants to prevent Black playing his queen to d7 with pressure on the h3-pawn.

35...♕xc1+?

Stronger was 35...♗c6 and White doesn't have much else against the decisive queen manoeuvre to d7 than to sacrifice the exchange on c6 – but then Black wins with his extra pawns.

36 ♖xc1 ♖xc1+ 37 ♔h2 ♗c6 38 ♕xa3 ♗xg5

39 ♕xd6??

It was necessary to play 39 ♘e2 to control the f4-square and only after 39...♖e1 play 40 ♕xd6.

39...♗f4

Black is now threatening a knight move followed by ...♖h1 mate.

40 ♗c5

40 f3 loses the knight after 40...♖c2+ 41 ♔g1 ♗xg3.

40...♘e7! White resigned.

A very nice defensive move to conclude the game in Black's favour. It stops the mate while setting up a mate threat himself that is impossible to parry. All this happened in a blitz game which makes it very impressive indeed. I actually watched this live and the tension and drama for all chess players sharing this moment was unforgettable.

150: Counterattack or Prophylaxis?

150

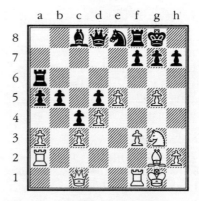

Anand – Carlsen
Game 9, World Championship,
Chennai 2013
Black to move

Black has to consider a delicate problem. Should the pawn push f4-f5 be allowed, while playing for the break ...b5-b4 as quickly as possible, or should it be prevented at all cost?

18...♘c7!?

Carlsen plays a cold-blooded move which requires precise

calculation since the position is very sensitive in terms of tempi due to the respective pawn masses marching forward. Understandably, Carlsen was worried how events might turn out, as he admitted during the post game press conference.

The normal move, in the spirit of Nimzowitsch, is 18...g6 with the plan ...♞g7 to stop the pawn march to f5. Then later Black can blockade the pawn with ...♞f5. The objective of such play is to destroy the white pawn majority, but the drawback is the weaknesses created on f6 and h6. Nothing is for free in chess – not even playing in accordance with Nimzowitsch's clever principles!

If Black tries an immediate blockade with 18...f5? White will obtain the clearly better position after the continuation 19 gxf6 gxf6 20 f4 f5 21 ♖b2 ♖b6 (*21...♞c7 22 ♞h5!*) 22 ♕d2 followed by ♖fb1 with positional pressure on b5, d5 and f6.

A serious option though was 18...b4 19.axb4 axb4 20.♖xa6 ♝xa6 21.cxb4 ♕b6 22.♕c3 ♞c7 with counterplay and an entirely different game.

19 f4 b4 20 axb4

Nakamura's suggestion 20 a4 avoids the opening of the a-file as well as preventing the knight manoeuvre to b5. However, Komodo calculates that Black is slightly better after 20...♖b6. The most precise was probably 20 f5 after which White's queen's rook could provide support from f2. Such a position would be very tense and in a state of dynamic equilibrium.

20...axb4 21 ♖xa6 ♞xa6 22 f5?

22 cxb4 ♞xb4 23 f5 should have been played, even though Black would land an annoying knight on the nice d3 outpost.

22...b3!

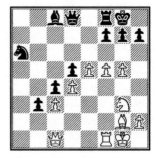

23 ♕f4?

Anand chooses to attack Black's king with pieces. Speelman advises a pawn storm instead: 23.h4 ♕a5 (*23...♞c7!*) 24 h5 ♞c7 25 h6 with the idea 25...g6? (*25...♞e8!*) 26 e6 and Black has huge difficulties. A difficult decision often has to be made in practical chess whether it's best to attack with pieces or pawns, since a lot of calculation is required in both types of attack.

23...♞c7 24 f6 g6?

24...gxf6 25 gxf6 ♚h8 was a better defensive option since Black will secure counterplay on the g-file. Now it is only the b3-pawn that is the objective of Black's offensive.

25 ♕h4 ♞e8

Not the routine 25...♚h8?? which loses quickly to 26 ♕h6 ♞e6 27 ♖f4! and 28 ♖h4.

26 ♕h6 b2 27 ♖f4! b1♕+

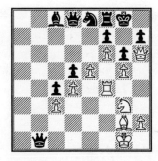

28 ♘f1??

It was necessary to enter the forced continuation 28 ♗f1 ♕d1 29 ♖h4 ♕h5 30 ♘xh5 gxh5 31 ♖xh5 ♗f5. Speelman analyses 32 g6 (After *32 ♗h3?! ♗g6 33 e6 ♘xf6! 34 gxf6 ♕xf6 35 ♖f5! ♕xe6* White doesn't have enough compensation for the pawn and his king is rather unsafe after a later *...♖a8* or *...♖b8*.) 32...♗xg6 33 ♖g5 (with the idea of h4-h5) 33...♘xf6 The knight on e8 is undoubtedly the hero of the day, not only has it covered the weak g7 square but now it even sacrifices itself for the annoying f6-pawn(s). 34 exf6 ♕xf6 35 ♖xd5 (*35 h4?* doesn't work here because the central files are opened and Black can reply *35...♖e8* threatening *...♖e1*.) 35...♕f3 36 ♖c5 ♕xc3 37 ♕f4 and the position is roughly equal even though White's king's position is not as well protected as Black's.

28...♕e1! White resigned.

Anand had forgotten this move and was mainly analysing 28...♕d1 29 ♖h4 ♕h5 30 ♖xh5 gxh5 31 ♘e3 ♗e6 32 ♗xd5! ♕xd5 (*32...♗xd5 33.♘f5*) 33 ♘xd5 ♗xd5 34 ♔f2 winning, since Black is in zugzwang and cannot prevent the advance of the enemy king to c5 followed by a pawn-push to d5.

This game showed that Magnus Carlsen played like a computer and brought the world title match to a logical conclusion which resulted in the crowning of a new champion. Even today (2020) without any doubt whatsoever he is the best player in the world and will probably remain so for quite some time to come.

Part 2:

150 most important tactical positions in the Endgame

151-168: Pawn Endings

The special features of pawn endings mean that they require precise calculation. The most common tactical themes are pawn races (transitions to queen endings), passed pawns, breakthroughs or stalemates.

151

Polerio/Balashov/Prandstetter
Basic Endgames 1992
White to move

1 c5!

Don't forget the well-known manoeuvre 1 ♔g5? ♔g3! 2 ♔xh5 ♔f4 and Black's king is inside the square of the pawn. It's easy to make the human mistake of thinking that Black should play his king to f3

instead of g3 since it's the quickest way to the white passed pawn.

1...h4 2 c6 h3 3 c7 h2 4 c8♕ h1♕

This position is winning as Polerio (1550-1610) discovered during the second half of the sixteenth century and which he demonstrated in a study from 1590. In accordance with Polerio's method White progressively approaches Black's king step by step. With Black's queen in the corner there is a forced mate if White's king is near enough and controls the key square g3.

5 ♕c2+

5 ♕g4+? ♔f2 and Black's king escapes.

5...♔f1

Or 5...♔h3 6 ♕d3+ ♔g2 7 ♕e2+ ♔h3 8 ♕g4+ ♔h2 9 ♕g3 mate.

6 ♕d1+ ♔g2 7 ♕e2+ ♔g1 8 ♔g3 ♕f3+

A last trick.

9 ♔xf3 Black resigned.

Now try Polerios's winning method by placing the white king on e3 instead of f4. This actually makes it easier since the key square is f2 and the queen can approach the enemy king faster by using the diagonal.

152

Selezniev
1930
White to move

This kind of position is normally lost, but by playing aggressively with the a-pawn White can, in this particular case, play for a stalemate by a method that is useful to know in practical play.

1 a5!

1 ♔c4? a6 eventually leads to the loss of the a-pawn which is too far advanced.

1...b5 2 a6!

White not only prevents Black from playing ...a7-a6 but also secures the a5 square for his king.

2...♔d5 3 ♔b4 ♔c6 4 ♔a5 ♔c5
Draw.

White is stalemated. Don't forget this pattern. Obviously 4...b4 5 ♔xb4 ♔b6 is an elementary draw.

153

Prokes
1944
White to move

Considering that White has the far more active king it seems he can win any way he wants but in reality only one narrow path secures victory.

1 ♔f6!

(1) 1 ♔f7? loses half a point due to 1...♔h7. For example after 2 g4 g5 3 ♔f6 Black secures the draw with the finesse 3...h5!. After the further 4 ♔xg5 hxg4 5 hxg4 ♔g7 Black holds the opposition with an easy draw.

(2) 1 g4? is also a mistake as if 1...g5 2 ♔f7 ♔h7! (Beware, don't play 2...h5? which loses after 3 h4!!.) 3 ♔f6 then 3...h5! and we come to the same position as in the 1 ♔f7? Line.

(3) After 1 h4? h5! White is unable to win.

1...♔h7 2 g4! g5 3 ♔f7 h5

With the king on f7 instead of f6 White has the surprise move **4 h4!!**

177

This tactical finesse is important to know in this kind of pawn ending. If you have seen it once you'll never forget it.

154

Kok
1935
White to move

1 ♔b5 ♔h4

If Black plays for stalemate with 1...a4 2 ♔xa4 ♔h4 3 ♔b3 ♔g3 4 g5 ♔xf3 5 g6 ♔e2 6 g7 f3 7 g8♕ f2 8 ♕g2 ♔e1 9 ♔c3 White's king is too close to the key square d2 and can deliver mate after 9...f1♕ 10 ♕d2 mate.

2 ♔a4!!

Instead 2 ♔xa5 ♔g3 3 g5 ♔xf3 4 g6 ♔e2 5 g7 f3 6 g8♕ f2 is a theoretical draw since White's king is too far away to create a mating net. Compare this with the continuation after 1...a4. A plausible continuation is 7 ♕c4+ (In the variation *7 ♕g2 ♔e1* it's easy to see that White would win with the king on b4 but now the king is one step away.) 7...♔e1 8 ♕e4+ ♔f1 9 ♔b4 ♔g1 10 ♕g4+ ♔h2 11 ♕f3 ♔g1 12 ♕g3+ ♔h1! 13 ♕xf2 stalemate.

2...♔g5

After 2...♔g3 3 g5 ♔xf3 4 g6 ♔e2 5 g7 f3 6 g8♕ f2 White doesn't need to worry about stalemate so White can approach Black's king and f-pawn with his queen and king. 7 ♕c4+ ♔e1 8 ♕e4+ ♔f1 9 ♔b3 a4+ 10 ♔c2 White obviously ignores the a-pawn which is White's ticket to a win. 10...a3 11 ♔d2 ♔g1 (11...a2 12 ♕h1 mate.) 12 ♕g4+ ♔h2 13 ♔e2 etc.

3 ♔xa5

Now is the right moment to capture the pawn.

3...♔h4 4 ♔b4 ♔g3 5 g5 ♔xf3 6 g6 ♔e2 7 g7 f3 8 g8♕ f2 9 ♕g2 ♔e1 10 ♔c3! f1♕ 11 ♕d2 mate.

155

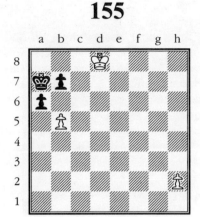

Joseph
British Chess Magazine 1922
White to move

This pawn ending looks very simple but Black has a stalemate resource which demands precise play for White to win.

1 b6+!

(1) 1 h4? axb5 leads nowhere. The key is to force Black to be left with a rook pawn.

(2) 1 bxa6?? even loses due to the eventual skewer on b8 after 1...b5.

1...♔b8!

Black plays for a stalemate. 1...♔xb6? 2 h4 and White wins the pawn race because after promotion the queen will control a1. A very important geometrical idea when there is pawn race between rook pawns.

2 h4 a5 3 h5 a4 4 h6 a3 5 h7 a2 6 h8♕

Obviously 6 h8♗? a1♕ 7 ♗xa1 is a draw since it's impossible to force the black king out of the corner.

6...a1♕ 7 ♕g8!

(1) 7 ♕xa1? is stalemate so the trick to win is to reach the position with the black king on a8.

(2) 7 ♕e8? fails to the clever 7...♕g7!! and White's king, as well as the queen, is unable to move along the eighth rank.

(3) 7 ♕f8? doesn't work either due to 7...♕a3! and a check will follow on d6 followed by the capture of the b6-pawn.

7...♕a2 8 ♕e8!

White exploits the fact that any queen check on the d-file fails to 9 ♔e7+.

8...♕a4 9 ♕e5+ ♔a8 10 ♕h8!

The geometry is very beautiful.

10...♕f4 11 ♔d7+ ♕b8 12 ♕a1+

and White mates next move.

156

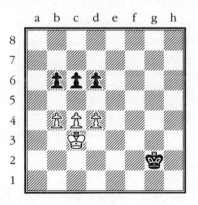

Kok
1939
White to move

Here it's not possible to win by an immediate breakthrough since Black has intermediate moves. White must prepare the breakthrough by first moving the king, but only one square is correct.

1 ♔d2!!

1 ♔d3? fails to 1...♔f3 2 c5 bxc5! 3 d5 cxd5 4 b5 c4+ 5 ♔d4 c3! with a draw since Black gets counterplay with his pawns at the right time. After 6 ♔xc3 ♔e3 7 ♔c2 ♔e2 8 ♔c3 ♔e3 9 b6 d4+ 10 ♔c2 ♔e2 11 b7 d3+ 12 ♔c3 d2 13 b8♕ d1♕ 14 ♕e8+ it's an easy draw.

1...♔f3

1...c5 doesn't help either after 2 bxc5 bxc5 3 dxc5 dxc5 4 ♔e3 with an easy win.

2 c5!

At least two pieces are needed for a combination to work so how is this combination possible when White has three pawns in a symmetrical position?

2...bxc5

2...dxc5 3 b5! cxb5 4 d5 makes no difference.

3 d5!

By creating double tensions White ensures himself that one of the other two pawns promotes by force, since Black's king is outside the square while White's is not.

3...cxd5 4 b5

Compare this variation with 1 ♔d3? where Black had a vital check on c4. This fact alone decides the battle of tempi. Black is one tempo short after...

4...c4 5 b6 c3+ 6 ♔xc3 ♔e3 7 b7 d4+ 8 ♔c2 ♔e2 9 b8♕ d3+ 10 ♔c3 and **White wins**.

157

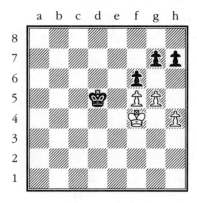

Chigorin – Tarrasch
Ostende 1905
White to move

Chigorin played like he thought the position was lost and we can assume that many other strong players might make the same incorrect assessment, but here there is an important tactical stalemate trick to remember.

1 ♔g4

Chigorin played the fatal 1 gxf6?? gxf6 2 ♔g4 ♔e4 3 ♔h3 ♔f4 and resigned since both pawns are lost.

1...♔e4 2 g6! h6

2...hxg6 3 fxg6 f5+ 4 ♔g5 f4 5 h5 f3 6 h6 leads to a draw in the forthcoming queen ending.

3 ♔h5

The position is a draw since there is no way for Black to repeal the stalemate by manoeuvring the king. White plays his king between h5-g4 and eventually Black must play **3...♔xf5** with a **draw**.

The stalemate is similar to the one we saw in the study by Selezniev, position 152. Don't forget such stalemate ideas where you put your own king in prison to avoid a loss. Sometimes chess isn't like real life!

158

Mitrofanov
Commendation, Vecherni,
Leningrad 1971
White to move

1 ♔f8!

It's vital to place the king on this square as will be clear when Black promotes on the white f1-square.

1...f3

1...♔h7 2 h5 f3 3 h6 g6 4 ♔f7 gxf5 5 g6+ ♔xh6 6 g7 f2 7 g8♕ f1♕ 8 ♕g6 mate.

2 f6!

This sacrifice is mandatory in order to avoid a future queen check on f5.

2...exf6 3 g6 f2 4 h5 f1♕ 5 h6 Black resigned.

A beautiful finish where Black cannot avoid mate since his queen cannot reach the relevant dark squares.

159

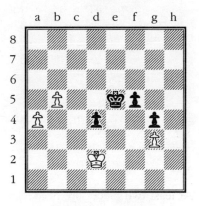

Stoltz – Nimzowitsch
Berlin 1928
Black to move

Stoltz had allowed a fatal exchange of his rook on d2 and reached a lost pawn ending.

52...f4 53.gxf4+ ♔d6!

A nice finesse by Nimzowitsch exploiting the fact that two passed pawns, with two squares between them, outfox two connected passed pawns.

Stoltz must have forgotten about this intermediate move which keeps the far advanced b-pawn under surveillance.

54 a5 g3 55 a6 ♔c7 56 ♔e2 d3+ 57 ♔xd3 g2 58 ♔e4 g1♕ 59 ♔f5 ♕b6 60 ♔g5 ♔d7 61 f5 ♔e7 White resigned.

160

Fine
Basic Chess Endings 1941
White to move

Is the tempo important in this position? According to Fine the position is winning so let's check if that is correct.

1 ♔e2!

It's also possible to play 1 ♔e1! since the key to the win lies in the fact that the king must be placed on g3 or g2 at the right moment in order to block the pawns. Surprisingly, the natural 1 a4? only leads to a draw after the plausible variation 1...h5 2 a5 ♔d7 3 a6 ♔c6 4 b4 ♔b6 5 b5 h4 6 ♔e2 h3 7 ♔f3 g5 8 ♔g3 g4 9 ♔h2!! ♔a7!!. Note that the natural 10 c4? loses after 10...f5 11 ♔g3 ♔b6 12 c5+ ♔a7 13 c6 ♔b6 and Black has blockaded all the pawns whereas White hasn't since it's his turn to move. After the further 14 ♔h2 f4 15 ♔g1 g3 Black wins. The player who manages to get all the pawns to the sixth rank is the winner in this type of ending.

1...♔d7 2 ♔f3 ♔c6 3 a4!

This is the principled move for White to play for a win. It takes a while for the computer to calculate 13 moves ahead and conclude that it is indeed a win. As a matter of a fact 3 ♔g4 also wins after 3...♔b5 4 b3! ♔b4 5 a4 g6 6 c4 (Despite the fact that White has gained a tempo he loses after symmetrical play: *6 ♔g5 h5 7 c3+ ♔a5! 8 c4 f6+ 9 ♔h4 f5! 10 ♔g3 ♔b4* and, compared to Black, White's options are limited.) 6...h5+ 7 ♔h4 f6 8 ♔h3! g5 9 ♔g3 f5 10 ♔g2!!. This is the key position to remember

...because here it's apparent that Black will reach a "zugzwang" after 10...h4 11 ♔h3 f4 12 ♔g4 and White wins.

3...h5 4 c4 f5 5 ♔g3!

5 ♔g2! wins too.

5...♔b6 6 b4 g6

Fine gives 6...g5 as the main line which ends with a mate. I think the variation I have chosen is more appropriate for the main line since it shows the important zugzwang position to remember, so the variations have been shifted compared to *Basic Chess Endings*.

7 a5+ ♔a6 (*7...♔b7 8 c5*) 8 c5 h4+
9 ♔h3 f4 (*9...♔b5 10 ♔h2!!* and
White wins.) 10 c6 f3 11 b5+ ♔a7
12 c7 g4+ (*12...♔b7 13 b6 g4+
14 ♔h2 g3+ 15 ♔g1 h3 16 a6+ ♔c8
17 a7*) 13 ♔xg4 f2 14 c8♕ f1♕
15 b6 mate.

7 a5+ ♔a6 8 c5 ♔b5 9 ♔g2 g5

Or 9...h4 10 ♔h2 f4 11 ♔g1!! g5
12 ♔g2 g4 13 ♔g1!!.

**10 ♔g3 g4 11 ♔f2 f4 12 ♔g2 h4
13 ♔g1!!**

The key position to remember!

It seems that White has problems
since Black's pawns are more
advanced, but as long as they don't
reach the third rank there is no
danger.

13...f3 14 ♔f2 h3 15 ♔g3 and
White wins.

Black cannot prevent the pawns
from reaching the third rank. An
incredible pawn ending which
primarily shows the value of
activating the king before doing so
with the pawns. It's important to
have a 100 percent understanding of
the key positions otherwise a won
position can turn into one that is lost.
This ending is difficult to solve but
once you are familiar with the

solution and its key positions there
shouldn't be any problems. This is
best done with the help of regular
reviews.

161

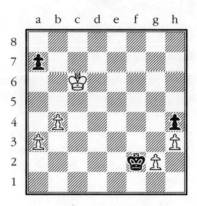

Mandler – Prochazka
Austria 1924
White to move

1 ♔d5!

1 ♔b7? ♔xg2 2 ♔xa7 ♔xh3 3 b5
♔g4! 4 b6 h3 5 b7 h2 6 b8♕ h1♕
leads to a queen ending in which
Black has good drawing chances.

**1...♔xg2 2 ♔e4 ♔xh3 3 ♔f3 ♔h2
4 ♔f2!!**

Superficially, 4 b5? looks like a
win but after 4...♔g1 5 ♔g4 ♔g2!!
it's a draw: 6 ♔xh4 ♔f3 7 a4 ♔e4
8 a5 ♔d5 9 b6 ♔c6 and Black's king
is inside the square of the a-pawn.

4...h3

4...♔h3 loses since Black's king
isn't inside the square of the a-pawn.
White queens after 5 b5 ♔g4 6 a4
♔f5 7 a5 ♔e6 8 b6 axb6 9 a6!.

5 b5 ♔h1 6 ♔f1 h2 7 b6!

A beautiful move. The natural 7.a4? leads to a draw after 7...a5.

7...a5

7...axb6 8 a4 b5 9 a5! b4 10 a6 b3 11 a7 b2 12 a8♗ mate.

8 b7 a4 9 ♔e2!!

An ingenious king move.

9...♔g1 10 b8♕ h1♕

The queen ending is winning according to Polerio's method as discussed in position 1.

11 ♕b6+ ♔h2 12 ♕d6+ ♔h3 13 ♕h6+ ♔g2 14 ♕g5+ ♔h3 15 ♕h5+ ♔g2 16 ♕g4+ ♔h2 17 ♔f2 ♕f3+ 18 ♔xf3 ♔h1 19 ♕g2 mate.

A very beautiful pawn/queen ending which involved several important tactical ideas.

162

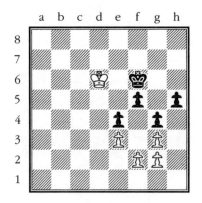

Pomar – Cuadras
Olot 1972
Black to move

When in possession of a qualitative pawn majority, that is pawns that are more actively placed than the opponent's on the same wing and in a symmetrical position, one must always look for possibilities of a breakthrough. The most famous position is the following where Black played the seemingly impossible move...

42...f4!!

Compare this move with Kok's study, position 156, where White had three pawns versus three and decided the game by sacrificing two pawns. This position is more spectacular since one pawn is sacrificed seemingly for no reason, but it's the same mechanism as in the study by Kok. Black tries to displace White's pawns so that one of his own pawns will become a deadly passer.

43 ♔d5

(1) 43 exf4 h4! 44 gxh4 g3! 45 fxg3 e3 and Black's last pawn promotes. Three pawns were sacrificed: one to displace the e3-pawn, one to displace the g3-pawn and lastly one to displace the f2-pawn.

(2) 43 gxf4 h4 and Black promotes on h1.

43...h4!!

Also 43...f3 44.gxf3 h4! 45.gxh4 g3!! (*45...exf3?? 46 ♔e4! and White wins.*) 46 fxg3 exf3 wins but the game continuation is more beautiful since maximum tension is maintained between the pawns.

44 ♔xe4

White has to stop the h-pawn but 44 gxh4 is answered by 44...g3 45 fxg3 fxe3 or 45...f3.

44...f3!

The purpose of this pawn thrust is to deny the white king access to the f3-square in order to avoid the following variation: 44...h3?? 45 gxh3 gxh3 46 ♔f3! and White contains the h-pawn.

45 gxf3 h3 46 fxg4 h2 47 f3 h1♕ 48 ♔f4 ♕h6+ 49 ♔e4 ♕g5 50 ♔d4 ♕e5+ White resigned.

163

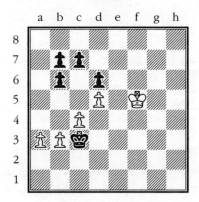

Schlechter – Marco
Vienna 1893
White to move

It seems incredible that White can save this position since he looks in really bad shape. Black appears to be way ahead in time and will collect the pawns on b3, c4 and d5 – yet the position is still a draw! The variation is not so difficult to calculate but it's vital to get acquainted with a particular finesse at the end.

52 ♔e6 ♔xb3 53 ♔d7 ♔xc4 54 ♔xc7 ♔xd5

Black has now captured all the pawns and White is ready to take his second pawn. The game continued:

55 ♔xb6

55 ♔xb7 ♔c5 obviously loses.

55...♔c4 56 ♔xb7 d5 57 a4 ♔b4

Here Black contains the a-pawn whereas White's king is outside the square of the pawn. It's still a draw though.

58 ♔b6! Draw.

This is the idea which is so important to know and which can be found in a most elegant study by Réti. It can be found in *300 Most Important Chess Positions*, position 158. Réti is said to have been inspired by this actual endgame when he constructed his immortal study. White plans to support his a-pawn and if Black captures it White's king is in time to reach the square of the passed pawn. The miracle has been achieved! Note that this idea can also be found in positions 151 and 161.

164

Kosteniuk – Savina
EC Rapid Chess,
Monte Carlo 2019
White to move

If White has a more active king on the fourth rank it usually pays to find invasion squares on the fifth with the help of a pawn sacrifice. An elementary but instructive example is the following where Kosteniuk played **43 a5!** with the idea of weakening the c5-square. Of course the fatal placement of the a6-pawn helps White in this specific case.

43...bxa5 44 ♔c5 a4

45 ♔c6!

A nice waiting move, which keeps open the option of whether to attack the f5-pawn or the a-pawns. A simple calculation produces the result that it takes White nine moves to pick up the a-pawns, including promotion, and that it takes Black eight moves to pick up the f-pawn, including promotion. It looks like both promote at the same time and this is correct if White goes for the a6-pawn: 45 ♔b6? ♔d5 46 ♔xa6 ♔e4 47 ♔a5 ♔xf4 48 ♔xa4 ♔e3 49 b4 f4 50 b5 f3 51 b6 f2 52 b7 f1♕ 53 b8♕ Both have queens on the board but White's king is badly placed on a4 and this can be exploited by 53...♕a1+ followed by a decisive skewer. However, if White picks up the a4-pawn first and then the a6-pawn, Black promotes

with a check on f1: 45 ♔b4?? ♔d5 46 ♔xa4 ♔e4 47 ♔a5 ♔xf4 48 ♔xa6 ♔e4 49 b4 f4 50 b5 f3 51 b6 f2 52 b7 f1♕+.

A general conclusion after looking at these two variations is that it's vital to check very carefully how the kings are placed after you have calculated who promoted first and who is to move when both have promoted. Here Tisdall's stepping stones, as discussed in the middlegame section, come to mind, since it's vital to focus on the position after promotion during your calculation process.

45...♔f7 46 ♔d5 ♔f6 47 ♔d6 a5 48 ♔d5 ♔f7

Black's pawn moves are finished so White's king can successively approach the f5-pawn and decide the game.

49 ♔e5 ♔e7 50 ♔xf5 ♔d6 51 ♔g6 ♔d5 52 f5 ♔c4 53 f6 Black resigned.

165

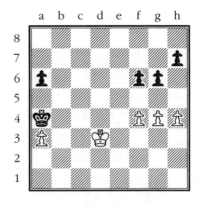

Van Doesburg – Maroczy
Zandvoort 1936
White to move

186

This pawn ending looks clearly lost for White but with the help of clever tactics White can save the position.

42 ♔e4 ♔xa3 43 f5! gxf5+

Otherwise White plays 44 fxg6 hxg6 45 h5 and establishes a passed pawn on the kingside.

44 ♔xf5 a5 45 ♔xf6 a4 46 ♔g7!

46 g5 ♔b4 47 h5?? (*47 ♔g7 is correct transposing to the game.*) loses after 47...a3 48 g6 hxg6 49 hxg6 a2 50 g7 a1♛+ with an elementary win.

46...♔b4 47 ♔xh7 a3 48 g5 a2 49 g6 a1♛

Black queens first but it's still a draw due to a tactical finesse.

50 g7 ♛a7 51 ♔h8

51 h5 followed by 52 h6 is a draw as well.

51...♛d4 52 h5 ♛f6 53 ♔h7 ♛f5+ 54 ♔h6!

The key move to save the ending.

54...♛f6+

54...♛f7 55 g8♛! ♛xg8 leads to stalemate and is the tactical finesse that White is relying on in this ending.

55 ♔h7 ♛f5+ 56 ♔h6 ♛e6+ 57 ♔h7 ♛f7 58 h6 ♔c5 59 ♔h8 ♛g6 60 g8♛ ♛xh6+ 61 ♛h7 ♛xh7+ 62 ♔xh7 Draw.

166

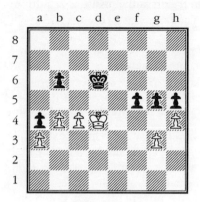

Réti – Barász
Hungary 1907
Black to move

It looks like Black is lost because of White's more active king but Black can save himself in a miraculous way.

41...g4!

In the game the fatal 41...gxh4? was played. White won after 42 gxh4 ♔e6 43 c5 bxc5+ 44 ♔xc5 f4 45 ♔d4 ♔f5 46 b5 f3 47 ♔e3 f2 48 ♔xf2 ♔e5 49 ♔f3 ♔d5 50 ♔f4 ♔c5 51 ♔g5 ♔xb5 52 ♔xh5 ♔c4 53 ♔g4 ♔b3 54 h5 ♔xa3 55 h6 ♔b2 56 h7 a3 57 h8♛+ ♔b1 58 ♛b8+ ♔a1 59 ♛e5+ ♔b1 60 ♛e1+ ♔b2 61 ♛b4+ Black resigned.

42 ♔d3!

White's goal is to place the king on d4 when it's Black to move with the king on d6. A mistake is 42 c5+? bxc5+ 43 bxc5+ ♔c6 44 ♔e5 ♔xc5 45 ♔xf5 ♔c4 and Black wins.

42...♔e6! 43 ♔d2 ♔f6 44 ♔e2 ♔e6 45 ♔d3 ♔d6 46 ♔d4

White has achieved his goal but nevertheless the position is a draw..

46...♔e6 47 c5 bxc5+ 48 bxc5 f4!!

This idea is the main point in Black's defence.

49 gxf4 g3 50 ♔e3 ♔d5 51 ♔f3 ♔xc5 52 ♔xg3 ♔d5! 53 ♔f3 ♔d4!

In this position White's extra pawn is irrelevant since White cannot reach the central square e4. Don't forget this important defensive idea when you are a pawn down in a pawn ending!

167

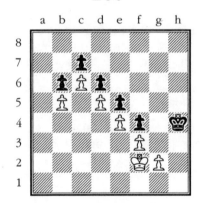

Horwitz
1851
White to move

1 g3+!

This tactical idea is the main theme up to move 10.

1...fxg3+

1...♔g5 doesn't stop White's plan to expand with his pawns. White's simplest continuation is 2 gxf4+ ♔xf4 3 ♔e2 ♔g5 4 ♔e3 followed by f4.

2 ♔g2 ♔h5 3 ♔xg3 ♔g5 4 f4+! exf4+ **5 ♔f3 ♔g6 6 ♔xf4 ♔f6 7 e5+! dxe5+ 8♔e4 ♔f7 9 ♔xe5 ♔e7 10 d6+! cxd6+ 11 ♔d5 ♔e8 12 ♔xd6 ♔d8 13 c7+ ♔c8 14 ♔e6!**

Obviously not 14 ♔c6 which is stalemate but all other available king moves win.

14...♔xc7 15 ♔e7

White wins the b6-pawn by force.

15...♔c8 16 ♔d6 ♔b7 17 ♔d7 ♔b8 18 ♔c6 ♔a7 19 ♔c7 ♔a8 20 ♔xb6 ♔b8 21 ♔a6!

21 ♔c6?! forces White to repeat the position after 21...♔a7! 22 ♔c7 (22 b6+?? ♔a8 is a well-known stalemate trap when the knight pawn is involved.) 22...♔a8 23 ♔b6 ♔b8 24 ♔a6!.

21...♔a8 22 b6 ♔b8 23 b7 ♔c7 24 ♔a7 Black resigned.

168

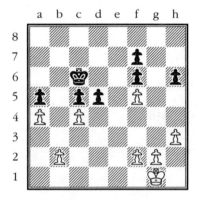

Capablanca – Condé
Hastings 1919
White to move

Capablanca played the cool move **32 b3!** obviously well aware that the seemingly strong **32...d4** was nothing to fear since White can create two distant passed pawns against two passed pawns which White easily contains with his king.

33 f4

White controls the e5-square and eventually prepares the break g4-g5 with g4 and h4 to establish a passed pawn on the kingside.

33...♔d6 34 g4 ♔e7 35 ♔f2 ♔d6 36 ♔f3 ♔e7 37 ♔e4 ♔d6 38 h4 ♔d7 39 b4!

This nice break secures White a passed pawn on the queenside.

39...axb4 40 a5 ♔c7 41 g5 fxg5 42 fxg5 hxg5 43 hxg5 ♔d7 44 g6 fxg6 45 fxg6 Black resigned.

Black is powerless against the two white passed pawns standing far away from each other. Compare these pawns with the black pawns White contains with his king. This is a more advanced example than Stoltz – Nimzowitsch, Bled 1931, position 159.

169-180: Knight Endings

Knight endings are unique and a good general rule is to think the same way as Botvinnik in that they are similar to pawn endings. Apart from the fork which makes a very strong impression in the first study by Ban/Benkö (6...♘c6!!) it's very much a matter of understanding the range of the knight, both its strength (for example, position 176) as well as its limitations (171, 173 and 177). Another common theme is seen in position 175 which must be considered one of the most beautiful breakthroughs ever played in a knight ending.

169

Ban/Benkö
1st Prize, *Tipografia* 1961
White to move

White's only chance to play for a win is to advance the pawns as far as possible before Black can blockade them, but is it enough to win?

1 d5 ♘f6 2 d6 ♔g7!

2...♔xh5? would lose control of the pawns after 3 g7 ♔g6 4 d7. However 2...♘xh5! works as will be clear after 3 d7 ♘f4+ 4 ♔g4 ♘e6 5 ♔f5 ♘d8 6 ♔f6

6...♘c6!! This knight really is a hero since it can also help in preventing the promotion of the g-pawn: 7 g7 ♔h7 8 ♔f7 ♘e5+ (Any other check will not work since after *8...♘d8+? 9 ♔e7 ♘c6+ 10 ♔f8* one of the pawns promotes. The principle of centralisation is still valid.) 9 ♔f8 ♘xd7+ What a super knight!

3 ♔h2!!

White's king must remain out of range of the super knight which explains this odd king move. Black nevertheless holds if he plays precisely. 3 ♔g2? makes Black's task too easy after 3...♘xh5 4 d7 ♘f4+ 5 ♔f3 ♘e6.

3...♔f8!!

190

The natural move 3...♔h6? fails to the extraordinary continuation 4 ♔g1! ♔g7 5 ♔f1! ♔h6 6 ♔e1 ♔g7 7 ♔d1 ♔h6 8 ♔c2. This square isn't mined! 8...♔g7 9 ♔b2! (White must be careful, not *9 ♔b3? ♘e4 10 d7 ♘c5+*) 9...♔h6 10 ♔a3 ♔g7 11 ♔b4! and White wins the knight by manoeuvring the king to c6 followed by playing d6-d7.

The important thing to learn from this position is that it's important to keep out of range of the knight wherever the king is on the board. This is something to be aware of in all phases of the game.

4 h6

White's h-pawn was doomed after Black's seemingly passive move.

4...♘g4+ 5 ♔g3 ♘xh6 6 ♔f4 ♔e8

The position is obviously a draw since both pawns are under Black's control. What is fascinating about this study is that the composers involved in it for a long time thought it was winning for White, yet there are even two ways for Black to hold the draw!

The knight is a very underestimated piece indeed. If skilful study composers can underestimate it and overlook defensive tactical possibilities then we can imagine how many mistakes are made by chess players over the board. Many games can be won just by strong tactical alertness and awareness of the knight's tactical abilities.

170

Benkö
Magyar Sakkelet 1989
White to move

1 ♔c8!

1 ♔c7? is a mistake due to 1...♔e7! 2 ♔c6 ♔e6 and White cannot hold the g-pawn.

1...♔f8

1...♔e7 also loses after 2 ♔c7 ♔e6 3 ♔d8! since Black cannot get the g5-pawn after 3...♔f5 4 ♘f7 ♔g6 5 ♔e8 ♔g7 6 ♔e7 ♔g6 7 ♔f8 ♔f5 8 ♔g7 ♔e6 9 ♔xh7.

2 ♘g6+!!

This key move is the only move to win. 2 ♔d7? is wrong because after 2...♔g7 3 ♔e6 it's a draw with 3...h6! (But not *3...♔xh8? 4 ♔f7* and White mates in four moves.) 4 g6 h5 5 ♔f5 ♔xh8 6 ♔f6 ♔g8!.

2...♔f7!

2...hxg6 leads to an elementary win after 3 ♔d8 ♔f7 4 ♔d7 ♔f8 5 ♔e6 ♔g7 6 ♔e7 ♔g8 7 ♔f6 ♔h7 8 ♔f7 ♔h8 9 ♔xg6 ♔g8 10 ♔h6!.

3 ♘f4!!

The second key move is also the only move to win. On the other hand 3 ♘h4?

...leads to a draw after the surprising 3...♔e8!! (*3...♔e6?* loses after *4 ♔d8 ♔e5 5 ♔e7 ♔f4 6 ♔f6*) 4 ♘g2 ♔e7 5 ♘f4 ♔d6 6 ♘h5 ♔e6 7 ♘f6 and now the simplest is 7...h6.

3...h6! 4 g6+

4 gxh6? ♔g8 is a simple draw since White's knight doesn't have time to manoeuvre to the relevant squares.

4...♔f6 5 ♔d7 h5 6 ♔e8 ♔g7

If 6...h4 then 7 ♔f8 h3 8 g7 h2 9 ♘h5+ ♔e5 10 ♘g3 and White wins by controlling the h1-square.

7 ♔e7 h4 8 ♔e6 h3 9 ♔f5 h2 10 ♘h5+ ♔f8 11 ♘g3

Now White is winnng because it's easy to gain the opposition or play for a mate in this kind of position where the knight has time and space for manoeuvres.

11...♔g8 12 ♔f6 ♔f8 13 g7+ ♔g8 14 ♘f5 h1♕ 15 ♘e7+

A very beautiful and intricate study by Benkö!

171

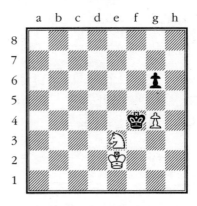

Zukertort – Blackburne
Game 13, match, London 1881
Black to play

In Fine's *Basic Chess Endings*, as well as Speelman's *Test your Endgame Ability*, Blackburne is given as the player with the white pieces but it's incorrect as has been discovered by Tim Harding in his excellent biography *Joseph Henry Blackburne*. Here Blackburne holds the draw with...

70...♔g3!

70...♔e4?? loses to 71 ♘g2 and 70...g5?? is most effectively met by 71 ♔d3 ♔f3 72 ♔d4 ♔f4 73 ♔d5! ♔xe3 74 ♔e5 ♔f3 75 ♔f5.

71 ♔e1 ♔f3 72 ♔d2 ♔f4 73 ♔d3 ♔f3 74 ♔d4 ♔f4 75 ♔d3

It's impossible for White to improve his position. 75 ♔d5 doesn't work with the pawn on g6. After 75...♔xe3 76 ♔e5 ♔f3 77 ♔f6 it's a draw but note that the natural 77 g5?? loses after 77...♔g4 78 ♔f6 ♔h5.

75...♔f3 76 ♔d2 ♔f4 Draw.

172

Palevic – Luzniak
Correspondence game 1984
White to move

1 ♘f6+!

The idea of the knight check is not only to lure the king away from the queenside, there is a deeper idea hidden in the position. The first time I was impressed by this position was 35 years ago but then I didn't know that White can draw with the less spectacular 1 ♘c3+! bxc3 2 bxc3 bxc2 3 ♔b2 ♔e4 4 ♔xc2 ♔f5 5 ♔b3 ♔g4 6 ♔c4 ♔xh5 7 ♔d5 ♔g4 8 ♔xd6 and both pawns promote in time.

1...♔e6 2 c3! bxc3

2...♔xf6 3 cxb4 ♔e5 4 ♔b1 ♔d4 5 ♔c1 ♔c4 6 ♔d2 ♔xb4 7 ♔d3 is a draw since Black cannot hold the b3-pawn. Note that White would have won with the d-pawn placed on d5 in this position!

3 ♘e4!!

This beautiful manoeuvre, which includes the next move too, is the main attraction of this knight versus

pawns endgame. 3 bxc3? ♔xf6 4 ♔b2 ♔g5 5 ♔xb3 ♔xh5 obviously leads to a win for Black.

3...c2 4 ♘c5+! dxc5 Stalemate.

4...♔d5 5 ♘xb3 ♔c4 is also a draw.

173

(board diagram – see image 173)

Balashov/Prandstetter
Basic Endgames 1992
White to move

1 ♘b7+! ♘xb7 2 a6 ♔c7 3 a7 Black resigned.

This tactical idea where a knight and a king cannot stop the a-pawn is not difficult at all but it's important to know since it shows the limitations of the knight when trying to control a rook pawn.

One can also reverse the reasoning and say that the rook pawn exploits the limitations of the board since there are no squares to the left of the pawn. The rook pawn is the cheapest material on the board, but there are situations when a rook pawn is to be preferred over any other pawn.

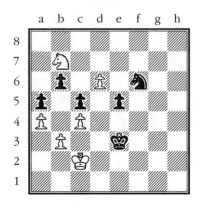

174

Zaikind
1926
White to move

175

Alburt – Lerner
USSR 1978
White to move

The endgame looks lost but White can exploit a stalemate finesse.

1 ♔b5!!

1 ♔c5 b3 2 ♘d4 b2 3 ♘b3 ♔d3 doesn't work.

1...b3

1...♔d3 2 ♘c1+ (2 ♘f4+ also holds in the same fashion.) 2...♔c2 3 ♘e2! (The only move. *3 ♘xa2?* loses after *3...b3 4 ♘b4+ ♔d2*) 3...♔d3 4 ♘c1+ ♔d2 5 ♘b3+! with an easy draw.

2 ♔a4 b2

2...♘c1 3 ♔a3 and the b3-pawn falls.

3 ♔a3

Not 3 ♘c3+? ♘xc3+ 4 ♔a3 ♘a4.

3...b1♕ 4 ♘c3+! ♘xc3

This stalemate, as well as the play which led up to this position, is useful to include in your repertoire of different stalemate patterns. There are quite a few in this book.

It seems that Black is in control of the situation but White has a surprising and unforgettable tactic which leads to a forced win.

64 ♘xc5!!

"Impossible move" number one!

64...bxc5 65 b4

"Impossible move" number two!

65...axb4

(1) After 65...♘d7 66 bxa5 White has two a-pawns and that is too much for the knight to handle since it has to attend to the d-pawn as well: 66...♔f2 67 a6 e4 68 a7 e3 69 a8♕ e2 70 ♕e4 e1♕ 71 ♕xe1+ ♔xe1 72 a5 ♘b8 73 ♔c3! (Not *73 a6? ♘xa6 74 d7 ♘b4+* followed by *75...♘c6* with a draw.) 65...cxb4 with the cheapo 66 c5 b3+ 67 ♔xb3 ♘e4 fails to 68 ♔c4.

(2) 65...e4 66 bxc5 ♔f2 67 c6 e3 68 d7 e2 69 d8♕ e1♕ 70 ♕xf6+ is a forced mate in 23 according to the computer.

66 a5

White's passers are faster than Black's.

66...e4 67 a6 ♔f2 68 a7 e3 69 a8♕ e2 70 ♕f8 e1♕ 71 ♕xf6+ ♔g3 72 ♕g5+ ♔h3

72...♔f3 73 ♕d5+ ♔g3 74 ♕d3+ ♔h4 75 d7 ♕f2+ 76 ♔b3 and White promotes to a second queen.

73 ♕d2! ♕a1

73...b3+ leads nowhere after 74 ♔c3 ♕a1+ 75 ♔xb3 ♕b1+ 76 ♔a4.

74 d7 ♕a4+

Or 74...♕a2+ 75 ♔d1 ♕b3+ 76 ♔e2 ♕xc4+ 77 ♕d3+.

75 ♔b1 ♕b3+ 76 ♔c1 ♕a3+

Or 76...♕xc4+ 77 ♔b2.

77 ♔d1 ♕b3+

77...♕f3+ 78 ♔c2 or 77...♕a1+ 78 ♔e2.

78 ♔e2

78...♔g4!

Black sets up a trap and this is obviously stronger than 78...♕xc4+ 79 ♕d3+ which makes White's task too easy.

79 ♕d1!

79 d8♕? is a draw by perpetual after 79...♕f3+ 80 ♔e1 ♕h1+ 81 ♔f2 ♕h2+ 82 ♔e3 ♕f4+ 83 ♔d3 ♕f5+. Note how the black pawns on c5 and b4 co-operate with the black queen to create a network of perpetual checks.

79...♕xc4+ 80 ♔e3 and **Black resigned.**

It's impossible to avoid the exchange of queens whatever king move Black chooses.

176

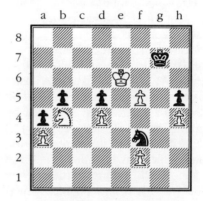

Schlechter – Spielmann
Vienna 1913
White to move

Knight endings require their own unique treatment as the following example demonstrates:

39 ♔xd5?!

The most effective win was the pawn rush 39 f6+ ♔f8 40 f7! as discovered by the Viennese master Dr. A. Kaufman.

The idea is to create a mating net with the king on f6 and the knight on d7, e6 or g6. Note that everything is about placing the white king on a square where the black knight cannot reach it.

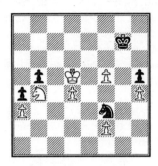

(1) After 40...♘xd4+ 41 ♔f6 White gains a lot of time by placing his king in a diagonal position and one square to the hostile knight because now it will take three moves for Black to disturb White with a check. 41...♘f3 42 ♘xd5 (A faster mate is the computer continuation *42 ♘d3!! ♘d2 43 f3!* followed by knight moves to c5, e5 or f4.) 42...♘d2 43 f3! The point is to use the doubled pawn so that White can mate Black's king without any trouble. This is how doubled pawns should be used! 43...♘xf3 44 ♘f4 and White mates next move with the knight on e6 or g6. It's interesting that a great player like Schlechter wasn't familiar with this idea and, as we have mentioned before, ideas that are missed by great players are the best ideas to learn because anyone else on earth can miss them too.

(2) 40...♘xh4 41 ♔f6 ♘f3 42 ♘xd5 ♘d2 43 f3! prevents the check on e4 so White can quietly play for mate while Black is unable

to do anything to prevent it. If 43...♘xf3 then 44 ♘f4 and mate next move.

39...♔f6 40 ♔e4 ♘xh4 41 ♘d5+ ♔f7

42 ♘c3?

Correct was 42 ♘e3 with the mini-plan to pick up the knight on h4 by ♔f4-g3.

(1) 42...♔f6? 43 ♔f4 puts Black in zugzwang since 43...♔f7 allows the decisive 44 ♔g3 and 43...b4 44 ♘d5+ ♔f7 45 ♘xb4 also doesn't save the game for Black.

(2) 42...♔g7 43 d5 ♔f7 44 d6 ♔e8 45 ♘d5 ♔d7 46 ♘c3 b4 47 axb4 a3 48 f4 ♔c6 49 f6 ♘g6 50 ♔f5 ♘f8 51 ♔g5 ♔d7 52 ♔xh5 ♔e6 53 ♔g5 ♘h7+ 54 ♔g6 ♘xf6 55 f5+ ♔e5 56 ♔f7 ♔xf5 57 b5 ♔e5 58 ♔e7 ♘g8+ 59 ♔d7 ♔d4 60 ♔c6! (After *60 ♘a2 ♔d5 61 ♘b4+ ♔c5 62 b6 ♔xb6 63 ♔e6 ♘h6 64 ♘d5+ ♔c5 65 d7 ♘f7! 66 ♔xf7 a2 67 d8♕ a1♕* White cannot profit from the extra piece in this position.) 60...♔xc3 61 d7 a2 62 d8♕ a1♕ 63 ♕xg8 with winning chances for White.

42...♔f6 43 ♘xb5 ♘xf5 44 d5 h4 45 f4 h3 46 ♔f3 ♘e3 47 ♔g3 ♘xd5 48 ♘d4 Draw.

177

Bonner – Medina
Olympiad, Haifa 1976
Black to move

Medina had played a very fine positional game against Bonner and now concludes with a nice tactic which exploits White's weakened queenside pawn structure.

41...♘c3!

This finesse only works because White has a doubled pawn on the b-file which means that Black gets a passed pawn on the a-file by force if the b2-pawn disappears.

42 bxc3

42 ♘xc3 dxc3 43 bxc3 a4 wins since White's king is outside the square of the pawn.

42...a4 43 cxd4 cxd4 44 c3 a3 White resigned.

One of many examples which, like position 173, shows that the rook pawn is the knight's number one enemy. A knight doesn't like rook pawns unless they are close to the king because when it captures an a7-pawn with a king on g8 the knight becomes decentralised.

"Pawns are the soul of chess", as the great French musician and chess player Philidor stated in the 18th century. With regard to this, in the search for the tree of knowledge, it's rewarding to play through the game from beginning to end to see how such an advantageous position could arise and noting the seemingly insignificant turning points. Here is the complete game up to the diagram position:

1 e4 e5 2 ♗c4 ♘c6 3 ♘c3 ♘f6 4 d3 ♗c5 5 ♘f3 d6 6 ♗g5 ♘a5 7 ♗b3 ♘xb3 8 axb3

The a2-pawn disappears, which improves the chances for the a7-pawn to promote in a future endgame, but at such an early stage this does not seem to be of any significance.

8...c6 9 d4 exd4 10 ♘xd4 h6 11 ♗h4 0–0 12 0–0 ♖e8 13 ♘f5?

An important turning point.

13...♗xf5 14 exf5 d5

Black now has an extra pawn in the centre.

15 ♕d3 ♕d6 16 ♖fe1 ♘g4 17 ♗g3 ♕d7 18 h3 ♘f6 19 ♗e5 ♗e7 20 ♖e1 ♘h7 21 ♖ae1 ♖ad8 22 ♕f3 ♗f6 23 ♗xf6 ♖xe2 24 ♖xe2 ♘xf6 25 g4 b5

Black starts to activate the queenside pawns in the spirit of the principles of Philidor and Nimzowitsch.

26 ♕f4 a5 27 ♘d1?

Passive play with the knight obviously increases Black's advantage.

27...c5

27...d4! would have literally killed the knight.

28 h4 Ee8 29 Exe8+ Wxe8 30 ⌖f1 d4! 31 g5 ⌘d5!

Black's last two moves are easy to find but are nevertheless important for the overall scheme and as preparation for the decisive sacrifice.

32 Wd6 We4

A really nice centralisation of the black pieces.

33 g6 ⌘f6 34 Wb8+ De8 35 Wg3 ⌘e4 36 Wg4 ⌘d2+ 37 ⌖g2 We1 38 Wf4 fxg6 39 fxg6 We4+ 40 Wxe4 ⌘xe4 41 ⌖f3

And the diagram position has been reached.

The best way to fully understand a combination, especially how it has arisen on the board, is to develop a feeling as well as a methodical procedure for creating combinations.

The drawback with books focusing solely on solving this and that combination is that they only explain the actual combinations, but not how to reach the decisive position – which is the most important thing,

We are all waiting for a book explaining how Alekhine managed to obtain those positions where it was possible to unleash a hidden combination.

178

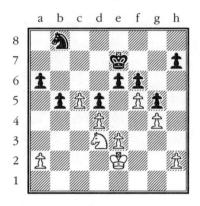

Pillsbury – Gunsberg
Hastings 1895
White to move

Superficially it's hard to believe that there is a forced win concealed in the position, as Pillsbury now demonstrated:

28 ⌘b4! a5

After 28...⌖d7 Romanovsky gives 29 fxe6+ ⌖xe6 30 c6 ⌖d6 31 c7 ⌖xc7 32 ⌘xd5+ followed by 33 ⌘xf6+ with a win.

29 c6! ⌖d6 30 fxe6!

The key to the combination lies in this move.

30...⌘xc6

30...axb4 31 e7 ⌖xe7 32 c7 is an important promotion idea to remember. You may recall the famous opening trap in the game Schlechter – Perlis, Carlsbad 1911, position 133, which featured the same idea.

31 ⌘xc6 ⌖xc6 32 e4!

White secures the win by defending the strong pawn on e6.

32...dxe4 33 d5+

And White won after the further **33...♔d6 34 ♔e3 b4 35 ♔xe4 a4 36 ♔d4 Black resigned.**

Despite the fact that there was so little material remaining on the board, Pillsbury's combination was regarded as the finest of the Hastings 1895 tournament.

179

Zahodyakin
White to move

In his famous book for Swedish chess players, *Schackpärlor* (Chess Pearls), Kristian Sköld (1911–1988), four times Swedish Champion between 1949–1963, headlines this fine study "Dam utan talan" (*The queen has no say*) as the two knights take command and stalemate the black king.

1 ♘a6

Necessary to allow the knight to take control over the promotion square e1.

1...e2 2 ♘c7+ ♔f8 3 ♘e6+

Another more demanding way to draw is 3 ♘g6+ ♔g7 4 ♘xe7 e1♕ 5 ♘ed5 and it's impossible to win according to Nalimov's tablebase. The main variation contains an idea which is useful to remember and is far more beautiful than other possible solutions.

3...♔g8 4 ♘f7!!

The key move which leads to a position where the black king will be imprisoned.

4...e1♕

Naturally the continuation 4...♔xf7 5 ♘g5+ followed by 6 ♘f3 keeps both pawns under control.

5 ♘fg5

Sköld writes here: "With the opponent's king cut off, White draws on the presumption that the knights cannot be dislodged. A useful concept."

180

Emanuel Lasker
1894
White to move

1 c4 ♘d2

A possible continuation after 1...♘a3 2 c5 ♘b5 is to play 3 ♘e6 and then continue with ♘f7-d6.

Play might continue 3...♔e2 4 ♘f7 ♔d3 5 ♘d6 ♘c3 6 c6 ♘d5 7 ♘f4+! ♘xf4 8 c7 and the c-pawn is promoted.

2 c5 ♘b3 3 c6 ♘d4 4 c7 ♘b5 5 c8♘ Black resigned.

It has been well-known since Reuben Fine's classic *Basic Chess Endings* (the most important endgame reference book before Averbakh's works) that three knights win against king and knight.

181-200: Bishop Endings

I was surprised to find more tactics in bishop endings than in knight endings when I did the preparatory work for this book. There are still more to come which might come in handy for a possible workbook. One common theme is how to lure the bishop away from a crucial diagonal. The most common themes otherwise are passed pawns, especially in endings with opposite coloured bishops (47...♗h3!! in position 195), breakthroughs and stalemates. I didn't know beforehand that stalemate was such an important tactical theme in bishop endings, more so than in knight endings.

181

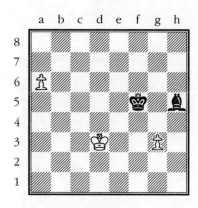

Mason
1894
White to move

1 g4+!

A beautiful but simple finesse to lure one of the pieces to a fatal square. Obviously 1 ♔e3? is met by

1...♗e8 2 a7 ♗c6 and Black controls both pawns. An immediate 1 a7? leads nowhere after 1...♗f3.

1...♗xg4

1...♔xg4 loses to 2 a7 since the king has blocked the light-squared bishop and it cannot enter the long diagonal via f3.

2 ♔e3

White controls the key f3 square and after the further **2...♗h3 3 ♔f2** White controls g2 as well so that it is impossible for the bishop to reach the crucial diagonal. This straightforward but instructive study shows how a simple pawn move can destroy the harmony in Black's defence. Such an idea is obviously valid for other positions as well.

182

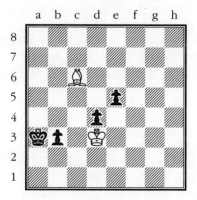

Gil – Erlandsson
Correspondence 1976
White to move

Black's main threat is 1...b2 2 ♔c2 ♔a2 so White's first move is forced.

1 ♗d5 b2

If Black moves the king White just holds the bishop on the same diagonal.

2 ♔c2 d3+

Note that 2...e4 3 ♗xe4 ♔a2 4 ♔d2 is also a draw.

3 ♔b1 d2 4 ♗b3!

The key move, exploiting the stalemate opportunity. The alternative 4 ♗f3? loses after 4...e4

(1) 5 ♗d1 e3 6 ♗e2 ♔b3 7 ♗d1+ ♔c4! and Black wins by triangulation via the squares b3-c4-c3. (*7...♔c3?! 8.♗e2 forces Black to repeat the position with 8...♔b3 and after 9 ♗d1+ triangulate with 9...♔c4!*) 8 ♗xb2 (*8 ♗e2+ ♔c3 9 ♗h5 ♔d3 10 ♗g6+ ♔e2 and Black promotes one of the pawns.*) 8...♔d3 9 ♗c2+ ♔e2 followed by 10...d1♛.

(2) 5 ♗e2 ♔b3 (*5...e3? 6 ♗d1 is a draw.*) 6 ♗d1+ ♔c3 7 ♗e2 e3. White is in zugzwang and has to allow the enemy king access to d3 if the bishop moves, or alternatively c2 if the king moves.

4...e4 5 ♗c2!

5 ♗d1? e3 and Black wins since Black's king manoeuvres to b3 next move after a bishop move along the d1-h5 diagonal.

5...♔b4

5...e3 6 ♗d1 is also a draw.

6 ♔xb2 ♔c4

7 ♗a4!

The only move to draw!

7...♔d3 8 ♗b5+

This check is necessary to avoid a loss.

8...♔e3 9 ♔c2 Draw.

An instructive bishop versus pawn ending which showed how White, with tactical means such as stalemate and zugzwang, was able to save himself despite the fact that Black had three far advanced pawns.

183

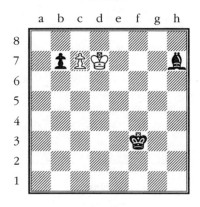

Sarychev
Shakhmaty Listok 1928
White to move

1 ♔c8!!

If White doesn't play this paradoxical move to force the black pawn to move Black will endeavour to place the bishop on c8 with an easy win. 1 ♔e6? leads nowhere after 1...♔e4 and 1 c8♕? ♗f5+ 2 ♔c7 ♗xc8 is obviously winning for Black as well since the b7-pawn is defended by the bishop.

1...b5 2 ♔d7!!

This move is probably more difficult to find than the first move, if one fails to understand that the e5-square is the key. 2 ♔b7? loses a tempo in the fight for the e5-square after 2...♗f5 3 ♔c6 b4 4 ♔d5 b3.

2...b4 3 ♔d6 ♗f5 4 ♔e5!

The key move which contains a double threat, since if Black moves the bishop along the h3-c8 diagonal White gains a tempo, which can be utilised to reach the square of the b4-pawn.

4...♗d7 5 ♔d4 b3 6 ♔c3 ♗e6 7 c8♕ ♗xc8 8 ♔xb3 Draw.

A beautiful study which touches on Réti's famous pawn endgame study from 1921, published as position 158 in *300 Most Important Chess Positions*. Someone might ask what this study has to do with tactics but it does according to Averbakh's clever defnition of tactics. He believes, and I'm inclined to agree, that the heart of tactics is the double threat. This means that the move 4 ♔e5! executes the tactical idea just as in the study by Réti. Averbakh's unique perspective on tactics means that also manoeuvres can be tactical and not only sacrifices according to Botvinnik's famous, but limited, definition that a combination is a forced variation with a sacrifice. You can read more about Averbakh's theories in his groundbreaking *Chess Tactics for Advanced Players.*

184

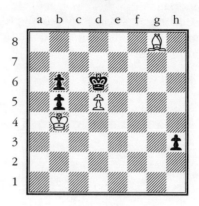

A. Larsen
White to move

In this beautiful study it seems that the h-pawn is like a runaway train but White can work a miracle thanks to the doubled b-pawns.

1 ♗h7 ♔xd5

After 1...♔e5

(1) 2 ♗e4? is bad because of the subsequent transfer to a lost pawn endgame after 2...♔xe4 3 d6 h2 4 d7 h1♕ 5 d8♕ ♕b1+ This check secures Black a forced exchange of queens on the d-file. 6 ♔c3 ♕a1+ 7 ♔b3 ♕a4+ 8 ♔c3 ♕c4+ 9 ♔b2 ♕d4+ 10 ♕xd4+ ♔xd4 11 ♔b3 ♔c5 and Black wins.

(2) Correct is 2 d6! h2 (*2...♔xd6 3 ♗e4*) 3 d7 h1♕ 4 d8♕ ♕xh7 5 ♕xb6 and the b5-pawn falls with a draw.

2 ♗f5 h2 3 ♗c8 ♔c6!

This is the tricky position because here it is vital to use the stepping stone technique and be sufficiently focused to find the stalemate.

4 ♗g4! h1♕ 5 ♗f3+!! ♕xf3 Draw.

The pawn on b6 was certainly important in this respect. It's fascinating that such a seemingly simple endgame can contain so many tactics!

185

Sallay – Honfi
Budapest 1973
Black to move

It seems Black is lost but there is a clever idea to save the draw.

46...h6! 47 ♗b2 ♔h5! 48 h3

48 ♔xf5? is met by 48...a1♕ 49 ♗xa1 stalemate!

48...♔g6!

In the game, Honfi must have forgotten the mate while in the process of queening his pawn, since he played 48...gxh3? 49 ♔xf5 h2 0 ♗f6! h1♕ 51 g4 mate.

49 hxg4 fxg4 50 ♔xg4 h5+ 51 ♔f4 ♔h6

This is actually a draw if Black goes back and forth between h6 and g6. The only way for White to prevent it is with **52 ♔f5** but then Black has **52...h4! 53.gxh4 ♔h5** and the pawn is lost.

186

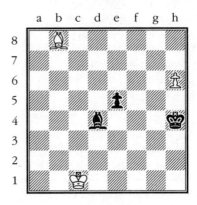

Heyecek
1930
White to move

Since there is a clear motif, the problem to be solved is to find a way to lure Black's bishop away from the long dark diagonal.

1 ♗a7 ♗a1

1...♗xa7 is met by 2 h7.

2 ♔b1 ♗c3 3 ♔c2 ♗a1 4 ♗d4!!

The key move and a very important idea to have seen. Indeed if you have seen it once you will never forget it. It's always important to look very carefully for such tactical opportunities when the passed pawn is only two squares from promotion.

204

4...♗xd4

4...exd4 would give White the chance to blockade the pawn and then the whole diagonal by 5 ♔d3! when Black has no defence to h7-h8♕.

5 ♔d3 ♗b2

If 5...e4+ then 6 ♔xd4.

6 ♔e4!

The final key move in this beautiful study. Black's e-pawn is blockaded and the bishop no longer has any influence on the key diagonal so the pawn promotes by force.

187

Kubbel
1914
White to move

White looks totally lost if it weren't for the beautiful turnaround:

1 c7 ♔b7

1...♗f5 2 ♗g6! h1♕. If Black moves the bishop to any reasonable squares along the c8-h3 diagonal White captures on e4. After 3 ♗xf5 ♕h4+ 4 ♔d7 it's not possible to prevent 5 c8♕+ so it's a draw after 4...♕h8 5 c8♕+ (*5 ♗e6!? is actually*

a draw as well, thus proving how strong White's position is.) 5...♕xc8+ 6 ♔xc8 e3 7 ♗d3+.

2 ♔d8

The king is a perfect supporter of a passed pawn since it not only defends the pawn on c7 but also prepares its promotion on c8.

2...♗f5 3 ♗g6! h1♕ 4 c8♕+!!

Here 4 ♗xf5? loses since White's king is on d8 instead of d7, and after 4...♕h8+ the pride in White's position falls.

4...♗xc8 5 ♗xe4+! ♕xe4

White is stalemated.

188

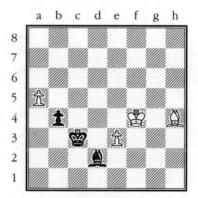

Vasiltsyikov
1952
White to move

If you are familiar with the previous study by Kubbel from 1914 you shouldn't have any problems solving this one.

1 a6

1 ♔e4? looks clever to prevent Black from playing his king to d3 but Black draws after 1...b3 2 a6

205

♔c2 3 ♗f6 ♔c3 4 ♗xc3 ♔xc3 5 a7 b2 6 a8♕ b1♕+ etc.

1...♔d3 2 ♗f2 b3 3 a7 ♗xe3+

3...b2 fails to the continuation 4 a8♕ ♔c2 5 ♕e4+ ♔c1 6 ♗e1!!. The key move must be played sooner or later and secures White two tempi with the king. 6...♗xe1 7 ♕c4+ ♔d1 8 ♔f3! ♗d2 (*8...b1♕ doesn't work with the bishop on e1 on account of 9 ♕e2+ ♔c1 10 ♕xe1+*) 9.♕d3 ♔c1 10.♔e2! b1♕ 11.♕xd2 mate.

4 ♗xe3 b2 5 a8♗! Black resigned.

Under-promotion to a bishop is obviously one of the exceptions in chess and important to be aware of since it might be a decisive weapon to avoid stalemates with the queen. We have already learned from Kubbel's study that 5 a8♕? b1♕ 6 ♕e4+ ♔e2 7 ♕xb1 is stalemate.

189

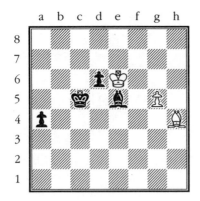

a b c d e f g h

Vasiltsyikov
Shakhmaty 1951
White to move

Amazingly White can save the draw by…

1 g6 a3 2 ♗e7! a2 3 ♗xd6+ ♗xd6 4 g7 a1♕ 5 g8♕ ♕a2+ 6 ♔d7! ♕xg8

White is beautifully stalemated. The king controls d6 and c6, the bishop e7 and c7, while the queen, working as a rook and bishop, controls the four squares e6, e8, d8 and c8, creating an economic stalemate. Such stalemates are the most difficult to see if you are not familiar with them. Note that Black cannot win this endgame with queen and bishop since it's impossible to win the queen or mate after 6...♕a7+ 7 ♔e6 ♕e7+ 8 ♔f5 ♕e5+ 9 ♔g6!.

190

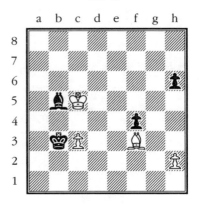

a b c d e f g h

Kostro – Adamski
1972
White to move

This position can be found in the preface by Bent Larsen to the Swedish book *Taktik & teknik i slutspelet* (Tactics and technique in the endgame) He writes: White has winning chances but it doesn't help that he wins the black bishop for the c-pawn, if the black king manages to reach h8. Kostro knows this, but he still captures on b5. Maybe he was sure that it was winning, maybe he didn't believe there were any chances in the position after 1 ♔d4. We will look at some moves which were played in the game:

1 ♔xb5

After 1 ♔d4 a plausible reply might be 1...♗d7.

Then:

(1) 2 ♗d5+ ♔c2! 3 c4 ♗g4! Black counters White's c-pawn with his own passed pawn: 4 c5 ♔d2 5 c6 f3 6 c7 f2 7 ♗g2 ♔e2.

(2) 2.h4 ♔a3! Black waits for the c-pawn to advance so as to be able to control it. After 3 c4 ♔b4 4 c5 ♔b5 White gets nowhere.

1...♔xc3 2 ♔c5 ♔d3 3 ♔d6 ♔e3 4 ♗b7

Here Adamski played...

4...h5!!

The idea is to make it easier for Black to reach h8 since it will be harder for White to stop this when the h-pawn advances compared with when it is on h6. Larsen thinks that Kostro routinely thought the development 4...f3 5 ♔e5 f2 6 ♗a6 ♔f3 7 ♔f5 was an easy win.

5 ♔e5

5 h4 ♔f2 leads to the loss of the h-pawn.

5...h4! 6 ♔f5 ♔d4! 7 h3 ♔c5 8 ♔e5 ♔b6 9 ♗d5 ♔c7

And the game ended in a draw after a couple of moves. It's not possible to prevent the black king from reaching h8 after White has captured the h-pawn. If the h-pawns had been placed on h5 and h6 and White's bishop a little further back on the classical diagonal White would have won. You should check this is correct because it is the whole point of advancing the h-pawn.

191

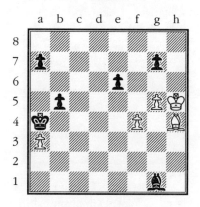

Selesnieff
Tidskrift för Schack 1917
White to move

1 g6 ♗c5

1...♗d4 is answered by 2.f5 exf5 (2...e5 3 ♗f6! and White wins.) 3 ♗f6!! (3...gxf6? 4 g7) 3...♗xf6 and White is stalemated.

2 ♗f6 ♗f8

2...♗xa3 3 ♗xg7 a5 4 ♔g5

(1) 4...♗b3 5 ♔f6! ♗b2+ 6 ♔xe6 ♗xg7 7 f5 a4 8 f6 ♗xf6 9 ♔xf6 and White promotes first with check.

(2) 4...♗e7+ 5 ♔f6 ♗f8 6 ♔e5 b4 7 ♔f6 b3 8 ♔xe6 ♔a3 9 f5 b2 10 ♗xb2+ ♔xb2 11 f6 a4 12 g7 ♗xg7 13 fxg7 a3 14 g8♕ a2 and it's a draw since the white king is too far away.

3 f5 exf5 4 ♗e7! ♗xe7

And White is stalemated in the same fashion as after 1...♗d4.

192

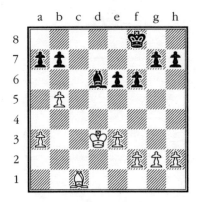

Spassky – Fischer
Game 1, World Championship
Reykjavik 1972
Black to move

29...♗xh2!?

Since it's a bishop ending and there is no king is on g1, the sacrifice cannot be called "a Greek gift". Many have argued over why Fischer played such a risky move and so spontaneously with a nervous demeanour. Maybe Reuben Fine was right when he stipulated that Fischer was so eager to show his genius (to make an "impossible move") that he made a miscalculation. Fine, who has written a book on this World Championship match, called the move an "edge blunder". The pragmatic course was to play 29...♔e7 and offer a draw.

30 g3 h5

30...♔e7, with the plan to manoeuvre to c5, is most easily stopped by 31 a4. If Black continues 31...♔d6? he must be careful because after 32 ♗a3+ ♔d5? he is mated in the centre after 33 e4+ ♔e5 34 f4 mate.

31 ♔e2

31...h4

In *Analysing the Endgame* Jonathan Speelman analyses the interesting continuation 31...g5 32 ♔f3 g4+ 33 ♔g2 h4 34 ♔xh2 h3. The idea is to tie White's king to the h-pawn but by manoeuvring the bishop to g1 White can still win. Nei gives 35 e4! ♔e7 36 f3 f5 37 e5!. White has limited Black's options by controlling the d6- and c6-squares. 37...a6 38 a4 axb5 39 axb5 ♔f7 40 ♔g1 ♔g6 41 ♔f2 ♔f7 42 ♗e3 ♔g6 43 ♔f1 Obviously White's king must be within the square of the h-pawn. 43...♔h5 44 ♗g1 The manoeuvre is completed so White wins easily after the further 44...♔g5 45 ♗h2 ♔g6 46 ♔e2.

32 ♔f3 ♔e7

If 32...h3 then 33 ♔g4 and in fact Fischer told Fine after the game that he had missed precisely this move. After the forced sequence 33...♗g1 34 ♔xh3 ♗xf2 35 ♗d2! White wins the bishop. I can understand why Fischer thought the bishop had been released on f2 so this is another theme – how to trap a bishop on f2 instead of h2.

33 ♔g2 hxg3 34 fxg3 ♗xg3 35 ♔xg3 ♔d6

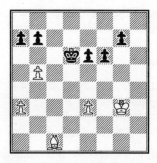

36 a4

Olafsson thinks that 36 ♔g4 was more precise than Spassky's move but Speelman doesn't agree: 36...♔d5 37 ♔h5 ♔e4! 38 ♔g6 e5 39 ♔xg7 f5 If Black gets a passed pawn he will automatically get the necessary tempi to hold the game.

(1) 40 a4 f4 41 exf4 exf4 42 ♗a3 b6 43 ♗e7 f3 44 ♗h4 ♔d5 45 ♔f6 ♔c4 etc.

(2) 40 ♔f6 f4 41 exf4 exf4 42 ♗d2 (*42 ♗xf4 ♔xf4*) 42...f3 43 ♗e1 ♔d5 44 ♔e7 ♔c4 45 a4 b6! This is the only move. It's important to prevent White from establishing a pawn on

b6. 46 ♔d6 ♔b3 and the position is a clear draw after 47 ♔c6 ♔xa4 48 ♗f2 ♔b4 etc.

36...♔d5 37 ♗a3

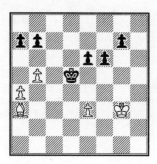

37...♔e4

Speelman thinks that this was the best time to start a counterattack on the kingside with 37...a6 38 b6 ♔c6 39 ♗f8 (*39 a5 ♔b5*) 39...♔xb6! 40 ♗xg7 ♔a5 41 ♗xf6 ♔xa4 42 ♔f4 b5 43 ♔e5 b4 44 ♔xe6 b3 45 ♔d5 ♔b4 but it's not correct because Speelman missed 46 ♗b2! a5 47 ♔d4! a4 48 ♔d3 a3 49 ♗f6 and White wins since Black's pawns are stopped.

38 ♗c5! a6

Of course not 38...b6? 39 ♗xb6 axb6 40 a5 ♔d5 41 a6 and Black's king cannot reach the square of the a-pawn.

39 b6 f5?

This seems to be the turning point of this ending. Speelman thinks that Black can hold by playing 39...e5.

(1) If then 40 ♔f2 f5 41 ♗e7! f4 42 ♔e2 ♔f5 43 ♔d3 (*43 ♔f3 e4+ 44 ♔f2 g5*) 43...g5 44 e4+ ♔g6 45 ♔c4 ♔h5!.

(2) One cannot trust the computer at this point because after 40 ♔g4 g6 41 ♗e7 ♔xe3 42 ♗xf6 ♔d4 43 ♗g5 ♔c5 44 ♗e3+ ♔b4 45 ♔g5 ♔xa4 46 ♔xg6 ♔b5 47 ♔f5 ♔c6 48 ♔xe5 ♔d7 it says that White is winning but this is in fact a well-known theoretical draw. Even if there is a white pawn on a5 it's a draw. If you are not sure about this conclusion check it yourself. It's these types of theoretical draws that are the main reasons why Fischer could have held the game.

40 ♔h4

60...f4?!

Black is lost but this move makes White's task much easier. Better is 40...♔d5! 41 ♗f8! ♔e4 42 ♗xg7 ♔xe3 43 ♔g5 f4 (After *43...♔d3 44 ♔f4 ♔c4 45 ♔e5 ♔c5 46 a5!* Black's king cannot reach c8 and so it's a win for White after *46...♔b4 47 ♔d6*) 44 ♗c3 ♔d3 45 ♗e1! e5 46 ♔f5 ♔d4 47 ♗f2+ ♔d5 48 ♗g1 Black is in zugzwang. Play might then continue 48...f3 49 ♔g4 e4 50 ♔f4 ♔c4 51 ♔xe4 ♔b4 52 ♔xf3 ♔xa4 53 ♔e4 ♔b5 54 ♔d5 and White wins by manoeuvring his king to c7.

41 exf4

Spassky needed 35 minutes to decide on his sealed move.

41...♔xf4 42 ♔h5 ♔f5 43 ♗e3 ♔e4 44 ♗f2 ♔f5 45 ♗h4 e5 46 ♗g5 e4 47 ♗e3

Black is in zugzwang since White's king will approach Black's pawns and pick them off one after another.

47...♔f6 48 ♔g4 ♔e5 49 ♔g5 ♔d5 50 ♔f5 a5 51 ♗f2 g5 52 ♔xg5 ♔c4 53 ♔f5 ♔b4 54 ♔xe4 ♔xa4 55 ♔d5 ♔b5 56 ♔d6

Speelman draws the conclusion that the capture on h2 was a bad choice but at the same time implies that it doesn't lose. Objectively the move is playable but in practical play only Spassky could benefit from it, since the complications are more difficult for Black to solve than for White.

Speelman mentions that when you analyse such a complicated endgame you decide on your moves by combining them with evaluations while calculating a number of concrete variations. What he means is that the evaluation is more important than delving too deeply into the variations.

193

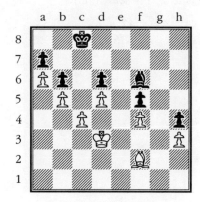

Spassky – R. Byrne
Candidates, quarterfinal 1974
White to move

50 c5!!

This "impossible break" makes it possible for White to play with the king on the light squares while exploiting the advanced pawns on d5, b5 and a6.

50...dxc5

50...bxc5 51 ♗e1! (The most effective move. *51 ♔c4 ♔c7 forces White to play 52.♔b3 and not 52 ♗e1? ♔b6 preventing White from penetrating Black's position.*) 52...♔b6 53 ♔a4 followed by manoeuvring the bishop to a5.)

(1) 51...♗d8 52 ♗c3 ♔b8 (The bishop has to be placed on d8 since a move like *52...♗b6 is met by 53 ♗f6*) 53 ♗g7. Black is helpless against the bishop manoeuvre to g5. 53...♔c8 54 ♗h6 ♔d7 55 ♗g5 ♗xg5 56 fxg5 ♔c7 57 g6 and White wins.

(2) 51...♔c7 52 ♗a5+ ♔c8 53 ♔c4 followed by 53 b6 and

White decides the game by manoeuvring the king to c6.

51 d6!

White evacuates the d5-square for his king. 51.♔c4? is wrong because of 51...♗e7.

51...♔d7

Otherwise White advances to d5. However, now White decides the game with...

52 ♗xc5! ♗d8

52...bxc5 53 b6 and White promotes on a8.

53 ♗b4 ♔e6 54 ♔c4 ♗f6 55 ♗c5 ♗d8

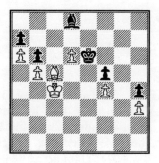

56 ♗d4!

A beautiful move which places Black in zugzwang and forces him to capture the d-pawn.

56...♔xd6 57 ♗e5+ ♔e6 58 ♗b8 ♔d7 59 ♔d5 Black resigned.

An endgame which shows the importance of advanced pawns placed on the opposite colour of the opponent's bishop.

194

Hindle – Mohring
Olympiad, Tel Aviv 1964
Black to move

195

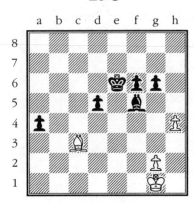

Topalov – Shirov
Linares 1998
Black to move

There is only one way to win this bishops of opposite colours ending and that is by a tactical stroke.

69...♗e3! 70 ♔xh6

(1) 70 fxe3 g4 and one of Black's passers queens.

(2) 70 f3 The main point of Black's 69th move was to provoke this pawn to advance to the third rank, because it enables Black to play 70...a2 71 ♗xa2 ♔xa2 72 ♔xh6 g4+.

70...g4+ 71 fxe3

71 ♔g6 ♗xf2 and the white bishop is overloaded.

71...g3 72 ♔h7 g2 73 h6 g1♕ 74 ♔h8 a2 75 ♗xa2 ♔xa2 76 h7 ♕g6 77 e4 ♕f7 White resigned.

It's mate next move.

47...♗h3!!

A characteristic move for Shirov who thereby puts on display his imaginative creativity. This is surely his immortal move with which he will always be associated. However, it wasn't the first time he was aware of the idea since he already knew it from analysing an endgame with Ulf Andersson. The main idea of the astonishing move is to manoeuvre the king to e4 as quickly as possible and then advance with his passed pawns.

48 gxh3

White has to accept the sacrifice since 48 ♔f2 ♔f5 49 ♔f3 will be met by the bishop sacrifice 49...♗xg2+ 50 ♔xg2 ♔e4 and, according to Shirov, Black is winning.

48...♔f5 49 ♔f2 ♔e4 50 ♗xf6

50 ♔e2 cannot stop White's three passed pawns after 50...f5.

50...d4

Shirov cuts off Topalov's bishop from control of the long dark diagonal.

51 ♗e7 ♔d3 52 ♗c5

White tries to stop Black's king from manoeuvring to c2 with an easy win.

52...♔c4 53 ♗e7 ♔b3 White resigned.

White has a hopeless struggle against the black passers. The game might have ended 54 ♗c5 d3 55 ♔e3 ♔c2 56 ♗b4 a3 and Black wins.

196

Bischoff – Khalifman
German Bundesliga 2001
Black to move

Black's two passed pawns aren't enough to win but if a third one is created it will be too much for White. Khalifman played the superb **56...g5!!** and **White resigned.**

Black not only creates a third passed pawn but also liberates his

king so it can support the pawns. 57 hxg5 is answered by 57...h4 58 gxh4 ♔xf4 and 57 fxg5 by 57...f4 58 gxf4 ♔xh4!. White's two passed pawns are harmless whereas Black's three separated ones are decisive. The key to remember when playing endings with bishops of opposite colours is to have as many disconnected passed pawns as possible!

197

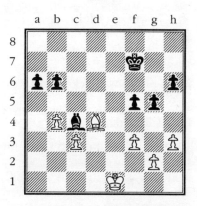

Unzicker – Botvinnik
Chess Olympiad, Varna 1962
Black to move

One can learn a lot how to play in opposite-coloured bishop endgames by the giants Botvinnik and Karpov who have collected many points in this specific ending.

The best chance to win when playing endgames with opposite-coloured bishops is to create a passed pawn even when a sacrifice is involved. Of course Black gets nowhere by keeping the material balance with 30...b5.

30...a5! 31 bxa5

It was possible to accept the pawn sacrifice and after 31 ♗xb6 a4 continue 32 ♔d2 (*32 ♗e3?* loses after *32...a3 33 ♗c1 a2 34 ♗b2 f4* since all of White's pawns are fixed. Black decides by advancing the king to the key square b1.) and then:

(1) 32...f4 33 ♗c7 ♗f1 34 g3 fxg3 35 ♗xg3 ♗xh3 36 b5 and the position is balanced with White's two connected passed pawns versus Black's two separated ones.

(2) 32...♗f1 33 g3 Even if Black gets two distant passed pawns following 33...♗xh3, the position is a draw after 34 c4.

31...bxa5 32 g3

White prevents Black from fixing his pawns with 32...f4.

32...a4 33 ♔d2

It would be natural to restrain the passer with 33 ♗c5. After 33...♔e6 a plausible continuation is 34 h4!. White wants to exchange as many pawns as possible. After all, Black has the wrong rook pawn if all the pawns are exchanged on the kingside. Then 34...gxh4 35 gxh4 h5 36 ♔f2 ♔d5 37 ♗b4 ♗b3 38 ♔e2 with a draw.

33...a3 34 ♔c2 h5

35 h4?

The losing move according to Botvinnik. 35 f4? also loses after 35...h4 36 gxh4 (36 ♗f2 g4) 36...gxf4.

35 g4! seems to hold. The goal is to reach an ending where Black only has the queenside pawn left with an easy draw. The most important variations are:

(1) 35...fxg4 36 hxg4! The exchange on g4 makes it easy for White to exchange all the pawns on the kingside. Then 36...h4 37 ♗f2 h3 38 ♗g3.

(2) 35...hxg4 36 fxg4! f4 37 ♗f2 etc.

(3) 35...♗e2! 36 gxf5 ♗xf3 37 ♔b3 h4! (*37...♗g2 38 h4!*) 38 ♔xa3 ♗g2 39 ♔b4 ♗xh3 40 f6 ♗d7 41 ♔c5! ♔e6 42 ♗e5! ♗e8 43 ♔d4!.

Without giving any variations, Botvinnik writes that the game probably could have been saved by a bishop manoeuvre to d8.

For example: 35 ♗b6!

(1) 35...♗f1 36 ♗c7! ♗xh3 37 f4 g4 38 ♗d8!.

(2) 35...♔g6 36 ♗c7! h4 37 gxh4 gxh4 38 ♗d6 a2 39 ♔b2 ♔h5 40 ♔a1 ♗d5 41 ♔b2 ♗xf3 42 ♔xa2 ♗g2 43 ♔b2 ♗xh3 44 ♔c2 ♔g4 45 ♔d2 f4 46 ♔e1.

(3) 35...♗d5 36 ♗d8! ♔g6 37 f4 h4 38 g4 fxg4 39 hxg4 h3 40 ♗c7! etc.

35...f4! 36 ♗e5

Botvinnik gives 36 ♗f2 gxh4 37 gxh4 ♔e6 followed by ...♔f5 and ....♗d5 with a win.

36...♔e6! 37 ♗c7 gxh4 38 ♗xf4

38 gxh4 ♔f5 and the f3-pawn falls.

38...h3 39 g4 h4 40 ♗h2 ♗e2 White resigned.

This endgame really does show the danger of being too passive in endings with bishops of opposite colours.

198

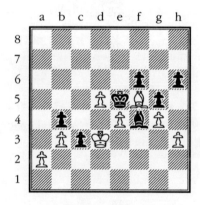

Zatulovskeya – Kozlovskaya
Gori 1969
White to move

Black plans to manoeuvre the bishop to c5 and then the king to g3 with decisive effect. However here White can construct a fortress and stop Black from penetrating on the white kingside.

52 d6!!

The game continued 52 ♗g6 ♗g3 53 ♗e8? (The turning point. White could have still held the game by sacrificing both central pawns by *53 d6! ♔xd6 54 e5+! ♔xe5 55 ♔e3*) 53...♗f2 54 ♗g6 ♗c5 55 ♗h7 ♔f4 56 ♔e2 ♔g3 57 ♗f5 ♔xh3 58 e5 fxe5 59 ♔f3 ♔h4 60 ♗g6 ♗d6 61 ♗e4 h5 62 gxh5 ♔xh5 63 ♔e3 g4 64 ♔d3 ♔g5 White resigned.

52...♔xd6 53 e5+! ♔xe5

53...fxe5 doesn't create any additional possibilities after 54 ♔e2.

54 ♔e2

The position is a draw since the light-squared bishop contains the c3-pawn and the king stops Black's king from advancing to f4 by playing ♔f3 next move.

The main point of the two pawn sacrifices was simply to open the f5-c2 diagonal for the bishop.

199

N.N.
Schaakwereld
White to move

I found the cleanest and most instructive position of a discoverer in Max Euwe's eminent book *Das Endspiel*.

The main variation is:

1 ♔a4 ♗b6 2 ♔b5 ♗a7 3 ♔a6 ♗b8 4 ♔b7

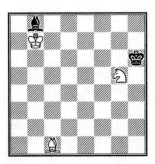

It's pretty amazing that despite the fact that the black bishop seems to have so many available squares the g5-knight can eat them all up.

What more proof can you get of the power of the discoverer?

200

Farago
L Echiquier de Paris 1947
White to move

1 ♗e4+! ♔xe4

1...♔xe3 2 ♗g2 and White can commute with the bishop along the f1-h3 diagonal since it will always be stalemate whatever Black does. And after 1...♔e2 2 ♗g2 the position is also a draw.

2 ♗xf2! gxf2 3 ♔g2 ♔e3 4 ♔f1

And Black cannot avoid stalemate or loss of his f-pawn.

201-210: Knight and Bishop Endings

The ending of bishop versus knight is obviously very much about who is dominating and who has the better pawn position so positions 202 and 206 show when it's possible to turn the tables. Sometimes the bishop is sacrificed as in 203-204 and it's a pawn race against the knight.

201

Stein – Dorfmann
USSR 1973
Black to move

1...♘a4!

Black exploits the fact that White cannot move the bishop otherwise it will be cut off either by ...♘b2 or ...♘c3. White therefore has to move the king and then there are opportunities for Black to manoeuvre in such a way that White's king will be in zugzwang. In the game followed 1...♔b1? 2 ♔d2 ♔xa1 (2...♘c4+ 3 ♔d1 ♔xa1 4 ♔c2!)

3 ♔c1! (3 ♔c2?? ♘d3!) 3...♘c4 4 ♔c2 and a draw was agreed.

2 ♔e2 ♔c1!!

This move forces White to lose a tempo. If 2...♔b1 then 3 ♗d1!.

3 ♔e1 ♘c5 4 ♔e2 ♔b1 5 ♔d1

5 ♔d2 fails to 5...♘b3+.

5...♘a4! 6 ♔d2 ♘b2!

The zugzwang is in place because now White wants to move the king to d1. It's White to move since Black earlier gained a tempo by moving the king to c1 first. Such a key position and how to reach it is obviously of paramount importance for understanding this endgame.

7 ♔c3 ♔xa1 8 ♔c2 ♘d3 and Black wins.

Note that this game was given as position 193 in *300 Most Important Chess Positions* with the declaration that it was a draw. It turned out to be a mistake to trust the players and not check the assessment in Nalimov's database. However, an attentive reader sent me an email and wrote

217

that the assessment was wrong and therefore I thought it would be a good idea to correct the mistake in this book.

202

Brenew/Ban
1934
White to move

Superficially it seems that Black's pawn is going straight on to f1 and it certainly does – so how can White still achieve a draw?

1 ♔g3 ♔g1 2 ♘e6 f2 3 ♘f4!

This is the point. White's knight is close enough to the vital points in Black's position to create chaos.

3...f1♕

3...♗e6 4 ♘e2+ ♔f1 5 ♘f4 ♗f5 6 ♔f3 leads to a funny zugzwang position where Black cannot escape without losing the f2-pawn.

4 ♘h3+ ♔h1 5 ♘f2+ ♔g1 6 ♘h3+

The magic words to saving the position are spelt "perpetual check". There is no way for the king to escape since Black only has two squares of different colours to

oscillate between. Such a bad state for the enemy king but just what the knight likes!

203

P. Littlewood – Kovacevic
Hastings 1982
White to move

46 ♗f3!!

A surprising move allowing the capture on a5 or the fork on d4. The positional way to win was 46 ♔a4 followed by 47 b4 but the move played is undeniably more spectacular and shows a more concrete and tactical method to secure victory. Of course such a decision is a matter of style.

46...♘d4+

46...♘xa5+ 47 ♔b4 traps the knight while other knight moves lose as well because of the two passed pawns.

47 ♔c4!

As soon will become clear, the king has to move here to secure the win.

47...♘xf3 48 a6 g4 49 a7 g3 50 a8♕ g2

It seems Black has a chance to draw due to the fact that the g1-square is under Black's control. However, now it's apparent why it's so important to place the king on c4.

51 ♕xf3 g1♕ 52 ♕d5+ ♔f6 53 ♕d4+

The transposition to a winning pawn endgame is the reason. Before playing his actual moves White had to visualise this position eight moves before, with one stepping stone after move 50. Since the variation is forced it's not so difficult to calculate for the experienced player. It's just a matter of technique. Even a positional player might choose this tactical variation because of its aesthetic appeal.

204

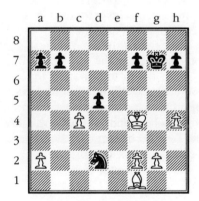

Duras – Rubinstein
Barmen 1905
White to move

34 cxd5?

A spectacular move but not the best. Stronger was the quiet 34 ♗e2!. Then:

(1) 34...dxc4? is answered by 35 ♔e3 c3 36 ♗d3! (Not *36 ♔d3?* because of the tricky knight move

36...♘e4! The player with the bishop must always be on the look-out for such tactical opportunities with the knight.) 36...b5 37 ♗xb5 ♘e4 38 ♗d3 f5 39 ♔d4 ♘xf2 40 ♗xf5 when White's bishop is stronger than the opponent's knight thereby giving him good winning chances.

(2) 34...♘xc4 35 ♗f3 and now Black must find 35...d4! to secure dynamic equilibrium.

34...♘xf1 35 ♔e5 ♘d2 36 ♔d6 ♔f6?

More precise was 36...♘e4+ 37 ♔c7 b5 38 d6 b4 39 d7 ♘c5 40 d8♘ a5 41 ♘c6 b3 42 axb3 ♘xb3 and Black has decent practical chances thanks to the distant passed pawn which is usually a significant factor in knight endings.

37 ♔c7 ♘e4 38 d6 ♘c5 39 d7 ♘e6+ 40 ♔xb7 ♔e7 41 ♔c8 h5 42 f3 f5 43 g3 a5 44 a4 ♘d8 45 ♔c7 ♘f7 46 ♔c8 ♘d6+ 47 ♔c7 ♘f7 48 ♔c8 ♘d8 49 ♔c7 ♘e6+ 50 ♔c8 Draw.

205

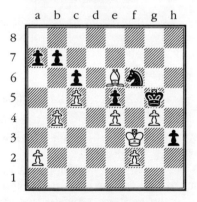

Åkesson – Barkhagen
Swedish Championship,
Linköping 2001
White to move

White's king on f3 is overloaded since it not only has to protect the e4- and g4-pawns but also to contain the h3-pawn. Black exploits the overloaded king by...

35...♘xe4!

Another idea, based on the same premise that the white king cannot leave f3, is 35...♔h4 36.♗f5 (*36 g5 ♘h7*) 36...♘d5!! 37 exd5 (Otherwise Black decides with 37...♘f4 followed by 38...h2.) 37...cxd5 and White has no defence against 38...e4 and 39...h2. It's a matter of taste whether one chooses the former or the latter, but the move played is the clearest.

36 ♗c8

If 36 ♔xe4 then 36...h2.

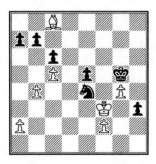

36...♔h4!

Black's 35th move was the prelude to a knight manoeuvre to g5.

37 ♗xb7 ♘g5+ and **White resigned** because of 38 ♔e3 h2 39 ♗xc6 e4!. The solution wasn't hard to find but the main point is to be on the alert for typical ideas of luring the enemy king away from a far advanced passed pawn.

206

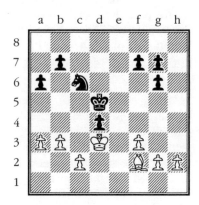

Abrahamyan – Foisor
USA Women's Championship,
Saint Louis 2011
White to move

The position appears balanced but White has a clever transition to a winning pawn endgame.

43 ♗xd4!

White overlooked this nice opportunity and played the inferior 43 f4? when after 43...b5 it was too late for the bishop sacrifice and a draw was soon agreed.

43...♘xd4 44 c4+ ♔e5

Or 44...♔c5 45 b4+.

45 f4+ ♔xf4 46 ♔xd4

White wins the pawn race with his extra pawn on the queenside.

46...f5 47 b4 g5 48 b5 axb5 49 cxb5 and White follows up with a4-a5-a6 etc.

207

Chéron
Journal de Geneve 1964
White to move

1 ♘f4! d4 2 ♗f6!

If White plays the natural 2 ♔g6? ♔c2 3 ♘g2! Black has to travel a narrow path to draw, namely 3...♔d1!! (*3...♔d2? 4 ♔f5 d3 5 ♔e4 ♔e2 6 ♘f4+ or 3...♔c1 4 ♘e1! ♔d2 5 ♔f5*) and White cannot win, for example 4 ♔f5 d3 5 ♘xe3+ ♔e2 and the d-pawn continues its advance.

2...e2! 3 ♘d3!

3 ♘xe2? d3 and the d-pawn can only be stopped by sacrificing the knight.

3...♔c2 4 ♘e1+ ♔d2 5 ♗h4 d3 6 ♔g6 ♔e3

Or 6...♔c3 7 ♗d8! d2 8 ♗a5+ and White wins.

7 ♗d8! ♔d2 8 ♗a5+ ♔e3 9 ♔f5 d2 10 ♗b6 mate.

What makes this study so amazing is primarily the economical mate. Each of the white pieces controls at least two flight squares and puts in maximum effort. The other amazing thing is that White did not make a single pawn capture and allowed the pawns to advance deeply into his own half of the board. A really unforgettable study by the French endgame master Chéron.

208

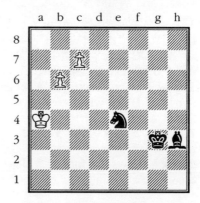

Speelman
Analysing the Endgame 1981
White to move

1 b7!

1 ♔b5? ♗d7+! (1...♘d6+? 2 ♔c6 ♘c8 3 ♔b5 (*3 ♔b7 also holds the draw, but not 3 b7? ♗g2+ and the b7-pawn falls.*) 3...♗f1+ 4 ♔a5! ♗g2 5 ♔a6 ♘d6 6 c8♕ ♘xc8 7 b7)

(1) 2 ♔a6 ♗c8+! 3 ♔a7 ♘d6 4 ♔b8 ♔f4 5 b7 ♗xb7 6 c8♕ ♗xc8 7 ♔c7 ♔e5 Note that his variation doesn't work with the king on h2.)

(2) 2 ♔c4 ♗c8! (2...♘d6+ 3 ♔d5
♘b7 4 c8♕ ♗xc8 5 ♔c6 ♘a5+
6 ♔b5! ♘b3 7 ♔c6) 3 ♔d5

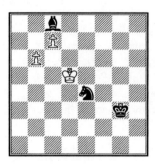

3...♘d2!! A very beautiful move.
(Not 3...♗b7+? 4 ♔e6 ♘c5+ 5 ♔d6
♘a4 6 c8♕! ♗xc8 7 ♔c7) 4 ♔c6
♘c4! 5 b7 ♘a5+ 6 ♔b6 ♘xb7 and
as the c7-pawn obstructs a king
move to c7 Black wins.

1...♘c5+ 2 ♔b5 ♘xb7 3 c8♘!

3 c8♕? allows the fork 3...♘d6+!
4 ♔c6 ♘xc8.

3...♗xc8 4 ♔b6!

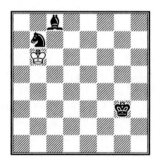

A useful position to remember.
White holds the draw since it's
impossible to avoid the loss of a
piece after 5 ♔c7.

209

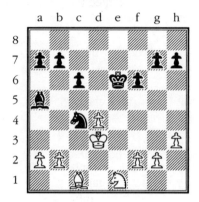

Lasker – Euwe
Nottingham 1936
White to move

Max Euwe always had a tough
time against Lasker. He played him
three times and lost every game.
Here he has just moved the bishop
from c7 to a5 instead of the standard
move 23...♘b6 with a technical
advantage to Black. Lasker's next
move turns the tables...

24 b4!

This decoy move lures the bishop
to b4 where it can be attacked by
♘c2. "The rest of the game requires
no comment" as Alekhine writes in
the tournament book.

24...♗xb4 25 ♘c2 ♗d2

Humour, disappointment or
desperation? Probably all three.
Sometimes it's difficult even for a
gentle person like Euwe to resign at
the right time. It might also be a way
of not becoming the victim of a

miniature game, but Euwe was unlucky if he wanted the game to be quietly forgotten.

Apart from the fact that Nottingham 1936 is one of the most famous tournaments of all time because of the clash of the old classical masters Lasker, Capablanca and Alekhine with the new generation from Russia (Botvinnik, Flohr) and America (Fine, Reshevsky) this game features a an immortal magnet combination.

It's the first example that comes to mind when you think about the most famous magnet combinations ever played – and where the king isn't the target.

26 ♗xd2 ♘b2+ 27 ♔e2 ♔d5
28 ♗c1 ♘c4 29 ♔d3 ♘b6 30 ♘e3+
♔e6 31 ♘c4 ♘c8 32 ♘a5 ♘d6
33 ♗f4 **Black resigned.**

210

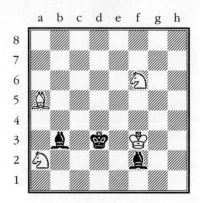

J. Fritz
Svobodne Slovo 1953
White to move

1 ♘c1+

1 ♘b4+? is a mistake due to 1...♔c4 2 ♔xf2 ♔b5 and Black wins the piece back.

1...♔c2

If 1...♔c4 then 2 ♔xf2.

**2 ♘xb3 ♗h4 3 ♘d4+ ♔d3
4 ♘g8!!**

This key move is the hardest to find but it's certainly aesthetically rewarding when one notices that after **4...♔xd4 5 ♔g4** the black bishop is beautifully dominated! It is trapped even though theoretically it has access to seven squares. The only move which doesn't allow an immediate capture is **5...♗f2** but then the skewer **6 ♗b6+** decides.

211-273: Rook Endings

The code words for rook endings are activity, activity and activity. It's all about understanding the peculiarities of the rook with its ability to exploit files and ranks. The rook is a super piece in the ending and really good at gobbling up pawns as well as creating threats against the enemy king, when it co-operates with the king and pawn(s). Most of these positions will show the value of activity in this particular branch of endgame play – but also how crucial it is sometimes to find the correct square or manoeuvre for the rook.

This is a really difficult endgame to conduct perfectly and the more we study the most important rook endings the better, because they are very common and abound in tactical and positional ideas. Hopefully these endings, as well as those published in *300 Most Important Chess Positions,* will inspire you to engage in further research. Capablanca claimed to have studied 1,000 rook endings which says something about its importance.

In the next example it looks like White will promote the passed pawn without any problems, since he controls both the d8- and c5-squares. However Black can put up pretty tough resistance by exploiting the resourcefulness of the rook along both file and rank. There are tactical opportunities like the check, the pin, the skewer and the stalemate at his disposal.

211

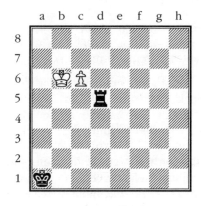

Saavedra
1895
White to move

1 c7 ♖d6+ 2 ♔b5

2 ♔b7? gives Black the opportunity to pin the pawn along the seventh rank by 2...♖d7 while 2 ♔c5? allows Black to exploit the c-file with 2...♖d1 and even win with a skewer if White promotes too early by 3 c8♕? ♖c1+.

2...♖d5+ 3 ♔b4 ♖d4+ 4 ♔b3

4 ♔c3 ♖d1 5 ♔c2 transposes to the main variation.

4...♖d3+ 5 ♔c2 ♖d4!

The key defensive move allowing the black rook to be maximally utilised for tactical purposes.

6 c8♖!!

This nice move is one of the most famous examples of under-promotion. It works because of the bad position of the king and rook.

6 c8♕? ♖c4+! 7 ♕xc4 leads to stalemate so White under-promotes to a rook to avoid this while creating a mating threat against Black's cornered king.

6...♖a4

The only move to prevent mate but 7 ♔b3! not only renews this but creates a second threat.

This study is quite incredible since Black first uses all his defensive resources associated with the rank and the file but then White concludes by exploiting all his attacking resources to threaten mate along the rank as well as the file. The secret of playing with a rook is essentially to use it both vertically and horizontally and there is no other study which shows this in its purest form than this masterpiece by the Spanish priest Rev. Fernando Saavedra (1849–1922). We will elaborate more on the Saavedra theme in position 217.

212

Lerner – Dorfman
Tashkent 1980
White to move

Lerner had done his homework because he played the stunning…

71 ♖f2!!

This is the only move to win. It's vital to stop Black from shielding White's king with ...♔f6 and ...♔e5. After the natural continuation 71 ♔b7? ♔f6! 72 ♔c6 ♔e5! White cannot win. Note that both Black's moves were forced to hold the draw. John Emms gives the following variation in *The Survival Guide to Rook Endings*: 73 ♖g2 ♔f4 74 ♔d5 g4 75 ♖f2+ ♔e3 76 ♖a2 g3 77 ♔e5 ♔f3 78 ♖a3+ ♔f2 79 ♔f4 g2 80 ♖a2+ ♔g1 81 ♔g3 ♔h1!.

71...♔h6 72 ♔b7 g4 73 ♔c6 ♔g5 74 ♔d5 g3 75 ♖f8 ♔g4 76 ♔e4 and White wins.

213

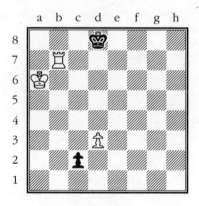

Kubbel
1927
White to move

White cannot initially hold the draw by using stalemate tricks since White has a pawn on d3 in this position.

1 ♖b8+ ♔d7 2 ♖b7+ ♔d6

2...♔c8 3 ♖b4 c1♕ 4 ♖c4+ ♕xc4+ 5 dxc4 ♔c7 6 ♔b5 ♔b7 7 ♔c5 ♔c7 with a draw shows why the d3-pawn is important.

3 ♖b6+ ♔d5 4 ♖b5+ ♔d4 5 ♖b4+ ♔xd3 6 ♖b3+

Now, as the d3-pawn has been liquidated, White must use tactical resources like the pin or the stalemate.

6...♔d4

6...♔d2 7 ♖b2 pins the pawn.

7 ♖b4+ ♔d5 8 ♖b5+ ♔d6 9 ♖b6+ ♔d7 10 ♖b7+ ♔c8 11 ♖b5!

The key move to draw without the d3-pawn.

11...c1♕ 12 ♖c5+ ♕xc5 Draw.

White is stalemated.

214

Grinfeld
1903
White to move

White has to sacrifice the rook, since if it moves along the first rank then 1...bxa4 leads to a simple draw. How can White sacrifice the rook in the most efficient manner?

1 ♖a3!

Very nice. The rook is given up on the most distant square from a1, so as to gain a tempo when White promotes the a-pawn.

1...♔xa3

1...b4 is too slow since after 2 ♖g3 b3 3 ♖g5 White wins the a-pawn as well as the b-pawn after 3...♔a3 4 ♖xa5 b2 5 ♖b5.

2 axb5 a4 3 b6 ♔a2 4 b7 a3 5 b8♕

White wins the queen ending since the pawn is only on a3 and not on a2.

215

Chekhover
1945
White to move

Normally such a position is lost for White since the black pawns are too far advanced, however in this particular case it's possible to hold the draw.

1 ♔f8!!

This key move is hard to understand if you haven't seen the

main variation to the end. The main idea is to avoid a check at move 5.

1...d2

1...e2 2 ♖e7 ♔c3 3 f5 d2 4 ♖xe2 d1♕ 5 f6 ♕xe2 6 f7 and White reaches an elementary draw. For example the normal continuation 6...♕g4 7 ♔e8 ♕e6+ 8 ♔f8 ♔d4 9 ♔g7 ♕e7 10 ♔g8 (*10 ♔h8??* *♕f8+*) 10...♕g5+ 11 ♔h7 ♕f6 12 ♔g8 ♕g6+ 13 ♔h8! ♕xf7 leads to stalemate.

2 ♖d7 e2 3 ♖xd2+ ♔xd2 4 f5 e1♕ 5 f6

In some positions it's possible to hold the draw with a bishop pawn placed on the sixth rank. Here Black cannot prevent 6 f7, because of the unfortunate position of the black king which stops Black from giving a decisive check on b4. Now it's understandable why White wanted to play his king to f8 rather than to g8 otherwise Black would have had a check on e8 or on the g-file.

216

Pogosyants
1962
White to play

1 ♖h8 ♔g7

1...♔f7 2 ♔g5 ♘f6 3 ♖f8+! ♔xf8 4 ♔xf6 ♔e8 5 ♔g7 wins the d7-pawn.

2 ♔g5!! ♘f6

2...♔xh8 3 ♔g6 A useful position to remember where both the black king and knight are dominated by White's king and far advanced pawn.

3 ♖d8!

Karpov/Matsukevich suggest 3 ♔f5 in *Find the Right Plan with Anatoly Karpov*, but that's met by the extraordinary move 3...♘e4!! and the endgame is a draw.

3...♘h7+

After 3...♘e4+ 4 ♔f4 ♘xd6 5 ♖xd7+ ♘f7 6 ♔f5 followed by 7 ♔f6 wins on the next move.

4 ♔f5 ♘f6 5 ♖a8!

White' plan is to place Black in zugzwang. Note that the seemingly winning 5 ♖f8? is countered by the amazing 5...♘e4!!. Such tactical ideas are easy to miss but they will be easier to detect if you are familiar with them!

5...♘d5 6 ♖a3! ♔f7

6...♘f6 7 ♖e3 ♘d5 (if *7...♘g8* then *8.♖g3+* followed by the capture on g8.) 8 ♖e5 ♘b6 9 ♖c5 ♔f7 10 ♖c7 ♔e8 (otherwise *11 ♖b7* decides.) 11 ♔g6 and it's mate in three moves.

7 ♖b3 ♘f6

Or 7...♔g7 8 ♔e5 ♘f6 9 ♖g3+ etc.

8 ♖e3 ♘g8 9 ♔g5 ♔g7 10 ♖e8

&f7 **11 ♖xg8 ♔xg8 12 ♔g6** and **White wins**.

An advanced and neat study where the difficulty wasn't finding White's best moves but Black's defensive resources – or rather the intricate trap linked to the hard-to-find move 5...♘e4!!. Only by thoroughly examining such studies can you really master precision in pawn endings, rook manoeuvres and not least tactical knight play. The secret of high level chess training is to have access to magical positions in which many different themes are intertwined.

217

Liburkin
Shakhmaty v SSSR 1931
White to move

The study by Saaavedra has been widely reproduced, and in *Test Tube Chess* John Roycroft calls it "unquestionably the most famous of all endgame studies". It has inspired many other composers. The many promotions and under-promotions in the studies of Harold Lommer, for example, were inspired by the Saavedra position. However, we will now turn our attention to another study composer, Mark Liburkin, who was also inspired of the Saavedra study according to Hooper and Whyld's *Oxford Companion to Chess*,

After the self explanatory **1 ♘c1** (Not *1 ♘b4? ♖xb5*) Black has two main defences; the first of which illustrates the Saavedra theme...

1...♖xb5

The other black defence features two new stalemate defences, and a second under-promotion, this time to a bishop. This is why this study is well-known whereas many other elaborations on the Saavedra position are forgotten: 1...♖d5+ 2 ♔c2 (*2 ♘d3? ♖xd3+ 3 ♔c2 ♖d5! 4 ♔c3 ♖xb5 5 ♔c4* is a draw. *2 ♔e2? ♖xb5 3 c7 ♖e5+* followed by *4...♖e8* is a draw as well.) 2...♖c5+ 3 ♔d3! (*3 ♔d2? ♖xb5 4 c7 ♖b2+! 5 ♔d1 ♖c2! 6 ♔xc2* stalemate, or *4 ♘b3+ ♖xb3 5 c7 ♖b2+!*) 3...♖xb5 (*3...♖xc1 4.♔d4* intending *5 ♔d5* and *6 b6* with a win.) 4.c7 ♖b8! White can win only by the under-promotion 5.cxb8♗! followed by the elementary procedure of mating with bishop and knight. All the other possible promotions lead to a draw. For example 5 ♘b3+ ♖xb3+ 6 ♔c2 ♖b2+! 7 ♔c1 (Not *7 ♔c3? ♔b1!* and Black wins.) only draws after 7...♖b1+ or the more spectacular 7...♖b4 8.c8♕ (*8 c8♖ ♖a4* is safe now.) 8...♖c4+!.

Nor does 1...♔b1 help after 2 ♘d3 ♖c4 (otherwise the knight manoeuvres to b4) 3 ♔d2 ♖c2+ 4 ♔e3 ♖c4 5 ♘e5 and White wins.

2 c7 Rd5+ 3 Nd3!! Rxd3+ 4 Kc2 Rd4

Here we have a position already seen in the Saavedra position. White wins with...

5 c8R!

5 c8Q? Rc4+! 6 Qxc4 is stalemate.

5...Ra4 6 Kb3! and **White wins**. The reason why this study is well-known whereas many other elaborations on the Saavedra position are forgotten is because Black's defence features two new stalemate defences, and a second under-promotion, this time to a bishop which is the most uncommon and surprising under-promotion.

218

Sjöberg – Kyhle
Hasselbacken Open 2000
White to move

One always has to be aware of stalemate tricks as the strong Swedish player Mats Sjöberg experienced in his game against Bo Kyhle. Sjoberg played the pragmatic...

58 g4?

...despite the fact that he had analysed 58 Rxg7! Kxg7 59 Kxh5 Kh7 60 Kg4 (An even simpler solution is *60 g4 Kg7 61 Kh4 Kh6 62 Kg3 Kg5 63 Kf3 Kh6 64 Kf4 Kg7 65 Ke4 Kf7 66 Kd5 Ke7 67 Kc6* and the f6-pawn is doomed.) 60...Kh6 61 Kf4 Kh5 62 g4+ Kh4 (or *62...Kh6 63 Ke4 Kg5 64 Kf3 Kh6 65 Kf4*) and now:

(1) 63 Kf3 Kh3 (*63...Kg5 64 Kg3 Kh6 65 Kf4*) 64 g5 fxg5 65 f6 g4+ 66 Kf2 Kh2 67 f7 g3+ 68 Kf3 g2 69 f8Q g1Q 70 Qh8 mate.

(2) The even quicker and direct 63 g5! fxg5+ 64 Ke4! (*64 Ke3? Kh5!* is a draw.) 64...Kh5 (*64...g4 65 f6 g3 66 Kf3 Kh3 67 f7 g2 68 f8Q g1Q 69 Qh8 mate.*) 65 Ke5 Kh6 (*65...g4 66 f6 g3 67 f7 g2 68 f8Q g1Q 69 Qh8+* wins the queen.) 66 f6 g4 67 Ke6 g3 68 f7 and White queens with check.

Unfortunately he thought that the text move was simpler.

58...Nxf5+! Draw.

58...hxg4? 59 Kxg4 loses in the long run and must have been what Sjöberg expected. He had completely missed this stalemate opportunity and had to concede half a point. The lesson to be learned is that one must always look for stalemate opportunities, whether on the attacking or defending side, especially when the king is short of space. I'm sure that if Sjöberg had focused more on the actual position he would have seen the stalemate. However he was focused on the sacrifice on g7 – but still didn't play it because he thought it was unnecessary and went for the more comfortable but mistaken solution.

219

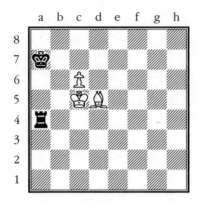

Ehrlich
1928
White to move

1 c7 ♖a5+ 2 ♔c4!

The only move to win as the alternatives lead to stalemate: 2 ♔b4 ♖b5+! 3 ♔xb5 and 2 ♔c6 ♖xd5! 3 c8♕ (or *3 ♔xd5 ♔b7 4 ♔d6 ♔c8 5 ♔c6*) 3...♖c5+! 4 ♔xc5.

2...♖a1 3 ♗c6!

Also this is the only move to secure the win.

3...♖c1+ 4 ♔d5

4 ♔b5? would be a draw after 4...♖b1+ 5 ♔c5 ♖b8.

4...♖d1+ 5 ♔e6

5 ♔e5 wins as well but if 5 ♔e4?! White has to repeat the position after 5...♖e1+ with 6 ♔d5 since the white king must be close to the c-pawn so that Black cannot save himself by 6...♖e8 7 ♗xe8 ♔b7 – but after the text move White would have 8 ♔d6.

5...♖e1+ 6 ♔f7

White wins by controlling the square on the last rank.

6...♖f1+ 7 ♔g7 ♖g1+ 8 ♔h7

White wins since there is no check available on h1. Note that White cannot play 8 ♔h8? due to 8...♖b1 9 c8♕ ♖b8 with a pin.

220

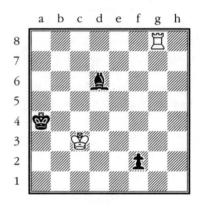

Mattison
1914
White to move

1 ♖g4+

1 ♖a8+? ♔b5 2 ♖a1 fails to 2...♗e5+ (*2...♗b4+? 3 ♔d3 ♗e1 4 ♔e2*) 3 ♔d3 ♗xa1 4 ♔e2 ♗d4.

1...♔a3

1...♔b5 2 ♖g5+ followed by 3 ♖f5 is an easy draw.

2 ♖g5 ♗b4+ 3 ♔c2 f1♕ 4 ♖a5+! ♗xa5

A beautiful and important stalemate picture to familiarise yourself with since it's unusual as well as economical. Note that all White's escape squares are controlled just once by Black's pieces. It is reminiscent of the stalemate pattern which arose in the simultaneous game between Kasparov and McDonald, although in that case the defending king was placed on the edge of the board.

221

Mattison
1914
White to move

White has the wrong rook pawn (or wrong bishop) so it's not possible to advance the e-pawn since Black simply sacrifices his rook for it and achieves an easy draw. More imagination and creativity are required to win this position.

1 ♗e3+ ♔b7 2 e7 ♖xa3 3 ♗a7!!

White obstructs the path of retreat for the rook with the same move as Karpov decided his game against Unzicker in the Nice Olympiad, 1974. Black must not be given full access to the a-file which was exactly the same mode of play Karpov adopted – but his was from a positional perspective. By placing

the bishop on a7 the a-file is blocked, at least temporarily, and that is enough to win with the e-pawn.

3...♖a1

Black's strongest defence prompts a further finesse from White.

4 ♔f4!

The only move to win.

4...♖f1+ 5 ♗f2!!

Really nice! 5 ♔e4? is only a draw after 5...♔xa7 6 ♔d5 ♖e1 7 ♔d6.

5...♖xf2+ 6 ♔e3 ♖f1 7 ♔e2 Black resigned.

A very beautiful study since all White's moves were necessary and included some exceptionally beautiful bishop moves. This is tactics in its purest form!

222

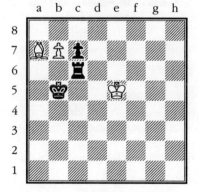

Troitzky
The end of a study 1895
White to move

Black cannot prevent White from promoting the b-pawn but thanks to special circumstances Black can hold the draw by playing for stalemate.

1...♖e6+!! 2 ♔xe6

2 ♔f5 ♖e8 is an obvious draw.

2...♔c6! 3 b8♕ Draw.

Black is stalemated. Under-promotion with 3 b8♘+ ♔b7 doesn't alter the result.

223

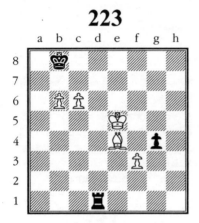

Goldstein – Shamkovich
Moscow 1946
Black to move

1...gxf3

It's in Black's interest to liquidate pawns so as to be able to create stalemate possibilities. 1...g3? would be a mistake because then White wins after 2 c7+ ♔c8 3 ♗f5+ ♖d7 4 ♗h3 g2 5 ♗xg2.

2 ♗xf3

2 c7+ ♔c8

(1) 3 ♗f5+ ♖d7 4 ♗h3 f2 followed by 5...f1♕ and 6...♖xc7 with a draw. After 2 ♗f5?! ♖c1 it's White who must be precise to hold the draw.

(2) 3 ♗xf3 ♖c1 4 ♔d6 ♖c6+! leads to another, more familiar

stalemate picture. Note that 4...♖xc7? fails to 5 ♗g4+ ♖d7+ 6 ♗xd7+ ♔b7 7 ♔c5. Such a position with a knight pawn on the sixth rank is only a draw with a bishop on a7.

2...♖d7!!

The only move and a pretty one! White obviously cannot capture the rook due to stalemate and if White plays...

3 ♗d5

Black has the stunning...

3...♖b7!!

Again, the only move and even prettier than before. Other rook moves lose, for example 3...♖h7? 4 ♔d6 ♖h6+ 5 ♗e6 ♖h8 6 c7+ ♔b7 7 ♔c5 ♖h5+ 8 ♗d5+ ♔c8 9 ♔d6. The rook moves are unusual but contain important stalemate ideas with which you can familiarise yourself for this kind of ending with bishop and two far advanced passers.

224

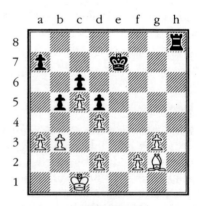

Chekhover
1947
White to move

The only way to hold the draw is by building a fortress. This is how it's done:

1 ♚d1!

If White keeps the bishop then the position is clearly lost. 1 ♚c2 is answered by 1...♖h2 2 ♗f1 (2 ♗f3 ♖xf2 3 ♗h5 ♖g2 4 g4 ♖g3) 2...♖xf2 3 ♗d3 ♖g2 and 1 f4 is met by 1...♖h2 2 ♗f3 ♖h3.

1...♖h2 2 ♚e2!!

Such an idea can't even be found by Komodo11 and that says something about the computer's limitations. 2 ♚e1!! also works in the same fashion.

2...♖xg2 3 ♚f1 ♖h2 4 ♚g1 ♖h3 5 ♚g2 ♖h8 6 f3

With this move White has built an impregnable fortress, making it impossible for Black's pieces to penetrate. White task is simple: he just oscillates his king between the squares g2 and g1 or f2 and f1 if Black's rook is on the e-file.

6...♖h7 7 ♚g1 ♖g7 8 ♚g2 ♖g6 9 ♚f2 ♖e6 10 ♚f1 ♚f6 11 ♚f2 ♚f5 12 ♚f1

If Black tries to win he can even lose as the following variations show:

12...♖e4?? 13 fxe4+ ♚xe4 14 ♚g2 ♚xd4 15 g4 ♚xc5 16 g5 ♚d6 17 d4 ♚e6 18 ♚g3 ♚f5 19 ♚h4 and it's obvious that White is winning. It's rare to construct a fortress where the opponent cannot win despite having an extra rook, but the main point is to show that such positions exist and they are certainly good for developing your imagination and

creativity. The use of fortresses is a well-known defensive method in all kinds of endings and you should know the most important of these.

225

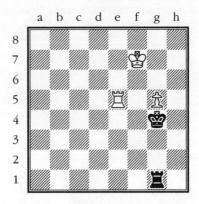

Kopayev
1958
White to move

1...♚h5 2 g6+

After 2 ♚f6 Black can go for the same idea as in the main variation by 2...♖g2 3 ♖f5 ♖g4 4 ♖f1 ♖f4+ 5 ♖xf4 with a stalemate.

2...♚h6 3 ♖e6

White's plan is to play ♖f6-f2-h2 with an easy win but Black has an effective antidote against this which is well worth remembering.

3...♖g2

Also the waiting moves on the g-file, 3...♖g3 or 3...♖g4, draw but beware because 3...♖g5? loses after 4 ♖f6 since the stalemate idea 4...♖f5 must occur with a check. Now it's White who checks with 5 g7+ and then the pawn ending is lost after 5...♖xf6+ 6 ♚xf6 ♚h7

7 ♔f7. The general rule to remember in rook endings is to keep the rook as far away from the opponent's king as possible.

4 ♖f6 ♖g5!

Black must carry out the stalemate idea since after 4...♖g1? 5 ♖f2 ♖xg6 6 ♖h2+ ♔g5 7 ♖g2+ White wins.

5 ♖f1

There is not much else White can do. After 5 g7+ ♔h7 the g-pawn is lost.

5...♖f5+ 6 ♖xf5

Remember this stalemate idea. Not knowing it would make it almost impossible for you to solve the next rook ending.

226

Grigoriev
1937
White to move

We know from the previous study by Kopayev that the rook must put pressure on the pawn from the rear

and that the king must advance to the h-file. What is most difficult is to find the first move.

1 ♖f5!!

It's interesting that it takes 17 moves before Komodo11 understands that the position is a draw. It's pretty difficult (and impractical) to calculate so many moves ahead but by knowing what position to strive for (Kopayev) our task will be much easier. The natural move 1 ♖g7? fails to 1...♖c4 since White cannot advance his king without suffering. For example 2 ♔d7 is met by 2...♖e4 3 ♔d6 ♔c3 4 ♔d5 ♔d3 and the king is cut off. The other attacking move 1 ♖f4? is just as bad due to 1...g3 2 ♖g4 ♖c3 3 ♔f7 ♔c2 4 ♔g6 ♔d2 5 ♔h5 ♔e2 6 ♔h4 ♔f2 7 ♔h3 ♖f3 and the rook is misplaced on g4 since it's White to move. With Black to move it's a draw as we saw in the previous study. The difference with placing the rook on g4, compared to g5 as in the main variation, is that 8 ♖a4 fails to 8...g2+ 9 ♔h2 g1♕ mate. This variation is not possible with the pawn one square back.

1...♔c2

1...g3 2 ♖g5 ♔c3 3 ♔f7 ♔c2 4 ♔g6 ♔d2 5 ♔h5 ♔e2 6 ♔h4 ♔f2 7 ♔h3 ♖f3 8 ♖g4! ♖f8 9 ♖f4+ and stalemate next move, which is exactly the same idea as in the study by Kopayev.

2 ♖g5 ♖c4 3 ♔f7 ♔d3 4 ♔g6 ♔e3 5 ♔h5 ♔f3 6 ♔h4 ♖f4 7 ♖a5

It's an easy draw due to the rook checks which will follow after 7...g3+ 8 ♔h3 g2 9 ♖a3+ ♔f2 10 ♖a2+.

227

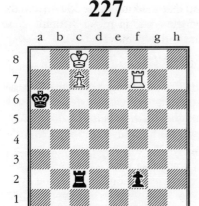

Emanuel Lasker
1890
White to move

With the black king on a7 the position is an easy draw but here White can manoeuvre the king and rook in such a way as to prepare a decisive tactical finesse.

1 ♔b8 ♖b2+ 2 ♔a8!

The point is to take the opposition and then drive the king back with a rook check on the sixth rank. Then White will repeat the same manoeuvre and check on the fifth rank etc.

2...♖c2 3 ♖f6+ ♔a5

Black must keep the b-file open for a rook check, otherwise White moves the king to b7 followed by promotion.

4 ♔b7 ♖b2+ 5 ♔a7 ♖c2 6 ♖f5+ ♔a4 7 ♔b6 ♖b2+

Black must defend against ♖xf2 when the c7-pawn is defended by the king.

8 ♔a6 ♖c2 9 ♖f4+ ♔a3 10 ♔b6 ♖b2+ 11 ♔a5 ♖c2 12 ♖f3+ ♔b2

White has managed to drive the king down to the second rank when White finally goes for the decisive **13 ♖xf2!** exploiting the pin. After **13...♖xf2 14 c8♕** the rest is a matter of technique, unless you are playing a computer when it's a tougher nut to crack. The elementary Philidor position must be mastered and it is presented as position 284 in *300 Most Important Chess Positions*.

228

Alekhine – Bogoljubow
World Championship match,
The Hague 1929
White to move

I have known this famous and important position ever since I was a young boy. The main principle when you have lost time in a pawn race is to prepare to push the passed pawn down the board by shielding off the enemy king.

70...♔e4!

Interestingly Bogoljubow missed what today must be regarded as a part of elementary endgame technique. This is why this position is so important. If Bogoljubow can fall into this, anyone can, unless you already know what happened in his world title match game against Alekhine: 70...♔g4? 71 b7 f5 72 b8♕ ♖xb8 73 ♖xb8 f4 74 ♔d5 f3 75 ♔e4 f2 76 ♖f8 ♔g3 77 ♔e3 and Black resigned.

71 b7 f5 72 b8♕ ♖xb8 73 ♖xb8 f4

The position is a draw since it's impossible to approach the pawn in an effective way. When you fully understand this rook ending it will be easier to understand the stunning example of position 212, Lerner – Dorfman.

229

Kok
1936
White to move

White obviously wants to give a deadly check but how can he evacuate the king?

1 ♔h7!!

White now has the opposition and wins by maintaining it. 1 ♔g7? ♔g1!! would have given Black the opposition.

1...♔h2

It's best to keep the pawn on d7 and the rook on b7 so White cannot attack the rook. If 1...d5+ 2 ♔g6 ♔g2 3 ♔f5 ♔f3 4 ♔e5 ♔e3 5 ♔xd5 ♔d3 (*5...♖e7 6 ♔d6*) 6 ♔c6 White wins by threatening the rook as well as a decisive check on d8. If the rook moves, White wins by 1...♖c7 2 ♔g6 ♔g1 3 ♔f5 ♔f2 4 ♔e5 ♔e3 5 ♔d6.

2 ♔h6 ♔h3 3 ♔h5 ♔h2 4 ♔h4 ♔h1 5 ♔h3

Black is not only in zugzwang but must also defend against the double threat 6 ♖f8.

5...d5 6 ♖f8!!

Note that the rook moves 6 ♖e8, 6 ♖c8 and 6 ♖b8 lead to a draw after 6...♖h7+ 7 ♔g3 ♖g7+ 8 ♔f2 ♖f7+. This is why the rook must be placed on the f-file.

6...♖h7+ 7 ♔g3 ♖g7+ 8 ♔f2 Black resigned.

White is threatening mate on h8 as well as a8♕. Do familiarise yourself with this very nice and useful study.

230

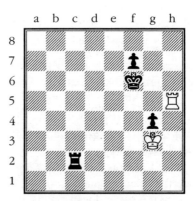

Sveshnikov – Sermek
Nova Gorica 1998
Black to move

In this position it seems that Black is winning after…

47...♚g6?

Correct was 47...♜c4 followed by 48...f5 with an easy win if it were not for the stalemate idea…

48 ♜g5+!

…whereupon the players agreed to a draw. Knowledge of such traps is obviously important for both the attacker and the defender. Towards the ending of games you are often more vulnerable to such traps so it is vital to be acquainted with them.

231

Wiedenkeller – Jung Min Seo
Gothenburg Open 2019
White to move

64...c4?

After this mistake it's a forced draw since White can exploit Black's passive king and badly placed rook. Correct was 64...♚f8! 65 ♚e6 ♚g8! 66 ♜c7 c4 67 ♚f6 b5 since the drawing manoeuvre which arose in the game doesn't work with a rook on c7. After 68 ♚g6 ♚f8 69 ♚f6 ♚e8 70 ♚e6 ♚d8 71 ♚d6 Black activates his rook by 71...♜b3

and after 72 ♜b7 manoeuvres the king towards the kingside to be able to check the white king at the right moment then sacrifice the b-pawn and transpose to an ending where the white king is cut off. The main variation is 72...♚e8! 73 ♚e6 ♚f8! 74 ♚f6 ♜f3+ 75 ♚e6 ♜e3+ 76 ♚f6 ♚e8 77 ♜xb5 ♚d7 78 ♜c5 c3 79 ♚f5 ♚d6 80 ♜c8 ♚d5 81 ♚f4 ♜h3 and wins.

65 ♚e6 ♚f8 66 ♚f6 ♚e8

66...♚g8 67 ♜g7+ ♚h8 68 ♜c7 is a draw since Black must sacrifice the c-pawn to parry the deadly threat of 69 ♚g6.

67 ♚e6 ♚d8 68 ♚d6 ♚c8 69 ♚c6 ♚b8 70 ♜h8+ ♚a7 71 ♜h7+ ♚a6 72 ♜h8 ♚a7 73 ♜h7+ Draw.

Here the players agreed to a draw since there is no way for the black king to escape the perpetual check. A complicated ending, especially with little time on the clock, but if have you seen and understood it, then it will not be so complicated for you next time.

232

Kamsky – Popov
World Rapid Championship 2019
White to play

Here Kamsky missed the fact that his best opportunity was to sacrifice the e6-pawn in exchange for the activation of his king.

59 ♔f5!

Kamsky wrongly played 59 ♖b6? whereupon Black replied 59...♔f6! and all White's winning attempts were in vain.

59...♖c5+ 60 ♔g6 ♖c4!

After 60...♔xe6 61 ♖e3+ Black can play 61...♖e5 to stop 62 f4 with an easy win but then White can win the pawn ending after 62 ♖xe5+ ♔xe5 63 ♔g5 ♔e6 64 f4 ♔f7 65 ♔f5 since Black loses the opposition.

61 ♖f3!!

Most probably it was this super move that Kamsky missed. The idea is simply to play 62 ♖f7+ followed by 63 f4 – or 62 ♖f6+ if Black captures the pawn.

61...♔xe6

61...♖g4+ upsets White's plans but then White can implement another idea. 62 ♔f5 ♖a4 63 ♖e3! The threat is 64 f4 which cannot be stopped. Black can try 63...♖a5+ 64 ♖e5 ♖a8 but White advances the f-pawn anyway, since after 65.f4 ♖f8+

66 ♔e4 is a theoretical win, e.g. 66...♖h8 67 ♔f3 ♖a8 68 f5 ♔f6 69 ♔f4 ♖a4+ 70 ♖e4 ♖a8 71 ♖e3 (White's plan is to manoeuvre the king to the queenside.) 71...♖a4+ 72 ♔f3 ♖a8 73 ♔e4 ♖a5 (After *73...♔e7* Black releases the pressure on the f5-pawn and White can exploit this by manoeuvring his rook to the kingside by *74 ♔e5 ♖a5+ 75 ♔f4 ♖a8 76 ♖h3*) 74 ♔d4 ♖a8 75 ♔d5 (It's sensible to keep contact with the e5-square while White's king heads for d6 to stop Black playing his king to e7.) 75...♖a5+ 76 ♔d6 ♖a6+ 77 ♔d7 ♖a7+ 78 ♔c6 ♖a8 (If the black king releases the pressure on the f5-pawn by *78...♔e7* it gives White the signal for a decisive rook manoeuvre: *79 ♖b3* followed by *80 ♖b7+*.) 79 e7! ♔f7 80 f6 ♔e8 81 ♔b7 ♖a1 82 f7+ and the e-pawn promotes.

62 ♖e3+

62 ♖f6+ ♔e5 63 ♔g5 also wins.

62...♔d6 63 ♔f5!!

63 ♔g5? ♖c8! leads to a draw since the pawn cannot advance due to checks from g8 and f8.

63...♖c8 64 ♖e6+ ♔d7 65 f4

With the rook on e6 White controls the sixth rank and the Lucena position is achieved by force. A likely continuation is...

65...♖f8+ 66 ♖f6 ♖a8 67 ♔g6 ♖g8+ 68 ♔f7 ♖g4 69 f5 ♖g5 70 ♔f8

Black is in a kind of zugzwang because whatever move Black makes White can improve his king or rook.

70...♖h5 71 ♔g7 ♖g5+ 72 ♔f7 ♖h5 73 ♔g6 ♖h1 74 ♖e6

The Lucena position with the king on f8 and the pawn on f7 cannot be prevented. Rook endings are difficult and it's vital to have as much understanding and knowledge of them as possible and be fully focused when specific situations arise. It will certainly be worth your while because 50 percent of all endgames feature rooks. In such endings tactics are intertwined with intricate rook and king manoeuvres and they can be tough for anyone on this planet!

233

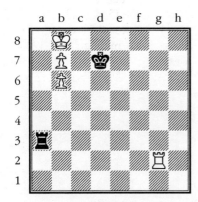

Duras
1905
White to play

If the b6-pawn is removed we would have a normal Lucena position on the board (See position 222 in *300 Most Important Chess Positions*) so the question is how White can get over this obstacle since it is hinders the path the white king normally wants to take.

1 ♖d2+ ♔e7 2 ♖d6!!

The key move to win. White has to play like this since the natural

building-a-bridge move 2 ♖d5 doesn't work on account of 2...♖a1 3 ♔c7 ♖c1+ and the path to b6 is obstructed.

2...♖c3

2...♔xd6 loses because of the check on b8 after 3 ♔c8 ♖c3+ 4 ♔d8 ♖h3 5 b8♕+.

3 ♖c6!!

Tactical point No.2.

3...♖xc6

3...♖d3 is met by 4 ♖c2 ♔d7 5 ♖a2 followed by a king move to the a-file.

4 ♔a7

The b7-pawn promotes. "A position for gourmets!" writes the Swedish writer Jostein Westberg when giving his impression of Duras's study in the Swedish endgame book *Slutspel i schack*.

234

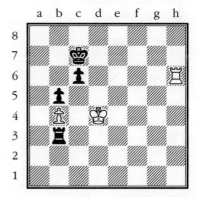

Motwani – Granda
Olympiad, Thessaloniki 1988
White to move

If you glance at this position it looks like Black is winning the b4-pawn by force, however with the help of a tactical, but far from obvious trick it's actually an easy draw.

1 ♖h4!!

The natural 1 ♔c5? fails to 1...♖c3+ 2 ♔d4 ♖c4+ and the pawn is lost. This kind of tactical device is useful to remember in rook endings as it is so common. The players immediately agreed to a draw since it will be stalemate after **1...♖xb4+ 2 ♔c5 ♖xh4 Draw.**

It is important to be aware of this stalemate idea since it does crop up every now and then. If you are not familiar with it then it's easy to miss the idea – which in this case saved an otherwise totally lost rook ending.

Note that 2...♖b1 doesn't help Black either after 3 ♖h7+ since then the c6-pawn is lost. 2...♖c4+ 3.♖xc4 bxc4 is also an elementary draw. Curiously all three legal king moves lead to a forced draw.

235

Tylor – Eliskases
Hastings 1936-37
White to move

Ragosin has analysed in *Shakhmaty* that White can draw with...

38 a8♕!

38 ♔xg6? would have been a mistake because of 38...f5+ followed by 39...♖xa7+. In the game 38 ♖b6? was played but White lost after 38...♖xa7+ 39 ♔xf6 (If *39 ♔xg6* then *39...f5* wins. The rook was clearly better placed on b5.) 39...g5 40 ♖b4+ ♔h5 41 ♖b5 ♔h4! 42 ♖b4+ (*42 ♖xg5 ♖a6+ 43 ♔f5 ♖a5+*) 42...g4 43 ♔f5 ♔h3! Black repeats the same motif. White resigned.

38...♖xa8

39 ♔xg6

And the f6-pawn is virtually lost. 39 ♔xf6? is the wrong pawn to snatch due to 39...♖a6+ and wins.

39...f5

If 39...♖f8 then 40 ♔g7.

40 ♖xf5 ♖g8+ 41 ♔f7

The reason an immediate promotion was so strong is that it displaced the black rook. However, as played in the game, the black rook had a perfect position on the sixth rank.

240

236

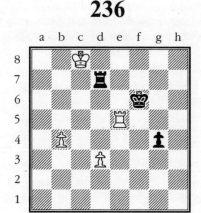

Ivkov – Kozomura
Sarajevo 1967
White to move

Sometimes three different endgames can arise in a game. White wins the pawn race in the pawn ending after...

54 ♔xd7

If White avoids the pawn ending then the rook ending is a draw because of the dangerous black passed pawn. After 54 ♖e4? Black replies 54...♖g7! and after the further 55 b5 g3 56 ♖e1 g2 57 ♖g1 ♔e5 58 b6 ♔d6 White must find the saving continuation 59 d4!! ♔c6 60 d5+ ♔xb6 61 d6 ♔c6 62 d7 to achieve the draw.

54...♔xe5 55 b5 g3 56 b6 g2 57 b7 g1♕ 58 b8♕+

The queen ending is winning for White since Black's pieces are misplaced.

58...♔f5

Forced. The alternatives 58...♔d5 59 ♕d6 mate and 58...♔d4 59 ♕b6+ were worse.

59 ♕f8+ ♔e5

Of course Black must avoid going to the g-file because of the deadly skewer on g8.

60 ♕d6+ ♔f5 61 ♕e6+ ♔f4 62 ♕f6+ Black resigned.

A beautiful ending, which at least leads to a queen exchange and a winning pawn ending. Note the great influence of the d3-pawn which controlled White's e4-square as well as enabling the placement of his king on d7 – which in turn assisted the queen when it checked on the e6-square. The variation is not so difficult to calculate but you must see nine moves ahead and use the position after move 58 as a stepping stone.

237

Ban
1954
White to move

After **1 g7** Black apparently has the saving resource **1...♖e6+ 2 ♔h5 ♖g6! 3 ♔xg6 g2**

However, White still wins after the nice rook manoeuvre **4 ♖h3+!**

Not 4 g8♕? g1♕+ 5 ♔f7 ♕xg8+ 6 ♔xg8 d3 with an elementary draw.

4...♔f4

If 4...♔f2 then 5 ♖h2 and the pawn is pinned.

5 ♖h4+! ♔f3 6 ♖g4! ♔xg4 7 g8♕ ♔g3 8 ♔f5+ ♔f2 9 ♕a2+ and White wins.

238

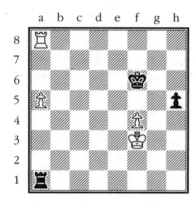

Kluger – Sandor
Budapest 1954
Black to move

This position look like a loss for Black because how can he prevent the elementary plan a6-a7 followed by ♖f8+? If Black places his king on g7 then f5-f6+ decides. Yet amazingly Black holds the draw thanks to his active play and opportunities for stalemate. The game proceeded...

1...♔f5 2 a6 ♖a3+ 3 ♔g2

After 3 ♔f2 ♔g4! 4 a7 ♖a2+ 5 ♔e3 ♖a3+ 6 ♔d4 ♖a4+ 7 ♔c3 Black does not play 7...♔xf4? which loses after 8 ♖f8+ ♔g3 9 a8♕ ♖xa8 10 ♖xa8 h4 11 ♔d3 h3 12 ♔e2 h2

13 ♖g8+ ♔h3 14 ♔f2 but 7...♖a3+! as it's essential to lure the white king to the b-file. Now after 8 ♔b4 ♖a1 9 ♖g8+ ♔xf4 10 a8♕ ♖xa8 11 ♖xa8 h4 the endgame is a draw.

3...♔g4! 4 a7 ♖a2+ 5 ♔g1 ♔f3 6 ♔h1

6 f5 is met by the rook manoeuvre 6...♖g2+ 7 ♔h1 ♖g7! 8 f6 ♖f7 with a simple draw.

6...h4! 7 f5 ♔g3!! 8 ♖g8+ ♔h3 a8♕ ♖a1+! 10 ♕xa1 and Black is stalemated.

239

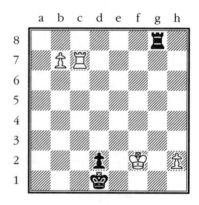

Zahorovsky
1989
White to move

Another example where it's necessary to under-promote is this rook ending, which might very well occur in a practical game.

1 ♖c8 ♖xc8 2 bxc8♗! ♔c2 3 ♗g4 ♔d3!

Black is obviously anxious to reach the black corner on h8 to salvage a draw, but White's king is just in time to stop that from happening.

4 ♔g3! ♔e4 5 ♔h4! d1♕ 6 ♗xd1 ♔f5 7 ♔h5 ♔f6 8 ♔h6 ♔f7 9 ♔h7 **Black resigned.**

240

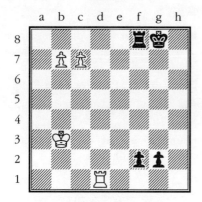

Walbrodt – Zinkl
Leipzig 1894
White to move

This position is on the front cover of the Swedish edition (1946) of a book (*Slutspelsteori Tornslutspel*) by Euwe about rook endings. It looks like a study but it's actually a game. Unfortunately White missed his way…

50 c8♕ f1♕ 51 ♕g4+

This is the reason White has to queen the more centralised c-pawn rather than the b-pawn.

51…♔h8

Black must avoid checks from the rook.

52 ♕h3+!

In the game, Walbrodt checked aimlessly on the h- and g-files but failed to understand that the check on h3 was the only way to win. The

game ended in a draw after 65 moves.

52…♔g7

52…♔g8 53 ♖xf1 gxf1♕ 54 ♕xf1 ♖xf1 55 b8♕+ is a win because the promotion comes with a check. Otherwise Black would win with a skewer.

53 ♖d7+ ♖f7 54 ♕g4+ ♔h7

54…♔h6 55 ♖d6+ ♖f6 56 ♖xf6+ .♕xf6 57 ♕h3+ followed by 58 ♕xg2+ and promotion of the b-pawn is the pragmatic solution. However, the non-human solution is 56 b8♕ which forces mate in eleven moves.

55 ♕e4+!

The key move to win because a queen check on b1 is prevented.

55…♔g7 56 b8♕

White can promote since the b1-square is protected.

56…g1♕ 57 ♕be5+ ♕f6 58 ♖xf7+! ♔xf7 59 ♕c7+ ♔g8 60 ♕eh7+ ♔f8 61 ♕c8+

It's mate next move.

The key to solving what Walbrodt failed to do was to see the decisive queen check on move 55. Such a move, which is both attacking and defensive, is crucial. Grandmaster moves are those with multiple effects. It was overlooked by the strong player Walbrodt and will doubtless be overlooked by other strong players too. The position after Black's 54th move should be a stepping stone in the mind of any player religiously searching for a win which must be there.

241

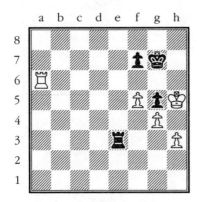

Speelman – N.N.
Simultaneous Exhibition,
Ostend 2006
White to move

1 h4!

Black's only salvation is if White plays 1 ♔xg5? because then Black has a stalemate trick after the forced line 1...♖xh3 2 f6+ ♔g8 3 ♖a8+ ♔h7 4 ♖f8 ♖h5+! 5 ♔f4 The capture on h5 results in an immediate stalemate. 5...♖a5 6 g5 (*6 ♖xf7+ ♔g6 7 ♖f8 ♖a6 and the f6-pawn is lost since 8 g5 is met by 8...♖a4+ 9 ♔e5 ♖a5+ etc.*) 6...♖xg5! 7 ♖xf7+ (*7 ♔xg5 is stalemate.*) 7...♔g8 (if *7...♔g6? then 8 ♖g7+*) 8 ♔xg5

♔xf7 9 ♔f5 ♔f8 with an elementary draw.

1...gxh4 2 f6+ ♔h7 3 ♖a7 ♔g8 4 ♖a8+ ♔h7 5 ♖f8 h3

The h3-pawn is completely harmless.

6 ♖xf7+ ♔g8 7 ♖g7+ ♔f8

7...♔h8 is answered by 8 ♔g6.

8 ♖h7 h2 9 ♔g6 Black resigned.

Having a knowledge of this relatively common position is especially useful, since tactics abound for both sides.

242

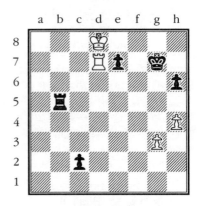

Zakhodiakin
Chigorin Memorial 1950
White to move

It is almost impossible to solve this study if you are not familiar with the positional draw. Here is the solution:

1 ♖c7!

1 ♖xe7+? loses after 1...♔f6 2 ♖c7 ♖b8+ 3 ♔d7 ♖b7! 4 ♖xb7 c1♕. Compare this position with the main

line. Here it's impossible for White to construct a fortress.

1...♖b8+ 2 ♔xe7 ♖b7 3 ♖xb7 c1♕ 4 ♔e6+ ♔g6

Of course it doesn't help to go to the last rank because of the ongoing checks.

5 h5+!!

This key move is a paradoxical pawn sacrifice whose purpose is to put the black king in jail.

5...♔xh5

5...♔g5 is met by 6 ♖g7+.

6 ♖g7!

Now it's a positional draw since there is no way for Black to force the rook away from g7. Black's king is imprisoned and Black can do nothing useful with a lone queen. Note that such fortresses are often associated with the stronger side's king being unable to penetrate the opponent's position. There is a further example of a positional draw in position 274.. The present position could well arise in a practical game and so it is very useful to know. If you haven't seen it before you might think the position can't be saved and so may not be

inclined to head for it. You cannot ask too much of creativity alone and that is why it's so important to know key positions and the end of this study is just that.

243

Schlechter – Perlis
Carlsbad 1911
White to move

41 e5!

This thematic move is the simplest way to secure the win. Black has to accept the sacrifice otherwise comes the decisive 42 e6. The prosaic 41 ♖xg7 h3 42 ♖h7 h2 43 b5 also wins but Schlechter's move is the most stylish and represents an important finesse to have up your sleeve.

41...♖d2+

41...♖xe5+ displaces the rook on e5 after which Black loses the opportunity to give check from the rear after 42.♔c6.

41...fxe5 is answered by 42 ♔e6 since the black pawn provides White with the necessary shelter from an annoying check on the e-file. This idea is a relatively common tactical idea in rook endings.

42 ♔e6

Of course a king on e6 is just as dangerous as a pawn in this position.

42...♔c8 43 d7+ ♔b8 44 ♖a6! ♔c7 45 ♖d6! Black resigned.

Perlis resigned after the simple calculation 45...♖xd6+ 46 exd6 ♔d8 47 b5 and White queens with an immediate mate.

244

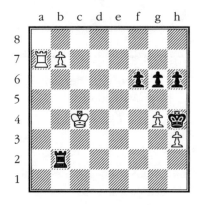

Galvenius – Stone
England 1952
White to move

1 g5!

A typical idea which it pays to remember. White clears the fourth rank for a decisive rook check. Of course not 1 ♔c5? ♔xh3 since White doesn't have 2 ♖a3+ followed by 3 ♖b3.

1...fxg5

1...♔xg5? doesn't even give Black the chance to play with pawns

against rook since 2 ♖a5+ ♔h4 3 ♖b5 promotes the pawn.

Nor does 1...hxg5 help after 2 ♔c3 ♖b6 3 ♖a4+ ♔xh3 4 ♖b4 ♖xb7 5 ♖xb7 f5 6 ♔d3. White's king is too close to the pawns and White can win in several ways, for example 6...g4 7 ♔e3 (*7 ♖g7 ♔g3 8 ♔e2!* wins since Black's only chance was to get the king to f2.) 7...g3 8 ♖g7 f4+ and here 9 ♔f3 is the simplest.

2 ♔c3 ♖b6 3 ♖a4+ ♔xh3 4 ♖b4 ♖xb7 5 ♖xb7

5...h5

5...g4 makes no difference: 6 ♔d2 Any move with the king on the d-file wins. 6...g3 7 ♔e2 (But beware, after *7 ♔e1?? ♔h2!* Black wins.) 7...h5 8 ♔f3

(1) If 8...g2 the rook picks up the pawn after 9 ♖b1 g5 10 ♔f2 g4 11 ♖b3+ (Passive play with the rook by *11 ♖g1?* is a draw by stalemate after *11...g3+ 12 ♔f3 h4 13 ♖xg2.*) 11...♔h2 12 ♖g3,

(2) 8...g5 9 ♖b5 g4+ 10 ♔e2 h4 11 ♖h5 g2 12 ♔f2 g3+ 13 ♔g1 ♔g4 14 ♖h8 h3 15 ♖h7 and Black is in zugzwang.

6 ♔d3 ♔g2 7 ♔e2 g4 8 ♖h7! g3 9 ♖h6

White wins by zugzwang. However note that this position is a mutual zugzwang, so if White is to move the position is a draw. Fascinating stuff!

245

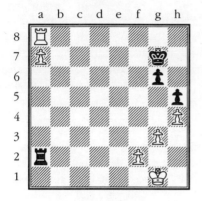

FIDE Master – N.N.
Club match
White to move

"White, a FIDE Master, had just played a6-a7 with an air of confidence, and after some deliberation Black resigned!" writes John Emms in his excellent endgame book *The Survival Guide Rook Endings*. Emms asked the white player what his winning plan would have been and he replied by shrugging his shoulders and moving his king to the queenside. It's clear that White must create a passed f-pawn to be able to win at all and that can only be done in one way. The most instructive and clear-cut variation to prove that this position is a draw is the following…

1 f3 Ra3 2 g4 hxg4 3 f4 Ra2 4 h5 gxh5 5 f5 h4 6 f6+ Kf7 7 Rh8 Ra1+! 8 Kg2

8 Kf2 is met by 8…g3+ 9 Kg2 Ra2+ 10 Kf3 Ra3+.

8…h3+!

If 8…Ra2+? then 9 Kf1 and Black loses since 9…Rxa7 fails to 10 Rh7+.

9 Kh2

Or 9 Kg3 Ra3+ 10 Kxg4 h2.

9…Ra2+ 10 Kg3 h2 11 Rxh2 Ra3+! 12 Kxg4 Kxf6 and Black draws.

246

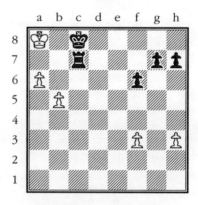

Milenkovic – Stankov
Yugoslavia 1968
Black to move

Black has many ways to win but the best and most spectacular is by preventing White from playing his pawn to b6 by…

1…Rc6!! 2 bxc6

If 2 Ka7 then 2…Kc7!.

2…g5!

The only move to win since it limits White's options on the queenside.

3 a7

3 ♔a7 is obviously answered by 3...♔c7 whereupon White will inevitably fall into a zugzwang position.

3...f5 4 c7

4 h4 was more venomous since it compels Black to find the only winning continuation 4...g4! 5 fxg4 f4! 6 g5 f3 7 g6 hxg6 8 h5 f2 and now after 9 hxg6 Black can even under-promote with 9...f1♗!! (The prosaic *9...f1♕* leads to a quick mate as well after *10 g7 ♕g2 11 g8♕+ ♕xg8 12 c7 ♔xc7* mate.) 10 g7 ♗c4 11 g8♕+ ♗xg8 12 c7 ♗d5 mate.

4...f4! 5 h4 g4 6 h5 h6! White resigned.

The whole idea of sacrificing on c6 would not have worked if Black were unable to place White in zugzwang on the kingside. At the same time Black needed to win the tempo battle so White didn't have time to stalemate himself.

The position is winning for White so is there anything Black can do? He played…

1...♖h1+!? 2 ♔xh1 gxf2

…and probably prayed to the gods that the winning boomerang combination 3 ♖f5!! ♔xf5 4 g4+ ♔xg4 5 ♔g2 went unnoticed. Naturally the gifted combinative player Richter saw it! Boomerang combinations by definition are those in which you need to see all the tactics within three moves. It's said that the American grandmaster Samuel Reshevesky (1911-1992) saw everything within the range of three moves. If you have the same ability to calculate flawlessly three moves ahead, as the great Reshevsky, you can really go far as a chess player. By the way, don't forget to check out Vallejo Pons – Kasparov, position 85 in the middlegame section, since it's a more advanced boomerang combination.

247

Richter – Amateur
Berlin 1930
White to move

248

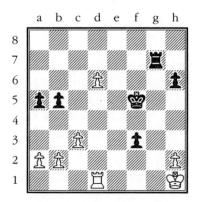

E. Berg – Engqvist
Stockholm 2007
Black to move

The only way to hold the position is to play actively with **45...f2!** and exploit the fact that White's king is out of play. The passive 45...♖d7? loses after 46 ♔g1 ♔e4 47 ♔f2 since the f3-pawn falls. In the game I played the fatal 45...♔e6? and resigned after 46 d7 ♖xd7 47 ♖xd7 ♔xd7 48 ♔g1 ♔e6 49 ♔f2 ♔d5 50 ♔xf3 ♔c4 51 ♔e3 a4 52 ♔d2 h5 53 h4 ♔d5 54 ♔d3 ♔c5 55 b3 axb3 56 axb3 ♔d5 57 b4 ♔c6 58 ♔e4.

46 ♖f1

46 d7? even leads to a win for Black in the pawn ending after 46...♖xd7 47 ♖f1 ♖d2 48 ♔g2 ♖xb2 49 ♖xf2+ ♖xf2+ 50 ♔xf2 ♔e4 because of Black's more active king.

46...♔e6 47 ♖xf2 ♖g5!!

This tactical idea can be difficult to find if you are not familiar with it and during the game I wasn't. However now I am, but I had to pay the price of a defeat to learn it. Capablanca said you learn more from your losses and that's certainly true.

Worse is 47...♔xd6? 48 ♖f6+ ♔c5 49 ♖xh6 ♖d7 50 ♖h5+ ♔b6 51 ♖g5.

48 ♖d2 ♔d7

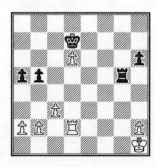

Black is two pawns down, but thanks to White's passive king,

which cannot be activated, Black has good drawing chances. Rook endings are often tactical in nature since they are often solely a matter of activity. For the sake of activity it's often possible to sacrifice a pawn and sometimes even two. In position 255, Kashdan-Alekhine, 1933, in *300 Most Important Chess Positions* an example of three pawn sacrifices is given!

249

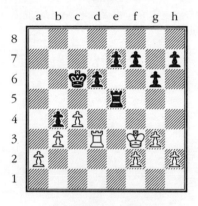

Te Kolsté – Réti
Baden-Baden 1925
White to move

29 a3!

A clever tactical pawn sacrifice, simplifying the position and nullifying the strength of the b4-pawn, which is practically as strong as the pawn duo on a2 and b3. In the game 29 ♖e3? was played but it led to a lost pawn ending after 29...♖xe3+ 30 fxe3 d5 since Black was practically playing a pawn up with his four against three majority on the kingside.

29...bxa3

29...♔c5 is met by 30 a4!, followed by 31 ♖e3, making a draw thanks to the protected passed a-pawn.

30 b4 a2 31 ♖a3 d5 32 ♖a6+!

An important intermezzo which makes it easier for White to achieve the draw, since Black's king is forced to go down the board and cannot protect the black pawn which will arise on c4. 32 cxd5+ ♔xd5 33 ♖xa2 ♔c4 34 ♖a4 is a theoretical draw but why play in a passive manner when there are more active and safer methods available?

32...♔b7 33 ♖xa2 dxc4 34 ♖c2 ♔c6 35 ♖xc4+ ♔b5 36 ♖f4 and it's an easy draw.

250

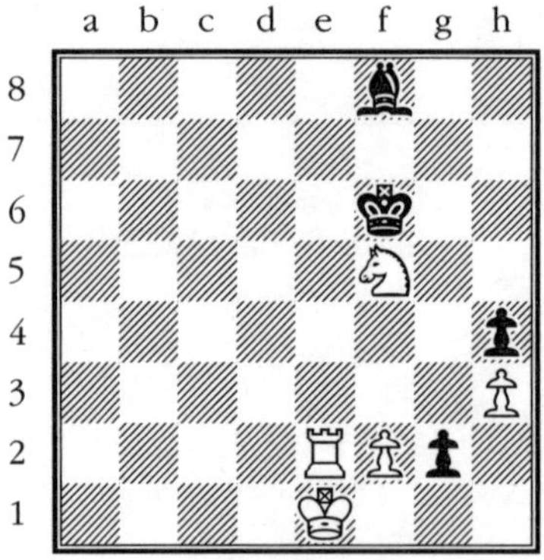

Schwere
1921
White to move

1 ♖e6+! ♔xf5

1...♔xe6 2 ♘d4+ ♔d5

(1) Note that 3 ♘e2? loses due to a zugzwang after 3...♔e4 4 ♘g1 ♔d3!

5 ♘f3 ♗d6 6 ♘g1 ♗h2 7 ♘f3 ♔e4 8 ♔e2 ♔f4.

(2) 3 ♘f3 ♗d6 4 ♔e2 ♗h2 5 ♔e3 and White is all right since it's impossible for Black to reach a zugzwang position.

2 ♖e5+! ♔xe5

2...♔f4 3 ♖g5! makes no difference after 3...♔f3. White holds with 4 ♖f5+ ♔e4 5 ♖e5+! or the more prosaic 5 ♖g5.

3 f4+ ♔xf4 4 ♔f2 Draw.

Also here White is helped by the fact that Black has the wrong bishop.

251

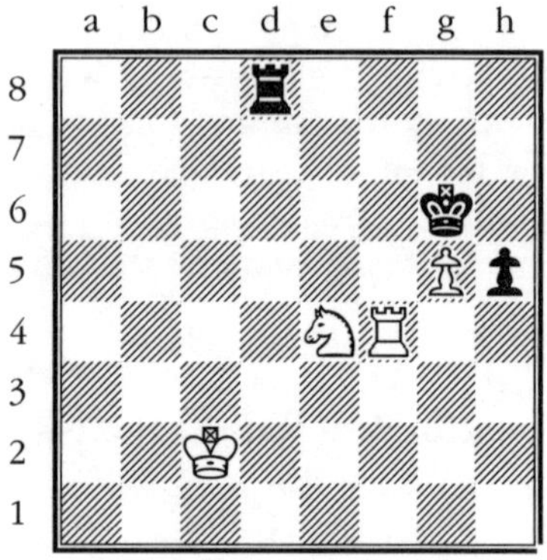

Ribli – Oszvath
Hungary 1971
Black to move

1...h4!

It's important that Black makes this move immediately, otherwise White decides the game with 1 ♖f6+.

1...♖xh4

(1) 2 ♖f3 ♚h5 3 ♔c3 ♚g4 4 ♖f1 ♚h5!!

...is also a fascinating positional draw.

(2) 2 ♖f6+ ♚h5 3 ♖h6+ ♚g4 4 g6 ♚f5 5 g7 ♖g8 6 ♘d6+ ♚g5 7 ♘f7+ ♚f5 is also a draw – by perpetual check.

2...♚f5!

The position is a positional draw and useful to know. White can only move his king to avoid immediate material loss. The game continued:

3 ♔c3 ♖d1 4 ♔c4 ♖d8 5 ♔c5 ♖d3 6 ♔c6 ♖d1 7 ♔c7 ♖d3

White's king cannot do anything constructive since it is cut off on the d-file whereas Black's rook has enough squares to oscillate between. White therefore tries a last trick.

8 ♖h1! ♖e3!

Here the players agreed to a **draw**. After 9 ♖h4, for example, Black just returns his rook to the d-file with a positional draw as previously mentioned. However, it should be noted that 8...♚xe4? would have lost after 9 ♖g1 ♖h3 10 g6 ♖h8 11 g7 ♖g8 12 ♔d6 ♚f5 13 ♚e7.

252

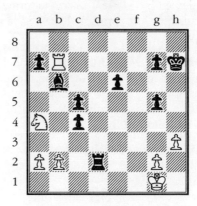

Ortueta – Aguado Sanz
Madrid 1934
Black to move

This is probably the most famous position showing the strength of passed pawns against a rook and knight.

31...♖xb2!! 32 ♘xb2 c3

Black exploits the fact that White cannot play the knight to d3 due to the discovered check.

33 ♖xb6

33 ♘d3 c4+ 34 ♚f1 (After *34 ♖xb6 cxd3* one of Black's two passers will decide.) 34...cxd3 35 ♚e1 ♗e3! followed by ...c2 next move.

33...c4!!

This key move creates maximum harmony between Black's pawns. The main threat is ...c2. White can only defend in one way.

34 ♖b4 a5!!

Another incredible move and the culmination of the combination.

35 ♘xc4

35 ♖xc4 cxb2 prevents White from controlling the b1-square since b4 as well as c1 are under Black's command. Note that the doubled pawn on g7 protects the king along the seventh rank so White cannot gain a decisive tempo after a check on c7 followed by ♖b7.

35...c2 White resigned.

253

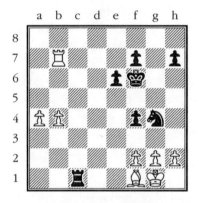

Kramnik – Anand
Game 5, World Championship
match, Bonn 2008
Black to move

As soon as Kramnik saw Anand grabbing hold of his knight, he understood what he had missed.

34...♘e3! 35 fxe3 fxe3 and **Kramnik resigned**, realising that there was no defence to 36...e2. It doesn't help to sacrifice the rook with 36 ♖c7 since Black can capture it and then return to c1, thereby renewing the threat. The combination is all the more beautiful when you consider that it was

actually the g-pawn which decided the game thanks to its tactically generated journey g5-gxf4-fxe3-e2-exf1♕. This example in the Meran variation proves that it's possible to create passers tactically (and not only positionally by qualitative or quantitative majorities) if you play in the spirit of Alekhine (Remember Marshall – Alekhine, position 139). This rather simple combination illustrates how three pieces are enough to create a combination: one which is sacrificed while the other two decide. Of course, the more pieces that are involved, the more tactical opportunities arise, which you have to see both as an attacker and defender.

254

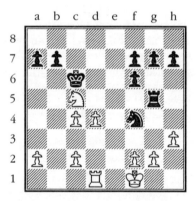

Andersson – Hörberg
Swedish Championship,
Sundsvall 1969
White to play

White has a passed pawn on the queenside but first the black knight must be lured away from the d-pawn.

27 g3! ♘xh3

(1) 27...♘e6 loses at least the exchange after 28 ♘e4.

(2) 27...♖xc5 28 dxc5 ♘e6 destroys White's pawn structure but the price is too high since sooner or later White will penetrate Black's position along the d-file after, for example, 29 ♖d6+ ♔c7 30 ♖d5 ♔c6 31 ♔e2 ♘xc5 (Otherwise *32 ♔e3* followed by *f4-f5* will harass the knight) 32 ♖d8.

(3) The most precise move was 27...♘g6 which makes it possible to stop the d-pawn if it tries to advance. However, White wins anyway after 28 ♖e1 as Black's pieces are completely misplaced.

28 d5+! Black resigned.

Hörberg resigned when he realised that the d-pawn promotes by force on d8, regardless of how Black plays. It's important not to forget that it takes five moves for a pawn to promote after leaving the second rank and if the pawn is placed on the fourth rank or on the fifth, as here, the distance is obviously shorter.

This tactical idea is typical for openings with this pawn structure and can arise in the Caro-Kann (1 e4 c6 2 d4 d5 3 ♘c3 dxe4 4 ♘xe4 ♘f6 5 ♘xf6+ exf6) or the Ruy Lopez (1 e4 e5 2 ♘f3 ♘c6 3 ♗b5 a6 4 ♗xc6 dxc6 5 d4 exd4 6 ♕xd4 ♕xd4 7 ♘xd4). If one has a pawn majority the chances are relatively good that a passed pawn will be crystallised. However, queening a pawn is a completely different matter – but here it worked.

255

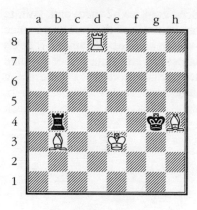

Petrov
The end of a study:
1st Prize, *Shakhmaty* 1959
White to move

It's important to avoid positions with rook and bishop against rook since they are a theoretical draw. The only way to win this position is by trapping the rook. It can only be done with the help of maximum co-operation between the king and the bishop pair. This is how to achieve such an astonishing feat...

1 ♖d4+!! ♖xd4 2 ♗e7!!

Such a position is good to have in your stockpile of ideas because it shows how strong the bishop pair can be in a totally open position. Despite the fact that the rook has several possible moves, it is trapped because the black king is placed on its worst possible square.

2...♖f4

Or 2...♖d7 3 ♗e6+.

3 ♗e6+ ♔g3

If 3...♖f5 then 4 ♔e4.

4 ♗d6

The rook is pinned and will be captured on the next move and then it's only a matter of mating with the bishop pair. So never underestimate the strength of the bishop pair, even if this position never occurs in your games.

256

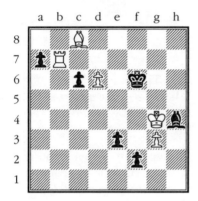

Korolkov
Trud 1935
White to move

It's not so difficult to see that White has to play…

1 d7 ♔e7 2 ♖b8

But it's harder to find Black's best defence, namely…

2...♗xg3!

2...f1♕ is met by 3 d8♕+ ♔xd8 4 ♗a6+ ♔c7 5 ♗xf1 ♔xb8 6 gxh4 and White's pawn promotes since the black king is outside the square of the h4-pawn.

3 ♖a8!

3 ♔xg3? leads to a draw after 3...f1♕ 4 d8♕+ ♔xd8 5 ♗a6+ ♔c7

6 ♖b7+ ♔c8 7 ♖b6+ ♔c7 8 ♖b7+ ♔c8 9 ♖xa7+ ♔b8 10 ♖b7+ ♔a8 since White has to give up the rook for the queen.

3...f1♕ 4 d8♕+ ♔xd8 5 ♗a6+

Now comes the most difficult move…

5...♗b8!! 6 ♗xf1

6 ♖xb8+ ♔c7 7 ♖c8+ ♔d7 leads to a draw.

6...♔c7 7 ♗a6 e2

It looks like Black is going to survive but here comes the climax of the whole study.

8 ♗xe2 ♔b7 9 ♗f3! ♔xa8

9...a6 10 ♗xc6+ ♔xc6 11 ♖xb8 with an easy win.

10 ♗xc6 mate.

This is one of the most beautiful studies I have ever seen. It's good practice to solve such intricate studies from time to time since it will not only help to improve your calculation skills but also your creative ability. From this study alone a lot can be learned about creativity and how to find the defender's best moves. White's moves were pretty easy to find but to discover super moves like 2...♗xg3!! and above all 5...♗b8!! indicates a very high level of skill, so you can be very pleased with yourself if you managed to solve the whole study up to the mate.

257

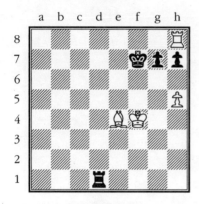

Sax – Kovacevic
Sarajevo 1982
White to move

56 ♗xh7?

The simple 56 ♔g3 followed by 57 ♗xh7 would have secured the win in the long run.

But not 56 ♖xh7? ♔g8 and White's rook is trapped with an inevitable draw.

56...g5+!!

White just fell into a really crude trap.

57 hxg6+

If 57 ♔xg5 then 57...♔g7 and White must give up his bishop, making it an easy draw.

57...♔g7 58 ♖g8+ ♔h6

Despite White's big material advantage the game soon ended in a **draw**. The reason for this was the ill-fated bishop on h7. Even after a rook exchange the position is a draw. Such positions are very useful to have in your repertoire since they can be used to draw lost positions – or the other way around if you can avoid falling into the same trap as Sax did.

258

Gorgiev
Shakhmaty 1929
White to move

This very beautiful study I found in John Montgomerie's book *The Quiet Game*. It is not White's moves but rather Black's that are the most difficult to find.

1 ♗f6+ ♔h7 2 ♖g7+ ♔h6 3 ♖f7 ♔g6

3...♘c6 4 ♗xd8 ♘xd8 5 ♖d7 and the knight is trapped.

4 ♖f8

The threat to move the bishop to h4 is not difficult to spot but one should also see **4...♘c6 5 ♗xd8 ♔g7!! 6 ♖e8 ♔f7 7 ♖h8 ♔g7 8 ♗f6+!! ♔xf6 9 ♖h6+** and White wins the knight, Beautiful, don't you agree?

259

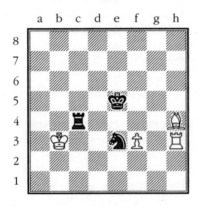

J. Fritz
Sachové 1954
White to move

1 ♗f2!

1 ♗g5? leads to a draw after 1...♖f4! 2 ♗xf4+ ♔xf4 since White cannot prevent the knight manoeuvre ...♘d1–f2 after which the f3-pawn is lost.

1...♖d4!

Despite this resource Black is losing by force after the further **2 ♗xe3 ♖d3+ 3 ♔c2 ♖xe3 4 ♔d2** Black's rook is trapped in a spectacular way.

4...♔f4

If 4...♖a3 then 5 f4+.

5 ♖h4+ ♔g3

Or 5...♔xf3 6 ♖h3+.

6 ♔xe3 ♔xh4 and White wins the pawn ending after **7 f4 ♔h5 8 ♔e4 ♔g6 9 ♔e5 ♔f7 10 ♔f5**

The position after the fourth move is useful to know. Don't forget such tactics – even in a seemingly simple rook ending.

260

Greco
1623
Black to move

Normally such a position is lost but at this particular moment Black can survive due to a well-known finesse.

1...♖a1+ 2 ♖f1 ♖xf1+ 3 ♔xf1 ♗h3!!

375 years later Shirov made this specific move even more famous in the chess world. His immortal move can be found in the ending which arose in Topalov – Shirov, Linares 1998, position 195.

4 ♔f2

4 gxh3 is obviously a draw since it's impossible to drive away the Black king from h8 without allowing stalemate.

4...♗xg2!

The only move to prevent the winning 5 g3.

Draw.

261

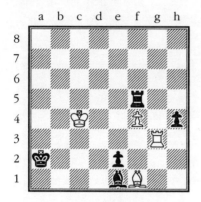

Herbstmann
Zvezda 1934
White to move

1 ♖g2!! ♖xf4+ 2 ♔d3 ♖xf1 3 ♔xe2 ♖h1 4 ♔f3+ ♔b3 5 ♖b2+!! ♔xb2 6 ♔g2

The end position is the key to the combination and even though it will probably never happen in a game it's useful to know that a lone king can hold the draw against rook, bishop and pawn despite the fact that the materially superior side is to move. It's quite amazing and one of many proofs that chess is an unbelievably rich game. The more such incredible exceptions you know, the closer you will come to gaining a true understanding of chess. By knowing exceptions to the rules you will already be ahead of chess players who are not familiar with these things. You know a position where it's impossible to win even though you are nine points ahead in material and have the move, which adds another half point! The more you are familiar with such positions, the more likely you will reach a true mastery of the game because chess isn't so simple. By having this key position constantly in your mind you can by analogy use its ideas in other scenarios where the exception is the rule. Chess, like language, is full of them and we must detect them as well as know them and then teach them to others who don't know.

262

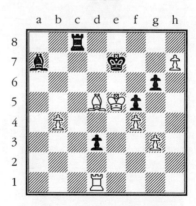

Koneru – Goryachkina
Women's Grand Prix,
Monaco 2019
White to move

I watched this game live on the internet and it's rather tricky since White must manoeuvre without falling into any of Black's traps.

60 ♖d2!

Correctly taking care of defence, while at the same time preparing a deadly rook move to h2. The obvious 60 ♗g8?! is met by 60...♖d8 and White must go back with 61 ♗d5. 60 ♖xd3? leads to a perpetual check after 60...♗b8+ 61 ♔d4 ♗a7+ since the d3-square is not available for White's king. 60 ♖h1 is playable but not as subtle as the move played since it allows Black to play 60...d2, preventing White playing 61 h8♕?? because of 61...♖xh8 and White's rook is overloaded.

60...♗b6 61 ♖h2 ♖h8 62 ♗g8

Black's fate is sealed with the trapped rook. White won after the further **62...♗e3 63 ♖h1 ♗d2 64 b5 ♗c3+ 65 ♔d5 ♔d7 66 ♔c4 ♗f6 67 ♔xd3 g5 68 ♖h5 Black resigned.**

263

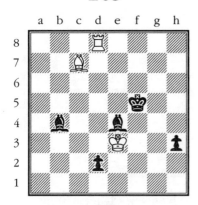

Nenarokov – Grigoriev
USSR Championship, 1923
Black to move

1...♗d6!!

Intersection-point combinations are common in problems but Grigoriev managed to play a move in a real game with the Novotny theme. The fundamental idea is to sacrifice a piece on the intersection-point (d6) and when the opponent captures the piece one of the lines is blocked, depending on which piece captures on d6.

2 ♖xd6

2 ♗xd6 would block the d-file, so d1♕ wins.

2...h2

This is decisive since the rook can cope with only one of the pawns.

3 ♖xd2 h1♕ White resigned.

264

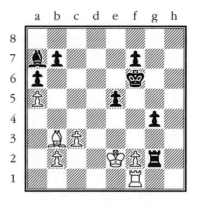

Lee – Tartakower
Ostende 1907
Black to move

In his comments to this endgame Tartakower writes that winning chances are far more limited because of the bishops of opposite colours. In most of these cases tactical finesses must be utilised. "Without sacrifices you can't continue!"

37...e4!

Tartakower makes the human move to which he attaches two exclamation marks. The idea is to block the h1-a8 diagonal. From d5 the white bishop can only work its way towards a8. If Komodo11 thinks 20 moves ahead it comes up with 37...♔f5!! 38 ♗xf7 ♔f4 but Black still has to move the e-pawn in the variation 39 ♗d5 e4 when after 40 ♗xb7 g3 41 ♗xa6 ♗xf2 the g-pawn will eventually decide the game, since the light-squared bishop cannot use the long white diagonal to stop it. The winning plan is simply to move the rook to h2, the king to e5, the bishop to an available square along the a7-g1 diagonal, when everything is ready for g2-g1♕. This variation illustrates to a high degree Tartakower's initial words about this endgame, where as many as three pawns were sacrificed in exchange for White's on f2. Black wins since the g-pawn is far too advanced and therefore unstoppable. White's pawns on the queenside are considerably slower and can also be stopped by the black bishop whilst it also supports its own g-pawn.

38 ♗d5

38 ♔e1 was relatively best, but as Tartakower mentions Black wins after 38...♔e7 39 ♗d5 f5 40 ♗xb7 ♔d6 41 ♗xa6 f4 42 b4 e3.

38...♔e5! 39 ♗xb7

If 39 ♗xf7 then 39...g3.

39...g3 40 ♗xa6 ♗xf2 41 ♔d1 f5

"The third musketeer" advances.

42 b4 f4 43 c4 ♖g1 44 ♖xg1 ♗xg1 45 c5 g2 White resigned.

265

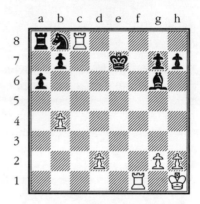

von Holzhausen
1910
White to move

1 ♖g8!

1 ♖ff8?? even loses the game since after 1...♘d7! there is no check on e8 available for the f-rook.

1...♔d7

Not 1...♗f7? 2 ♖xg7.

2 h4!

White needs to avoid back rank issues before hunting down the knight. 2 ♖ff8? is still too early due to 2...a5!! but not 2...♔c7? 3 ♖c8+). Then:

(1) 3 bxa5 ♖xa5 Black saves the knight since White is occupied with defending against the back rank mate.

(2) 3 b5 ♔c7 leads nowhere after 4 ♖xg7+ ♔b6 5 ♖f6+ ♔a7.

(3) 3.♖xg7+ is met by 3...♔c6.

(4) 3.♖xb8 ♖xb8 4 ♖xb8 ♔c7 This is the point. The b4-pawn falls and Black obtains counterplay thanks to his passed pawn. A plausible variation is 5 ♖a8 axb4 6 ♖a4 b3 7 ♖c4+ ♔d6 8 ♖b4 ♗f7! 9 ♖xb7 ♗d5 10 ♖b8 ♔c5 and Black has enough counterplay to draw.

2...♔c7 3 ♖ff8 b5 4 ♖xg7+ ♔b6 5 d4! and White wins since Black is unable to move his rook and knight.

266

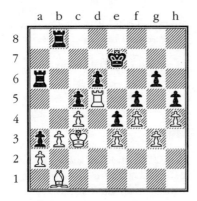

Brzozka – Bronstein
Miscolc 1963
Black to move

The only way for Black to play for a win is by the amazing...

48...♖xb3+!! 49 ♔xb3

49 axb3 a2 50 ♗xa2 ♖xa2 51 ♖d2 ♖a1 wins at least a pawn in the rook ending.

49...♖b6+ 50 ♔c2 ♖b2+ 51 ♔c1 ♖e2

The main point of the incredible sacrifice is to harvest two more pawns and obtain three pawns and more activity than the opponent.

52 ♖d1 ♖xe3 53 ♖g1 ♖c3+ 54 ♔d2 ♖xc4

Mission accomplished. Now it's only a matter of advancing the three passed pawns.

55 ♗c2 d5 56 ♖b1 d4 57 ♗d1 ♖c3 58 ♖b3 e3+ 59 ♔e2 ♖c1 60 ♖xa3?

60 ♖d3 would have prolonged his resistance.

60...c4 61 ♖a7+ ♔d6 62 ♗a4 ♖h1 63 ♖d7+ ♔c5 64 ♖c7+ ♔b4 65 a3+ ♔c3 66 ♗b5 ♖h2+ 67 ♔f1 d3 68 ♖xc4+ ♔b2 69 ♔g1 e2 70 ♔xh2 e1♕ White resigned.

267

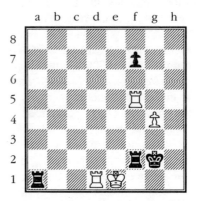

Dake – Bernstein
USA Championship 1936
Black to move

When playing for a transition to a rook ending one must calculate precisely the ensuing pawn ending.

48...♖f1+!

In the game 48...♖xd1+? was played but then the pawn ending is a draw as it's White who will gain the opposition: 49 ♔xd1 ♖xf5 50 gxf5

f6 (*50...♔f3 51 f6*) 51 ♔e2 ♔g3
52 ♔e3 ♔g4 53 ♔e4 ♔g5 54 ♔e3
♔xf5 55 ♔f3 ♔e5 56 ♔e3 f5 57 ♔f3
f4 58 ♔f2 ♔e4 59 ♔e2 f3+ 60 ♔f2
♔f4 61 ♔f1 ♔g4 62 ♔f2 ♔f4
63 ♔f1 ♔g3 64 ♔g1 ♔h3 65 ♔f2
♔g4 66 ♔f1 ♔f4 67 ♔f2 ♔e4
68 ♔f1 ♔e3 69 ♔e1 f2+ 70 ♔f1 and
a draw was agreed.

49 ♖xf1 ♖xd1+ 50 ♔xd1 ♔xf1

Now White remains with a g-pawn
and that makes all the difference
between a loss and a draw, since it's
impossible for White to gain the
opposition. A plausible variation
is...

**51 ♔d2 ♔f2 52 ♔d3 ♔f3 53 g5
♔f4 54 ♔e2 ♔xg5 55 ♔f3 ♔f5**

Black has achieved a well-known
book win. Incidentally, after
examining thousands of games
played by amateurs, the great writer
Fred Reinfeld said he was struck by
the frequency of transitions to
unfavourable endings.

268

Gufeld – Andersson
Camaguey 1974
Black to move

In this position Black missed an
extraordinary possibility to force a
checkmate in ten moves beginning
with...

80...f3!!

In the game 80...♖a2? was played
and after the further 81 ♖bxe3+ fxe3
(*81...f3* no longer works due to a
subsequent sacrifice on g2 followed
by a stalemate idea: *82 ♖b3 ♖a8
83 ♖b2! ♖h8 84 ♖xg2+ fxg2
85 ♖e3+ ♔f4 86 ♖f3+!*) 82 ♖xe3+
♗f3 83 ♔f1 a theoretically drawn
position arose.

However, Gufeld lost his way and
resigned after 95 moves.

80...♖xb3? would have made it too
easy for Gufeld because of
81 ♖xe3+ with stalemate.

81 ♖bxe3

81...♖a8!

This is the point. White is helpless
against the incursion on h1. Such
rook manoeuvres are easy to miss
even for famous grandmasters.
Karpov made a similar mistake
against Taimanov as we have
seen in the middlegame section,
position 24.

269

Radevich – Donskikh
USSR 1972
White to move

1 ♗xe4!!

1 ♗c2? ♖a2 2 ♖c1 ♘e2 wins for Black but the move played secures the draw due to the poor placement of the black king.

1...♖xf1 2 ♗f5!

This is the point. The players agreed to a **draw** since 2...♖a1 leads to a perpetual check by oscillating between the squares e6 and f5. Note that with a black pawn on h7 Black would have even been mated. Always be careful of the bishop's ability to create such possibilities. The main reason players miss such an opportunity is because of the nice "zwischenzug" 2 ♗f5!. Due to bad technique, it's a very common to miss this kind of intermediate move when exchanging pieces. An experienced player is always looking for alternatives to a natural recapture in a quest for an exception to the rule. The key is to calculate half a move at a time instead of one move, which can be too hasty.

270

Caruana – Nakamura
Wijk aan Zee 2013
Black to move

The first thing we notice is the pin on the h7-b1 diagonal. Is there any way to profit from this? Nakamura pulled off a very beautiful undermining combination.

54...g4!!

A lesser imaginative mind than Nakamura might have played 54...♖d4? 55 ♖e1 ♗b4 56 ♖e2 but then White has an easy defensive task by shuffling his king between c1 and c2.

55 hxg4 h3 56 ♖d1

After 56 gxh3 the protection of the bishop is undermined and Black wins a piece by force with

56...♖f8 57 ♔d3 ♖f4 as there is no way to defend against 58...♗xe4+. A very instructive example – when White could no longer increase his attack on the e4-knight, he hit its defender instead.

56...♖f8 57 ♔d3 h2

A prettier win was 57...♖f4 followed by 58...♖xe4 59 ♗xe4 ♗xe4 60 ♔xe4 hxg2. Then Caruana would probably have resigned on the spot.

58 ♖h1 ♗g1 59 ♔e2 ♗xe4 60 ♗xe4 ♔f6 61 ♗f3 ♖d8 White resigned.

271

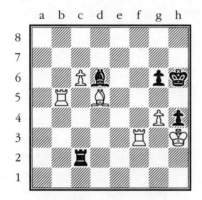

Shamkovich – Visier
Palma de Mallorca 1966
White to move

48 g5+

The natural move to prevent mate.

48...♔h5

Black renews the threat but White has the killer blow **49 ♖g3!** and Black has no effective antidote against the threatened bishop mate on f3, apart from giving up the rook on h2 and prolonging his suffering.

By the way 49 ♖f4! is also winning after 49...♔xg5 50 ♗e4+.

272

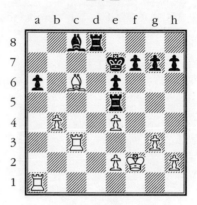

Anand – Wang Yue
Linares 2009
White to move

Black has just played the fatal 23...♔e7? which Anand exploited with...

24 b5! axb5 25 ♖a7+ ♔f6

25...♔f8 is met by the clever 26 ♖c7!, putting pressure on the weakest spot in Black's position, the c8-bishop, with the decisive threat of 27 ♖d3. Black has no effective antidote. He can try 26...♔g8 (*26...♗a6 27 ♖a3 ♖c8 28 ♖xc8+ ♗xc8 29 ♖a8* with a decisive pin along the eighth rank.) but then 27 ♖a3 (Not *27 ♖d3? ♖f8*) 27...♖c5 28 ♖a8 wins.

26 ♖f3+ ♔g6 27 ♖fxf7 ♖g8 28 ♖fc7 ♖h5

Black has no other defensive resources than one-move threats.

29 h4 ♔f6 30 ♖a8 ♖c5 31 ♖cxc8 ♖xc8 32 ♖xc8 b4

White has one tactical problem left to solve and that is to stop the b-pawn while retaining the extra piece.

263

33 ♗d7! and **Black resigned** after he realised that 33...♖xc8 34 ♗xc8 b3 35 ♗a6 b2 36 ♗d3 stops the pawn just in time.

273

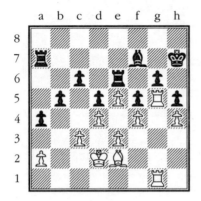

Averbakh – Hug
Palma de Mallorca 1972
White to move

52 ♗xh5!

If White should have any practical winning chances, then this positional sacrifice is the best choice – even though the computer disagrees.

52...gxh5 53 ♖xf5

White's goal is obviously to get two connected pawns on the fifth rank with f4-f5.

53...♗g6

An illuminating variation is 53...♖ae7? 54 ♖fg5 ♗e8 55 f5 ♖h6 56 f6 ♖f7 57 e6 and Black will be mated if the f7-rook captures the f6-pawn.

54 ♖f8 ♔g7 55 ♖c8 ♖f7

Black must prevent the pawn-push to f5.

56 ♔c1!

White systematically plays according to the principle of the two weaknesses, since there is no immediate breakthrough on the kingside. White's goal is to advance with his king to c5 and then capture the c6-pawn.

56...♔h6 57 ♖g5 ♔h7

(1) 57...♖f5? 58 ♖h8+ ♔g7 59 ♖hxh5 wins since the pawn-rush to f5 cannot be stopped. This was the tactical point of move 57.

(2) 57...♗h7! followed by ...♖g6 was the best defence since it's in Black's interest to exchange a pair of rooks.

58 ♔b2 ♖f5 59 ♖g1 ♖f7 60 ♖g5 ♖f5 61 ♖c7+

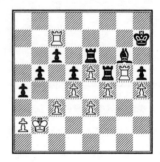

61...♔g8

(1) 61...♔h6? 62 ♔a3 and Black cannot exchange on g5 because he will be mated.

(2) 61...♖f7 62 ♖xf7+ ♗xf7 63 f5 ♖e7 64 ♔a3 ♗e8 65 ♔b4 ♖g7 66 ♖xg7+ ♔xg7 leads to a variation where all the rooks have been exchanged but also where White can exploit the possibility of zugzwang: 67 ♔c5 ♗d7 68 f6+ ♔f7 69 ♔d6 ♗c8 70 a3! ♗e6 71 ♔xc6 ♗e8 72 ♔xb5 ♗d7+ 73 ♔c5 ♗e6 74 ♔b4 ♗d7 75 c4 dxc4 76 ♔xc4

and White wins easily with his four pawns.

62 ♖g1 ♔f8?

The key to salvation is to exchange a pair of rooks with 62...♖f7, even though after 63 ♖xf7 ♔xf7 64 ♖g5 Black cannot prevent White's pawn-push to f5 or the loss of his h5-pawn. Nevertheless, according to Komodo this was the best defence as can be seen after the further 64...♗d3 65 ♖xh5 (*65 f5 ♖h6*) 65...♖g6 66 f5 ♖g3 which leads to an equal game.

63 ♔a3 ♗f7 64 ♔b4 ♔e8 65 ♔c5 ♔d8

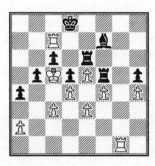

66 ♖a7!

Note that White continually exploits the dark squares to avoid the bishop's radius of action. However, another way to win is 66 ♖xc6 because after 66...♖xc6+ 67 ♔xc6 ♔e7 68 ♔xb5 ♗e8+ 69 ♔c5 ♔e6 70 ♖g8 Black has no effective defence since he cannot avoid the further loss of a pawn.

66...♗g6 67 a3

White is in no hurry and places the last pawn on a dark square.

67...♔c8

67...♖f7 is met by 68 ♖xg6!.

68 ♖g7 ♗e8 69 ♖h7 ♖f8

After 69...♖g6 70 ♖xg6 ♗xg6

71 ♖g7 ♗e8 72 ♔d6 Black cannot prevent ♔e6 followed by f5.

70 ♖gg7 ♔b8

White's position is very active with two rooks on the seventh rank and a king on the fifth. How can he profit from this?

71 ♖b7+ ♔a8

71...♔c8 72 ♖a7 leads to the same position as in the game.

72 ♖a7+ ♔b8 73 ♖hb7+ ♔c8 74 ♖b6

A very nice manoeuvre. White plans a doubling of rooks on the b-file, followed by a check on b8 and a mate on b7 with the b6-rook, or alternatively a rook check on a8 followed by ♖ab8 (after ...♔c7). 74 ♔b6?! is not so effective as the king is driven back by 74...c5+ 75 ♔xc5 ♖c6+, although White is winning after 76.♔xd5. But why prolong the game when there are more effective methods available?

74...♖g6

Black evacuates the e6-square. Can you see the most effective win?

75 f5

Good enough – but stronger was 75 e6! ♖xe6 76 ♖a8+ ♔c7 77 ♖ab8 and it's mate next move. 77 ♖ba6 and then 78 ♖6a7 mate also works.

75...♖xf5 76 ♖a8+ ♔c7

76...♔d7 77 ♖b7+ ♔e6 78 ♖xe8 mate.

77 ♖ab8

Two rooks on the seventh is normally a deadly force but with the king on c5 obviously more so. After all, White could choose how to win in several ways which is an indication of just how strong White's position is here. By the way, 77 ♖ba6 also mates in two.

274-300: Queen Endings

274

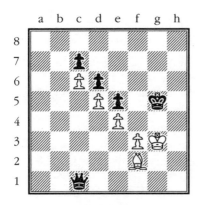

Chekhover
14th Comm., USSR Ch. 1948
White to move

It's important to know the exceptions to rules in chess, as for example the fact that two knights are unable to mate a lone king or that a light-squared bishop cannot win with a rook pawn if Black's king is placed in a dark corner. However these positions are very fundamental and so we naturally have to turn to more advanced ones as we become stronger. When we have become acquainted with these we don't necessarily want them to crop up in our own games since they are very rare, but they should rather be studied with the aim of developing our imagination and creativity, since that is what separates the really good players from the rest. It's all about the exceptions – but you cannot learn them all so you have to focus on improving your own abilities, such as fantasy and creativity, and find similar fortresses in other positions.

1 ♗a7!

This position is a simple draw if White oscillates between the f2 and a7 squares and doesn't allow the black king to enter the fourth rank. Note that all Black's queen checks are useless due to the fact that the bishop controls g1 and also that it has the possibility of going to f2 after a check on e1. If Black checks on f4 Black cannot use that square for his own king. Black has no possibility of penetrating White's position which is a perfect fortress despite the fact that he has only one bishop and a pawn for a queen. This represents a really nice exception to the rule that the queen is superior to a bishop and a pawn. We must constantly search for these exceptions, search, search, search...

1...♕f4+

1...♕e1+ is met by 2.♗f2.

2 ♔g2! ♕d2+ 3 ♔g3

Black cannot improve his position so the position is a clear **draw**.

275

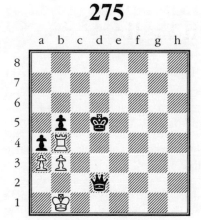

Yates – Tartakower
Bad Homburg 1927
Black to move

276

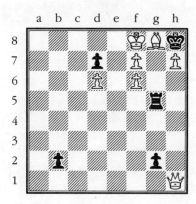

Korolkov
Shakhmaty v SSSR 1936
White to move

56...♕xb4?

The simplest solution to winning this endgame is to play for the notorious endgame, queen versus rook. This could have been achieved by force after 56...♕c3 57.♖xb5+ ♔c6 58.bxa4 ♕xa3. The a4-pawn cannot be defended without losing the rook. In the game, Tartakower most probably made a miscalculation.

57 axb4 axb3 58 ♔b2 ♔c4 59 ♔a3 b2 60 ♔a2!

Tartakower probably missed this key move. It pays to be careful when calculating variations in pawn endings, since it's easy to make an automatic calculation such as 60.♔xb2? ♔xb4 and overlook the clever waiting move.

60...b1♕+

60...♔c3 doesn't change anything after 61.♔b1 ♔xb4 62 ♔xb2.

61 ♔xb1 ♔xb4 62 ♔b2 Draw.

It's not so difficult to find the initial moves in this incredibly imaginative study composed by Korolkov.

1 ♕g1 b1♕ 2 ♕xb1 g1♕ 3 ♕xg1

The most difficult thing is to find Black's strongest defensive move.

3...♖g3!

3...♖xg1 leads to an easy win for White since the stalemate motif disappears in the variation 4 ♔e7 ♖e1+ 5 ♔xd7

(1) 5...♖e7+ 6 fxe7 and Black's king isn't stalemated. 3...♖g2 4 ♔e7 ♖e2+ 5 ♕e3! White's queen must leave the g7-square to avoid stalemate motifs (*5 ♔xd7? ♖e7+*) 5...♖xe3+ 6 ♔d7 and White wins in the same way as after 3...♖xg1.

(2) A funny but longer variation, not given by Petrosian when he wrote about this study in *Petrosian's Legacy*, is 5...♖e8 6 f8♕ ♖xf8 7 f7

(*7 ♔e7? ♖xf6!*) 7...♖b8 8 ♔e7 ♖f8 9 d7 ♖a8 10 d8♕ ♖xd8 11 ♔xd8 ♔g7 12 ♔e7 ♔h8 13 ♔e6 ♔g7 14 f8♕+ ♔xf8 15 h8♕ ♔e8 16 ♗f7 mate.

4 ♕g2!

4 ♔e7 ♖e3+ 5 ♔xd7 ♖e7+ 6 ♔c6 ♖c7+ 7 ♔d5 ♖c5+ 8 ♔e4 ♖e5+ leads to a perpetual check since White cannot avoid stalemate.

4...♖g4! 5 ♕g3! ♖g5! 6 ♕g4! ♖xg4

Black has to capture the queen since 6...♖g6 is met by 7 ♔e7 and Black has no check on the e-file.

7 ♔e7 ♖e4+ 8 ♔xd7 ♖d4 9 f8♕ ♖xd6+ 10 ♔e7 ♖d7+ 11 ♔e6 ♖e7+ 12 ♔f5 ♖e5+ 13 ♔g6 ♖g5+ 14 ♔f7 ♖g3 15 ♕g7+ ♖xg7+ 16 fxg7 mate.

A very aesthetic study – it's easy to understand why Petrosian was so fond of it.

277

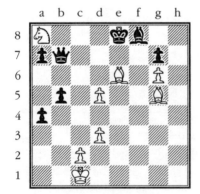

Simkovich
Pravdi 1927
White to move

1 ♗f7+ ♔d7 2 ♗e6+ ♔d6 3 ♗f4+ ♔c5 4 ♗e3+ ♔b4 5 ♗d2+ ♔a3 6 ♔b1! ♕xa8

After the capture of the knight there is no longer any perpetual check so how can White hold the draw from here?

7 ♔a1!!

The most difficult as well as the most beautiful move. White effectively makes no moves at all – in the spirit of tao (nothing = everything). It's because of such rare and astonishing ideas that it feels wrong to exclude studies from this book – because the obvious drawback with games is that two people are creating instead of one.

7...♕b7 8 ♔b1 ♕a6 9 ♔a1!!

The reader and the solver will probably understand by now that the main point is that as long as the queen is placed on light squares White only needs to oscillate between a1 and b1 with his king. If Black's queen is placed on a dark square, White wins the queen or draws by perpetual check.

An important variation is **9...b4?? 10 ♗c1 mate** and that bishop moves lead to a perpetual check.

The study is so exceptional that even the "American Capablanca", Isaac Kashdan (1905-1985), couldn't believe his eyes when he saw the solution, admitting: "I still can't believe it!".

The code words for queen endings are "king safety" (position 285) and "far advanced passed pawn" (which is more important than a whole bunch of pawns). Calculation abilities are very important due to the many variations with checks. Sometimes decentralising queen checks are the path to victory. Common tactical themes are mate (position 278 and 284), stalemate, zugzwang (position 279 and 281) pawn race, transition to a pawn ending (position 283) and perpetual check.

278

Neumann – N.N.
Vienna 1887
White to move

This beautiful ending can be found In Max Euwe's famous endgame manual *Das Endspiel*. Euwe was a great pedagogue, a teacher by profession, and very thorough. Unfortunately his book was never translated into the English language. He had an excellent feeling for illustrative examples and this position is one of the most impressive ones which I haven't

seen published elsewhere. It shows how to win a queen ending when the defending king is in the corner. Such a position might very well arise in a practical game since it's common knowledge that on principal the defending king should manoeuvre to the corner to avoid as many fatal checks as possible when the attacking side has a rook- or a knight-pawn. You can read all about this in another high calibre book, *John Nunn's Chess Endings – Volume 1*. Here Black has placed his king prematurely on h1 since White's king is too close and can profit from this by co-operating with the queen to create mating threats.

1 ♕d5!!

Euwe writes that it's extraordinary to give up the pawn with check.

1...♕g6+

1...♕xb4+ would have led to mate by the amazing move 2 ♔f3!!

This is the main point. Surprisingly Black cannot prevent mate. A very useful position to know by heart. The main variation goes 2...♔h2 3 ♕h5+ ♔g1 4 ♕g6+ ♕g4+ 5 ♕xg4+ ♔f1 6 ♕g5! (More beautiful than the routine blitz continuation *6 ♕g2+ ♔e1 7 ♕e2*

mate.) 6...♔e1 7 ♕c1 mate. This economical mate is the most beautiful one that I learned as a young boy. Note that if Black tries to be clever with 1...♕g3 White can force an exchange of queens by 2 ♕d1+ ♔h2 3 ♕e2+ ♔g1 4 ♕e3+ ♔h1 5 ♕f3+!.

2 ♔f4+

White has to be careful because if 2 ♔f3?? Black wins with the only move 2...♕g2+.

2...♔h2 3 ♕e5!

This thematic idea is important to remember when handling this kind of ending.

3...♕d3

Black must prevent the white king from advancing to f3, otherwise Black is soon mated.

4 b5

Now is the right time to advance the pawn.

4...♕d1 5 b6

A quicker win is 5 ♔g5+ with mate in 17 moves. Euwe recommends 5 ♔e3+ which is far better than the move played as it's mate in 18 moves. Now it takes nearly twice as long to clinch the win with perfect play.

5...♔h1 6 ♕e4+ ♔h2 7 b7

And **Black resigned** In fact it will be mate in 30 moves. The whole ending is very pleasing to study and I would not have known about it if it were not for Euwe's eminent work on the endgame.

279

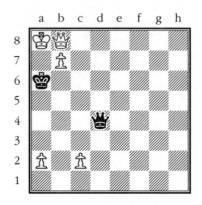

Kok
1991
White to move

Black has tactical co-ordination between his queen and king but White can destroy it by precise play with the pawns and turn the tables by creating his own tactical co-ordination.

1 c3!

The only move, otherwise Black will win. White's goal is to control two of the critical squares d4, c5 and b6.

1...♕c5

1...♕b6 is answered by 2 a4! (*2 a3? ♕c5 3 a4 ♕b6 4 a5 ♕c5 and it's White who is under the compulsion to move.*) 2...♕c5 3 a5 placing Black in zugzwang since he cannot avert a decisive check on a7 or d6.

2 a3! ♛b6 3 a4 ♛c5 4 a5

White now controls b6 and d4 and with the opposing queen placed on the remaining critical c5 square, Black is lost.

4...♛d5 5 ♛c7! ♛c5! 6 b8♛! Black resigned.

280

Afek
9ch WCCT 2011–2012
White to move

This position looks like a draw since the d7-pawn will fall. If White protects the pawn with the queen Black will attack it with the king by going nearer the pawn. However this reasoning will fail to hidden tactical finesses. White wins after the important zwischenzug…

1 ♛f1+!

(1) The direct 1 ♛xh3? ♛f6+! is a draw by perpetual since White cannot escape the checks without sacrificing the candidate on d7. After 2 ♚e2 ♛e5+! 3 ♚e3 ♛h5+ 4 ♛f3 ♛e5+! 5 ♚f1 ♛a1+! 6 ♚g2 ♛g7+ the advanced pawn falls.

(2) 1 ♛c1+? ♚b5 2 ♛c7 h2 3 ♚g2 ♛e2+ 4 ♚h1 ♛e1+ 5 ♚xh2 ♛xd2+ also leads to perpetual check.

1...♚c5! 2 ♛xh3

After 2 ♛d3? ♛d8 3 ♚g3 ♚c6 the arising pawn ending is a draw because of White's decentralised king.

2...♚b6!

The obvious 2...♚c6? loses after the tactical finesse 3 ♛e6+! ♛xe6 and the under-promotion 4 d8♘+. The pawn ending is winning for White after 4...♚d5 5 ♘xe6 ♚xe6 6 ♚e4 ♚d6 7 ♚d4.

3 ♛h6+!

This is probably the most difficult move to find. 3 ♛f5? is refuted by 3...♛a3+! 4 ♚g2 ♛d6 and Black cannot lose if 5...♚c7 is the next move and not the fatal 5...♚c6?.

3...♚b7!

3...♚c7 allows an exchange of queens in spectacular fashion by using the seventh and the last ranks, as well as the a3-f8 diagonal and the e-file: 4 ♛f4+! ♚xd7 5 ♛a4+! It's fascinating that Black cannot avoid the exchange of queens whatever king move he plays. Such a tactical idea is important to know in queen endings. 5...♔d8 6 ♕a8+ ♔c7 7 ♕a7+ ♔d8 8 ♕xe7+ ♔xe7 9 ♔e4 ♔e6 10 ♔d4 ♔d6 11 d3 and White gains the opposition and thus wins the pawn ending.

4 ♕e6!!

This finesse is the only move to win.

4...♕f8+

Otherwise 4...♕xe6 5 d8♘+ or 4...♕a3+ 5 ♔e2!.

5 ♔e2 ♔c7 6 ♕e8 ♕f6 7 ♕c8+

The pawn is promoted next move.

281

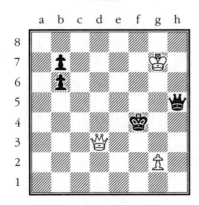

Kok
1941
White to move

This wonderful study by Kok is pretty tricky to solve since there are many options to analyse for White. However the first move suggests itself.

1 g3+ ♔g5!

1...♔g4 makes it too easy for White to place Black in zugzwang

by 2 ♕e2+ ♔g5 3 ♕e6. The following decentralising move is the key to solving the position.

2 ♕b5+!

(1) 2 ♕e3+?, with a subsequent exchange of queens, is a mistake since White cannot profit from any pawn race. Black replies 2...♔f5! and after 3 ♕f4+ ♔e6 4 g4 ♕e5+! 5 ♕xe5+ ♔xe5 6 g5 b5 7 g6 b4 8 ♔f8 b3 9 g7 b2 10 g8♕ b1♕ 11 ♕g7+ it's a draw by perpetual check.

(2) 2 ♕d6?, threatening mate on f4, doesn't work after either 2...♔g4 or 2...♔f5.

2...♔g4 3 ♕e2+ ♔g5 4 ♕e6!

The tactical co-ordination of White's three pieces helps to create a zugzwang position, since the remaining black pawns must advance to the critical b5-square.

4...b5 5 ♕e5+ ♔g4 6 ♕e2+ ♔g5 7 ♕xb5+

White repeats the queen manoeuvre until all Black's pawns are eliminated.

7...♔g4 8 ♕e2+ ♔g5 9 ♕e6! b6 10 ♕e5+ ♔g4 11 ♕e2+ ♔g5 12 ♕e6 b5 13 ♕e5+ ♔g4 14 ♕e2+ ♔g5 15 ♕xb5+ ♔g4 16 ♕e2+ ♔g5 17 ♕e6!

There are no pawns left for Black and under a compulsion to move it's impossible for him to avert mate.

17...♕d1

The quickest way to avoid torture!

18 ♕g6 mate.

A really beautiful study which can help you to practice queen manoeuvres where decentralising queen moves are involved.

282

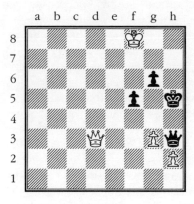

Kok
1938
White to move

If Black's pieces are in constrained positions it pays to look for a win. Here White claims victory by increasing his space with...

1 ♔g7!

White improves his position considerably by taking control of the h6- and g6-squares as the following variations show:

1...♛g4

Other queen moves lose quickly:

(1) 1...♛xh2 2 ♛f3+ ♔g5 3 ♛f4+ ♔h5 4 g4+ wins the queen.

(2) 1...♛g2 2 ♛d1+ ♔g5 3 h4 mate.

(3) The pawn move 1...g5 opens the e8-h5 diagonal and it's mate in

three after 2 ♛e2+ g4 (*2...♛g4 3 ♛e8 mate.*) 3 ♛e8+ ♔g5 4 ♛g6 mate.

King moves doesn't help either:

(4) 1...♔g4 2 ♛e2+ ♔g5 3 ♛e3+ ♔h5 (*3...♔g4 4 ♛f4+ ♔h5 5 g4+!*) 4 ♛h6+ ♔g4 5 ♛f4+! (The key move to win. Note that *5 ♛xg6+? ♔f3* is a drawn queen ending and *5 ♛xh3+ ♔xh3 6 ♔xg6 ♔xh2 7 ♔xf5 ♔xg3* a dead draw!) 5...♔h5 6 g4+ ♔h4 (The g4-pawn is taboo due to immediate mate.) 7 gxf5+ ♔h5 8 ♛h6+ ♔g4 9 ♛xh3+ ♔xh3 and White can choose one of three winning moves in the pawn ending.

(5) 1...♔g5 leads to the same thing as in the last variation: 2 ♛e3+ ♔h5 3 ♛h6+ ♔g4 4 ♛f4+! ♔h5 5 g4+.

2 h3!

An instructive example of tactical co-ordination between all of White's pieces. It's aesthetically pleasing when the least employable unit, the rook pawn, participates in such a decisive way in the overall scheme – and just by taking one small step forward!

2...♛xh3

Or 2...♛e4 3 ♛d1+ ♔g5 4 h4+.

3 ♛f3+ ♔g5

3...♛g4 4 ♛h1+ ♔g5 5 ♛h6 mate.

4 ♛f4+ ♔h5 5 g4+ ♔h4

5...♛xg4 6 ♛h6 mate.

6 gxf5+ ♔h5 7 ♛h6+ ♔g4 8 ♛xh3+ ♔xh3

And now **9 fxg6!** is the quickest way to mate.

What's important to understand from this study and what might very well happen in a real game, is how to work with the pawns on h2 and g3. The co-operation between king and queen we have already learned to master as beginners but to play with pawns as well requires a higher level of skill. "The pawns are the soul of chess" needs to be repeated until we really understand the significance of Philidor's immortal maxim.

283

a b c d e f g h

Cardenas – Engqvist
Swedish Team Championship 2018
Black to move

72...♛d7+?

Correct was GM Jon Ludvig Hammer's suggestion of 72...c1♛! 73 ♛xc1 ♛d7+ and Black wins the h4-pawn by force. After the further 74 ♔e3 ♛e7+ 75 ♔f2 ♛xh4+ 76 ♔g2 IM Jonas Barkhagen remarked that the position is a theoretical draw according to Nalimov's tablebase. However, in a practical game the winning chances are nevertheless pretty good, especially since we normally have very little time left to defend well in this phase of the game. This knowledge I had already acquired since I wrote about it in *300 Most Important Chess Positions*. If you have the book you can look at position 289, Ribli – Spassky. However, this important knowledge didn't help me because I thought the continuation I chose was simpler.

73 ♔xc2 ♔g7

Here, to my horror, I discovered too late that 73...♛f5+ 74 ♛xf5 gxf5 75 ♔d3 ♔g6 76 ♔d4 ♔f6 77 ♔d5 leads to a draw. If Black continues 77...♔g7 then White plays 78 ♔e5 ♔g6 79 ♔d4! and Black cannot win since it's impossible for him to reach the critical e5-square without any help from his opponent.

This idea was presented in position 166, Réti – Barasz, but unfortunately I had forgotten about it despite the fact that I wrote a book on Réti in 2017. This fact alone proves how important it is to **collect** the most important ideas and **repeat** them on a regular basis. And this is also the reason you can find the same idea in this book, since it is clearly an important one judging from my experience.

74 ♔c3

The position is now a fairly simple draw and we did in fact agree to a draw, albeit after 93 moves.

284

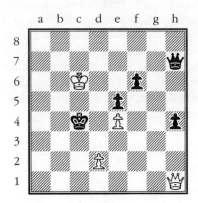

Rinck
1906
White to move

1 ♕b1!

White plans to mate with a check on b5 and then mate on d5.

After 1 ♕f3? Black's king escapes by 1...♔b4 2 ♕c3+ ♔a4.

1...♔d4

1...♕g8 defends the d5-square but loses the queen after 2 ♕a2+.

2 ♕b3!!

The key move.

2...♕xe4+ 3 ♔d6

White is threatening mate on c3, so Black has to prevent it while defending the d5-square.

3...♕a8

3...♕g2 4 ♕c3+ ♔e4 5 ♕c6+ loses the queen.

4 ♕e3+ ♔c4 5 ♕c3+ ♔b5 6 ♕b3+ ♔a6 7 ♕a4+ ♔b7 8 ♕b5+ ♔a7

If 8...♔c8 then 9 ♕d7+ ♔b8 10 ♕c7 mate.

9 ♔c7

A beautiful study which not only shows how to create a mating net to catch the enemy king in the centre but also how to systematically drive the enemy king down the board by using the queen and king together. All these themes in just one position!

285

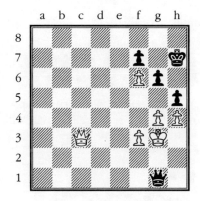

Larsen – Keres
San Antonio 1972
White to move

Larsen played the natural **59 ♔f4?**

After all, White has an extra pawn and the more active position so how can this move be wrong? Correct was 59 ♔h3 whereupon Black has a draw by perpetual.

59...♕h2+ 60 ♔g5?

Also this move seems to be in harmony with White's more aggressive position, but it's actually a decisive mistake. It was necessary to fight for a draw by 60 ♔e3 ♛xh4 61 gxh5 gxh5 62 ♕d3+ ♔h6 63 ♕d8 when Black has the advantage since he has good chances of winning the f6-pawn and/or advancing his h-pawn.

60...♛g3!!

This quiet and treacherous move was probably missed by Larsen. It may not have the same appeal as Marshall's beautiful queen sacrifice 23...♛g3!!, position 111 (Levitsky-Marshall) since it's only a quiet move but nevertheless it's absolutely decisive because there is no way to stop 61...hxg4. White cannot simultaneously defend the g4- and f3-pawn.

61 ♕e3 hxg4 62 ♕f4 ♛xf3 63 ♕xg4 ♛e3+ 64 ♕f4 ♛e2

White's king is in a very unhappy position on g5 and the f6-pawn will eventually be lost since the king must withdraw.

65 ♕g3

Not 65 ♕g4? ♛e5+.

65...♛b5+ 66 ♔f4 ♛f5+ 67 ♔e3 ♛xf6 and **Black won** after 91 moves.

How is it possible to win this endgame a pawn down in a meeting between two strong grandmasters? Yes, it's possible if the materially stronger player plays too hard for a win and tries to penetrate too early, because then he may get hit with a heavy boomerang. White goes

headlong into an attack which brings him in contact with Black's pawns and king but when there is a black queen on the board it's by no means impossible to get mated or suffer loss of material. It is therefore important to consider the implications very carefully when starting an attack with the king and queens are still on the board. Queen endings are completely unique in this respect. They can actually mate in conjunction with a king and pawns. Remember the study by Kok, position 281.

286

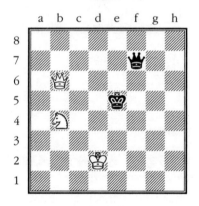

Dehler
1908
White to move

In his classic *Basic Chess Endings* Reuben Fine writes about material advantage, stating that the main rule in endgames without pawns is that one must be at least a rook up to be sure of a win. However here we are going to look at two exceptions to this rule. Naturally the actual placement of one's forces ultimately decides whether an extra minor piece is enough to win or not.

1 ♘c6+

To be able to win this type of ending the knight must be placed in such a way that its radius of action reaches the enemy pieces.

1...♚f5!

The strongest defence – and it's enough to analyse this variation to fully understand the study.

2 ♕f2+ ♚e4!!

This clever stalemate idea is the hardest thing to discover when you try to solve the study. It's well-known when calculating variations that the hardest part is to find the opponent's best defensive moves. Most players would be satisfied with having found 2...♚e6 3 ♘d8+ or 2...♚g6 3 ♘e5+ but then they would have missed Black's clever defence and the main point of the study.

3 ♕e3+

A very beautiful stalemate arises after 3 ♕xf7. The stalemate pattern is economical since White's pieces control each of the flight squares only once. If you haven't seen this stalemate before it's easy to miss it.

3...♚d5! 4 ♕b3+ ♚e4!

Black repeats the clever defence but it doesn't hold in the long run

against White's beautiful queen manoeuvres along the third rank.

5 ♕d3+! ♚f4 6 ♕e3+ ♚f5

6...♚g4 is met by 7 ♘e5+.

7 ♕f3+

White has to check one square at a time from d3-e3-f3 on the understanding that the e4-square will not be available to Black.

7...♚e6

Or 7...♚g6 8 ♘e5+.

8 ♘d8+

At last White manages to decide the game with a fork but on the last rank, exploiting the board as much as possible during the process.

287

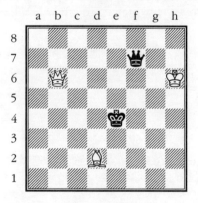

Horowitz
1872
White to move

Black's pieces are not placed on good squares and White can exploit this by means of a series of checks to place Black in zugzwang.

1 ♕e3+ ♚f5

After 1...♚d5 the skewer 2 ♕b3+ decides.

2 ♕f3+ ♚e6 3 ♕b3+ ♚e7

If 3...♚f6 then 4 ♗g5+ wins the queen.

4 ♗g5+ ♚f8

4...♚e8 loses after a series of checks: 5 ♕b8+ ♚d7 6 ♕b7+ ♚e6 (*6...♚e8 7 ♕c8 mate.*) 7 ♕b3+.

5 ♕b8+ ♚e8 6 ♕d6+ ♚g8

6...♚f7 7 ♕f6+ ♚g8 8 ♕g7 mate.

All of Black's moves have been forced and now White wins with a beautiful zugzwang:

7 ♗e7!

This is the key move to the whole study and must be seen before the first move is made. It's psychologically easier to see checks and captures compared with quiet moves which require more discipline and creativity.

288

Troitzky
Shakhmatny Zhurnal 1901
White to move

1 ♕h7+ ♗f7

(1) 1...♚d6 2 ♕h2+ followed by promotion next move.

(2) 1...♚d8 2 ♕h8+ and b8♕.

2 ♕h4+!

It would be a mistake to centralise with 2 ♕e4+? because White cannot win after 2...♚f6! since the king can then escape to the kingside.

2...♚e6!

(1) 2...♚f8 3 ♕b4+

(2) 2...♚d6 3 ♕b4+ or 3 ♕f4+

(3) 2...♚d7 3 ♕a4+ ♚e6 (3...♚d8 4 ♕a8+) 4 ♕b3+ ♚d7 5 ♕b5+! (5 ♕xf7+? is wrong due to 5...♚c6)

(4) 2...♚e8 3 ♕h8+.

3 ♕h3+!!

This move is the hardest to find in the calculations.

3...♚d5!

(1) 3...♚f6 4 ♕h8+ is the important point which explains the need to check on h3.

(2) 3...♔e7 4 ♕a3+ ♔d7 5 ♕a4+.

4 ♕b3+!

Once more it's wrong to centralise the queen since White cannot exploit the placement of Black's king. 4 ♕f5+? ♔c6! (4...♔d4! also works) 5 ♕c8 looks like a win if it weren't for the very beautiful 5...♗e6!!.

4...♔c6

If Black's queen wasn't defended White could just promote the pawn, ignoring the threat on b3.

5 b8♘+!!

The under-promotion is another key in this amazing study.

5...♔c5

If 5...♔d6 then 6 ♕g3+.

6 ♘a6+ ♔d4 7 ♕d1+!

The only move where White can check so Black cannot interpose with his queen. The study is quite incredible considering that it's very hard to solve it fully since the human brain (i.e. the experienced chess player) is drawn to centralising moves. In this study it's important to understand that the key square is h8 and therefore the two checks on

move 2 and 3 are important. If you understand that the decisive check on h3 is the key to the study you will solve it. It's all about finding keys!

289

Speelman
Jon Speelman's Chess Puzzle Book
2008
White to move

1 ♔e1!

This clever move gains a tempo so that White can reach the a1-square with an elementary draw after the exchange of queens. An immediate 1 ♕xd5+? ♔xd5 2 ♔e1 fails to 2...♔c4 3 ♔d2 ♔b3 4 ♔c1 ♔a2 and Black is just in time to cover the critical squares b1 and b2.

1...♔c5

1...♕xg2 leads to a nice economical stalemate, which might easily be overlooked if one is not familiar with it.

2 ♕xd5+ ♔xd5 3 ♔d2 ♔c4 4 ♔c1 ♔b3 5 ♔b1

The king oscillates between a1 and b1 with an easy draw.

290

```
   a  b  c  d  e  f  g  h
8              ♖           ♚   8
7  ♟  ♛              ♟     ♟   7
6     ♟     ♙  ♙              6
5                    ♙        5
4     ♙  ♕                    4
3                    ♙        3
2                       ♔     2
1                            1
   a  b  c  d  e  f  g  h
```

D. Cramling – Blomqvist
Hasselbacken Open 2006
White to move

In this instructive position two connected passed pawns on the sixth rank show they can be stronger than a rook. Try to solve the position before you look at the solution. This is the only way to really improve your tactical abilities. Even if you fail to complete the task you are doing the right thing because you are getting into the habit of trying to solve rather than just looking at the solution first without any thoughts of your own. The best way to learn is to feel a little uncomfortable and learn from your mistakes, rather than being complacent and lazy.

50 ♕d3!!

In the game, 50 e7? was played but then the talented Swedish player Erik Blomqvist got the chance to defend with 50...♖c8 and after another mistake 51 b5? (Correct was *51 ♕f1 ♔g8 52 ♕f5 g6 53 ♕e6+ ♔g7 54 e8♕ ♖c2+ 55 ♕e2!* when White has good winning chances in the queen ending after *55...♖xe2+*

56 ♕xe2) 51...♕d7 the position was objectively a draw but Dan Cramling still managed to win the game.

Alexander Kotov, in *Think Like a Grandmaster*, describes the kind of move played here as insidious. It's a simple move which is easy to overlook when you glance at the position and yet it contributes to the collapse of the opponent's position. However the co-ordination of the pieces is only changed a little. Such moves are easy to miss since they are so treacherously quiet. "It is in the calmest waters that the biggest fish go" is a famous saying to shed light on the best move in this position. The idea is simply to prepare e6-e7 followed by d6-d7. According to Stockfish the main variation is **50...♕c6 51 e7 ♖e8 52 d7 ♖xe7 53 d8♕+** and White wins.

Why is this kind of position important? It's a clear example of pawns placed on adjacent squares on the sixth rank having at least the same value as a rook. In my previous book *300 Most Important Chess Positions* I discussed at length how to play with knights versus three pawns. Such positions are instructive and useful when it comes to learning the value of the knight when compared with the pawn(s). When pawns are placed on the fifth rank they are stronger than the knight but on the fourth rank they have the approximately same value and so on and so forth. The better we play chess the more we need to understand such relative values and how they change with every move. One instructive way to do just that is to look at positions where the values are pretty clear, for example in the endgame.

We constantly need to develop our own chess thinking and thus use appropriate analogies to improve our scale of correct values of pieces, which will obviously differ from position to position. The present ending can be regarded as a key position where two pawns on the sixth beat a rook. However, precise play with the queen is required in order to co-operate fully with the pawns and triumph against Black's queen and rook.

I'm inclined to agree with Réti that chess is all about exceptions (on a higher level) but one can add that tactical positions in particular come into this category. Remember his famous pawn endings, positions 158 and 160 in *300 Most Important Chess Positions.*

291

Mitrofanov
1967
White to move

1 ♕g5!!

White's queen sacrifice lures the black queen to a dark square and makes the vital check on the f1-a6 diagonal impossible.

Not 1 ♔a6? ♕e2+.

1...♕xg5+ 2 ♔a6 ♗xa7

The best defence against 3 b7 mate.

3 c7 ♕d5

Black needs a move like 3...♕e6 to be able to win the game but it's not available – and then Black is lost. It only remains to prevent the mate on b7.

4 c8♕+ ♗b8 5 b7+

But Black is mated anyway.

Simply expressed, this study shows the importance of having control of the square on which the queen is placed since it can have a decisive influence in many positions. After all, the queen cannot play on the white and black squares at the same time – it always has to make a decision, move by move. Can you find a more pure and beautiful example than this to illustrate the queen's weakness (the colour it doesn't control) as well as strength (the colour it does control) whatever square it stands on?

Studies are often more educational than games since all the pieces have an important function.

292

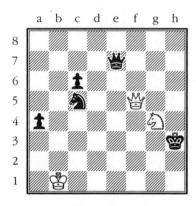

Kubbel
150 Endpielstudien 1925
White to move

This position is excellent both for developing imagination and calculation of variations. First it's important to note that Black's queen is undefended, while the white queen is seeking co-operation with the knight to try to weave a mating net. An experienced problem solver then searches for mating patterns at the same time as calculating variations. It's easy to see that White's first move must be the centralising **1 ♘e3+** forcing **1...♔g3**.

After other king moves Black will be quickly mated. Now it's natural to look at queen checks.

2 ♕g4+ ♔f2 3 ♕f4+!

Of course White must look at the right checks and quickly realise that 3 ♕g2+? fails to 3...♔xe3.

3...♔e2 4 ♕f1+!

White exploits the fact that the knight is taboo because of the skewer at e1.

After **4...♔d2 5 ♕d1+ ♔c3** it gets more difficult. This position is an excellent stepping stone to focus your mind. What are you thinking about here?

It's natural to calculate…

6 ♕c2+ ♔b4

6...♔d4 is met by the fork 7 ♘f5+, showing that we are on the right track.

7 ♕b2+ ♘b3

Or 7...♔a5 8 ♘c4+ ♔a6 9 ♕b6 mate.

Yes, we should be on the right track, so what are we missing? We have reached the zenith of the study which now requires familiarity with a neat mate.

8 ♕a3+!! ♔xa3 9 ♘c2 mate.

Wow!

A very nice study by the great composer Kubbel, which is suitable for calculation of variations, stepping stones and economical mate pictures. Can anyone ask for more from just one position? I don't think so and therefore this kind of position, from which you can learn so many things, is the right one to improve one's overall chess thinking.

293

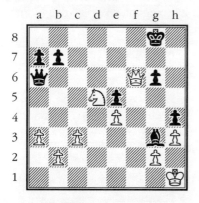

Engqvist – Wambach
Novi Sad 2016
White to move

In this position White's queen and knight has the possibility of attacking the black king and there is indeed a forced mate. Can you see it? I couldn't.

34 ♘e7+

In the game I chose the pragmatic, comfortable and lazy solution: 34 ♕xa6 bxa6 35 ♔g1. Had I seen there was a forced mate hidden in the position I would obviously have gone for it. Indeed, it concludes the game more quickly and with an aesthetic touch.

34...♔h7 35 ♕f7+ ♔h6 36 ♘g8+ ♔g5

Or 36...♔h5 37 ♕h7+ ♔g5 38 ♕h6 mate.

37 ♕f8!!

This mating pattern with the queen on h6 might be rather difficult to see since it's an unusual mate, which also requires help from the h3- and e4-pawns. It can be easy to forget that pawns are often important ingredients when constructing a mate and who would have thought that the h3-pawn was so important? It's also important that the f1-square is under control. In my private annotations I wrote: It's a pity I missed this quiet move in the spirit of Rubinstein. I made the classical mistake of looking only at checks, despite the fact that I had seen the mate on h6 in another variation.

Now it's a good idea to be reminded about positions 281 and 285.

294

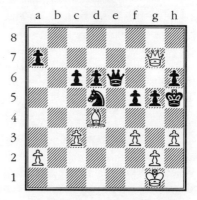

Schlechter – Dr Meitner
Vienna 1899
White to move

Black has just made the seemingly natural queen move from e8-e6 but it turns out to be a decisive blunder which Schlechter promptly exploited.

31 g4+ fxg4

31...♔h4 32 ♕xh6+!! ♕xh6 33 ♔h2 fxg4 34.hxg4 leads to the same position as in the game. Not 34.fxg4?? however because after 34...♕f8! the tables are turned.

32 hxg4+ ♔h4 33 ♕xh6+!! ♕xh6 34 ♔h2 Black resigned.

As mate by ♗f2 follows.

Always look for mate when the king is on the edge of the board! And refer to positions 281, 285 and 294 as well.

295

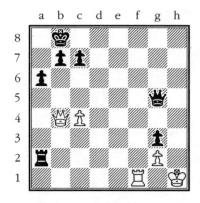

Lolli
1763
White to move

When the king is very constricted and many pawns have been eliminated it might pay to check for stalemate ideas. Here White can draw by sacrificing all his major pieces.

1 ♖f8+ ♔a7 2 ♖a8+! ♔xa8 3 ♕f8+ ♔a7 4 ♕c5+! ♕xc5

White is stalemated since the king cannot move due to the fact that the queen controls g1 and simultaneously blockades the c4-pawn.

4...♔b8 5 ♕f8+ continues the perpetual as does 4...b6 5 ♕xc7+ ♔a8 6 ♕c8+.

Obviously White cannot capture the hanging queen on g5 due to mate on the first rank.

In those days they knew what kind of tactic was important!

296

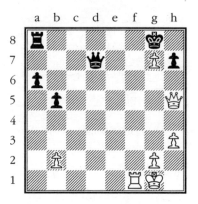

Labone – N.N.
1889
White to move

1 ♖f8+ ♖xf8 2 ♕xh7+! ♔xh7 3 gxf8♘+!

This under-promotion to a knight might very well arise in a practical game and is also a common idea in studies. If you have seen the idea once you will never forget it. I have never played it myself but I remember having looked at a position where this happened on the queenside. It's undoubtedly an important idea since it involves under-promotion in a relatively normal position.

297

Alekhine – Keres
AVRO tournament,
Holland 1938
White to move

Alekhine missed a win against Keres when he didn't play...

41 ♖xb4!

In the game the players agreed to a draw after 41 ♕g6+? ♔f8 42 ♕h7 ♔f7.

41...♕xd6

Not 41...♖xd6? 42 ♕g6+.

He now missed a forced win by **42 ♕c4+!**

It's important to prevent Black from carrying out the defensive setup ...♔g8 and ...♕f8. Wrong would be 42 ♖b7+? ♔g8! 43 ♕g6 ♕f8 and Black has a defence.

2...♔e7!

The strongest defence.

(1) 42...♕d5 43 ♖b7+ ♔e8 (*43...♔f8 44 ♕c7! ♕xh5+ 45 ♔g2 ♕d5+ 46 f3 ♕a2+ 47 ♔h3 ♕e6+ 48 g4 and Black has no defence to the double threat on g7 and d8.*) 44 ♕e2+ ♕e5 45 ♕xe5+ fxe5 46 ♖xg7 leads to a winning rook ending since in the long run Black cannot simultaneously defend his pawn islands with his two pieces.

(2) 42...♔f8 43 ♖b7 ♖d7 44 ♕c8+ ♔e7 (*If 44...♖d8 then 45 ♕g4. It is important to master such long and forceful queen moves which utilise the queen's potential to the maximum – both as an attacker and defender when playing with only major pieces on the board.*) 45 ♖b3! Note the flexibility of the rook: first it utilises the seventh rank and now it's the e-file which is the centre of its attention. 45...f5 (*If 45...♔f7 then 46 ♖b8! as the eighth rank is the most important route to get to Black's king.*) 46 ♖e3+ (*46 ♕g8 also wins.*) 46...♔f6 47 ♕e8 ♖f7 (Black must prevent the mate on g6) 48 ♖c3 followed by 49 ♖c6 decides the game.

43 ♖b7+ ♖d7 44 ♕g8 ♖xb7 45 ♕xg7+ ♔e6 46 ♕xb7

285

White now has a winning endgame in which a weakness on h6 has arisen. What is fascinating about the position at move 42 is that yet again it proves that three pieces are enough to win by a mating attack. White has two major pieces while the third piece is the strong h5-pawn.

Normally one doesn't count on pawns when engaged in an attack, but according to Kasparov one should do so. In this case the h5-pawn secures control of the very important g6-square.

298

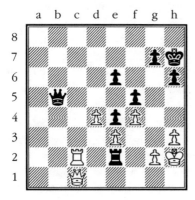

Bellon Lopez – Engqvist
Team Championship,
Stockholm 2014
White to move

I had just moved the queen from b8 to b5 when, to my horror, I discovered that White can win on the spot with a simple pin. **39 ♕f1!**

Happily for me, in the game 39 ♖xe2? ♕xe2 was played and the queen ending petered out to a draw after further 20 moves.

But how come that two experienced players missed the queen move? My only explanation is that I wanted to keep my active rook on e2 and that's why I didn't want to exchange it on c2. On the other hand, Bellon must have thought the same way and was glad to exchange his passive rook for Black's active one. This is why we missed this pin. We were not thinking about tactics but were rather dealing with positional considerations.

Some other influential factors might have been that we were playing in the morning and no spectators were watching the game in such a way as to alert Bellon that something was going on in the position. We were actually playing a team match and that sort of thing is pretty common when team-mates are following the games. However, luckily for me no one at all was present when these horrific moves were played.

So even if you have a good understanding of fundamental tactics, you can still make oversights because of other things like focusing exclusively on positional matters, tiredness or even the psychological impact of not expecting a strong player to make such an oversight.

All this means that it's important to be attentive even – or especially – when the position (or the player) seems calm and when you don't expect a blunder. The undeniable conclusion is that in chess anything can happen!

299

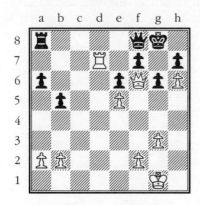

Janowski – Saburov
Ostende 1906
White to move

White wants to simplify the position with a timely ♕e7 and win the rook ending with his more active rook, king and strong h6-pawn, but to make the exchange all the more effective the king wants to manoeuvre to g5 in order to protect the h6-pawn.

38 ♔g2!

This is the simplest solution to win the game. Another idea is to place Black in zugzwang by grabbing as much terrain as possible with the pawns.

One plausible variation is the following: 38 b4 ♖c8 39 ♔g2 ♖a8 40 a3 ♖c8 41 g4 ♖b8 42 g5 ♖c8 43 ♖d6 ♖a8 44 ♖b6. Black's rook cannot defend the last rank as well as the a6-pawn so defeat is inevitable.

38...b4 39 ♔f3

Another winning plan is to advance on the kingside with 39 f4 followed by g5 and f5.

39...a5 40 ♔g4 a4 41 ♔g5 a3 42 b3 ♖b8 43 ♕e7

White has achieved the goal of his 38th move.

43...♕xe7+ 44 ♖xe7 ♔f8 45 ♔f6

A dream position for the king when in an attacking position.

45...♖b5 46 ♖xf7+ and **Black resigned.**

300

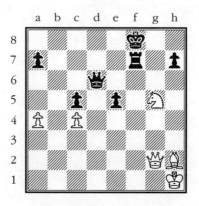

Petrosian – Simagin
USSR Championship,
Moscow 1956
White to move

44 ♕a8+

This beautiful long queen move along the light-squared diagonal decides the game.

44...♔g7 45 ♗xe5+!

Note that 45 ♕h8+? would be a mistake since Black doesn't have to accept the sacrifice. After 45...♔g6 46 ♘xf7 (*46 ♕g8+? ♖g7*) 46...♕d1+ it's a draw by perpetual check.

45...♕xe5

46 ♕h8+!

By moving the queen from one corner to the other White is constructing a position where a fork will be the crowning climax.

46...♔xh8 47 ♘xf7+

What is remarkable with this aesthetically appealing combination is that Petrosian won in the same manner in the tenth game of his world title match with Spassky in 1966. There it was unleashed along the long dark-squared diagonal when the white queen decided the game by moving from b2-h8. And in that game it was a rook that was captured on f7 with a resulting knight fork on the king and queen.

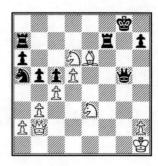

White decided the game with **29 ♗xf7+ ♖xf7** (*29...♔f8 30 ♕h8+ ♔e7 31 ♘ef5+* and White wins the queen or delivers mate next move.) **30 ♕h8+!** A nice concluding stroke! **Black resigns**.

This type of combination is pretty common not only in Petrosian's games but also in studies by Troitzky, for example, and so solving such studies is an effective method of learning the technique of similar combinations where queen and knight are involved. It's no coincidence that Petrosian played this combination twice!

Other chess books available from Batsford

BATSFORD

www.pavilionbooks.com

300 MOST IMPORTANT CHESS POSITIONS

Thomas Engqvist
9781849945127 | £16.99 | PB
304 pages

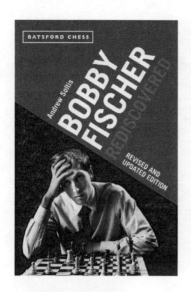

**BOBBY FISCHER
REDISCOVERED**
Andrew Soltis
9781849946063 | £16.99 | PB
312 pages

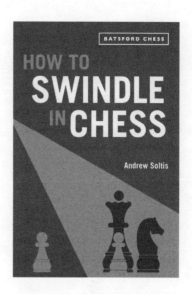

**HOW TO SWINDLE IN
CHESS**
Andrew Soltis
9781849945639 | £16.99 | PB
240 pages

A TO Z CHESS TACTICS
George Huczek
9781849944465 | £17.99 | PB
352 pages

**365 CHESS
MASTER LESSONS**
Andrew Soltis
9781849944342 | £16.99 | PB
384 pages

DAVID VS GOLIATH CHESS
Andrew Soltis
9781849943574 | £15.99 | PB
238 pages

WHAT IT TAKES TO BECOME A CHESS MASTER
Andrew Soltis
9781849940269 | £14.99 | PB
208 pages

PAWN STRUCTURE CHESS
Andrew Soltis
9781849940702 | £16.99 | PB
286 pages

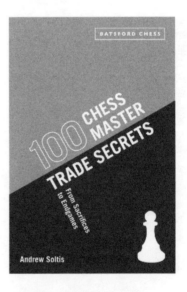

100 CHESS MASTER TRADE SECRETS
Andrew Soltis
9781849941082 | £14.99 | PB
208 pages

YOUR KINGDOM FOR MY HORSE: WHEN TO EXCHANGE IN CHESS
Andrew Soltis
9781849942775 | £15.99 | PB
208 pages

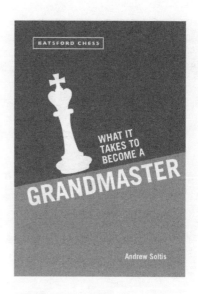

WHAT IT TAKES TO BECOME A GRANDMASTER
Andrew Soltis
9781849943390 | £15.99 | PB
320 pages

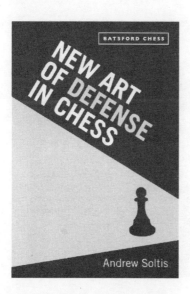

NEW ART OF DEFENCE IN CHESS
Andrew Soltis
9781849941600 | £15.99 | PB
288 pages

MY 60 MEMORABLE GAMES
Bobby Fischer
9781906388300 | £16.99| PB
384 pages

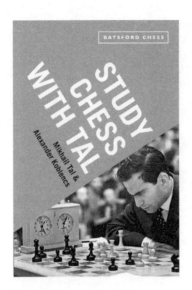

STUDY CHESS WITH TAL
Mikhail Tal, Alexander Koblencs
9781849941099 | £15.99 | PB
272 pages

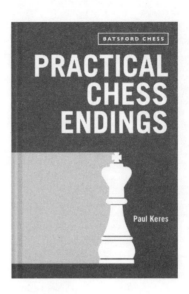

PRACTICAL CHESS ENDINGS
Paul Keres
9781849944953 | £16.99 | PB
352 pages

THE MOST INSTRUCTIVE GAMES OF CHESS
Irving Chernev
9781849941617 | £15.99 | PB
320 pages

THE ART OF CHECKMATE
Georges Renaud, Victor Kahn
9781849942706 | £15.99 | PB
224 pages

**THE WISEST THINGS
EVER SAID ABOUT CHESS**
Andrew Soltis
9781906388003 | £15.99 | PB
304 pages

**BATSFORD'S MODERN
CHESS OPENINGS**
Nick De Firmian
9781906388294 | £22.95 | PB
720 pages

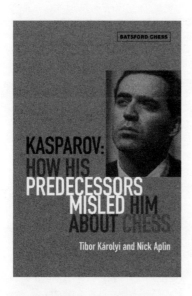

**KASPAROV: HOW HIS
PREDECESSORS MISLED
HIM ABOUT CHESS**
Tibor Karolyi, Nick Aplin
9781906388263 | £14.99 | PB
272 pages

**CRITICAL MOMENTS
IN CHESS**
Paata Gaprindashvili
9781906388652 | £15.99 | PB
288 pages

THE BATSFORD BOOK
OF CHESS
Sean Marsh
9781849941648 | £14.99 | HB
208 pages

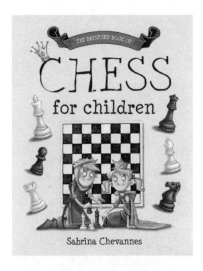

THE BATSFORD BOOK OF
CHESS FOR CHILDREN
Sabrina Chevannes
9781849940696 | £12.99 | HB
128 pages

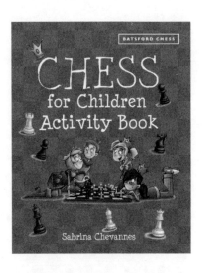

CHESS FOR CHILDREN
ACTIVITY BOOK
Sabrina Chevannes
9781849942843 | £9.99 | PB
120 pages